345 MAT

JUSTICE AND PUNISHMENT

# Justice and Punishment
## *The Rationale of Coercion*

MATT MATRAVERS

OXFORD

UNIVERSITY PRESS

# OXFORD

UNIVERSITY PRESS

Great Clarendon Street, Oxford OX2 6DP

Oxford University Press is a department of the University of Oxford.
It furthers the University's objective of excellence in research, scholarship,
and education by publishing worldwide in

Oxford New York

Athens Auckland Bangkok Bogotá Buenos Aires Calcutta
Cape Town Chennai Dar es Salaam Delhi Florence Hong Kong Istanbul
Karachi Kuala Lumpur Madrid Melbourne Mexico City Mumbai
Nairobi Paris São Paulo Singapore Taipei Tokyo Toronto Warsaw

and associated companies in Berlin Ibadan

Oxford is a registered trade mark of Oxford University Press
in the UK and in certain other countries

Published in the United States
by Oxford University Press Inc., New York

British Library Cataloguing in Publication Data

Data available

Library of Congress Cataloging in Publication Data

Data available

ISBN 0–19–829573–1

1 3 5 7 9 10 8 6 4 2

Typeset by Hope Services (Abingdon) Ltd.
Printed in Great Britain
on acid-free paper by
Biddles Ltd.,
Guildford & King's Lynn

*For Anne, my mother*

# ACKNOWLEDGEMENTS

I have been thinking about many of the questions discussed in this book for some time. My wife Julika has endured spoiled weekends and holidays and has put up with me through the highs and lows of the writing process. I am glad, and very grateful.

I would like to thank my teachers in the Government Department at the LSE, and the members of the 'Tuesday' and 'Thursday' Seminars—Russell Bentley, Vittorio Buffachi, Duncan Ivison, Charles Jones, Tim Stainton, and Subu—where the earliest formulations of some of these ideas received their first airings. My colleagues in the Department of Politics at York have provided a friendly and stimulating atmosphere in which to undertake research and I would like to thank them in general, and Alex Callinicos, David Edwards, (until recently) Duncan Ivison, Sue Mendus, Peter Nicholson, (and now) Jon Parkin, who constitute the 'political philosophy' research group in particular. Political philosophy thrives at York in no small measure because of the generous support of the C. and J. B. Morrell Trust, and I would like to thank the Trustees for this and for their encouragement. I am also grateful to my students, Ajaye Black and Robert Wavre, and to Tom Baldwin, Gordon Finlayson, and Christian Piller of the Philosophy Department at York who have contributed to various seminars at which some of these ideas were presented and who, together with those of us in the Politics Department, make York such an interesting and fun place to do moral and political philosophy.

A number of people have kindly provided comments, both written and spoken, on parts of this manuscript. Often this has been in the context of seminar and conference discussions, and I am grateful to the many audiences who have been prepared to listen and to talk about earlier versions of parts of this book. Catriona McKinnon kindly offered written comments on an early version of Chapter 4 following one such meeting. Antony Duff has followed the development of my ideas from their earliest inception, when he examined my Ph.D. thesis, to their near final form, when he acted as a reader for Oxford University Press. I am grateful for the comments he has sent me at various stages, for his support and encouragement, and also for the inspiration that his own work has often provided. Another reader, whose identity is unknown to me, also provided useful and challenging comments.

Whilst working on this book I spent periods of leave at the Department of Political Science and the Program in Ethics, Politics and Economics at Yale University and at the Bentham Project at University College, London. I am grateful to my colleagues at York for making this possible and to Ian Shapiro and Fred Rosen at Yale and UCL respectively for their hospitality.

Various friends and members of my family have sustained me and picked me up during the darkest days of the last few years. I would especially like to thank Joy Drucker, Derek and Amanda Matravers, and Stephanie Norfolk.

My greatest debts are to four people: Brian Barry and Anni Parker, John Charvet, and Sue Mendus. I have discussed much of what follows and a great deal else besides with Brian. In person, and through his work on justice, he has taught me a great deal. He has also provided advice and support on numerous occasions over the last few years. In addition, he and Anni have often rescued me from despair, filled me with fine foods, and generally provided sanctuary from this book and the world. John Charvet gave me my first taste of political philosophy when I was a first year undergraduate and later supervised my Ph.D. thesis. He has been a guide and partner in philosophical enquiry and a friend from the beginning. Although this book bears little relation to the Ph.D. that he supervised, the ideas it contains owe a great deal to his work and to the many meetings and discussions that we have had over the last few years. When I moved from the LSE to York my colleague, Sue Mendus was allocated the job of acting as my 'mentor'. I don't suppose that either of us knows now what this means any more than we did then. However, I am confident that Sue's actions then and since would fall into the category of the supererogatory. She has read and commented on the whole manuscript, much of it in several drafts. Her comments have proved invaluable. More than that, through conversation, discussion, argument, and stand-up fight, she has encouraged, cajoled, and supported me. She has also lifted my spirits and kept me going when it all looked pretty bleak. Without her, this would have been a much worse book, if a book at all. Some people make all the difference and for me Brian and Anni, John, and Sue fall into that category. I am deeply indebted to them.

The feeling on seeing one's own ideas mangled, distorted, and put to a use entirely different from the one intended is a familiar one to all who teach undergraduates. I can only apologize to those mentioned above for the many times that this reaction will be appropriate in what follows. Their contribution to this book has been so great as to make me hesitant to add the normal academic formula to absolve them of responsibility for what follows. However, as Scanlon says, it is right sometimes to hold a person

responsible even where judgements of substantive responsibility are difficult to make. On this basis I must take responsibility for the arguments presented here.

Parts of the Introduction and of Chapter 4 borrow from my
'Introduction' and my ' "What to Say?": The Communicative Element in
Punishment and Moral Theory', both in Matravers (ed.), *Punishment and
Political Theory* (Oxford: Hart Publishing, 1999). Other parts of Chapter 4
come from my 'Contractualism and the Moral Significance of Human
Well-Being', in A. J. Coates (ed.), *International Justice* (Aldershot: Ashgate,
2000). I am grateful to the editor and to Ashgate Publishing for permission
to reproduce this material.

M.M.

# CONTENTS

## Contents

# Introduction

He asked a very simple question: 'Why, and by what right, do some people lock up, torment, exile, flog, and kill others, while they are themselves just like those they torment, flog, and kill?' And in answer he got deliberations as to whether human beings had free will or not; whether or not signs of criminality could be detected by measuring the skull; what part heredity played in crime; whether immorality could be inherited; and what madness is, what degeneration is, and what temperament is; how climate, food, ignorance, imitativeness, hypnotism, or passion affect crime; what society is, what its duties are—and so on . . . but there was no answer on the chief point: 'By what right do some people punish others? (L. Tolstoy, *Resurrection*)[1]

The aim of this book is to answer Tolstoy's question: why and by what right, do some people punish others? This is not a new question. The problem of punishment is one of the most enduring in political theory. Whilst other topics—political obligation, power, democracy, and the like—go in and out of fashion, there is a seemingly constant and substantial stream of contributions to the discussion of punishment.[2] The result is that penal philosophy can now reasonably make a claim to being a separate subdiscipline of moral and political philosophy and, indeed, it has been treated as such. In part, my argument is that this separation of punishment theory from the wider concerns of moral and political philosophy is damaging to both. For a theory of punishment to be adequate, it must be rooted in a broader moral theory, and that broader moral theory will, I believe, be constructivist.

An advantage of this approach is that it explains a puzzle. Political theory has been dominated over the last three decades or so by the topic of justice. However, recent theories of justice have for the most part concentrated on distributive justice and have excluded retributive or corrective justice. Indeed, the term 'justice' as used in the literature has almost come to be

---

[1] Quoted from Pincoffs 1966: epigraph. It is also quoted in Duff 1986: 187.
[2] For useful summaries of the contemporary state of punishment theory see Duff and Garland 1994; Duff 1996.

synonymous with 'distributive justice'. Yet the right to punish, and the role of punishment in understanding the state and political legitimacy, was once taken to be central in political philosophy.[3] The question then arises, why has distributive justice become separated from retributive justice?

My argument is that this separation has occurred because contemporary theories of justice cannot explain the relationship of justice and morality more broadly conceived. As it is this relationship which a theory of punishment needs to explain, it is in examining the problem of punishment that the limitations of contemporary theories of justice are most starkly exposed. Moreover, those limitations are not confined to the response of contemporary theories of justice to the problem of punishment, but are such as to undermine also the accounts of justice. Put bluntly, the argument pursued here is that it is through the discussion of punishment that the inadequacies of contemporary theories of justice are demonstrated and it is therefore through the discussion of punishment that those inadequacies can be rectified.

The claim that punishment theory needs a wider moral context is controversial. The first part of this Introduction begins the defence of this claim (a defence that is completed by the rest of the book). The second, describes the argument that follows from its being true.

For some, the thought that the question of punishment is 'relatively independent' (cf. Davis 1989) of moral and political theory more broadly is encouraged by what appears most obviously problematic about punishment. This is that punishing someone involves doing to her things that would normally be in violation of her rights. As one commentary puts it, 'it is usually wrong to lock people up, to take their money without return, or put them to death' (Duff and Garland 1994: 2; cf. Knowles 1999: 29).

---

[3] Michael Davis makes the strange claim that before the latter half of the 18th century punishment was of little or no concern to political and moral theorists. He writes, in support of the idea that punishment theory is independent of political theory, that 'Hobbes was unusual in giving it [the topic of punishment] two chapters of *Leviathan*. Most political philosophers (for example, Locke in *The Second Treatise* or Rousseau in *The Social Contract*) said much less, and what they said was perfunctory' (Davis 1989, 321). In this he is surely mistaken. Locke grants man in the state of nature (only) 'two Powers', one of which is 'the *power to punish the Crimes* committed against [the] Law [of Nature]' (Locke 1988: ii, § 128), and it is this power—or right—that is given up to the political association and thus forms the basis of the State. Indeed, Locke defines political power to be '*a Right* of making Laws with Penalties of Death, and consequently all less Penalties, for the Regulating and Preserving of Property' (Locke 1988: ii, § 3). Rousseau is less explicit in placing punishment at the centre of his concerns but, in the famous opening paragraphs of *The Social Contract*, it is clear that what is to be 'made legitimate' is the 'chains' on people, which are backed up by the threat of force.

Given this, it might be taken that the central questions for the penal philosopher are, 'when it is appropriate to do such things?'; 'to whom should they be done?'; and 'in what quantities?' However, this is to miss an important point. Punishment follows from the contravention of a rule that has attached to it a provision that those who contravene the rule will be liable to punishment. Before asking whom, under what conditions, and how much, what is needed is, as Stanley Benn puts it, 'to ask what can justify punishment in general'. That is, 'to ask why we should have the sorts of rules that provide those who contravene them should be made to suffer: and this is different from asking for a justification of a particular application of them in punishing an individual' (Benn 1958: 326; cf. Hart 1959).

To give a very rough picture: three distinct sets of questions can be discerned: (i) questions about the rules and their foundations, scope, and authority; (ii) questions about what justifies the threat that those who contravene the rules under certain conditions will be liable to punishment; (iii) questions about what justifies the particular application of the threatened sanctions.

For those about whom Tolstoy complains, the primary enquiry of punishment theory is into (iii). For what is at stake in questions of skull size, heredity, and passion is whether the conditions for liability are met in full by some particular offender. Similarly, consider the following example offered by the Oxford philosopher John Mabbott:

I was myself for some time the disciplinary officer of a college whose rules included a rule compelling attendance at chapel. Many of those who broke this rule broke it on principle. I punished them. I certainly did not want to reform them; I respected their characters and their views. I certainly did not want to drive others into chapel through fear of penalties. Nor did I think there had been a wrong done which merited retribution. I wished I could have believed that I would have done the same myself. My position was clear. They had broken a rule; they knew it and I knew it. Nothing more was needed to make punishment proper. (Mabbott 1939: 42)

Mabbott clearly distinguishes between the rule and the threat of a penalty attached to the breach of that rule. He clearly believes the rule compelling attendance at chapel to be unjustified, but that is for him not relevant to the question of the justification of punishment, which he takes to be the question, 'under what circumstances is the punishment of some particular person justified and why?' (Mabbott 1939: 39). As is clear, Mabbott believes that the punishment of a person is justified by that person having culpably broken a (correctly instituted) rule. The punishment falls on that particular person because it is he who has broken the rule. Presumably having established that a given student did not attend chapel the only question for Mabbott is whether the student was culpable in so doing. This is surely insufficient. Although Mabbott's account might be taken to be a comment on the proper application of punishment—if Mabbott had always pardoned one favourite offender whilst punishing all the others he would have done something unjustifiable—it cannot seriously be taken to be a justification of punishment in the sense in which such a justification is required.

However, it might be thought that whilst an adequate theory of punishment must do more than address (iii), penal philosophy can nevertheless limit its enquiry to (ii) and (iii), but need not engage with those questions grouped under (i). It might be argued, for example, that the content, source, and nature of the rules that govern a community is a matter for political and moral philosophy. Assuming that some set of rules can be justified then it is a reasonable assumption that it would be a good thing, other things being equal, to reduce the incidence of rule breaking. Preventing, or diminishing the number of acts of rule breaking provides the rationale for appending to the rules the threat of sanctions, and penal philosophy concerns the subsequent questions that arise about that threat. Alternatively, it might be thought that whatever the source, nature, and authority of the rules the failure to abide by them on the part of the offender calls for some response. This response may be one of condemnation; or it may be best captured in the language of 'cancelling' or 'annulling' the act of the offender; or in the claim that justice needs to be restored to the relations of the offender and her community.

These two examples of how punishment theory might be thought to be relatively independent gesture towards the traditional way of conceiving of the 'punishment debate': that is, as a debate between consequentialism and retributivism. It is doubtful that this picture was ever accurate and it certainly now fails to capture the subtle and sophisticated ways in which punishment theory has developed.[4] However, one reason for the continuing resonance of the consequentialist versus retributive presentation of the problem of punishment is undoubtedly that each position seems to contain something that is essential. Another is that neither retributivism nor utilitarianism need, at first sight, to address those questions grouped under (i). My argument is that neither can, in fact, escape this requirement, but before considering that it is worth commenting briefly on what it is of importance that is captured by each position.

---

[4] So much so that the labels 'consequentialist' and 'retributive' are of increasingly little use as the theories that they are meant to group together have become so diverse.

Retributivism, in looking to the past act of the offender, connects the punishment of the offender to what it is that he has done and thus captures two important intuitions: that punishment is justified if (and only if) it is deserved—if it is 'of an offender for an offence'—and that the amount of punishment imposed ought to be in some way proportional to the wrong done. Yet, retributivism is also a strange doctrine. It no doubt appeals to a strong intuition that 'the guilty deserve to suffer', but it contradicts another, that 'two wrongs do not make a right'. Moreover, retributivists do not seem to be able to explain why the guilty deserve to suffer, and when asked to do so they often do no more than restate this basic proposition in different, and often 'mystical' terms (Lacey 1987: 410; Chapters 2 and 3 below). The consequentialist argument that if it were certain that punishment yielded absolutely no benefit in either social or individual terms it would be wrong to continue to punish is, for many, quite compelling.[5]

For their part, utilitarian justifications of punishment capture the idea that one purpose of having rules that threaten sanctions against those who contravene them is to reduce the incidence of prohibited acts. In addition, as with all consequentialist arguments, utilitarian theories of punishment appeal to two further intuitions: that human well-being matters and that moral rules ought to be evaluated in light of their effect on human well-being (Kymlicka 1990: 11; Chapter 1 below). Where consequentialist theories seem to fail our intuitions is in being entirely forward looking. Taking into account only future consequences appears to ignore the importance of the past act. Furthermore, because of its concern for aggregate human well-being, utilitarianism appears to be blind to distributive concerns. It is unjust to punish an offender's family even if doing so would deter future offending and, thus, bring great gains in aggregate human well-being (Chapter 1 below).

The insights captured by retributivism centre on who should be punished (those who deserve it) and on the quantum of punishment that may justifiably be imposed (that which is in proportion to desert). The problems associated with the account stem from the question of why punish at all. Consequentialism, conversely, appears best to address the question of what justifies having a system of punishment, and its difficulties emerge when considering the distributive questions of whom and how much to punish. One well-established way of responding to these features of the debate is to separate what Hart calls the question of the general justifying

---

[5] Although not, of course, for Kant who notoriously writes that even on the point of the dissolution of society 'the last murderer remaining in prison would first have to be executed' (see Kant 1991: § 333, 142).

aim of punishment from the question of its distribution (Hart 1959: 4; see also Benn 1958; Clark 1997). This allows the combining of consequential-ist and retributive approaches in a 'mixed theory', the most common form of which takes the answers to the distributive questions ('Whom?' and 'How much?') to be side constraints on a utilitarian understanding of the general justifying aim of punishment (see Benn 1958; Hart 1959; Clark 1997).[6] Whether such a mixed theory can be successful is a question taken up later, the crucial test being whether the theory can successfully integrate its consequentialist and retributive (or other distributive) components. What is of interest here is whether such mixed theory can sustain the claim of relative independence.

On the usual understanding of mixed theory—a preventive rationale for the general justifying aim of punishment constrained by retributive dis-tributive principles—the argument remains in the domains of questions (ii) and (iii). The argument begins not with the nature, scope, authority, etc. of the rules, but with the need to prevent breaches of those rules (the pursuit of that preventive aim being constrained by distributive concerns). However, despite its very widespread use, Hart's formula contains an ambi-guity remarked upon at least as early as 1961. 'It is important to notice', Armstrong argues,

that the moral justification of a practice is not the same thing as its general point or purpose, except in the eyes of those who have travelled so far down the utilitar-ian road that they never question the means if the end is desirable. . . . An act or practice may have a very sound point indeed and still lack moral justification . . . . There is an ambiguity in a phrase like 'The general justifying aim of punishment', between *why* we do it, and why it is morally permissible—if it is—for us to do it. (Armstrong 1969: 141; cf. Dolinko 1991: 541)[7]

---

[6] For one example of an argument that the right to punish is derived from retributivism, but the quantity from consequentialist considerations, see Bradley 1927: 27: 'Having once the right to punish, we may modify the punishment according to the useful and the pleasant; but these are external to the matter, they can not give us a right to punish, and nothing can do that but criminal desert. This is not a subject to waste words over: if the fact of the vul-gar view is not palpable to the reader, we have no hope, and no wish, to make it so.'

[7] In addition to arguing that Hart's formula of 'the general justifying aim of punishment' is ambiguous, Dolinko claims the separation of the distributive question of 'whom to pun-ish' from the question of the moral permissibility of the practice of punishment to be 'pre-posterous' for 'to split off . . . the question of who may be punished . . . suggests that we can decide what punishment is and why we engage in it without knowing who is supposed to receive punishment'. As Dolinko correctly notes, Hart surreptitiously builds the answer to the distributive question into 'the supposedly separate "definition" of punishment' as 'of an actual or supposed offender for an offence" (all quotations from Dolinko 1991: 541).

What Armstrong points towards is the claim that punishment theory must concern itself with the morality of attaching the threat of sanctions to rules (as well the morality of imposing those sanctions on particular people). And whilst it seems plausible to think that the point of threatening sanctions must have something to do with preventing offending (see Chapter 3 below), that is not the same as arguing that preventing offending through the threat and imposing of sanctions is morally permissible.

Nevertheless, it might still be argued that the question of the moral permissibility of attaching threats to rules can be addressed without the need to consider questions concerning the rules themselves. The argument that this is not so is, in a sense, presented throughout this book. However, that it is not so is surely plausible. That what informs the moral justification, rather than practical rationale, of attaching the threat of penalties to rules is only that such penalties reduce the incidence of rule breaking is implausible. The argument must be more complex and part of the complexity can only be unravelled by considering the rules to which those threats are to be attached and the agents to whom they are to apply. Addressing the question of why it is a good thing to prevent the breaking of some rules would seem to require addressing the question of what is the nature and content of those rules.

Even were prevention the major component of a moral justification of punishment, questions would still arise as to who ought, or has the authority, to threaten such sanctions. In addition, whether it is morally permissible to prevent offending by threat of sanctions, even where that threat is made by a legitimate authority, is, in part, a matter of whether it is morally permissible to alter the behaviour of agents by threatening them. In turn, this question raises the issues of the relationship of prudential and moral reason and of their relationship to agency.

The case is perhaps even clearer when it comes to the retributive claims that some action in contravention of some rule calls for a response, an annulment or cancellation, or other corrective to right the wrong committed. If these claims are to be made meaningful the strategy must be to link them with the wrongdoing in the offending act. Retributivism, if it is not to be either circular and mystical or irrelevant to the moral justification of punishment must show that such responses are morally permissible (or obligatory) by a correct understanding of what is morally owed to responsible agents or by such an understanding of the nature of the rules.

The claim that a moral justification of punishment needs to give an integrated account of questions (i) and (ii), just as it does for (ii) and (iii), is plausible. In the first three chapters that follow the claim is substantiated.

It is argued that existing approaches to the theory of punishment have failed successfully to justify punishment either because they have not taken seriously the need to integrate the account of punishment and a broader moral theory or because the moral theory on which they do rely is itself inadequate. Chapter 1 examines the utilitarian account of punishment. Utilitarians, of course, have available a complete moral theory: an account of the rules, of what considerations determine whether those rules should have a threat of sanctions attached to them, and of when the use of those sanctions is morally permitted. Treated as a straightforward teleological theory in which first the good is identified and then the basic moral command is to do that which will maximize that good, utilitarianism can be quickly dispensed with. It makes little sense to claim that there is a moral obligation owed to states of affairs. Treated more seriously as a way of giving content to the demand that equal respect is shown to individuals, utilitarianism is a much more attractive theory than is commonly recognized. However, the counting of all wants in a social decision function raises a problem of external preferences that ultimately undermines the account. The utilitarian account of punishment fails because it relies on a utilitarian moral theory that is ultimately indefensible.

Chapters 2 and 3 focus on retributive theories. Retributivism looks initially to be the most plausible candidate for being an independent account of punishment, focusing as it does on the idea that, in some sense or other, culpable offenders deserve punishment. Chapter 2 examines what is arguably the most important retributive school of recent years, which ties punishment to the restoring of a just balance of benefits and burdens between law-abiding citizens and free-riders. Chapter 3 looks at expressive and communicative retributive accounts. In all these cases the argument is that in order to maintain the relative independence of punishment theory and the claim that punishment is to be understood as deserved by the past act of the offender, retributive theorists separate the understanding of the wrong done in the offence from the wrong to which punishment responds. Such a strategy is untenable. Moreover, insofar as they surreptitiously appeal, or need to appeal, to an understanding of the rules to which the threat of penal sanctions are to be attached, what they provide is inadequate.

Given that the argument of the first three chapters is that much punishment theory does not succeed because it fails to take sufficiently seriously the need to integrate a justifying account of punishment with a larger political and moral theory, the next chapters look to contemporary accounts of justice to provide such a theory. It is here that the puzzle referred to above appears. Although concerned with the topic of justice, recent work on distributive justice by Rawls and his followers has very little to say about punishment theory and penal justice. The argument pursued in Chapters 4 and 5 is that this is because theories of justice, at least those that can be classed as 'impartialist', cannot adequately explain the relationship of justice to morality more widely. In Chapter 4, it is argued that such theories, if they are to give an adequate account of the public domain, must appeal to considerations that fall outside the narrow confines of an impartialist account of distributive justice. However, if they do so appeal then they must give up the claim of impartiality. Chapter 5 focuses on the structure of impartialist theories and brings to the fore a distinction between *faux* and genuine constructivism that underpins the remainder of the book. *Faux* constructivists do not, as the name suggests, attempt to construct moral norms, but rather use the techniques of constructivism to explicate the demands made by an initial assumption of the fundamental equality of persons. The result is that the demands of justice, or of morality, appear to the agent as alien restrictions on the pursuit of his good. Although *faux* constructivists attempt to fill the 'gap' that they open up between the agent's personal perspective and the demands of morality they cannot adequately do so. The result is that the threat of sanctions is needed to attempt to fill this gap. Such threats must be attached to existing moral rules and the justification for so doing must appeal to one or other of the theories discredited in Chapters 1–3. The problem with the account of punishment lies with the *faux* nature of the constructivism adopted by these theorists.

Given the identification of the problem as lying in the separation of the demands of morality and the agent's self-interest, the argument turns to an attempt to ground moral reasons in prudential ones; to the genuine constructivism of David Gauthier. Gauthier sets out to show that there are rationally compelling reasons for a non-tuist rational agent to adopt the constraints of morality. However, in Chapter 6 it is argued that he does not succeed. Given the resources that he has available to him, Gauthier cannot show that the rational non-tuist has reason to treat moral norms as anything but instrumentally useful to the pursuit of his narrow self-interest. Obedience to those norms is thus a matter of prudential calculation and this is inadequate. A theory of morality must be able to explain moral norms' 'imperatival force' (Charvet 1995: 1): the authority that such norms have over the pursuit of narrow self-interest. Gauthier closes the gap between morality and self-interest only by dissolving the former into the latter.

However, in recent work Gauthier has suggested that meeting the demands of constructivism may not require constructing morality from concerns quite as narrow as those that he allowed himself in his 1986 book, *Morals by Agreement.* This idea is pursued in the development of a genuine constructivist account of morality in Chapters 7 and 8.

The central claim of these chapters is that the closing of the gap between self-interest and morality does not require that morality can be shown to be rationally compelling even to the egoist. There are no rationally compelling reasons to be moral. However, if the constructivist enterprise begins with an already social agent, standing back from her commitments, asking whether she has reason to endorse the priority of moral reasons, then there surely are reasons that can be given to show that such a commitment to morality is not a mistake or a confidence trick. The commitment to morality must be a commitment that goes beyond what is dictated by reason, but that is not to say that reason is impotent. The argument of Chapters 7 and 8 is that there are important and substantial reasons to be moral that can be understood from the perspective of self-interest. These reasons are not decisive, but are sufficient to meet the challenge that morality is a fraud, a mistake, or a confidence trick.

The constructivist theory sketched in these chapters ties together self-interest and morality, not by reducing the former to the latter nor by surreptitiously appealing to *faux* constructivist assumptions. It claims that morality must be understood as the product of a commitment by agents to recognize the imperatival force of moral norms. Such a commitment is only possible where each agent understands his good as best pursued together with others in a community regulated by such norms. Of course, this commitment can only be reasonable when it is made together with others. To commit oneself to the authority of moral norms in circumstances in which one is surrounded by those who would exploit and free-ride on that commitment would be nonsensical. In such circumstances, morality is indeed a confidence trick, which the agent would do better to avoid.

Given this understanding of morality and of the moral community, the argument is that the will to commit to morality also commits the agent to renouncing free-riding (understanding moral norms as merely of instrumental value in the pursuit of one's narrow self-interest). Social norms that govern co-operation can only be understood as moral in conditions in which agents are secure and know that the commitment to morality will not lead to their being taken advantage of. Moral norms are, thus, necessarily coercive, for the commitment of those participants in the moral community to the authority of moral norms is also a commitment to coerce those who would jeopardize the moral project by free-riding. Thus, the account of morality integrates the coercive threat of sanctions and the broader moral theory. It does so only because it is able to close the gap between the personal perspective and the demands of moral reasons. Rather than being alien constraints on the pursuit of self-interest (as they are in *faux* constructivist theory) or being 'evils' from which the rational self-interested being 'would be free' (as they are in Gauthier's account), the agent commits himself, together with others, to understand and to pursue his good through the demands of moral reasons. What is achieved is the integration of rules of justice, coercion, and morality in a single, genuinely constructivist account.

Although the place of coercion is central to the argument of Chapters 7 and 8, the answer to Tolstoy's question is not complete until Chapter 9. In understanding morality as a product of a commitment, the theory must allow that some will reject that commitment and the idea of moral co-operation. Such people stand in no moral relation to others and, thus, although they may be coerced and suffering may be inflicted upon them, this cannot be done in the name of punishment. Rather, these people stand in a state of nature relationship to the moral community. However, those who do make the commitment to morality will, of course, need to be assured that by doing so they do not make themselves vulnerable. In integrating self-interest and morality the account does not obliterate the demands of narrow self-interest and, given that agents will sometimes give in to temptation and behave immorally, an account is needed of the coercion and punishment of those members of the moral community who do not renounce their commitment, but sometimes fail to abide by its demands. Chapter 9 develops such an account. There I argue that in constructing the norms of co-operation, the contracting parties in this constructivist theory would adopt an understanding of punishment which is coercive, which threatens hard treatment, but which is also both communicative and educative.

In short, the strategy pursued in this book is to examine the problem of punishment both for itself and for what it reveals about contemporary theories of justice and of morality. That some such theories cannot give an adequate account of punishment is evidence, or so it is claimed, of deeper flaws in their accounts. Avoiding these flaws ought, therefore, to provide not merely an account of morality, but also an adequate account of punishment. Chapters 1–3 reveal what is needed in an account of punishment. Chapters 4–6 reveal why it is that contemporary theories of justice cannot provide what is needed. Chapters 7–9 attempt to develop a theory that meets the demands of an account of punishment and through this the attempt is made to develop a more adequate moral theory.

# 1

# Consequentialism

## INTRODUCTION

As noted in the introduction, utilitarian accounts of punishment have available to them the resources of a utilitarian moral theory. Consequentialism (of which utilitarianism is a particular variety) holds that the justification of any action is to be found in its consequences. A straightforwardly utilitarian theory holds that an act is right only if its consequences are as good as or better than those that would have resulted from any alternative action (including doing nothing). That is, utilitarianism is a form of consequentialism in which the right act is defined as being that act which will maximize expected net utility. Utilitarianism has a number of attractions as an account of morality and of punishment. Not least, as mentioned in the Introduction above, it captures two important features of any plausible account of morality: that human welfare matters and that one way in which a policy or practice ought to be evaluated is in terms of its consequences for human welfare (see Kymlicka 1990: 11).

The post-war intellectual landscape of political and penal philosophy was dominated by consequentialist reasoning until the 1970s when John Rawls's *A Theory of Justice* changed the face of political and moral philosophy. In the field of punishment the revolt against consequentialism was as much in response to practice as to theory. The revival of retributivism or 'desert theory'[1] in the 1970s was not, as it became, a politically right-wing response to perceived rising crime rates, but rather grew out of a left of centre campaign to eradicate the use of indeterminate sentencing. Apart from the claim that such a sentencing practice was prima facie unjust, it placed the power of setting a release date for incarcerated offenders in the hands of bodies such as parole boards and these were thought (often accurately) to misuse this power so as systematically to discriminate against black, poor, and otherwise 'difficult' offenders (cf. von Hirsch 1976).

---

[1] See, for an important example, von Hirsch 1976.

Philosophically, utilitarianism suffered not just at the hands of Rawls's work but from a more general attack that alleged that it was incompatible with widely held intuitions about the requirements of justice. In this attack examples drawn from punishment were common and so, contemporaneous with utilitarianism's fall into disfavour as a comprehensive account of morality, it also suffered as an account of punishment.

## SECURING HAPPINESS

In a formulation which has become famous Jeremy Bentham begins his *Introduction to the Principles of Morals and Legislation* with the following: 'Nature has placed mankind under the governance of two sovereign masters, *pain* and *pleasure*. It is for them alone to point out what we ought to do, as well as to determine what we shall do' (Bentham 1970: 11). Bentham's utilitarianism is hedonistic, defining the good to be maximized as happiness (which is taken to be the sum of enjoyable experiences an individual has less any painful experiences). It also includes a hedonistic account of motivation; human beings are motivated by their desire to avoid pain and to attain pleasure. This creates a problem for if each agent is motivated by her pain and pleasure, but the good to be maximized is the sum total of pain and pleasure, then there is likely to be a conflict between what the agent is morally obliged to do and what she is motivated to do. Unless she takes pleasure in what happens to others (whether what happens to others is pleasurable or painful) the account of motivation given by Bentham means that each person pursues her good indifferent to every other. There is then a gap between the account of what is morally right and the account of motivation; the morally right act is that which will maximize general utility whilst the agent is motivated to advance her individual utility.

One function of government is to bridge this gap, to ensure that the balance of pain and pleasure anticipated by each individual when thinking of what to do is such that she will be motivated to do that act which will not only be to her greatest advantage, but also to the greatest advantage to the community of which that person is a part. To this end, the government has the use of physical sanctions (supplemented by the manipulation of moral and religious sanctions). The function of law and punishment is to deter actions that are likely to be in the interest of particular individuals but that are detrimental to the good of the community. As Bentham puts it: 'the

general object which all laws have, or ought to have, in common, is to aug-
ment the total happiness of the community; and therefore, in the first
place, to exclude, as far as may be, everything that tends to subtract from
that happiness: in other words, to exclude mischief' (Bentham 1970: 158).

Punishment, then, has only contingent value. In itself, as the infliction of
pain, it is wrong. Its value, and what when it is correctly administered
makes it right, is that it can prevent a greater evil (Bentham 1970). This is
a structural feature of this form of consequentialism: given an independently identified end (however defined), actions or policies have value only
insofar as they promote that end. Thus, utilitarian accounts of punishment
need to show not just that the promotion of utility can be served by the
infliction of punishment, but that a system of punishment is better than
any alternative form of social control at promoting that end. Insofar as utilitarians assume that the 'problem' is to justify punishment (in some form
broadly similar to that which currently exists in much of the developed
West), they beg the question. They need first to show that a utilitarian society would have a system of punishment (cf. Duff 1986: 157–8).

In addition to incorporating the benefits of consequentialism mentioned above (the concern for human welfare and the importance of
human welfare in the evaluation of acts or policies), Bentham's theory of
punishment has the attraction of seeming to respect the idea that the government may legitimately concern itself with how an individual (within its
jurisdiction) acts but not with how she thinks. That is, the aim of government in Bentham's scheme is to ensure that individuals act in such a way
that they do what will promote the greatest good of the community; how
each individual thinks or what private beliefs each individual holds is not a
matter of public concern. The state defines certain actions as wrong, and
attaches penalties to those actions so as to deter potential offenders. The
actions that the state may legitimately class as wrong are only those that if
permitted would lead to a decrease in net utility (in comparison with the
level that would be reached in the absence of such a prohibition).[2] In addition, given that punishment is for Bentham a necessary evil there should be
a tendency to parsimony in the setting of penalties; the quantum of punishment attached to any given act ought to be just sufficient to deter the
potential offender from committing the act of offending and certainly
ought not to be so great as to encourage him to commit a more serious
crime.[3]

[2] Indeed, this, for Bentham, is the definition of wrong, see Bentham 1970: ch. I, § X.
[3] This feature of Bentham's work is often overlooked. His argument is simple: if the
penalty for robbery is similar to that for armed robbery then the potential offender might

Utilitarianism has, of course, come a long way since Bentham, but nevertheless the essential features of this form of utilitarianism remain the same: punishment is one of many ways of trying to alter the calculation of individual advantage so as to bridge the gap between the pursuit of individual good and the general good and to assure others that this gap has been closed. Its function is to attach an extra potential cost to particular activities so as to deter potential wrongdoers and thus secure a situation in which each can generally rely on every other. It is a theory of specific and general deterrence aimed at preventing crime and securing 'stability of expectations'.[4]

This simple form of utilitarianism in which the morally right act is that which will maximize aggregate utility has a number of less attractive features. The importance of human welfare is transformed in utilitarianism into the command to maximize the good (in this case happiness) and this is independent of considerations of distribution. The locus of value lies in the state of affairs that results from a given action or policy and this has led to the allegation that utilitarianism is insensitive to what Rawls has called 'the separateness of persons' (Rawls 1971: 27). That is, to considerations of the distribution of welfare motivated by our sense that the locus of value lies not in some state of affairs but in individuals.

This feature of utilitarianism is at the heart of many criticisms and is often captured through the use of examples drawn from the realm of punishment. Thus, it is claimed, in certain circumstances utilitarianism would determine that the morally obligatory action would be to frame and punish an innocent person in order to avoid some greater evil; to inflict disproportionate penalties on some offenders so as to deter others; and so on. In short, as long as it is true that the only morally significant fact is the total of a given good (utility) that is realized it is conceivable that utilitarianism

as well carry a firearm when he goes to commit the crime. If the penalty for armed robbery is raised so that it becomes close to that for murder (in order to avoid this problem) then the armed robber has reason to kill the policeman pursuing him, and so on (see Ch. 9 below).

4 Utilitarians also often argue that punishment can be incapacitative and rehabilitative. That is, it can stop potential offenders by geographically separating them from places in which there are the opportunities to offend and it can try to alter the agent in such a way as to encourage him not to offend. The second of these is consonant with the characterization of the function of punishment given above. The first also seems to be so. Incapacitation is needed when the agent cannot be relied upon to calculate correctly and see that crime will not pay or, in the even that crime does pay, it is needed to secure the general good from an individual who does not have the necessary social, moral, or religious scruples to stop him pursuing his pleasure through criminal activity.

will demand the sacrifice of some in order to achieve a greater sum total of utility to be enjoyed by others.

The second unattractive feature of this kind of utilitarianism is the use of pain and pleasure (or even a slightly more complex measure such as 'enjoyable states') as the measure of welfare and as the foundation of human motivation. Bentham's view that the pleasures of poetry were identical to those of pushpin and that such an account was sufficient to explain human motivation was famously found wanting by John Stuart Mill who subsequently introduced qualitative distinctions into the idea of happiness. However, the more sensitive and realistic the maximand is the less likely it is that the utilitarian will be able to perform the interpersonal comparisons that are needed.

The third, related, worry is that for all the apparent liberalism of allowing the government legitimate concern only in people's public actions (rather than in their thoughts or private behaviour), there is something manipulative in the proposal that the government try to deter the performance of utility decreasing actions by threatening sanctions. To try to affect the way people behave by threatening to make them suffer if they choose certain actions is to offer prudential reasons that coerce rather than moral reasons that persuade (cf. Chapter 9 below). This fails to respect the idea of free choice which is essential to the liberal view of the individual. No liberal could endorse Bentham's remark—made with reference to his projected prison (the *Panopticon*)—'Call them men, call them monks, call them soldiers, call them machines; I care not so long as they be happy ones' (Bentham quoted in Ryan 1987: 33).

Of course, the form of utilitarianism described above is no longer representative of utilitarianism generally, if it ever was.[5] Utilitarianism has become a great deal more sophisticated and the following sections deal with some more developed accounts and their response to the three criticisms mentioned above: the problem of distributive insensitivity; of defining the maximand; and of manipulation. The earlier sections deal mainly with the first and third of these objections. In the final sections of the chapter a different understanding of utilitarianism is offered, one which tries to address these objections and to present a more plausible moral theory. It is an account of utilitarianism in which rather than offering an account of the good to be maximized utilitarianism is formulated so as to be a theory of the right designed to cope adequately with the need to respect people in a world characterized by the reasonableness of pluralism.

---

[5] For a sympathetic view of Bentham see Kelly 1990.

## THE IMPORTANCE OF RULES

One of the allegations made above is that utilitarianism demands that aggregate utility is maximized irrespective of the equity or otherwise of the distribution of utility because it locates value in states of affairs rather than in individual agents. As a result in particular circumstances utilitarianism permits, or makes obligatory, the sacrifice of some to promote a valued state of affairs. One of the most common examples used in such arguments is the claim that utilitarianism can justify the punishment of the innocent. One standard story in the literature concerns a sheriff in a small town in which there are two racial communities and a degree of underlying tension. A woman is raped and the members of the community to which she belongs threaten to riot. The sheriff realizes that he can avert the riot by framing an innocent member of the other community who happened to have been near the scene of the rape. Assuming that more disutility will be produced by a race riot than by the punishment of the innocent man, utilitarianism, it is alleged, makes it morally obligatory for the sheriff to frame the innocent man.[6]

Examples such as this form the basis of certain critiques of utilitarianism.[7] There are a number of ways in which utilitarians can respond to this kind of criticism two of which are of special relevance to the argument that follows. The first is that examples such as the above only show that there can be, in certain (fairly extreme) circumstances, conflicts between our intuitions about justice and the demands of utilitarianism. Some further argument is needed to show why in such circumstances it is not our intuitions that should give way. This is not, of course, to say that our ordinary moral intuitions about punishing the innocent are wrong, merely that they are intuitions grounded in, and relevant to, ordinary experience. The constructed examples of philosophers are, so some defenders of utilitarianism claim, so far from reality that there is reason to doubt the appropriateness of using our intuitions in such cases (cf. Nielson 1971).

This objection is linked to the second defence of utilitarianism: that the example of the sheriff given above is a parody or caricature of utilitarian

---

[6] This is a very common example. It was first introduced into the literature (I think) by McCloskey 1968.

[7] Others, not drawn from punishment, include circumstances in which it appears morally obligatory for a very successful transplant surgeon to kill a healthy visitor to her ward so as to use the visitor's organs to save a number of critically ill patients each of whom requires a (different) organ transplant.

reasoning. The fact of the matter is that no genuine utilitarian theory would endorse the arbitrary use, or even the holding, of such extensive power by a sheriff. The knowledge that the law officers in a town held such power would itself be a disutility as the inhabitants would worry about the possibility of being framed. Additional disutility would result from leaving the real culprit free (a consequence of convicting the innocent), and so on. Insofar as the example is changed—or more conditions are added (such as that nobody ever finds out about the sheriff's actions, or knows of his powers, the real perpetrator of the rape never reoffends, etc.)—the example moves further from the 'real world' and the objection outlined above (that in fantastic cases our intuitions are no longer relevant) becomes more plausible. If further specifications are not added the claim is that the reasoning attributed to the utilitarian sheriff simply gets the nature of utilitarianism wrong. Act, or direct, utilitarianism of the kind on which the above example relies misses the point; utilitarianism is best interpreted as applying to systems or practices not individual acts. This can either be stipulative—utilitarianism is then interpreted as a theory of public morality, a means of deriving morally correct rules—or derived from utilitarian reason itself. A society in which utility is maximized will have established rules so as to promote what Bentham called 'stability of expectations' (as such stability is essential to the promotion of utility) and so as to eliminate excessive costs in calculating the correct act in broadly similar situations.[8]

In the first instance, this move to rules can be made without having to endorse consequentialism as a complete moral theory. Such is the nature of John Rawls's argument in his seminal paper 'Two Concepts of Rules' (Rawls 1955) which includes a detailed argument about the punishment— or 'telishment'—of an innocent scapegoat.[9] Rawls distinguishes between 'justifying a practice and justifying a particular action falling under it' (1955: 144). His argument is, essentially, that once a practice is up and running the participants cannot coherently appeal outside of the rules that govern and define the practice, even to considerations that inform the structure of the practice itself.

Rawls's simplest example is of a game of baseball. He notes that if a batter were to ask whether he could have four strikes this would normally be

---

[8] For a stirring attack on the 'nonsense' of assuming that a commitment to utilitarianism requires that the agent 'test each individual action directly by the first principle' see Mill 1987: 296–7.

[9] Rawls 1955: 144–70. 'Telishment' is the term Rawls adopts in order to avoid definitional problems. There are numerous discussions of rule- (or indirect-) utilitarianism (e.g. Smart and Williams 1973; Lyons 1965); for a discussion which is historically informative, see Gray 1989: ch. 8.

taken to be a request to have the rules clarified for him. If, when told that the rules only entitled him to three, he said that he knew this but he thought that on this occasion it would be better for all concerned if he had four, 'this would be most kindly taken as a joke' (1955: 164). Rawls makes a logical claim, that if one does not follow the rules of a practice, one is simply no longer doing the same thing; 'the rules of practices are logically prior to particular cases.'[10] Thus, although one can swing a piece of wood at a ball and run if one hits it, one cannot play baseball unless one is engaged in the practice of baseball, and following the rules that define it. Of course, this does not stop the player trying to change the rules of baseball in the out season if he believes that it would be a better game if four rather than three strikes were required to dismiss the batter. The justification of the rules is independent of the justification of any particular act that falls under them.

With respect to punishment, Rawls argues that instituting a practice of 'telishment'—in which officials 'have authority to arrange a trial for the condemnation of an innocent man whenever they are of the opinion that doing so would be in the best interests of society' (1955: 151)—would be so hazardous that a 'utilitarian justification for this institution [would be] most unlikely' (1955: 152). Instead, Rawls believes, the practice most likely to receive utilitarian backing would be one similar to the practice of punishment as we know it, with all the checks of the right to audience, the presumption of innocence, etc. in place. 'It happens in general', Rawls remarks, 'that as one drops off the defining features of punishment one ends up with an institution whose utilitarian justification is highly doubtful' (1955: 152).

Assume that Rawls is right, and that empirical conditions would mean that a consequentially justified system of rules for regulating society and dealing with offenders would include something which resembles a system of just punishment (but see McCloskey 1972). Rawls's argument, then, is that having established the practice of punishment with rules governing who may be punished and how, those rules must take precedence over any direct appeal to the consequences in any particular instance. The result is something that looks very much like Hart's 'mixed account' in 'Prolegomenon to the Principles of Punishment' (1959), in which the

---

[10] It is important to distinguish this logical claim from the argument, often ascribed to Kant's view on promise breaking, that if one allowed the breaking of the rules in any given practice then that practice would wither away because people would lose confidence in it. Rawls explicitly rejects this argument with reference to promise keeping, Rawls 1955: 154–5.

general justifying aim of punishment is consequentialist, but the principle governing the distribution is derived from demands of fairness.

At its simplest the idea is that, for example, given the circumstance in which an innocent individual is charged with an offence in a magistrate's court, the magistrate is not at liberty to convict and punish that individual because, in this instance, there would be a net gain in utility, because she can only operate on the rules that define and constitute the practice of punishment. She cannot appeal to the utilitarian grounding of the practice itself. Thus, the practice of punishment that would receive a utilitarian justification makes the statement 'you are innocent but, for the benefit of society, I am going to punish you anyway', nonsensical (cf. Duff 1986: 162–3).

Such a statement is nonsensical, but would anyone say such a thing? Consider the practice of promise keeping, Rawls's argument must be that if anyone said, 'I have no intention of doing $x$, but I promise to do $x$', they would be speaking nonsense. They would not understand what it is to make a promise. However, if one thought that all things considered it would be better to make a false promise one would not say such a thing, or describe one's actions in such terms. As Antony Duff points out, what one would think is, 'all things considered, it would be better if I *pretended* to promise to do $x$, even though I know that I will be unable to do $x$ when the time comes' (1986: 163).[11] This is not logically incoherent, it is simply deceitful, and, of course, if one is trying to realize consequentialist ends it is likely that such deceit will be necessary. Similarly, the magistrate would not admit in open court, 'I know you to be innocent, but for the good of society I am going to punish you', rather she would say, 'you are guilty and I am going to punish you', although she knows the person to be innocent.[12]

Rawls's argument that there is a logical failure in the criticism of rule-utilitarianism cannot then be sustained. However, that does not blunt the force of the utilitarian claim that utilitarianism may be able to generate a fair system of punishment, a system of punishment compatible with the intuitions of a given set of people, given the world in which such people live.[13] If this is the case then it seems as if utilitarians can justify all that is

[11]  What one would say, of course, is 'I promise to do $x$'.

[12]  Cf. Duff 1986: 163. As Duff makes clear, the importance of this argument is that it emphasizes that punishing the innocent violates criteria which are internal to the concept of punishment; deliberately punishing an innocent is a perversion of punishment, and this is why it must be accompanied by dishonesty and deceit on the part of the punishing authorities.

[13]  There is clearly a connection between the intuitions people will have about 'fair' punishment and the conditions in which they live. In the democratic first world the

asked of them and such a conclusion leaves the utilitarian in a very strong position. However, there are a number of questions that can be raised about the two-level structure of rule utilitarianism even where it is reinterpreted so that it makes claims contingent on the way the world is rather than on the more solid ground of logic. First, once one rejects the logical impermissibility of appeals to direct utilitarian reasoning the insistence that a given agent ought never to break the rules seems questionable and the whole two-level structure seems liable to collapse. Second, even if the world is such that the rules that would be justified by a utilitarian scheme are fair ones, and such that there are never good utilitarian reasons for disobeying those rules, the reliance on the contingency of circumstance has led some to argue that utilitarianism is an inappropriate moral theory.

The first point is this: given that there is no logical inconsistency in appealing to utility circumstances might plausibly arise in which utility would be better served by an agent ignoring some (justified) rule and acting as she would if she were an act utilitarian. To deny that the agent should do this, to insist that she follow the rule, seems to introduce a kind of moral schizophrenia. The agent knows that the right thing to do is, say, to punish this individual given the utility maximizing purpose of the system of punishment, but knows that the rule requires that she release him. If it is not logically incoherent, why should she give precedence to the rule instead of breaking it and 'keeping it dark' (Mabbott 1955: 128)?[14] It seems very difficult to believe that the world will always be such that a direct appeal to utility is not justified. Obedience to the rules is itself reduced to an action that must be assessed by direct appeal to utility and this undermines the distinction between the two levels.[15]

circumstances are such that utilitarianism will generate the normal structures of the criminal justice system. In more pressing circumstances it may be that the intuitions people have about fair punishment are different, but also that utilitarianism delivers different answers.

[14] See also Mabbott 1939 and Ten 1987: 71. This argument applies, *mutatis mutandis*, to Hart's (1959) thesis. The point is that 'mixed theories' of the Hart type offer no account of how the different demands of yielding good consequences and matching moral desert can be reconciled. Instead they try to confine them to different spheres of punishment (see Goldman 1979, 1982: 62).

[15] The analogy with games, which is a very common and powerful argument deployed by rule utilitarians, is somewhat misleading in that games (ignoring for the moment professional sports) do not have a point (a participant in a game might think that the point is to win but this is internal to the playing of the game, for the most part playing games itself does not have a point). The rules of a game cannot then conflict with the purpose of the game. In the case of two-level utilitarianism, in contrast, obedience to a particular rule may conflict with the purpose of having the system of rules. It is interesting that where the playing of games does have some point, for example where an experienced player is trying to teach a less experienced one, often rules will be bent or ignored in pursuit of the overall purpose of playing.

The second objection to the defence that utilitarianism can deliver all the safeguards of fair distribution that might be wanted given a realistic assessment of the world as it is is that it fails to understand what is at the centre of the critics' worries. Arguing in reply to the allegation that utilitarianism can sanction the punishment of the innocent by claiming that there are unlikely to be 'real world' circumstances in which this is true is somehow missing the point. The allegation is that any moral theory that can consider the rightness or wrongness of punishing the innocent as a moot question contingent on circumstance is mistaken (irrespective of whether, as a fact about the world, utilitarianism would demand such a thing). This is surely what has motivated utilitarianism's most severe critics to write as if it is only a matter of time before utilitarianism is thought to be so wrong-headed as to be on a par with phrenology (cf. Williams 1973). Of course, there is a hint of circularity in the critics' argument: consequentialism is wrong because the reasons it gives are consequentialist. However, it captures the worry underpinning two of the three objections above, that utilitarianism fails to give sufficient weight to the distribution of utility (if it does so it is only for contingent reasons), and that in so doing it fails to respect persons and their individual importance.

The arguments above are of the kind that dominate the punishment literature and they will be relevant to what follows. However, the difficulty with assessing them comes from their separation from a broader utilitarian framework. The questions, 'can utilitarian justifications of punishment protect the innocent?', 'Can they deliver proportionality in punishments?', etc. are important, but their importance lies in demonstrating that an overall utilitarian theory cannot be adequate. What punishment theorists assume when they ask these questions is that the answers demonstrate the following fundamental difficulty with utilitarianism: if utilitarianism ascribes fundamental value to states of affairs and not to individual agents then it cannot, except by chance, satisfy distributive criteria based on the value we ascribe to individuals. The individual appears in utilitarian theory as nothing other than a place holder of a certain quantum of utility. Although this interpretation of utilitarianism is not uncommon, it is only one reading and a fairly implausible one at that.[16] It is implausible because, as Kymlicka points out, one cannot have a moral duty to maximize utility

---

[16] For example: 'C[onsequentialism] ascribes intrinsic value to states of affairs. The value of everything else . . . is extrinsic' (Anderson 1996: 539–40). Rawls in *A Theory of Justice* at times interprets utilitarianism in this 'teleological' way (Rawls 1971: § 5) and it is the basis of his famous critique that utilitarianism 'does not take seriously the separateness of persons (1971: 27).

for there is nothing to which such a moral duty could be owed (Kymlicka 1990: 33). Instead utilitarianism is more plausibly interpreted as a mechanism through which the ideal of respect for persons is realized. Put in general terms: one ought to do what is best and what is best is to realize the best consequences for the most people as it is human welfare that matters. In the next two sections two different types of consequentialist theory that try to develop this general conception are examined. The first retains many of the features of the kind of utilitarianism discussed above, but attempts to avoid the criticisms by expanding the maximand. The second alters the structure of the theory more fundamentally. However, before looking at these theories it is necessary to say something about the nature of the utilitarian maximand.

If the concern is to do what is best for the most people then it is necessary to offer an account of how 'bestness' is to be defined. There are, it seems, two ways that this might be achieved. One might ask people what they want and how happy it makes them to get it, or one might give some account of some goods that every person wants and then draw up a list of these interpersonal goods. These two options, between a subjective measure such as preference satisfaction and an interpersonal one such as 'functionings', have been much discussed in the literature and will structure the remainder of this chapter. Each has its attractions; if one is to do what is best for people (because people matter) then the idea that things should be organized so that people get what they want seems intuitively plausible. However, it raises difficulties concerning how interpersonal comparisons of utility can be measured, and also problems given what people might want. If utility is measured in terms of some set of general goods that everyone is thought to want then it might be easier to do the calculations required by utilitarianism, but it may create an odd situation in which a given individual is said to be better off even when she explicitly denies this and denies ever wanting the things that are said to have contributed to her increased utility. This issue, of what is to be counted, will reappear in the examination of the two consequentialist theories discussed below.


## MAXIMIZING EQUAL CONTROL


In a recent book on the justification of a criminal justice system an eminent criminologist and an equally well-respected philosopher, John Braithwaite and Philip Pettit, attempt to combine two important strands in the history of moral philosophy; republicanism and consequentialism.[17] In many ways Braithwaite's and Pettit's book, *Not Just Deserts*, tries to relocate penal philosophy back within a broad moral philosophy, an aspiration that is shared by the current enquiry.

Although Braithwaite and Pettit are consequentialists they differ from the standard position discussed above in that the account that they offer of the maximand of their consequentialism is one of 'republican freedom' or what they call 'dominion' (Braithwaite and Pettit 1990: 61–9). This is defined as follows:

A person enjoys full dominion if and only if: (1) she enjoys no less a prospect of liberty than is available to other citizens. (2) it is common knowledge among citizens that this condition obtains, so that she and nearly everyone else knows that she enjoys the prospect mentioned, she and nearly everyone else knows that the others generally know this too, and so on. (3) she enjoys no less a prospect of liberty than the best that is compatible with the same prospect for all citizens. (Braithwaite and Pettit 1990: 64–5)

Despite the formality of the above definition it does not capture the real flavour of dominion. Dominion is something close to the capacity to determine the shape of one's own life. It is different from both negative liberty and self-determination in the sense of autonomy because it is not opposed to interference in principle, only interference that is arbitrary. Education, for example, is on some accounts a restriction of autonomy because it is an 'outside' influence, but it increases dominion because it improves the agent's capacity to shape his own life (the same is true of some paternalistic interventions). Similarly, and more relevantly, a law restricting, say, murder does not diminish the agent's dominion (even though it may be a restriction on the agent's negative freedom) because so long as it is correctly instituted, publicly known, etc., it does not impose any arbitrary restriction on the agent and so the agent can shape his life in the knowledge that murder cannot be part of it. In addition, such a law enhances the agent's dominion because it creates a more stable environment in which, others things being equal, an agent's reasonable expectations of what the future will be like will, in fact, in the future obtain.

Although dominion is an interpersonal measure—it is an account of something that is assumed to be good to promote independent of whether

---

[17] Philip Pettit has subsequently produced a book offering a fuller account of republicanism (Pettit 1997) which incorporates and develops many of the arguments of *Not Just Deserts*. John Braithwaite is responsible for much of the most interesting work in what has become known as restorative criminology (see, e.g. Braithwaite 1989, 1999).

every individual expresses a desire for it—it also contains within it an important subjective element: 'crucially . . . to enjoy dominion you must know that you enjoy all that it otherwise involves' (Braithwaite and Pettit 1990: 9). Thus, for example, both crime and the fear of crime undermine the agent's dominion by reducing the agent's control or sense of control over the shape of her life.

This change in the maximand would seem to meet a number of the criticisms mentioned above. It is, on the face of it, an interpersonal measure which nevertheless allows each individual space to want different things (that is, it is an interpersonal measure that does not seem to obliterate the evident differences in what people want and the ways in which they wish to live their lives). It seems to avoid the manipulation problem by making (a form of) human freedom the maximand, and, perhaps most importantly, it has within it a distributive condition so that a (formally) egalitarian distribution (of dominion) is not in conflict with the aggregative demand to maximize dominion. With such a robust maximand Braithwaite and Pettit use the notion of dominion not only to explain what is wrong with crime (it diminishes dominion), but also to justify the practice of punishment (having it secures greater dominion than not having it), the correct methods of policing, the nature of sentences, and a host of other questions related to the criminal justice system.[18]

On closer examination each of the above advantages is questionable. One reason to prefer a subjective to an interpersonal measure of utility is that if one endorses a straightforward interpersonal measure (like money) then it raises the problem that for various reasons some people will be able to convert a certain sum of money into a lot of satisfaction, others into only a little. It seems unfair then to measure utility in terms of money (in this example) rather than in the satisfaction that the money brings. However, one reason to prefer money as a measure is that it is difficult, perhaps impossible, to make interpersonal comparisons of satisfaction. Dominion combines both approaches but is also vulnerable to both associated sets of problems.

Dominion combines both approaches by being so broad a measure. The problem in the above example is that money is worth less to some people than it is to others if one measures worthiness in terms of the satisfaction

---

[18] For a list of all the questions addressed see Braithwaite and Pettit 1990: 12–15. The fact that one theory, developed over 209 pages, can have something to say about every aspect of the criminal justice system, from the justification of punishment, to who should be taxed to pay for it, to prosecutorial and parole practices, is described by the authors as 'incredible but true' (but cf. von Hirsch and Ashworth 1992).

brought. Dominion seems to escape this problem. By being the condition of being able to do what one wishes with one's life—subject only to the limitations of variable circumstance (see Braithwaite and Pettit 1990: 66), reasonable expectations, and non-arbitrary interference—dominion is sufficiently broad that it precludes being of unequal value to different people. Choice of lifestyle (within those restrictions), even the choice not to value choice of lifestyle, is what is secured. However, Braithwaite and Pettit must accept that dominion is made up of many different elements each of which can be manipulated independently. This is explicit in their analysis of law. Laws restrict one aspect of dominion, one's negative freedom, but by doing so increase overall dominion by providing stability and assurance of one's dominion. However, if each aspect of dominion can be traded off against the other then this raises the problem that the rates at which people will trade off these elements will be different. One agent may desire greater restrictions in freedom of movement, say a night curfew, because he does not greatly value going out at night, but he does value feeling secure. Having such a rule will greatly increase his dominion because he will feel more secure. Another agent might prefer few restrictions on freedom of movement, but wish to inhibit the freedom of speech of people who denigrate the ethnic group of which she is a member. She may, for example, feel threatened or feel that her capacity to develop fully is reduced by living in a community in which such speech is allowed. Braithwaite's and Pettit's problem is that the attempt to be fair to everyone by making the maximand so broad undermines the claim to be able to make the necessary interpersonal comparisons. Ruling such trade offs out in favour of declarations of how the elements of dominion are hierarchically structured would resolve this problem, but only at a cost to the claim that dominion represents a measure that is fair to all because it is desired to a similar degree by all.

The problem that the social decision mechanism is imperfect is hardly unique to the theory offered by Braithwaite and Pettit and might be thought to be addressed to the wrong part of their argument. What is needed is to address the plausibility of the moral theory that they endorse not the difficulties inherent in putting it into practice. Criticisms of the overall theory can be made. They concern issues of manipulation and distribution.

One of the presumptions of Braithwaite and Pettit is that the criminal justice system is reprobative. As might be expected from a book co-authored by the author of *Crime, Shame and Reintegration* (Braithwaite 1989) Braithwaite and Pettit are concerned to show that punishment is about censure, blame, and restoration. However, as the title of their book (*Not Just Deserts*) suggests their conception of blame and censure is not the standard one. Rather than couple blame and desert they endorse an instrumental view of the former. Blame and censure are valuable parts of the criminal justice system because they are efficient ways of influencing the future behaviour of the offender and of others. Braithwaite and Pettit present a theory that is reminiscent of Bentham's account. Each individual cannot be relied upon to pursue her life choices in a manner compatible with the promotion of general dominion so extra disincentives are necessary to try to alter the individual's behaviour. These disincentives can range from criminal sanctions to social disapproval. Thus, as Andrew von Hirsch and Andrew Ashworth have pointed out, if a white collar offender and a 'street criminal' are convicted of offences of comparable gravity then there is according to Braithwaite and Pettit nothing wrong with punishing the white collar offender more leniently than the other whilst publicizing the white collar offender's name and crime. This is because white collar criminals are generally more affected by social stigma (von Hirsch and Ashworth 1992: 93). Indeed, given that punitive sanctions are dominion diminishing such a policy might be required so as to minimize the use of punitive sanctions where others will be equally effective.

This use of blame as 'dispraise' has been advocated by J. J. C. Smart and is for many a *reductio* of consequentialism (see below, Chapter 2). The reason is that it is explicitly manipulative and, although this is not troublesome for someone who thinks human freedom a mirage, it therefore fails to respect the idea of agency central to liberal theory and to the republican tradition to which Braithwaite and Pettit appeal. Censure, blame, and reprobation are intimately connected to the idea of desert and to decouple them from it is to endorse a conception of agency that is very different from the one that underpins the concern for dominion. After all, why should one think dominion valuable if one thinks it satisfactory to manipulate the choices individuals make through the threat of coercion rather than through persuasion? Braithwaite's and Pettit's theory cannot escape the accusation that it involves manipulation.

Moreover, Braithwaite and Pettit cannot avoid the claim that their theory is insensitive to distributive concerns. The problem stems from the fundamentally aggregative heart of the account. Although dominion contains within it a formal egalitarianism it remains true either that the promotion of dominion is best achieved by sacrificing the interests of some so as to improve the overall position, or that if this is not the case it is for contingent rather than principled reasons. The first of these accusations can be substantiated by thinking of the relationship of the severity of punishment and the subjective element of dominion. The fear of crime is not necessarily rational, indeed often the groups the members of which fear most being the victims of crime are also the statistically least likely to suffer any such attack.[19] Assume, as Ralf Dahrendorf (1985) suggests, that increased penalties may reduce fear of crime even if they have no effect on crime rates (cf. von Hirsch and Ashworth 1992: 91). If this is true then Braithwaite and Pettit are in a position where if they do not advocate the increasing of penalties it can only be for some contingent reason. Perhaps there may be more dominion protecting methods of reducing this fear. If there were no such mechanisms (and there may very well not be) then there is nothing in their account that could be used to stop the ratcheting up of the sentences for some offenders to a point well beyond that demanded by proportionality.

A similar criticism can be made of Braithwaite's and Pettit's discussion of the punishment of the innocent. Braithwaite and Pettit consider the case (discussed above) of the sheriff, the innocent man, and the mob. They argue, in the normal two-level way, that given the circumstances that are likely to obtain the promotion of dominion is best achieved by indirect reasoning. The sheriff should aim at the protection of rights and the upholding of the law, not directly at the promotion of dominion. However, the degree of indirectness that they endorse is open to question. At one point Braithwaite and Pettit seem to suggest that the dominion promoting agent (the sheriff) ought to become so disposed that he is incapable of considering any option that breaks the rules under all circumstances. They write that 'the sheriff who takes the promotion of dominion seriously will deny himself the possibility of offending against such [uncontroversial] rights' (Braithwaite and Pettit 1990: 72). However, they cannot mean that the sheriff should become the sort of person who is in some sense psychologically incapable of thinking in this way (even were that possible). What they must mean is rather that the sheriff who is concerned to promote dominion must be disposed to maintain the law (or 'uncontroversial rights') and must be known to be so. Of course, the sheriff might consider whether in a given case he ought to break the law to ensure some good outcome, but he is aware when he thinks this that even the fact that he thinks such thoughts (were it to become known) might undermine the subjective element of dominion.

However, as discussed above, this argument seems heavily dependent on assertions about the way the world is. In addition, it seems an inappropri-

---

[19] Elderly women fearing violent crime often fit this category.

ate response when considering the punishment of the innocent. It may be the case that framing an innocent man is likely to undermine dominion in the long run, but there is a large distance between all the protections of a liberal criminal justice system and framing a complete innocent. The sheriff is much more likely to try to use, for example, what ought to be inadmissible evidence to ensure the conviction of someone whom he has independent reasons to think guilty and in so doing he may very well have the support of a proportion of the population. So long as it is generally believed that the police only bend the rules when they are dealing with people who they are confident are guilty of some crime, even if not the particular one in question, many people might feel more not less secure. 'The balance has tilted too far to the offender and too far from the victim and the police' is a currently popular rallying cry and was used in the UK to defend getting rid of what were thought to be basic rights (such as the right to remain silent under questioning and not have this be to one's disadvantage in one's defence). The point here is not to allege that removing this right promotes dominion or that the regular bending of the rules of evidence will do so. The point is that given the failure of the logical argument of Rawls and of the psychological impossibility argument of Braithwaite and Pettit, all that one needs to allege is that there are circumstances that are not fantastic in which dominion might best be promoted by the sacrificing of the rights of one or a group of agents. In such a circumstance Braithwaite's and Pettit's aggregating strategy cannot but endorse the sacrifice.

In any case, as noted above, even if it is granted that no non-fantastic circumstances are likely to obtain in which the promotion of dominion will best be served by keeping to rules that resemble those of a system of just punishment, the reasons offered for why, for example, the innocent should not be sacrificed are not satisfactory. Considering the sacrifice of the innocent, Braithwaite and Pettit write that to promote dominion in such a direct way is nonsensical because 'once it becomes a matter of common suspicion that the authorities use the promotion of overall dominion to justify particular invasions, then the dominion of ordinary people in the society is jeopardized' (Braithwaite and Pettit 1990: 74). However, what is wrong with sacrificing the innocent is not that it will endanger the dominion of others, what is wrong with it is that an innocent person is sacrificed.

Braithwaite's and Pettit's position is untenable because its structure remains that of identifying a good (in their case dominion) and promoting the aggregate of that good. It is essentially the same theory as is discussed in the early sections of this chapter and it suffers from essentially the same flaws.

## SECOND-ORDER UTILITARIANISM

Above it was said that it was implausible to think of having a moral obligation to a state of affairs and that instead utilitarianism should be interpreted as a way of realizing the ethical commitment of equal respect. The
basis of the criticisms of utilitarianism discussed above is that utilitarianism offers an account of the good and adds the demand that the good be
maximized. This structure is flawed. A different approach is offered by
what one might call second-order utilitarianism.

Assume that there are many people in a society who disagree about the
nature of the good and whose disagreement is reasonable, that is it cannot
at the moment be resolved by reason. What all the people agree upon is that
they need to make certain decisions which will affect them all and which
will establish rules or norms that will govern their future interactions. Such
people might agree that what they should do is ask each person what she
wants and then do those things or institute those rules that will satisfy the
most of these wants. Although certain shared assumptions, to be discussed
below, are needed, these people need not agree on a particular substantive
account of the good. They need merely to endorse utilitarianism as a standard of rightness. Specifically a way of giving content to the idea that we
should treat everyone with equal respect. On such an account the command to maximize utility is derived from the more fundamental idea that
each person deserves equal consideration (see Kymlicka 1990: ch. 1). As
such, utilitarianism can be interpreted as a theorem of justice as impartiality, a reaction to what Rawls has called 'the fact of pluralism' (see Chapter
4 below).

More formally: if the fundamental problem of contemporary political
philosophy is taken to be the finding and justifying of public rules of justice to govern societies in which there is reasonable, profound, and seemingly irresolvable conflict between people on the question of what
constitutes the good life for human beings, or on the question of the best
way to live, then one seemingly fair way of achieving this goal is to institute
a system which gives equal weight to each person's preferences regardless of
the content of such preferences. Indeed, one might think with Richard
Hare that it is difficult to think of a way of showing equal respect other than
by treating the preferences of each person as worthy of equal consideration
(Hare 1984).

Such an account of utilitarianism can be characterized as second-order,
by which it is meant that this is not an account of the sort offered at the

beginning of this chapter in which an account of value is given (e.g. happiness or utility) and then the morally right action is that action which will maximize the amount of that value in the world. Rather, second-order utilitarianism allows that each person may have his own idea of what the good is for him (and possibly for others). The job of the theory is to provide a way of collecting together the different claims of different people. At its simplest the idea is this: imagine a group of people trying to decide where to have dinner. They differ in that some would prefer Indian food, others Chinese, etc. The obvious and fair way to decide this, the utilitarian claims, is to add up the preferences for each type of food (and perhaps the intensity of the preferences) and then go to the restaurant that will satisfy more of the preferences than any other. This is fair because nobody is excluded from consideration (nobody's preferences are discounted because they are, for example, black or female), not because the result will treat each person equally, for clearly some people are going to get more of what they want than others. In contrast to the teleological view discussed in previous sections the group does not go to the restaurant that will satisfy most preferences because they have a duty to realize a state of affairs in which most preferences are satisfied, but rather they maximize preference satisfaction as a result of a commitment to treat each person equally by giving each person's preferences equal consideration.

This move to utilitarianism as derived from equal respect, and understood as a means of addressing the fact of pluralism, has been challenged as misrepresenting the relationship of the agent to her commitments and beliefs. This is because the method requires that all commitments and beliefs are converted into the common currency of preferences and this seems to violate an important element of our self-understanding. A version of this argument can be found in Brian Barry's *Justice as Impartiality* (1995*a*). Barry's example is a good one for his purposes as it involves invoking a value (the integrity of the natural world) which is only with difficulty translated into a human want. Many people hold an ecocentric conception of the good part of which is the belief 'that nature, as an object of reverence, love and respect, itself has a moral worth and therefore should be protected for its own sake and not simply for the "satisfaction" or "benefits" it offers human beings' (Sagoff 1988: 149; quoted in Barry 1995*a*: 21). The example Barry gives is of a community that must decide whether to build a dam given that to do so will destroy the habitat of an endangered fish, the snail-darter.[20] Consider an agent who thinks that the dam ought not be built

---

[20] This is a 'real life' case (see Kelly 1998: 49).

because she holds an ecocentric conception of the good. Barry comments that if the decision is made in accordance with want-satisfaction (that is, using the common currency of human wants) then such an agent will have to argue that 'the case against building the dam is that a lot of people . . . want to save the snail-darter, and that, if enough people want to save it, want-satisfaction will be increased by not building the dam' (Barry 1995*a*: 151). This, Barry thinks, 'is enough to show how absurd is the assumption that the rationale of the referendum must be a want-satisfying one. For the basis of your opposition to the dam is that, from the point of view of an ecocentric conception of the good, it would be wrong to extinguish a species in pursuit of human interests of less than critical importance' (1995*a*: 151).

Barry's argument is that if the agent endorses utilitarianism as the means by which to decide the issue of whether to build the dam (via a referendum) then this entails that the agent endorse a second-order conception of the good as want-satisfaction (what is of value is the satisfaction of wants). As Barry can find no reason to think that the agent does have such a second-order conception of the good (indeed it is absurd to think such a thing) utilitarianism is revealed as unsatisfactory.

Barry is right to think that the agent does not have, nor does she need, a second-order conception of the good as want-satisfaction, but wrong to think this a criticism of second-order utilitarianism. The only thing that the agent must be committed to is a conception of the right as aggregate want-satisfaction. Putting this point more clearly: second-order utilitarianism can be interpreted as a theorem of impartial justice (see Chapters 4–5 below) in which in response to profound and continuing disputes about the good, social decisions are decided in accordance with maximal aggregate want-satisfaction. The commitment to this form of decision procedure stems from a belief in the equality of persons; from a commitment to treat each person as deserving of equal respect. Aggregating preferences reveals what is the right (or, if this is told as an account of justice, what is the just) thing to do, it does not decide issues about the good. The agent with an ecocentric conception of the good can, therefore, argue with her fellow citizens that it would be morally wrong to build the dam because the ecosystem has value greater than the value that would derive from building the dam, and nevertheless accept that it is just to build the dam if a majority of her fellow citizens[21] remain convinced that it should be built. She does not have to commit herself to a second-order conception of the good

---

[21] Ignoring, as I have above, intensities of preference.

as want-satisfaction, merely to the idea that a fair and just decision making procedure is one which respects each person equally through considering each person's wants in the calculation. Second-order utilitarianism as a theorem of justice as impartiality has the structure of such a theory, endorsing the priority of the right over the good (see Chapter 4 below). If it is to be shown to be inadequate, therefore, it must be shown that it is an inadequate account of the right (which is the project of the rest of this chapter).

Before engaging with that question, however, it is worth emphasizing one point. It might be thought unlikely that a person who holds a conception of the good in which is included the belief 'that nature, as an object of reverence, love and respect, itself has a moral worth and therefore should be protected for its own sake and not simply for the "satisfactions" or "benefits" it offers human beings' (quoted above) would accept as a fair decision procedure a system that attempts to capture a commitment to the equal value of human beings (however that is achieved) and nothing else. Part of what such a person believes is likely to be that much of the destruction of the environment that has occurred has happened precisely because of the arrogance of thinking that it is only human beings that matter. Interpreting utilitarianism as a way of implementing a commitment to equal respect means taking it for granted that people are equal and entitled to treatment as equals. Anyone who modifies this, either by expanding the set of things entitled to such consideration (for example, by including the environment in itself not the environment as it affects human beings present or future) or by restricting the set (for example, by denying that Jews are worthy of being considered), will not accept the move to an equality (of human beings) based theory of the right.

## Second-order utilitarianism and punishment

Taken as a second-order theorem of justice as impartiality utilitarianism does not immediately provide a theory of punishment. This is because a society may have people within it who think that criminals ought to suffer for past acts of wrongdoing, others who think that the only function of punishment is individual and general deterrence, or that punishment is only justified if it serves rehabilitative goals, and so on. In addition some people may think that it is more important to protect one's house from burglary because of the emotional cost of having one's home invaded whilst others consider only the economic costs. Thus when considering increasing expenditure on security some people might think that the expenditure is worth it even if the economic costs of burglary are smaller than the cost of the security system, others not. What second-order utilitarianism does provide is a procedure for determining the system of punishment for a given society. This is because all relevant preferences can be weighed against one another (assuming that this is possible) and the just system of punishment will be that which ensures maximum preference satisfaction.

It is, of course, impossible to say what the criminal justice system that results will look like without knowing the preferences of the people who would determine it. However, utilitarians can make a strong case that it would not be the nightmare scenario painted by most anti-utilitarians. Assuming that most people most of the time want to be free from invasions of their bodily integrity, of their private space, and of their possessions the system that is likely to result will have many of the normal prohibitions of the criminal law as it is found in the West. Whether it would have additional prohibitions is something to be examined below. In addition, assuming that most people would wish to have access to a fair trial, to legal representation, to an assumption of innocence, etc., given that they might find themselves (mistakenly or otherwise) the objects of attention of the criminal justice system, utilitarians can plausibly conclude that the procedures of the system will also be broadly in line with those with which we are familiar. Further, this reasoning can be extended to one of the objections to rule-utilitarianism outlined above. Given that most people fear the operations of government and are suspicious of the motivations of those who hold public office, it is not implausible to claim that there will be a widespread preference for the open operation of public functions. The magistrate, concerned to further the prevention of crime, could not then sacrifice an innocent person in a given case and 'keep it dark' not because it would be incoherent to appeal to the preventive ends of the criminal justice system (if such they are) but because the system would be such as to make the possibility of keeping something dark very remote.[22]

Finally, utilitarians can argue, even if the quantum of punishment imposed primarily aims at preventing crime (through individual and gen-

---

[22] A further extension of this reasoning may also account for why maximal preference satisfaction would most likely yield something like a criminal justice system rather than some alternative general method of social control such as 'Adults' Panels' charged with assessing and incapacitating or deterring likely future offenders (cf. Duff 1986: 166–7). Given the imperfect techniques for such assessments and the level of surveillance and interference in citizens' lives that would be needed to make even rough guesses of future conduct it is unlikely that such a system would satisfy the demand of maximal preference satisfaction.

eral deterrence), it will not include the excesses of pure preventive systems. Here the assumptions that have to be made about people's preferences become more questionable, but the case might be as follows. Given the widespread desire not to suffer invasions of one's bodily integrity or of one's possessions it is a safe assumption that people would wish the criminal justice system to have at least in part a preventive purpose. Indeed it is hard to see why else such a system would evolve from the demand to maximize preference satisfaction. However, given the imperfection of any system of criminal justice it is also likely that people will wish for protection against suffering great harm should they mistakenly be convicted of an offence, or indeed should they be correctly convicted for a minor offence that they may commonly commit (such as road traffic violations).[23] Finally, it is open to the utilitarian to argue that the intuition (much used by anti-utilitarians) that the guilty (and only the guilty) deserve to suffer in proportion to the gravity of the crime they have committed is itself a strong and widespread preference that would need to be taken into account in the assessing of what kind of system of criminal justice achieves the maximal level of preference satisfaction.

Combining the idea that utilitarianism is best interpreted as a standard of rightness, the insights of rule utilitarianism applied 'as a public philosophy',[24] and some basic and more or less plausible assumptions about the actual preferences of people (at least of most people in reasonably stable, developed, societies) it is possible to derive the skeleton of an account of criminal justice that is satisfactory. At least, it seems as if the account delivers the right answers. However, two assumptions have been made both of which are open to question. First, that the analogy with the group deciding where to eat is an adequate one for deliberation when it comes to moral matters. Second, that preferences can be aggregated.

---

[23] Minor violations are often the stuff of anti-utilitarian critiques. The argument runs that if prevention is the goal of punishment it must be the case that the quantum of punishment for a given offence is a factor of the level of temptation to commit that offence and the likelihood of the offender being punished. Classically, road traffic violations are tempting even for people who would regard it as unthinkable to commit crimes against property or persons, and the rate of convictions for such violations is comparatively low (when compared to murder, armed robbery, etc.). Therefore, it would appear that the quantum of punishment imposed for such offences ought to be comparatively great.

[24] This phrase is taken from the title of Goodin's book defending rule-utilitarianism (Goodin 1995).

## FAIRNESS AND THE CONTENT OF PREFERENCES

In the above it is assumed that people's preferences are for the guilty to suffer, for the protection of liberty and property and so on. Based on such an assumption plus some others concerning the way the world is, it is noted that utilitarianism seems to deliver the right answers. However, not all preferences are so benign. Imagine a society in which there is a widespread belief that homosexuals ought to be excluded from bars and other social places, as well as from employment, and that homosexual sexual practices ought to be illegal. If such an external preference (that is a preference over the goods, opportunities, etc. open to others) is shared by the majority of the population then designing social institutions so as to maximize preference satisfaction will involve criminalizing or discriminating against homosexuals.[25]

The problem of external preferences has been central to recent writing on utilitarianism. As Ronald Dworkin frames the problem: 'external preferences . . . present a great difficulty for utilitarianism. That theory owes much of its popularity to the assumption that it embodies the right of citizens to be treated as equals. But if external preferences are counted in overall preferences, then this assumption is jeopardized' (Dworkin 1977: 236). The question is whether to count objectionable external preferences, for example that homosexuals or Jews receive less than their fair share of the resources available. The claim to count each preference once and only once is important if utilitarianism is to be thought of as fair, yet there is something bizarre about thinking that a preference for all Jews to be killed should count in a moral theory, and even worse should it turn out to be the case the preference satisfaction is maximized through enacting such a policy. It is as if someone in the example given above of a group deciding where to eat does not have a preference for any particular kind of food, but does have a desire that the group should not eat at whatever place is chosen by one of the others.

Utilitarian theorists have been keen to show that there is way to deal with such preferences. The attempts have been usefully classified by Robert Goodin into 'input' and 'output filters'. An 'output filter' is a means of rejecting certain outcomes of the utilitarian calculus, for example by saying that all individuals have certain rights and no preference

[25] Other examples drawn from recent history in the Anglo-American world might be preferences about the goods, opportunities, etc. available to blacks and other ethnic minorities.

maximizing strategy is allowed to override those rights. An 'input filter' by contrast, attempts to limit the input of preferences, that is, it refuses to count certain kinds of preferences when performing the calculus (Goodin 1995: 134).

Put to one side output filters. The most common output filter, the attempt to protect certain rights from the outcome of the utilitarian decision making procedure, requires a justification of those rights. Contemporary Rawlsian contractarianism provides one such theory. The attempt to combine a concern for consequences with individual rights is, then, the subject of later chapters. Input filters require no such additional non-consequentialist element, instead they focus on the nature of preferences. In order to launder individual preferences through an input filter one has to show that there is some reason not to consider objectionable preferences when aggregating individual preferences. That is, one has to find a way of distinguishing between types of preferences such that objectionable preferences can justifiably be filtered out. Goodin has suggested, or grouped together, a number of ways in which this might be achieved and it is worth examining these in some detail as without some acceptable account of input filters there is reason to look towards contractarianism (or some third option) rather than consequentialism as providing an adequate account of the right (Goodin 1995: 137–41).

Input filters all attempt, in some way or another, to depict agents' 'real' preferences in some way that excludes objectionable preferences. The first input filter described by Goodin he calls 'protecting preferences from choices' (1995: 137). Some people sometimes express preferences which are not really in their best interests, or not really what they want. Perhaps they have been misinformed about some state of affairs, or they are unaware of some crucial fact, or they have failed to deliberate correctly or for long enough. For example, if an agent expresses a desire for a glass of liqueur that she sees on the table it is not respecting her real preference to give it to her if, in fact, one knows the glass to contain liqueur-coloured weed killer. This is the clearest case of when respecting an agent's preferences may involve ignoring her expressed desires. However, it is worth noting that it is not always true that in such cases one is justified in ignoring the expressed preference in favour of some 'real' preference. It is sometimes important (and right) to let someone make her own mistakes. Given that second-order utilitarianism counts each person's preferences as a way of respecting persons it needs further argument if it is to be established that one shows greatest respect not by counting the expressed preference of the agent, but rather some other unrevealed preference.

Even given that a distinction can sometimes be drawn between someone's expressed and their real preferences, it is nevertheless not obvious
how this argument would apply to objectionable external preferences. Take
as an example the preference mentioned above, that homosexuals should
have a smaller share of available resources (including freedom as a
resource). It may be that this preference is held by someone because they
believe that the HIV virus is air-travelling and what they really desire is to
be protected from this (but note this is not an external preference). In such
a case it seems clear that the agent is mistaken and his preferences regarding homosexual activity can be laundered. However, if we take the more
plausible scenario that the agent instead argues that the Bible records that
a man 'shall not lie with a male as with a woman; it is an abomination'
(Leviticus 18: 22) and that it is this fact which informs his preferences then
there is no question of this desire being based in false information or a mistake in reasoning. It is true that the Bible records that a man lying with a
man 'as with a woman' is an abomination. Of course, it might be argued
that the reason it is important to the agent is that he believes that the Bible
records the word of God and this claim is false. However, such a move
undermines the use of second-order utilitarianism as a response to the fact
of pluralism. If the project is to find public rules of justice that display or
are derived from a basic demand that each person is treated with equal
respect then it is surely not an admissible move to declare one view of the
nature of the good life (especially a view some variant of which is held by
so many people) to be false.[26] However the laundering of this preference is
to be achieved it is not the case that the revealed preference for anti-homo-
sexual activity is not a good indication of the 'real' preference of the agent.

Goodin's second category of 'input filters' also relies on some distinction
between the agent's expressed and her real preferences. Goodin argues that
often people have second-order preferences (preferences about preferences) and these might explicitly or implicitly contradict their expressed
preferences. In such cases one can launder objectionable first-order preferences by discounting them in favour of the real, second-order, preference.
Thus, an agent may find himself incapable of not feeling revulsion whenever confronted by thoughts of homosexual activity and, for this reason,
want such activity to be banned, but he may wish that he did not feel that
way; he may have a second-order preference for his first-order preference
to be different.

---

[26] Even if this is not the fundamental project of political philosophy and the agent's
belief can be treated as false it is implausible to suppose that all objectionable external preferences are based in false beliefs.

This analysis of preference structure owes much to the work of Gerald Dworkin and Harry Frankfurt on autonomy (Dworkin 1970, 1988; Frankfurt 1971), but just as it is not clear in their work why a second-order endorsement of first-order preferences is autonomy conferring (because there is no obvious difference in the formation or importance of first- and second-order preferences), so it is not clear why respecting the 'real' preferences of the agent means ignoring those of the agent's first-order preferences which are incompatible with her second-order desires and counting only those first-order preferences which have second-order endorsement. Perhaps much of the initial plausibility of this view comes from the language of 'higher' and 'lower' (as against first and second) as in the following from Goodin: 'No violation of want-regarding principles is entailed [when laundering preferences through this kind of input filter], since we choose which preferences to count and which to ignore on the basis of the individual's own (higher-order) preferences' (Goodin 1995: 138). The language of 'higher-order' lends credibility to the thought that really respecting the agent means respecting only those preferences which receive second-order endorsement. This may sometimes be the case. Sometimes it may be true that the best assessment of what a person really wants is found through asking which of her expressed preferences she would endorse as ones that she wants to hold, but it is also true that sometimes people are self-deceiving. Judging what someone really wants when her first- and second-order preferences conflict is a difficult task—and one to which there is probably no non-case-specific answer—but it is certainly not true that second-order preferences just by virtue of being such reveal the person's real wants. Even if it were, as with protecting preferences from choices, it is hard to see how this would help in the case of external preferences. It is unlikely that many people who express the preference for homosexual practices to be outlawed regret that they have that preference.

This kind of input-filter becomes even more troublesome when the second-order preference is not explicit. Goodin thinks it possible to 'generalize important conclusions about the whole class of "second-party preferences" from Hegel's master–slave paradox' (1995: 139–40). The master–slave paradox is that if the master exerts his mastery over the slave he gains no non-economic benefit because by reducing the slave to the level of a thing he negates the possibility of gaining recognition from an agent (as opposed to a mere thing). If he treats the slave as an agent, however, then he loses his mastery over the slave. Goodin takes from this the thought that an agent with sadistic preferences can find satisfaction in the realization of his 'second-party preferences' only if the relevant second party is 'acknowledged . . . by one's own behavior or by some larger system of social values' (1995: 140) to be a person. This leaves Goodin with the dramatic conclusion (when considering the case of a sadist) that:

The sadist's preferences for humiliating men in everyday life, then, imply a preference that others' dignity be acknowledged and respected in public policy. Even though he insistently demands the contrary, the social decision-maker is obliged to respect this logically central implication of the sadist's first-order preferences. His utilities are still controlling, however. No violation of want-regarding principles has occurred. (Goodin 1995: 140)

Whatever the truth of the claim that what the sadist really wants is that the dignity of others be respected (this may be just part of what defines a sadist) it is difficult to understand why this particular class of people (sadists) provide an argument that can be generalized 'across the whole class' of external preferences. The sadist is peculiar if, as is alleged, he gains satisfaction out of the humiliation of another agent just because the victim is another agent. Not everyone who holds an objectionable external preference is like this (indeed, very few are). The racist who thinks that blacks should receive fewer resources and opportunities than similarly situated whites does not, or need not, gain satisfaction from the subsequent humiliation of black people whom he encounters.

Nevertheless, the idea of digging into someone's preferences in order to find out what they really want is a familiar one. In his seminal essay 'Paternalism',[27] Gerald Dworkin argues that there are certain goods that everyone can be thought to want (under normal conditions) such as health, life, etc. (Dworkin 1971). Thus, Dworkin argues, it is reasonable to assume that the agent desires these goods even when that agent does not recognize that this is so, or that such goods are at stake in some action he is performing. The example Dworkin discusses is whether it is justified to enact and enforce compulsory seat-belt wearing in cars. Dworkin's argument is, in short, that given that the agent has an interest in his health and life—as these are necessary to the fulfilment of his life-plans and commitments (assuming that the agent is not suicidal)—then it is justified to impute to this agent a desire to remain alive and healthy. Given this imputed desire and the reduction in the risk of injury or death when wearing a seat belt the agent can be said to have a desire to wear a seat belt.

It is difficult to see how such a laundering technique would work on the external preferences mentioned above. It may be that some people wish to live in a tolerant society in which all are free to pursue their own concep-

---

[27] Cited with approval by Goodin (1995, 139).

tions of the good, but that they simply have a moral blind-spot when it comes to homosexuals and think that such people should be excluded. However, it is unlikely that this is commonly the case in any straightforward way. Of course, it is the case that people's preferences for the kind of life that they want to lead depend upon certain features of the society in which they live and, therefore, that they must be prepared to endorse certain other preferences which they may not immediately recognize. However, calculating from this what such people really want is not just a problem of deciding whether certain goods desired by an agent necessarily require (or are best promoted by) some other good. This is because people may trade off the satisfaction of their various preferences.[28]

Smoking, it is now universally agreed, is bad for one's health. Most people who smoke will die of a smoking-related disease. Given that such people have similar interests in life and in being able to fulfil their commitments to those of Dworkin's car driver, why is it not equally plausible to argue that what smokers really want is not to smoke, and that this is true even of those who express no desire to give up? The answer, of course, is that it is accepted that people also have an interest in the quality of their lives—their productivity, their remaining calm and not suffering from stress, etc.—and smoking has benefits in such areas. It is thus up to the individual[29] to trade off her satisfying her desire to smoke against her desires to be healthy and to live to an old age. Similarly, in the setting of speed limits on roads. There is an inverse correlation between safety on the roads and the speed of traffic (except at very low speeds) so that if speed limits on the roads were reduced from, say, 60 to 40 miles per hour there would be a decline in the number of accidents and of fatalities when accidents occur. The same would be true for a reduction from 40 to 30 mph. Why then do policy makers not confidently say that what road-users (including drivers) really want is to have lower speed limits? Again, the answer is because people are willing to trade off their safety (and the risk of causing harm to others) against their ability to get from one place to another quickly.

This does not show that Dworkin is wrong to assert that if an agent wants $x$ it is reasonable to assume that he also does not want things that make $x$ impossible and that he does want the means to $x$ (or that assuming these things does not violate a demand to show respect for the agent). However, because the situation is that an agent may want $x$ and $y$ where $y$

---

[28] The following borrows from Matravers 1997.
[29] Ignoring questions that arise because of secondary smoke.

might deleteriously affect the chances of her getting *x* then the fact that different agents will be prepared to risk *x* to different degrees in order to have more or less *y* means that this feature of preferences cannot be of any significant help in laundering preferences in a utilitarian social decision function. Everyone might want social peace so that they can pursue their projects in conditions where reasonable expectations are, other things being equal, likely to be reliable guides to the future, but some people will be prepared to sacrifice a little of this in order to maintain prejudicial laws against a minority community; others might be prepared to sacrifice more, others less.

Input filters, it will be remembered, are needed because without them utilitarianism must either rely on some account that will justify ring-fencing certain individual rights or else it will have to include objectionable preferences of various kinds in the calculus of what is the morally right thing to do. However, input filters rely on a separation between an agent's revealed preferences and her 'real' preferences. Although in some cases such a move seems both consonant with the desire to respect agency and reasonable as an interpretation of what the agent really wants, it is not unproblematically so nor does it seem to apply to the standard case of a bigot who, for example, wishes to criminalize homosexual activity. Before concluding this section, it is worth commenting on one final version of utilitarianism that tries to counter both the problem of objectionable preferences and the measurement problem (the second of the assumptions that is suggested above as being problematic).

## Measuring utility

It has so far been taken for granted that utility is to be measured in preference satisfaction. However, there is a widely accepted view that interpersonal measurements of preference satisfaction are impossible, and although that does not mean that utilitarianism must be wrong as an account of morality (it merely raises an epistemological problem about how we would know what the morally right act or rule is), it does raise serious questions about how utilitarianism could be implemented as a decision procedure. One riposte to this measurement problem that has consequences for the issue of what to do about objectionable preferences is to change the maximand from a subjective measure (preferences) to an interpersonal one (like capabilities).[30] If what is to be counted is whether

[30] The term 'capabilities' is from Amartya Sen's work (see, e.g., 1985*a*, 1985*b*, 1993) although what follows is not in any sense an interpretation of Sen.

people have, say, adequate food, shelter, and political freedoms for normal life then not only are interpersonal measurements possible, but also there is no reason to consider people's objectionable preferences. This approach has generated a huge literature and this is not the place to attempt to review it. Although it seems incompatible with the initial claim that respecting people requires respecting each person's preferences, it is surely possible to argue that if respecting people means not respecting any old preference but rather, say, the preferences that they would have were they fully informed and rational, then the preference set of any given person would probably include preferences for those things that are included in any given description of capabilities.

However, the move to this kind of interpersonal account seems to face a similar problem to that found in Dworkin, and in Braithwaite and Pettit: people will trade-off elements of their capabilities at different rates. This makes an interpersonal measurement that remains a valid means of respecting persons difficult to construct. Reducing what is measured so that the test would be whether people had some baseline of capabilities and ignoring those that fall above the baseline would leave utilitarianism impotent as a social decision-making mechanism for the developed world (except in its relations with the underdeveloped) and remove its claim to be an account of morality and its interest for punishment theorists. There is no answer to the question of whether to build the dam or protect the snail-darter that can be established through the use of an uncontroversial interpersonal measure of well-being. The alternative is to try to find a very broad maximand that can act as an interpersonal measure that is so comprehensive that it can avoid controversy. As was demonstrated above, in the discussion of Braithwaite and Pettit, such a solution is not viable because the elements that make up the maximand can themselves be traded off and this introduces a necessarily subjective dimension.

Second-order utilitarianism appears to offer a different structure to teleological utilitarianism that corrects many of the faults of the latter. However, if it is a way of reflecting the idea of the equality of persons through using maximal preference satisfaction as a means of establishing the right then it seems inadequate to the initial premiss to which it tries to give content; the assumption of the equal worth of persons. If it cannot exclude objectionable preferences then it cannot avoid the problem that maximal preference satisfaction might involve discrimination or worse. The problem that has run through this chapter has reappeared: even second-order utilitarianism may legitimize some receiving considerably fewer resources and freedoms than others simply because in doing so others are made better off. No principled objection can be given against this sacrifice of the few just so as to increase the utility of the many.

## CONCLUSION

Teleological utilitarianism cannot provide an adequate account of punishment. In both its act and rule forms it cannot explain what is wrong with sacrificing an individual just so as to benefit others. No deployment of logic in support of a two-level structure or expansion of the maximand so as to internalize distributive criteria can rescue this understanding of the utilitarian project. Taken seriously as a second-order account of justice, utilitarianism is far more defensible than its critics have often alleged. However, its fundamental thesis—that the way to resolve the problem of finding justified rules to govern societies is to convert people's commitments into wants and then aggregate them—is unsatisfactory. Even understood as a second-order theory, utilitarianism cannot deliver a principled objection to the sacrifice of one person's essential interests to further the interests of others.

The utilitarian account of punishment reveals the problem that besets utilitarianism. Moreover, utilitarianism, like all forms of consequentialism, is forward looking and, although a system of punishment that had no regard for consequences would be a very odd one, punishment seems to have an essential backward looking component. The punished offender is punished at least in part because she committed an offence and that is not adequately understood in terms of a contingent claim that punishing only those who have offended will advance utility given the way the world is. The inadequacy of the account of punishment is, in this case, a symptom of the inadequate moral theory in which it is embedded.

# 2

# Retributivism I: Fair Play Theory

## INTRODUCTION

There is something about the claim that punishment has an essential back-ward-looking element that goes beyond its being merely a conceptual or definitional point. No doubt it is in part conceptual; when Anthony Quinton argues that punishment is of an offender for an offence, that therefore 'retributivism . . . is not a moral but a logical doctrine' (Quinton 1969: 55) and that the infliction of suffering (even on an offender) for the sake of some future state of affairs cannot be punishment he has a point, at least of a sort.[1] However, the backward looking element in punishment runs deeper than this. Confronted with the perpetrator of some horrific crime many people respond with the thought that he deserves to suffer for his act. In Michael Moore's rather blunt prose, 'the good that punishment achieves is that someone who deserves it gets it' (Moore 1997: 87).[2] Even in debates as divisive as that over capital punishment the centrality of desert is for the most part taken for granted by both sides.[3]

The nature of the 'retributive reaction'[4] to (many) crimes suggests simi-larities between it and Strawson's 'reactive attitudes' (Strawson 1982: 63). Confronted with someone who has deliberately failed to respect the claims

---

[1] Quinton (1969) uses the definitional argument to deny the very possibility of conse-quentialist justifications of punishment, but this kind of 'definitional stop' (Hart 1959: 5) hardly seems interesting.

[2] Or, in the equally blunt but somewhat less informed prose of the UK Home Office (1990, para. 1.6), punishment is justified because 'criminals get their just desserts [sic]'.

[3] On the one hand there are those who think that offender x deserves to die for crime y on the grounds that he is guilty of y. On the other, the argument often revolves around questioning not whether those who are guilty of y-type crimes deserve to die, but whether x is in fact guilty (or guilty of a y-type crime). Arguments are produced to show that x did not commit the crime, that the process by which he was found guilty was questionable, or that although x did perform the deed there are mitigating circumstances such as mental ill-ness, poverty, lack of education, having suffered abuse as a child, and so on.

[4] The term 'retributive reaction' is used in what follows to describe the reaction that the wrongdoer ought to suffer for the wrong he has committed.

of another (without the presence of excusing or mitigating factors) a normal reaction is one of blame, resentment, and an accompanying thought that the offender should, in some sense, (be made to) pay for his act. Of course, it is possible to think of this as being a reaction that is socially useful and as having a justification that is tied to this forward-looking usefulness, but (as noted in Chapter 1 above) such an analysis is commonly thought to be a *reductio ad absurdum* of consequentialism. There may be a valid account of blame as 'dispraise', but it is not widely thought to be plausible.[5]

Nevertheless, there is a problem in accounting for the reaction that the offender deserves to suffer. Holding someone to have the status of an agent may require that she is held to be responsible, and that judgements of praise and blame are applied to her,[6] but a great deal more argumentative work would need to be done to convert this into the claim that an offender ought to suffer and that this itself can provide a justification for imposing that suffering. The retributive reaction would seem to be less a consequence of our regarding one another as capable of agency, and more a matter of appeal to some kind of ' "celestial mechanics" in which every criminal action . . . deserves an "equal and opposite reaction", in the shape of punishment' (Fleischacker 1992: 204).[7]

The difficulty of giving sense to some brute notion of desert and the political sensibilities of various times have meant that retributivism has had a decidedly mixed history. Traditionally regarded as one of the 'great schools' of punishment theorizing, nevertheless in 1969 one standard text on punishment recorded that 'there no longer are defenders of the traditional retributive theory. . . . At any rate, there are no defenders writing in the usual places' (Honderich 1969, 148). In the mid- to late 1970s things changed.[8] In 1976 Martin Gardner entitled a piece 'The Renaissance of

---

[5] The language of 'dispraise' is borrowed from J. J. C. Smart (1973: see esp. 47–54). Smart's response to the *reductio* argument is simply to deny that the position that he is defending is reduced to an absurdity. This move is captured (using another famous *reductio*) in the following entry in *The Philosophical Lexicon* (Dennett 1987): 'Outsmart, v. To embrace the conclusion of one's opponent's *reductio ad absurdum* argument. "They thought they had me, but I outsmarted them. I agreed that it was sometimes just to hang an innocent man".'

[6] Or, on Strawson's account, that one applies to her judgements such as resentment, blame, etc., and these are constitutive of responsibility.

[7] Fleischacker borrows the phrase 'celestial mechanics' from Cohen 1939: 279.

[8] Politically and philosophically. The rise of 'just deserts theory' was an early indication of a general rise in the political appeal of individual responsibility and desert. Right-wing governments under Mrs Thatcher, Chancellor Kohl, and Ronald Reagan were elected in the UK, Germany, and the USA in 1979–80 and each preached the priority of the individual and

Retribution: An Examination of Doing Justice' and by 1984 the new edition of the text cited above had a postscript dedicated to the 'new college industry [which] turns out theories of retribution' (Honderich 1984: 10). Of these new accounts only a few have survived the critical scrutiny to which they have been subjected and the claim that no retributivist theory is viable is still relatively common.[9] Yet the project of justifying punishment cannot do without accommodating its essential backward looking component and, once again, retributive theory and practice is back in fashion. As David Dolinko puts it:

The retributive theory is arguably the most influential philosophical justification for the institution of criminal punishment in present-day America. Yet it is curiously difficult to articulate this theory in a perspicuous fashion. . . . Concise efforts to characterize retributivism risk collapsing into 'it's right to punish criminals because doing so is right'. (Dolinko 1997: 507)

In the following section some distinctions are introduced in the idea of retributivism so that it can be determined what it is exactly that stands in need of justification. In the remainder of this chapter an attempt to capture the essential claim of retributivism within a framework of distributive justice is assessed and criticized. In the next, some recent retributive theories grounded not in distributive justice but in the retributive response to wrongdoing are discussed. The aim is twofold: first, to investigate the nature of retributive theory and current accounts that try to 'articulate this . . . in a perspicuous fashion'. Second, to enquire further into the relationship of punishment theory and moral theory more generally.

In the Introduction a distinction is drawn between those questions that refer to the nature, scope, authority, and so on of the rules and those that arise because of the addition of a threat of sanctions addressed to those who would transgress. The argument of Chapter 1 is, in part, that the only plausible utilitarian accounts of punishment are those that are embedded in a broad utilitarian moral theory and that as this theory is flawed the account of punishment fails. Retributivist theory appears to be a paradigm

---

of individual responsibility to the social and collective (for an interesting discussion of the failure of left of centre political philosophy to speak to this desert-based individualism see Scheffler 1992). Ironically, as noted above (Ch. 1) the rise of retributivism was in part a left-wing response to the abuse of consequentialist sentencing practices, which tended to result in offenders from ethnic minorities and from poor socio-economic groups suffering disproportionately to white, middle-class, offenders convicted of similar crimes.

[9] See e.g. Ellis 1997: 81. The denial of the plausibility of retributivism as a moral justification of punishment is not to be confused with the claim that retributivist theory has no role in establishing the correct quantum of punishment for a given offender or offence.

of the independent approach to punishment in that it explicitly addresses only the question of what justifies the threat and imposition of sanctions. As noted in the Introduction, if the argument that culpable disobedience makes the infliction of suffering on the offender morally permissible or obligatory can be defended in terms that do not depend on the particular account of the rule disobeyed then the basis for an independent justification for punishment would have been found.[10]

Arguments of the form of John Mabbott's (discussed above in the Introduction)—that the justification of punishment is only that the offender has broken a correctly instituted rule—and those arguments that depend on some claim about the meaning, or definition, of punishment being 'of an offender for an offence' are paradigm instances of the claim that punishment theory can be independent. Nevertheless, even putting these to one side leaves a number of retributive theories that make the claim to relative independence. It is to one of these that the chapter turns after some comments on the question of what retributivism is and, thus, of what claims stand in need of justification.


## RETRIBUTIVISMS


One standard problem with considering the retributivist justification of punishment is that there is no consensus on what retributivism actually is.[11] Retributivism has no clear definition, resembling an 'essentially contested concept' rather than a rigorous term which can be used to distinguish clearly one non-consequentialist theory from another. Indeed, given the bewildering number of writers who lay claim to the ascription 'retributivist', it is difficult to imagine giving anything but an affirmative answer to Antony Duff's question, 'has the label "retributivist" been applied to such a diversity of views and principles that it now lacks any unambiguous or unitary meaning?' (Duff 1986: 4).[12]

Retributivism, as it is of concern here, is a thesis about the moral justification of the practice of punishment. Retributivists are closely associated

[10] 'The basis' because questions of whether, and how much, punishment should be inflicted would still need to be determined.

[11] John Cottingham distinguishes nine varieties of retributivism in his 1979 paper, 'Varieties of Retribution'.

[12] Cottingham likewise remarks that, 'the fact is that the term "retributive" as used in philosophy has become so imprecise and multi-vocal that it is doubtful whether it any longer serves a useful purpose' (Cottingham 1979: 238). See also Ten 1987: ch. 3.

with the *lex talionis*—the idea that the punishment received by a given offender should be directly equivalent to the wrong that she has committed—but this is not the position of all, or even most, retributivists. The *lex talionis* is but one answer to Hart's second question, 'how much?', and is only incorrectly thought to be at the heart of retributivism.

Although the answer to the question of the correct quantum of punishment for a given offence can in some sense be detached from retributivism the same is not true of the answer to Hart's third question, 'whom should we punish?'[13] Retributivism is closely linked with culpability and desert, and thus who qualifies as an object of punishment is entailed by any retributive theory, although the question of whether the offender ought then to be punished may depend upon the precise formulation of the theory in question.

Simply because of the vast array of self-proclaimed retributivists it is necessary to stipulate what is under discussion when attempting any general critique. In what follows the defining feature of retributivism is taken to be the claim that the moral justification of the practice of punishment is to be derived from the status of offenders as deserving of punishment. The existence of offenders, of people deserving of punishment, may be taken to justify the practice of punishment directly, as in the claim that punishment is morally justified only because the offender deserves it and we are morally justified in giving such people their 'just deserts'. Alternatively, the justification of punishment may flow indirectly from the desert claim, as in the argument that punishment is justified because inflicting suffering in accordance with desert realizes some moral value (that is intrinsically related to the infliction of suffering[14]) in the world. These two routes to retributive punishment are discussed below, as clearly they stand in need of unpacking, but first it is necessary to comment on what is left out of this characterization of retributivism.

As noted above, arguments over the correct quantum of punishment can be left to one side as inessential to retributivism, and thus do not feature in the characterization of that theory given above. Of course, in unpacking

---

[13] Indeed the necessary link between the moral justification of the practice of punishment and the question 'whom should we punish?' is, as noted above, one of the reasons that Dolinko thinks Hart's widely used tripartite division of the questions of punishment unhelpful (see n. 7 in the Introduction above).

[14] That is, the moral value realized is not, for example, a reduction in future criminal acts. The second route from desert to punishment is, in part, forward looking, but is also retributive (it aims to bring about some good state of affairs, but only by responding in some intrinsically appropriate way to the past act of the criminal (cf. Duff 1996: parts iii and iv).

various accounts of retributivism arguments as to how a given offence or offender should be punished will appear, but no particular answer to these questions (such as the rule of *lex talionis*) ought to be regarded as a defining characteristic of retributivism.

What might be taken to be much more important is the absence of reference in the above to the question of whether punishment is morally permissible or morally obligatory. This distinction is one of the most common in discussions aimed at distinguishing retributive theories. Unfortunately, all too often two different arguments are run together: first, an argument as to whether desert is a necessary or sufficient condition for justified punishment. Second, whether retributivism gives the appropriate authority the moral right, or imposes on that authority the moral duty, to punish a deserving offender. Michael Moore, for example, claims that,

retributivism is a very straightforward theory of punishment: We are justified in punishing because and only because offenders deserve it. Moral responsibility ('desert') in such a view is not only necessary for justified punishment, it is also sufficient. Such sufficiency of justification gives society more than merely a *right* to punish culpable offenders. . . . For a retributivist, the moral responsibility of an offender also gives society the *duty* to punish. (Moore 1997: 91)

However, *pace* Moore, the question of whether desert is a necessary or sufficient condition for morally justified punishment must be clearly separated from the question of whether society has a right or both a right and a duty to punish.

Amongst those who hold that desert is merely a necessary condition for justified punishment a distinction needs to be drawn between those for whom it is a necessary condition of the moral justification of inflicting suffering on a particular individual that that person has culpably performed some wrong, and those for whom a necessary part of the moral justification of the practice of punishment itself is derived from the existence of persons who deserve punishment. The former position is endorsed by a wide variety of theories. A rule-utilitarian, for example, holds that the moral justification of having coercive rules, and in general for imposing the penalties stipulated in those rules, is to be found in the promotion of good consequences and that, given the way the world is, good consequences will only be promoted if the guilty, and only the guilty, are punished. Desert, as this is understood by the rule-utilitarian, is thus a necessary condition for the infliction of a particular punishment being morally justified, but desert plays no role in the justification of the practice of punishment itself (see Chapter 1 above). The latter position is that part of the moral justification of the practice of punishment is derived from the desert of offenders, but that there are also other conditions that need to be met for a system of punishment to be fully justified. Two such accounts are discussed below. Thus the question of whether they can be classified as retributive in any useful sense can be postponed for the present.

It should be noted that in neither case is there an easy overlap between this discussion and the question of whether the relevant authority has a right or a duty to punish. A rule-utilitarian, of a particularly strict kind, will hold that, given a system of rules that stipulate sanctions in response to their contravention, the authority is morally obliged to inflict the stipulated sanction on an offending individual. Someone who holds that the system of punishment can only be fully morally justified where certain non-desert-related conditions are met (in addition to the necessary desert-related conditions) will hold that in the absence of the former being met the authority has neither the right, nor the duty, to punish.

Finally, it is worth stressing that those who hold that desert is both a necessary and sufficient condition for morally justified punishment do not necessarily hold that those who under the theory have authority to punish thereby have a duty to punish the deserving. Admitting of no distinction between actions that are morally justified and those that are morally obligatory (as in the case of crude utilitarianism) is not often thought to be a favourable characteristic in a moral theory, not least because of such things as the possibility of conflict between morally justified courses of action, and because of the existence of supererogatory acts.

The question of whether desert is a necessary or necessary and sufficient condition for the moral justification of the practice of punishment is an important one and is discussed below. The question of whether the appropriate authority has a right or a duty to punish is not taken to be of the same importance. What matters is whether the practice of punishment can be given a moral justification through the idea of desert. If so, it is of course important whether punishment is merely morally permissible or whether it is morally obligatory, and whether, even if the latter, the obligation is such as to override other moral obligations with which it might conflict, all things considered. However, no particular answer to these questions can plausibly be held to be a defining characteristic of retributive theory.[15]

---

[15] Not least because whether a moral obligation is decisive, all things considered, may depend upon contingent features of the world. Even amongst those retributivists who hold that punishment is a duty, none, with the possible exception of Kant, holds that it is of a kind that overrides all other possible considerations. It is always possible to conceive of a situation (e.g. where carrying out the punishment of a particular individual will cause a

The preliminary claim to be made sense of, then, is that the moral justification for punishment stems from the past performances of certain acts
by individuals[16] such that those responsible deserve punishment and/or
such that the response of inflicting suffering on offenders realizes some
intrinsically related good. In this and the following chapter various
attempts to explicate and to defend this claim are examined, beginning
with an account that seems, at first sight, to support the argument for the
relative independence of punishment theory.

## FAIR PLAY THEORY

As noted above, the dominant concern of political theory in the last thirty
years has been the issue of distributive justice yet this has had little impact
on theories of retributive justice. However, a number of writers have
responded to Ted Honderich's claim that the completion of punishment
theorizing is dependent on finding 'a clear principle of *distributive* justice,
an answer to the question of how all the benefits and burdens in society are
to be distributed' (Honderich 1984: 239).[17] The most famous such
attempt, described in a 1996 review of research as 'for a time widely
accepted as the most plausible version of retributivism' (Duff 1996: 26), is
what is known as 'fair play' theory. Despite this, or perhaps because of it,
fair play theory has been subject to a great deal of criticism and its critics

---

visiting alien to destroy the planet) where the duty to punish ought not to be decisive (cf.
Moore 1997: 172).

[16] Or, in some cases, by collective bodies (such as firms) capable of being treated as a single unit.

[17] In Honderich's case the appeal is motivated by a particular view of the free will/deter-
minism debate; a view which is wholeheartedly determinist (see Honderich 1988, 1993). In
addition to those in the fair play school cited below, a small number of writers have written
on retributive justice using the techniques of distributive justice. Jan Narveson (1974)
argues that if one removes the assumption of risk aversion from Rawls's original position
the contractors will adopt utilitarian principles of punishment (a similar argument is used
by Harsanyi (1982) to derive a utilitarian alternative to the difference principle). James
Sterba (1977) argues for a 'morally adequate form of retributivism' derived from a con-
tractual situation. His argument is challenged by Reed (1978). Hoekema (1980) also applies
Rawlsian analysis to punishment. See also Davis (amongst others, Davis 1983, 1986*a*,
1986*b*); Sadurski 1989. For some sceptical comments on the attempt to derive principles of
punishment from a Rawlsian starting point see Duff 1986: 217–28 (although this discussion
focuses primarily on Jeffrie Murphy's (1973) mistaken reading of Rawls).

now include some of those responsible for its early development.[18] In what follows the idea of fair play theory is first described and then defended against some of its opponents. However, although fair play theory is shown to have the resources to meet some of the criticisms levelled against it, it cannot sustain its claim to give a justification for punishment that is independent of any substantive theory of justice or account of morality. Fair play theory is incomplete and, to anticipate the argument, the nature of its further development depends upon what understanding of society, and of the character of the benefits and burdens enjoyed by, and imposed on, citizens, is embraced. Locating the principle of fair play in, as it were, a particular understanding of the game being played invalidates the claim that the principle of fair play can underwrite a relatively independent justification of punishment.

It may seem in what follows that disproportionate space is accorded to this theory given that it is widely thought to have been discredited. However, the aim is to show that some of the problems of fair play theory stem from the understanding of reciprocity that underpins it and it is argued in later chapters that these problems recur in contemporary contract theories. The failure of fair play theory is not particularly interesting because of what it tells us about punishment, but because it is informative about the structure of our relations, one to another.

In its modern form, fair play theory developed from Herbert Hart's paper 'Are There Any Natural Rights?' (Hart 1955) in which he argued that the obligation to obey the law was derived from a 'mutuality of restrictions'.[19] That is, 'when a number of persons conduct any joint enterprise according to rules and thus restrict their liberty, those who have submitted to these restrictions when required have a right to a similar submission from those who have benefited by their submission' (Hart 1955: 85). The idea is that fair play theory—the mutuality of restrictions—should be a new and independent mechanism for creating rights and duties;

[18] The two most influential fair play accounts of punishment were Morris 1968, and Murphy 1973. Among others, contributions have been made by Finnis 1972; von Hirsch 1976; Sadurski 1989; Sher 1987: ch. 5. Both von Hirsch and Murphy have since expressed dissatisfaction with the theory; von Hirsch 1985, 57–60, 1990: 264–5; Murphy 1985. For critical discussions see (again, among others) Duff 1986: ch. 8; Dolinko 1991; Fingarette 1977; Wasserstrom 1980. More constructive critiques can be found in Burgh 1982; Dagger 1993.

[19] Hart later repudiated this paper. An earlier statement of much the same view can be found in Broad 1915–16; a later, more influential, statement in Rawls 1964.

'independent' in the sense that it 'differs from other right-creating transactions (consent, promising)' (Hart 1955: 85).[20]

Hart's basic principle has been developed and debated at some length in the forty years that have followed its publication,[21] but as Richard Dagger points out, most of that debate has remained centred on the question of whether one has an obligation to obey the law (Dagger 1993: 474). The application of the principle to the justification of punishment has had, by comparison, a relatively short popular life.

The starting points of a fair play justification of punishment are a conception of society as a co-operative endeavour for mutual advantage and a particular view of the nature of that co-operation and of its benefits and burdens. Co-operation brings advantages to the members who compose the society. However, these advantages can only be realized if the members of the society interact on the basis of shared rules that govern their co-operation. The basic idea, then, is that insofar as each enjoys the benefit of the co-operative enterprise, each is obliged to co-operate in accordance with the rules. This means that each member is obliged to undertake activities that are burdensome—paying taxes for example—if such activities are commanded by the rules that regulate and make possible the co-operative enterprise.

The law, which is to be thought of as the form given to the norms and rules governing co-operation, provides enormous benefits to the participants, most notably in attempting to secure the conditions of 'peace, security and freedom' (Duff 1986: 206) for them. It protects the individual from interference, and thus allows her to formulate and attempt to carry through her chosen desires or plan of life in conditions in which her legitimate expectations are likely to be fulfilled and in which she will be free from unwanted and unwarranted interference from others. However, the law secures these benefits for the individual only by imposing on her a burden of self-restraint. That is, the individual must restrain herself should she

---

[20] This is the claim that it will be argued below is unsustainable and even Hart, in the formulation given above, seems to indicate the incompleteness of the idea of reciprocity with his talk of 'joint enterprises' and 'rules'. What is more, although Hart is concerned to distinguish obligations derived from fair play from those derived from consent, he none the less in the sentence immediately before introducing the idea states that he believes that 'it is true of all special rights that they arise from previous voluntary actions'. Whether he means that the agent needs to have voluntarily joined the 'joint enterprise' or voluntarily accepted its benefits is unclear. On this point see Simmons 1979.

[21] See, broadly in support, Arneson 1982; Becker 1986; Dagger 1993; Fishkin 1992: § 3.3; Gibbard 1991; Klosko 1992; Sadurski 1989; Sher 1987. Broadly against, Nozick 1974: 90–5; Simmons 1979: ch. 5; Smith 1973. Other references appear below.

desire to act in ways that are illegal. She must respect the prohibitions of the law and moderate her behaviour accordingly.[22]

In brief, the argument that the principle of fair play can underwrite a relatively independent account of punishment is this: assume that the benefits and burdens of social co-operation are justly distributed. For example, given some kind of egalitarianism (and ignoring issues concerning children, the insane, and so on), the law provides (or attempts to provide) the benefits of peace, security, and freedom for everyone. Likewise, the burden of having to obey the law falls equally on everyone. The criminal, in benefiting from the protection of the law whilst failing to restrain himself in accordance with its demands, free-rides on the system of co-operation and thereby disrupts the just distribution of benefits and burdens. The function of punishment, it is claimed, is to restore the status quo ante; to re-establish the just distribution of society's benefits and burdens.

This account of punishment can stand apart from the justification of the distributive scheme which it is the function of punishment to restore. For although if there is to be a moral justification for punishment in the idea of restoring some distribution of benefits and burdens it must be the case that the pattern of distribution to be restored is just, what defines such a distribution is not a question that fair play theory need address. Indeed, if it is to retain its character as a justification of punishment based on Hart's simple idea it must not do so. This is important because fair play theory essentially holds that given a just society it can justify punishment as a second, independent, stage of moral theorizing. That is, the derivation of just norms and rules of co-operation (and their legal analogue, laws) is a different matter from the derivation of just punishment.

As characterized, fair play theory combines a contract-based understanding of social co-operation and a retributive account of punishment. Present suffering is deserved by the offender because of his past act in that the past act creates a situation of imbalance (in the benefits and burdens of social co-operation) that justice demands be rectified. Contract theory provides the account of benefits and burdens. The argument below is that the requirement that justice restore the status quo ante is insufficient to justify punishment and that this is recognized by fair play theorists. In

---

[22] See Duff 1986: 206, 1993: p. xii; Sadurski 1989: 355–6. It should be noted that this understanding of the benefits and burdens of co-operation, and especially of the law as imposing a burden, is a premiss of fair play theory (one taken from the assumption of a particular kind of contractarianism). It is not entailed by a conception of society as a co-operative venture for mutual advantage. Such a conception of society is compatible with a number of ways of understanding co-operative benefits and burdens some of which are non-contractarian.

response these theorists call upon the resources of (an under-specified) contract theory. However, there are reasons to think that the appeal to contract theory introduces a separate and distinct justification of punishment that is in tension with the retributive idea of restoring the balance of benefits and burdens. To understand why this is the case it is first necessary to examine fair play theory more closely.

The argument is that punishment is a requirement of justice, for (given a just starting point) it is just that each carry his share of the burdens of cooperation and should someone fail to do so a situation of injustice results that has to be rectified. The criminal disturbs the just distribution by refusing to mediate the pursuit of his self-interest by the laws that regulate the society; that is, the criminal does not bear his burden of self-restraint whilst he continues to enjoy the benefits of others doing so. He is 'a *parasite* or *freerider* on a mutually beneficial scheme of social cooperation' (Murphy 1985: 7). It is important to note that the relevant benefit to the criminal is not, for example, the property he steals or the pleasure he gets from raping someone. Rather, the relevant benefit is, in Duff's word, '*intrinsic*'.[23] It is the evasion of self-restraint. The justification for punishment is that it imposes on the criminal an extra burden, in some way equivalent to the burden that she evaded, and thus it restores the balance of benefits and burdens in the society. Punishment is this restoring of the balance, just as the crime was the disruption of that balance. On this account, then, punishment is a demand of justice; it falls on those who fail to shoulder their burdens or those who claim a greater share of benefits than that to which they are entitled. As Richard Dagger puts it:

Criminals act unfairly when they take advantage of the opportunities the legal order affords them without contributing to the preservation of that order. In doing so, they upset the balance between benefits and burdens at the heart of the notion of justice. *Justice requires that this balance be restored*, and this can only be achieved through punishment or pardon. (Dagger 1993: 476, emphasis added; cf. Morris 1968: 478)

This is a retributive conception of punishment. Justice demands punishment in response to some past act. This might have deterrent effects—presumably co-operators will know that the society operates a system of punishment and this will make it less plausible that they will find it in their

---

[23] Duff 1986: 207. Of course, the criminal does benefit from the gain in property or from the pleasure of raping someone. What is being claimed here is that the benefit which the fair play theorist—as against, for example, a restorationist—is concerned with is that of the offender not mediating his behaviour in accordance with the norms the obeying of which by others leads to benefits for the offender. This argument is set out in greater detail below.

interests to break the law—but the reason for punishing is not that it serves to increase or decrease the likelihood of disobedience.[24]

Before considering objections to the fair play account it is worth pausing to consider precisely what is demanded by justice. For although fair play theory appears to have the great virtue of simplicity (from a just pattern of distribution, to a disruption of that pattern, to its restoration), the argument is not so straightforward. On the one hand, justice is said to demand that the balance of benefits and burdens be restored. On the other, justice demands that the individual free-rider 'pay a debt', shoulder some extra burden, or get his 'just deserts'. These are different kinds of arguments; one directed to the achievement of some state of affairs, the other to some claim of, or concerning, a particular individual. The imposing of suffering on an offender may be a means to restore the relevant pattern of distribution, but it is not the only means to so doing. Moreover, how the role of justice is conceived makes a considerable difference to the understanding of the theory. This ambiguity is discussed below. However, it stems from the understanding that fair play theorists have of the benefits and burdens of social co-operation and these can be best understood by considering some misdirected objections to the fair play account.

## Intrinsic and extrinsic benefits

Consider three criticisms of fair play theory. First, given by Fingarette, that fair play theory fails to capture the nature of legal prohibitions:

On [the fair play[25]] view . . . I would seem to have two equally legitimate options— paying my debts earlier in cash, or paying later in punishment. But surely that is not the intent of the law *prohibiting* stealing. The intent is precisely to *deny* us a legitimate alternative to paying the storekeeper for what we take. (Fingarette 1977: 502)

---

[24] Andrew von Hirsch has argued that fair play theory generates a prima-facie reason for punishment based on the desert of the offender. Against this prima-facie reason he argues is a 'countervailing moral obligation of not deliberately adding to the amount of human suffering'. To get to justified punishment he thinks that one needs the assumption that punishment has deterrence effects, and thus in fact punishment reduces rather than increases the total of human suffering. Although these extra steps are interesting they do not, it seems to me, change the basic justification for punishment offered by von Hirsch as being based on desert generated by fair play. 'Step 3', the deterrence argument, merely makes 'Step 2' (subtract from rather than add to human suffering) irrelevant; 'the prima-facie case for punishment . . . based on desert . . . stands again' (von Hirsch 1976: 54). This is the theory that he has since retracted, see n. 18 above. Dagger thinks that the general justifying aim of fair play theory is deterrence (see Dagger 1993), but this is because he fails to distinguish fair play theory from contractarian accounts of punishment.

[25] Fingarette's discussion is of Morris's 1968 paper.

Second, that fair play gives rise to a theory of compensation or restitution, but not of punishment. Again Fingarette provides such a criticism when he says, continuing from the above: 'and even if I restore the balance by returning the stolen goods, and by paying back any incidental losses incurred by the storekeeper, it still remains intelligible and important . . . to ask whether I should *also* be punished' (Fingarette 1977: 502).

If it were the case that the balance could be restored solely by (this kind of) restitution, the critic claims, the theory would be severely undermined. Apart from the obvious difficulties posed by crimes such as rape, it is not even satisfactory in apparently straightforward cases such as theft. If a criminal steals a car and is caught, it is not a punishment for him to be forced to return the car, paying the owner for any wear and tear, petrol used, and inconvenience caused; that is not punishing the criminal, it is making the victim into an (unwilling) car hire firm.[26]

Third, the critics of fair play ask in what sense the rapist, for example, claims more than his fair share of something that is generally desired. Antony Duff claims that the fair play theorist has it that the rapist has done something that the law-abiding members of society all would want to do, but which they do not do because they mediate their acts in accordance with the demands of the norms of co-operation. Duff argues that this is simply not true. Most people do not wish to rape or murder so obeying those laws is not a burden:

talk of the criminal's unfair advantage implies that obedience to the law is a burden for us all: but is this true of such *mala in se*? Surely many of us do not find it a *burden* to obey the laws against murder and rape, or need to *restrain* ourselves from such crimes: how then does the murderer or rapist gain an unfair advantage over the rest of us, by evading a burden of self-restraint which we accept? (Duff 1986: 213)[27]

The response to all three of these objections (and without a response fair play theory would be fatally undermined) can be encapsulated in the claim that all three rest on a fundamental misunderstanding of the benefits and burdens in fair play theory. As noted above, fair play theory understands the benefits to the offender as intrinsic to disobeying the law. What the criminal gains is that, unlike non-free-riders, she pursues her self-interest unconstrained by law. The burden imposed by the co-operative scheme is, likewise, to be understood as that of having to mediate the pursuit of one's

---

[26] I am grateful to John Charvet for this example.
[27] A similar criticism appears in Wasserstrom 1980: 143–6.

self-interest in accordance with the demands of the law (the rules of the co-operative enterprise).

Thus, the fair play theorist can respond to the first criticism that it is not that the shoplifter may either pay for his goods now in cash or later in punishment, because the debt he owes if he steals the goods is not for the goods. Likewise, to address the second criticism, the benefit (to be considered in justifying punishment), is not the illicit gains of material possessions, or the pleasures of rape, it is the benefit of not regulating one's actions by the norms of co-operation established in law.[28] Thus, the criminal would not 'restore the balance by returning the stolen goods' because those are not the goods that punishment addresses (cf. Dagger 1993: 478, 484–7). Finally, Duff's argument that most people do not find the prohibition on rape (and similar *mala in se*) burdensome can likewise be rejected. It is not the case that what the criminal has done that the law-abiding members would want to do is rape or murder, but that he has acted as a free-rider. This is something that law-abiding citizens also want to do, but don't because they recognize their obligations.[29]

In short, the defence against the three criticisms lies in the conception of obedience to the law as a burden; a restraint on the direct and unmediated pursuit of self-interest. The relevant burden in fair play theory is the requirement to mediate the pursuit of one's self-interest in accordance with the demands of the co-operative scheme from which one gains the benefits of 'peace, security, and freedom'. The failure on the part of the criminal lies in her direct pursuit of her self-interest regardless of the burden that she should fairly carry. The criminal, in John Finnis's words, 'permit[s] himself an excessive freedom in choosing' (Finnis 1972: 132). Characterizing the benefits, burdens, and the nature of criminality thus is not merely central to the correct understanding of fair play theory as a whole, but also deflects the three criticisms discussed above.

However, this understanding of fair play theory is also subject to criticism. Two related questions arise: first, given that the above correctly characterizes what is wrong in criminal acts, how can punishment (the deliberate infliction of suffering by an appropriate authority on an offender

---

[28] Cf. Sadurski 1989: 360–2. Clearly from the criminal's point of view the benefits of crime are primarily the material or physical gains achieved in robbing or raping someone. A fair play system of punishment would presumably advocate the restoring of possessions and compensating of the victim (insofar as it is possible), but this would be in addition to punishment (see n. 23 above). The punishment itself must be conceived in the terms given above if fair play theory is to avoid the three objections described.

[29] Cf. Dagger 1993: 479–80; Sadurski 1989 offers a similar defence of fair play theory caged in the language of choice options, 357–60.

for an offence) be justified as the appropriate response? Second, is the characterization of crime as free-riding at all plausible?

## Punishment and free-riding

The argument of those who wish to apply the principle of fair play to penal philosophy is that punishment is supposed to restore the balance of benefits and burdens, but it is difficult to understand how it does this. In the ordinary language of morals 'two wrongs do not make a right' and it is not clear that in this case punishment (a prima-facie harm) can achieve the desired end. Three related problems arise: first, 'restoring a balance' does not entail correcting the thing that created the imbalance. Second, fair play theory must show that punishment is (uniquely) appropriate as the means of restoration. Third, fair play theory must generate an account of proportionality between crime and punishment. It is worth considering each of these problems.

The function of punishment in fair play theory is to restore a just balance, as was emphasized in the quotation given from Dagger above.[30] It follows that, as with all such projects, other things being equal there is no compelling reason to alter what lies only on a particular side of what ought to be in balance. Consider, for example, an election between two candidates each of whom is permitted to spend £1,000 and in the middle of which it is discovered that one candidate has spent £1,500. In such a case there may be reasons to censure the overspending candidate, to throw him out of the race, etc., but there may also be a case for restoring the fair balance between the candidates by allowing the other candidate to spend an extra £500.

It might be objected that this example forgets what has been already argued for, that what is to be considered is not the tangible stuff involved in breaking the rules (in this case the benefit of spending more money), but the extra freedom gained in pursuing directly one's self-interest. However, in principle the same argument must apply. If what the offender has done to disrupt the balance of benefits and burdens is 'permit himself an excessive freedom in choosing' then the restoration of the status quo could be achieved by licensing such excessive freedom to be enjoyed by all the others in the co-operative enterprise (cf. Dolinko 1991: 548–9). The difficulty

---

[30] Jeffrie Murphy's paper 'Marxism and Retribution' provides a reminder that the assumption of a just baseline is problematic given the inequalities in the distribution of income and wealth in most contemporary liberal democracies and given the social and legal consequences of those inequalities (see Murphy 1973).

is that in focusing on the restoration of some state of affairs the important retributive connection between the act of the offender and that offender's punishment is threatened.

Even if, for the moment, it is granted that the correction required must be achieved through some change to the condition of the offender, the theory is faced with a second problem. The claim that punishment is an appropriate way to restore the balance of the relevant benefits and burdens is hard to understand. The intuition traded on by fair play theory is that the criminal has allowed himself some extra 'freedom in choosing'—the extra freedom of pursuing his self-interest directly—and so by punishing him, by taking away some of his freedom, the situation is restored. However, this seems little more than a play on words. In depriving the offender of some tangible liberties (such as to spend his income as he wishes, or his freedoms of movement and association), society does not extract from the offender some 'repayment' of liberty to the co-operative venture. Self-restraint and the freedom to do certain things are not substitutable goods.

One possibility,[31] if what is of concern is that the offender has not carried his share of the burden of sustaining the benefits of 'peace, security, and freedom', might be to treat the punishment of the offender as a contribution to the system of deterrence that is part of the means by which these benefits are secured. This, at least, has the advantage of tying punishment to the idea that the offender owes something to a system from which he has benefited and that punishment should be aimed at extracting this debt. In being punished the criminal contributes to the co-operative venture whilst being deprived of its benefits. Such an account would be complicated, involving a retributive claim that justice demands that each shoulder her fair share and, in addition, the claim that the means by which this burden can be extracted when it is not voluntarily embraced is through the use of the punishment of the offender to deter others. However, such an account is unlikely to be successful. One problem is that the marginal effects of individual punishments on deterrence are hard, if not impossible, to determine. In any case, the account is liable to the other criticisms of fair play theory. It is mentioned only to illustrate the treacherous nature of the conversion of the claim that the offender claims some freedom or benefit to which he is not entitled to the claim that restricting some particular freedom(s) of the offender will deprive him of the relevant benefit and thus restore the balance of benefits and burdens that holds between him and the rest of the co-operative community.

---

[31] Although, as far as I know, not one that is discussed in the literature.

Finally, if it is not quite obvious how punishment restores the status quo ante neither is it obvious that it is the only mechanism for attempting such a goal. For example, one alternative to punishment, considered by fair play theorists such as Herbert Morris and taken seriously also in Dagger's review of fair play theory, is pardoning.[32] Another, as mentioned above, is the licensing of others to enjoy an 'excessive freedom in choosing'.

The third problem (the problem of proportionality) arises even if it is granted that the balance is to be restored through altering the condition of the offender and that this is to be done by imposing on the offender some restriction on her freedom (some punishment). The problem results from the characterization of the benefits and burdens of social co-operation. By treating criminal actions as free-riding, as avoiding the burden of self-restraint, and thus abstracting from what the agent has actually done—rape, murder, drive recklessly, or park illegally—fair play theory risks reducing all criminal actions to the same act: the non-mediation of one's

---

[32] 'Forgiveness—with its legal analogue of a pardon—while not the righting of an unfair distribution by making one pay his debt is, nevertheless, a restoring of the equilibrium by forgiving the debt. Forgiveness may be viewed, at least in some types of case, as a gift after the fact, erasing a debt, which had the gift been given before the fact, would not have created a debt. But the practice of pardoning has to proceed sensitively, for it may endanger, in a way the practice of justice does not, the maintenance of an equilibrium of benefits and burdens. If all are indiscriminately pardoned less incentive is provided individuals to restrain their inclinations, thus increasing the incidence of persons taking what they do not deserve' (Morris 1968: 95; cf. Dagger 1993: 476). This is not pardoning as traditionally understood. Traditionally pardoning is not an alternative to punishment, but is something done once it has been established that the offender is deserving of punishment; it is, in the strict sense, an act of grace. (It is true that sometimes there are calls for pardoning when it is thought that there are mitigating circumstances, such as that the offender is young or naïve. In such cases the offender is said to 'deserve pardoning'. Such calls, it seems to me, are in fact motivated by something like the thought that the criminal justice system has failed to take such things into account (perhaps because of a mandatory sentencing policy), but rather than amend the system to meet a particular need it is easier to circumvent it by means of an extrinsic intervention such as a pardon. In such cases, the offender may be legally pardoned, but in fact the offender deserved less punishment, and pardoning is being used to achieve this. It is thus not the case that the offender deserved pardoning.)

However, Morris accepts that pardoning restores the balance of benefits and burdens rather than being (as it would be on the traditional picture) an acceptance of the disequilibrium as the new status quo. But on Morris's account, pardoning is an alternative to punishment (both being justified only by appeal to their efficacy at restoring the status quo ante) and this makes Morris's distinction between the righting and restoring of an unfair distribution (and, by extension the difference between 'the practice of pardoning' and 'the practice of justice') difficult to understand. Morris's argument for punishment as the uniquely appropriate restorative of equilibrium is explicitly consequentialist and thus is unacceptable if fair play theory is to retain its retributive character. For Morris we must punish because the indiscriminate use of pardon would not deter individuals from 'restrain[ing] their inclinations' (cf. Duff 1986: 216).

self-interest by the duty of fair play.[33] This is problematic for a theory of punishment because, in the absence of any additional argument, it seems that if there is only one crime then there should be only one punishment. Worse still, in the attempt to distinguish between crimes—by differentiating the degree to which offenders permit themselves an 'excessive freedom in choosing'—the most promising line of enquiry would seem to be connected to the degree of temptation. Where an offender has done something that many people are tempted to do (for example, jump a traffic light) she has done something that it takes others a significant effort not to do. Where she has done something that most others find repellent rather than tempting, such as commit murder, she has not claimed a freedom from self-restraint of a kind that others would wish to have for (as Duff points out) others do not find the 'burden' of self-restraint in such instances too burdensome. However, this would suggest that the repayment due for traffic violations is greater than that for murder.[34] In sum, if all crimes are equal failures of self-restraint the theory cannot account for differential punishments. If the seriousness of the violation of the law is to be proportional to the average degree of restraint needed to stop the performance of the action then the theory supports the deeply counter-intuitive view that traffic offences are more serious than crimes such as rape and murder. The characterization of benefits and burdens needed to rescue fair play from criticisms of the type mentioned on pp. 57–8 seems merely to put it at the mercy of another set of telling objections.

Richard Dagger, in an enquiry into the strengths of fair play theory admits that the theory cannot adequately account for the difference in types of offence (most importantly between *mala in se* and *mala prohibita*), but argues that this does not undermine fair play theory because the difference in the nature of offences is in addition to their character as acts of free-riding.[35] Moreover, it is only when the rule of law applies, when offences are, at least in part, acts of free-riding, that punishment can be

---

[33] This reduction of all crimes to a single offence mirrors Klosko's argument that one has a duty to obey all laws (including those whose function is to provide discretionary goods) because (if the principle of fair play applies) one has an obligation to play one's part in the provision of the presumptive good of the rule of law. Klosko 1992: 101–3.

[34] These objections to fair play theory are common. See, for example, Burgh 1982; Dolinko 1991: 545–6; Ellis 1997; Wasserstrom 1980: 141–6. Note, punishment would still be imposed for the 'intrinsic' offence of not bearing one's burden of self-restraint. The degree of punishment would reflect the degree of temptation.

[35] 'All crimes, I have said, are in some sense crimes of unfairness. They may be *more than* crimes of unfairness, as rape, robbery and murder surely are, but they must be *at least* crimes of this sort' (Dagger 1993: 479).

justified. In the absence of the rule of law, and of a fair play justification of punishment, the additional wrongness of an act might legitimately be the subject of 'punishment of the gods' or 'revenge' (Dagger 1993: 479), but the law has no business replicating the former and once society has come into being the right to private revenge is replaced by the rule of law. Nevertheless, Dagger rejects the conclusion that all crimes are equivalent in terms of the punishment they are to receive. His argument is that the duty of fair play is a necessary but not sufficient grounding for a full account of justified punishment:

This is not to say that the murderer and the tax cheater should receive the same punishment *tout court*. For the murderer has committed two crimes, in a sense, but the tax cheater only one. The murderer has simultaneously committed a crime of unfairness (a *malum prohibitum*) *and* a crime against her particular victim (a *malum in se*). For these two offenses, as it were, she must suffer two punishments. The first serves to discharge her debt to society by restoring the balance of benefits and burdens under the rule of law. The second punishment must be justified and established on other grounds. (Dagger 1993: 484)

Apart from the difficulty that this position deprives fair play theory of much of its force as a theory of punishment, it reveals once again the feature of fair play that makes the account vulnerable. The offence of relevance to fair play theory is, at least for many criminal acts, one that is disconnected from the moral character of the act (cf. Duff 1986: 212). The punishment for the offence that it might be thought would be of most interest to a retributive account of punishment—the rape, murder, or whatever—is, according to Dagger, yet to be determined. The offence of claiming more 'freedom in choosing' than that to which one is entitled turns out to be common to all offences and the only one to which fair play theory is able to respond.

However, perhaps this is too quick. George Sher, in his defence of fair play theory, argues that both the characterization of the extra benefit claimed by the offender as the intrinsic benefit gained through pursuing one's self interest unmediated by the demands of a co-operative venture of which one is a member, and that of the associated burden borne by members of the co-operative venture, are correct. Nevertheless, he argues that the benefit gained by the offender can be connected to the particular act performed thus allowing a differentiation between crimes, and satisfying better the demands of retributivism.

Sher's argument is captured in the following passage:

a person who acts wrongly does gain a significant measure of extra liberty: what he gains is freedom from the demands of the prohibition he violates. . . . as the strength of the prohibition increases, so too does the freedom from it which its violation entails. Thus, even if the murderer and the tax evader do succumb to equally strong impulses, their gains in freedom are far from equal. Because the murderer evades a prohibition of far greater force . . . his net gain in freedom remains greater. And for that reason, the amount of punishment he deserves is greater as well. (Sher 1987: 82)

The importance of this is that Sher connects the conception of the benefit accruing to the offender with the offending 'act's degree of wrongness' (1987: 81). However, this raises important questions that go to the heart of the fair play account (and that lead to the objection that fair play theory misconceives the nature of the wrong in criminal acts). The questions concern the sense in which the offender gains something, some benefit, from his offending behaviour and the connection of this to the role of punishment in restoring the balance of benefits and burdens and/or in extracting from the offender the debt that he owes to others in the co-operative venture.

On the one hand, the intuition that the law constrains those within its jurisdiction and that, therefore, to break the law is to shrug off some restriction and make a gain in freedom is common, especially in the liberal tradition. Those who jump traffic lights do get ahead, and some of those who do not do so may envy them. On the other hand, the thought that to break a law is to gain in freedom, and that the gain is greater the more serious is the prohibition enshrined in the law that is broken, is in many ways mysterious.[36] The offender does not gain the freedom to break the law by his actions. He is, like most other citizens, free to break the law in the sense that the fact that he is able to do so reveals that although there are constraints on his ability to do what he wants (there are policemen, locked doors, burglar alarms) these are (sometimes) insufficient. However, the same applies to many others who do not choose to break the law. Nor does the offender gain freedom in the sense that he is freed from the obligation that he has not to break the law. In short, the idea of a 'gain in freedom' cannot, in any strict sense of those terms, be made plausible. Rather, the sense of the phrase that allows it to pass without evoking suspicion is that sense in which it loosely overlaps with the original fair play claim that the offender free-rides; allows himself to take something from a co-operative venture to which he shows himself to be unwilling to contribute his fair share. Despite the apparent clarity and the whiff of logic in Sher's argument his claim that the offender 'gains freedom' in proportion to the seriousness

[36] The remainder of this paragraph follows Dolinko 1991: 548–9.

of the prohibition he breaks is metaphorical.[37] There is no actual increase in options available to the free-rider (others have the option of jumping the red light, but they choose not to do so) or decrease in his obligations.[38]

Finally, although the idea that there is something wrong in free-riding and the claim that the free-rider owes something to the co-operative venture that she has cheated appeal to common intuitions there is surely something distorting in thinking that what is common to all wrongs is that they are instances of free-riding (cf. Duff 1986: 212, 1996: 27). It may be true that some crimes can be understood as taking unfair advantage of others, but others are surely wrong in some more fundamental sense. To return to the examples of rape and murder, these acts are wrong in some other way than because they violate a principle of fair play.[39] Sher's argument that the more serious the wrong the greater the gain in freedom only adds to the sense of distortion.

The examination of the above three objections reveals a flaw at the heart of fair play theory. This is that it fails to connect the punishment to the crime. Both the focus on restoring the balance of benefits and burdens, and the interpretation that it is necessary to give to what constitute the relevant benefits and burdens, lead to the disconnection of the offence and the offender; the crime and the punishment. For that reason, fair play theory cannot show that the balance must be restored by addressing only the position of the offender; that punishment, penal hard treatment, is the appropriate response to the creation of imbalance in the distribution of benefits and burdens; or that different offences merit different responses.

The difficulty for fair play theory stems from the characterization of the benefits and burdens that it employs. Abstracting from the act that the offender actually performed and instead focusing on the failure of the offender to restrain the pursuit of his self-interest in accordance with the norms of the co-operative enterprise of which he is a member separates the punishment from the 'real wrong' done and undercuts the theory's claim to be able to justify the practice of punishment. However, fair play theory does appeal to an intuition that there is something wrong with free-

---

[37] It is hard to avoid Dolinko's thought that it is a metaphor that 'betrays us at every turn' (1991: 549 n.).

[38] It is worth noting that Sher's argument, in making proportional the gain in freedom and the seriousness of the offence (rather than in treating all offences as comparable instances of free-riding) makes fair play theory vulnerable to Duff's criticism that fair play theory is committed to the view that what people most want to do is those things that are most seriously wrong, and that this is false (see above).

[39] The precise nature of such wrongness depends, of course, on the grounding that one gives to morality. I shall argue for a particular moral theory below in Chs. 7–9.

riding; Murphy's claim that the free-rider reveals herself by her actions to be a 'parasite' does not ring false. Moreover, the idea that justice requires not the restoring of some balance of freedom, but the repayment of a 'debt' or a 'gain' by the offender is similarly attractive. Examining the retributive reaction to free-riders not only reveals what it is that fair play theory fails to capture, and why, but is also useful for the analysis of reciprocity and contractarianism that follows in the later chapters.

## WRONGNESS AND FREE-RIDING

The claim that the free-rider does something wrong is, in the context of the above discussion, uncontroversial. However, the claim that free-riding is all that there is to wrongdoing is implausible. Nevertheless, understanding the attraction of fair play theory is important in determining at least part of what an adequate theory of punishment must capture. However, what it is that the free-rider does wrong, and what it is that underpins the intuitive reaction that free-riding both creates a disequilibrium in the pattern of benefits and burdens and makes the free-rider deserve to suffer, is hard to determine. One difficulty is that the response to the free-rider may contain two separate and distinct arguments: that someone who defects from some co-operative venture achieves some illegitimate gain over and above the immediate booty realized by the defection, and (separately) that the free-rider does something wrong in failing to respect the moral value of the other participants. This combination contributes to the ambiguity mentioned above in the role ascribed by fair play theory to justice (as requiring, on the one hand, the re-establishing of a particular state of affairs and, on the other, the payment of a particular debt by a particular person).

Consider an example of a group of associates who agree to some co-operative enterprise, say the waiters in a restaurant who agree to pool their tips each evening and then to divide them equally at the end of the night. All of them regularly comment on the advantages of this arrangement and they congratulate one another on the cordial atmosphere that is generated by it, and that is owed to the self-restraint of each. Some time after the practice has been established it is discovered that one of their number, Fred, has been withholding most of his tips. One response of the other waiters may be that Fred should pay back the estimated sum that he has gained by his illicit behaviour. Another might be disappointment that Fred has failed to constrain his behaviour in accordance with the agreed norm. However, it is also surely likely that the other waiters will feel that Fred has not merely taken advantage of them financially, but that he has treated them shoddily. What he has done is wrong because he has failed to treat his associates appropriately given their status. Insofar as the others believe Fred should be punished or should suffer beyond paying back his illicit gains it is surely for this; for his failure to respect the equal value of those with whom he interacts. The resentment felt by the other waiters is not directed at Fred for having allowed himself an option in choosing that the others through their own self-control did not permit themselves, but at Fred's failure to respect their moral standing. Moreover, it not only badly misrepresents, but undermines, the reaction of Fred's fellow waiters to say that Fred has done something that they wish to do. Resentment can be a mask for envy, but it would be an impoverished world in which this were always the case.

The point of this example is to highlight two different ways of understanding the co-operative arrangement into which the waiters have entered. The model adopted by fair play theorists of punishment has it that the contract is one of mutual advantage. Each participant enters because she calculates that over time her interests will be better served if she co-operates rather than acts as an independent. Fair play theory commits itself not merely to this model, but to an understanding of interests such that individual co-operators may, at times, be better able to pursue their interests by free-riding. They perceive the rules of co-operation as limiting the pursuit of their self-interest and, therefore, obedience to the rules as a burden. For the most part, what the individual contractor wants is that others should co-operate, that she should benefit, but that she should be able to do so without carrying her share of the burdens necessary to sustain the co-operative enterprise.

The adoption of this model of contractarianism is attractive to fair play theory because it delivers the characterization of benefits and burdens necessary to avoid the objections detailed above.[40] However, it is problematic in two distinct ways. First, in characterizing the wrong in criminal acts as the avoidance of self-restraint (or the permitting for oneself of 'an excessive freedom in choosing') it adopts a distorted understanding of (many) crimes with the consequences discussed above. In addition, the adoption of this contractarian model introduces a distinct route to the justification of punishment: rational individuals will not agree to constrain the direct pur-

---

[40] The adoption of contractarianism may also be attractive to fair play theorists because through it they have access to a notion of (hypothetical) *consent*, which can be used in answering some of the objections to the whole idea of a 'mutuality of restrictions' raised by such people as Nozick (see n. 21 above).

suit of their self-interest unless they are sure that others will do the same and the threat of punishment is one way to assure the co-operating parties that there will be general compliance. On this model, then, the system of punishing is not based in fair play, but is designed to contribute to an environment of stable expectations.[41]

The contractarianism described above is one that cannot capture entirely the reaction of Fred's colleagues to his behaviour. On the above understanding Fred has acted in accordance with his perception of his interests (given that his duplicity is discovered he may well have calculated incorrectly when deciding what action would best serve his interests). In pursuing directly his own interests he has done something that the others would want to do, but don't because they lack the courage or because they think the risks of being caught are too great. The crucial claim is that each, Fred and those who obey the norms of co-operation, thinks of the norm of combining their tips as imposing a burden adherence to which will, over a

---

[41] The argument is this: in coming to understand one's relations with others as governed by norms and rules that (if these are legitimate) would have been the subject of agreement in some suitably constituted hypothetical choosing situation each person commits herself to obedience to the rules on the condition that every other does the same. In order to deter free-riding each person would agree to a system of compulsion. This, then, forms the basis of an account of punishment.

Among fair play theorists this feature of the contractarianism they import goes largely undiscussed. Dagger is exceptional in explicitly drawing attention to it, describing 'punishment as a practice' as 'justified because it is necessary to the maintenance of the social order' (Dagger 1993: 475). Morris implies much the same when he argues, as noted above (n. 32), that pardon, although an alternative to punishment as a restorative of justice, should be used cautiously because it does not have the deterrence effects of penal hard treatment.

Dagger's suggestion is that the maintenance of the social order explains the general justifying aim of punishment, but the question, 'Whom to Punish?' is correctly addressed by fair play theory. Dagger's adoption of Hart's typology of questions is, for reasons given in the Introduction, unhelpful, but the argument can be restated in Armstrong terms as: the maintenance of the social order explains why we punish; the argument from fair play explains what makes it morally permissible for us to do so (Morris, also, seems to have some similar division in mind). However, this leaves far too many questions unanswered, not least those concerning how the two parts of the theory are to be integrated. Moreover, although the importing of a deterrence rationale as the point of punishment may explain why hard treatment of the offender is to be preferred to other means of restoring the balance of benefits and burdens, it can do nothing to address the problem that fair play theory seems to misconstrue the wrong to which punishment is the appropriate response. Looked at unsympathetically, the best that might be said of the Dagger proposal is that it merely combines two unsatisfactory theories of punishment. Fair play theory, as it stands, does not have the resources to deliver priority rules or to integrate an assurance-based explanation of 'why the system of punishment?' and a 'benefit and burden' based account of individual punishment. However, it is worth noting (as it will be the subject of discussion in later chapters) that a natural reading of contractarianism leads to an assurance/deterrence component in punishment.

period of time, serve their interests (relative to universal non-cooperation), but which they conceive of as an imposition that frustrates the most profitable pursuit of their self-interest (which on this model would be achieved by benefiting from the restraint of others whilst not restraining oneself). What this leaves out is the possibility that involvement in the co-operative enterprise may alter the view that the individual has of his interests. In brief, one reaction of Fred's colleagues may be disappointment that Fred should have thought in the way that he has. The others may think of their interests as aligned with the interests of the whole, or they might value the co-operative norm such that they do not conceive of it as being a restriction on the pursuit of their self-interest, but rather a means through which they pursue a good that they share together. Fred's failure, then, is not a failure of self-restraint, but a failure to be the kind of being who is not disposed to consider the norms in accordance with which he lives together with others, and indeed his relations with those others, as of merely instrumental value. The disappointment and retributive reaction of Fred's colleagues is not based in the thought that Fred has given in to the understandable and rational temptation to defect from the agreement, but that his actions reveal that he thinks of them, and of his relations with them, as merely self-serving. Fred is revealed to be a cad, not something that the others would want to be, even if they thought that they could, unlike Fred, get away with it. The intuition that there is something amiss in the situation that obtains after Fred's actions is not that what needs to be 'put right' is the material gain that Fred has made, but it is also not that Fred owes a debt for the freedom that he has taken. The intuitive reaction that a wrong has been done that needs to be undone is common, and needs to be made sense of, but it is a reaction that is best, if only inchoately, understood in terms of the restoring of the social fabric that has been torn by Fred's actions.[42]

The development of an account of co-operation that allows the understanding of co-operative relations briefly sketched above is a complex matter, and is pursued below. The point to be made here is just that fair play theory adopts a particular account of co-operation. One to which it is pressed by having to incorporate a particular understanding of benefits

---

[42] This conception of what needs to be restored makes sense of the thought that pardoning could be an alternative to punishment. If what needs to be set right is the social fabric then pardoning, given that a pardon must come from the injured party or her representative, might be considered to play this role. If this is the case it would have interesting implications for the understanding of such things as the Truth and Reconciliation Commission in South Africa.

and burdens. However, with this account it cannot adequately characterize what the agent does wrong when she does not behave in accordance with the law. Instead, fair play theory is forced toward an entirely unconvincing account of wrongness as 'the gain in freedom' of allowing oneself to pursue one's interests directly.

It is worth noting that this not only distorts the notion of wrongdoing, but is also implausible as an understanding of the structure of social relations. In portraying all rules as constraints on the individual and in assuming an account of motivation that makes obeying rules a burden and (successful) disobedience a 'gain', fair play theory conceives of societal relations as a continuing battle between self-interested beings held in check only by rules that threaten punishment for defectors. For this reason fair play theory is pushed (albeit unwillingly) toward the assurance/deterrence understanding of the function of punishment. If the system of punishment is effective it provides what Hobbes called the condition of 'sufficient security'(Hobbes 1991: part i, Ch. 15, 215), it answers an assurance problem, by convincing each party that the others will not free-ride. However, this is implausible: our relations one to another and to the rules that govern our co-operation are not as described above, and, as even Hobbes recognized, were they to be so the threat of punishment would be insufficient to hold society together.[43]

It is argued below that the discussion of fair play theory presents, in microcosm, the problems and choices that afflict contract theories more generally. The development of a more adequate contractarianism must learn from the failure of fair play theory, and ensure that the relationship of reciprocity that underpins it is not one in which each regards every other and the norms that regulate their co-operation as of merely instrumental

---

[43] Men, Hobbes says, 'need to be diligently, and truly taught; because [civil society] cannot be maintained by . . . terrour of legal punishment' (Hobbes 1991: part ii, ch. 30, 337; see Ch. 6 below). In a book that post-dates his article on fair play theory Richard Dagger explicitly juxtaposes the cultivation of 'civic virtues' and punishment as two means of holding society together. He writes, 'one way to avoid this outcome [the outcome of people thinking of free-riding as the most effective means to further their interests] is to compel people to obey the law—to force them, if not to be free, then at least to bear their share of the burdens. In this way the practice of punishment seeks to ensure that "those who would voluntarily obey shall not be sacrificed to those who would not". A more positive way to secure cooperation is to cultivate the desire to do one's part in the cooperative endeavour. This desire fosters a form of civic virtue—of acting for the common good even when it proves personally painful. The more we can rely on people to exhibit this virtue, the less we shall have to rely on punishment and other forms of coercion to secure their cooperation. Punishment may be a necessary evil, but civic virtue is a positive good' (Dagger 1997: 79). I am grateful to John Maynor for bringing this passage to my attention.

value to the realization of his self-interested projects. The rules that structure our relations must not be conceived of as alien impositions against which individual self-interest strains, but must be integrated with self-interest. This is the project attempted in later chapters.

## CONCLUSION

Fair play theory appeals to a common understanding of the retributive response in linking the state of affairs brought about by the wrong done and the restoring of the status quo through the annulling of that wrong and the punishment of the offender. It appeals to an idea that people are held together by a moral fabric, or social glue, and that the criminal's actions tear that fabric and his punishment repairs it. It is in this way that the two requirements of justice—that some state of affairs be restored and that some particular individual be punished—are supposed to be linked. However, in appealing to the crude contractarian understanding of social co-operation that they do, fair play theorists ensure that they cannot explain or justify this account. The account of social co-operation separates the two functions of justice and undermines the theory. Moreover, the contractarianism that fair play theory adopts brings with it an account of punishment that, whilst it might be thought to capture some important part of the function of punishment, is far removed from the central retributivist intuition described above. The retributive response that fair play theory fails to capture requires further examination, which is the task of the next chapter. The model of social relations that underpins it—a model that must go beyond the instrumental relations of self-interested contractors assumed in fair play theory—is the subject of what remains thereafter.

# 3

# Retributivism II:
# Resentment, Guilt, and Censure

## INTRODUCTION: THE WRONG IN WRONGFUL ACTIONS

The argument of Chapter 2 is, in part, that fair play theory incorrectly characterizes what is wrong in (many) criminal actions because of the account of benefits and burdens on which it depends. Moreover, the assumptions concerning benefits, burdens, and motivation distort the understanding of wrongdoing and the 'retributive reaction' to it, as is illustrated in the example (from that chapter) of Fred. Fair play theory holds that what Fred has done is something that his associates, too, would wish to do, and that his associates must therefore understand him as having given in to a rational temptation to free-ride that all share (the temptation to pursue one's self-interest unmediated by the terms of the agreement that govern one's cooperative relations). In fact, Fred's associates think him shabby and, far from envying him his 'gain in freedom', they resent the way that he has treated them.

The purpose of this chapter is to examine some recent attempts to articulate a retributivist theory, again both to assess their credibility and to examine the relationship between punishment theory and moral philosophy more generally. Interestingly, a number of retributive writers have recently focused on resentment and retributive emotions as the starting point for justifying punishment. Amongst these is one of those who originally led the development of fair play theory, Jeffrie Murphy.[1] Murphy argues that resentment is an appropriate reaction to wrongs against oneself. Not to feel resentment is to fail to treat oneself, and one's entitlements, seriously. It is to fail to respond in a way compatible with self-respect (Murphy and Hampton 1988: 16–17; cf. Baldwin 1999: 130; Butler 1969: Sermons VIII and IX; Strawson 1982). Such resentment, in Murphy's view,

---

[1] Although see Ch. 2 n. 18 above.

can sometimes be linked to the desire to see that 'the wrongdoer gets his just deserts', that he is 'brought low' and '*hurt*' (Murphy and Hampton 1988: 95, 89, 94). This 'natural, fitting, and proper response to certain instances of wrongdoing' Murphy describes as 'retributive hatred' (Murphy and Hampton 1988: 108).

Murphy's phenomenology of the retributive reaction that many people have to various crimes is more compelling than the account given by fair play theory. It better describes the intuition that the wrongdoer deserves to suffer. However, insofar as retributive hatred, unlike resentment, is in part defined by the claim that the offender ought to suffer some harm—ought to get his 'just deserts'—it cannot contribute to the justification of a retributive account of punishment. As Murphy accepts, retributive hatred is a morally permissible response to wrongdoing only if one presupposes that there is some truth in the retributive claim that wrongdoers deserve to suffer (Murphy and Hampton 1988: 94–5; cf. Baldwin 1999: 130). Nevertheless, because Murphy does make the claim that retributive hatred as he describes it is 'appropriate', his description of it ought to prove useful in discerning the outline of what he would hold to be a justified account of punishment, notwithstanding that he is cautious in drawing any conclusions for accounts of state punishment from his analysis of hatred, resentment, and forgiveness. It is possible to identify such an outline. Unfortunately, it betrays evidence that Murphy has not entirely shaken off his fair play roots; whilst he considers resentment as a response to 'direct violations of one's rights . . . *or* [an individual having] taken unfair advantage of one's sacrifices by free riding on a mutually beneficial scheme of reciprocal cooperation' (Murphy and Hampton 1988: 16), he links retributive hatred to the removal of the offender's 'unfair advantage' and to the restoring of the 'proper moral balance of whatever goods are in question' (1988: 89).

There are two separate and distinct arguments here (cf. Duff 1996, 30–1). The removal of some intrinsically related unfair advantage that the offender has gained (which, it is argued above, is an untenable theory), and an inchoate claim that a situation in which those who have done wrong nevertheless flourish is somehow 'out of kilter'. These arguments are of different kinds. Moreover, if what is said above in relation to fair play theory is correct, the phenomenological accounts of the retributive reaction in the two theories pull in opposite directions. Unfortunately, Murphy provides little more elucidation of the idea of retributive hatred and its connection to the justification of imposing suffering on the offender. Nevertheless, as Duff puts it, is there not something to the idea that one who has committed some serious wrong should not be able to live a life of 'freedom and contentment'—should not be able to carry on as if she had done no wrong . . .? She should suffer; which leads naturally to the thought that we may or should make her suffer. (1996: 31, quoting Murphy and Hampton 1988: 91)

Duff is surely right. What is more, this common response to many acts of wrongdoing lies at the heart of the appeal of retributivism and in one form or another it has a long and distinguished philosophical and cultural pedigree. Something like it allows moderns to understand the role of the *Erinyes* in the myths of ancient Greece; it appears in Kant's idea of punishment as the returning of a wrong done; and in Hegel's claim that punishment annuls the crime. However, as noted above, the problem is to explain this claim, and the route by which that is to be accomplished, through the idea of desert, remains elusive.

Murphy's co-contributor to *Forgiveness and Mercy*, Jean Hampton, attempts the development of what she calls an 'expressive' retributive theory in that book and in a series of subsequent papers (Murphy and Hampton 1988; Hampton 1991*a*, 1992*a*, 1992*b*).[2] Hampton, like Murphy, finds fair play theory inadequate because it fails to connect the punishment to the actual wrong done. She also builds on the idea that there is something in wrongdoing that requires a response; that requires, in Hegel's terms, to be annulled. Her argument revolves around an account of wrong (or that element of wrong that is relevant to retributivism) as 'moral injury'. This is defined as 'damage to the realization of a victim's value, or damage to the acknowledgement of the victim's value, accomplished through behavior whose meaning is such that the victim is diminished in value' (Hampton 1992*b*: 1679).

This is a difficult idea to understand. By damage to 'the realization of a victim's value' Hampton refers to forms of wrongdoing that diminish the victim's ability to secure 'that to which his value entitles him—where that can include his autonomy, his bodily integrity, the possession of property, and even his life' (1992*b*: 1678). Thus, in attacking his victim's bodily integrity the assailant conveys a message that the victim is of no great value and, thus, claims to justify his failure to respect the victim's (apparent) entitlements. This same message can be conveyed even in cases where no direct harm is done (for example, where the attempt to harm fails). In

---

[2] In addition, Hampton is justly renowned for her paper on the educative function of punishment (1984).

such cases what is damaged is the 'acknowledgement of the victim's value'.[3]

Hampton argues that the infliction of a moral injury calls for a retributive response that is 'intended to vindicate the value of the victim denied by the wrongdoer's action through the construction of an event that not only repudiates the action's message of superiority over the victim but does so in a way that confirms them as equal by virtue of their humanity' (1992*b*: 1686). This she glosses as a reaction designed to 'defeat' the wrongdoer. The argument is an interesting one, not least because it seems to offer a relatively independent basis for punishment. Whatever one's account of morality, so long as one endorses a normative commitment to equal human value then Hampton offers an understanding of (certain types of) wrong as the denial of that value and an account of punishment as a reassertion of it. The murderer (for example) conveys by her actions that her victim is of no great value. The punishment of the murderer ought to re-establish the value of the victim by destroying the claim to mastery made by the murderer (1992*b*: 1691).[4] However, both parts of this account are problematic.[5]

With respect to Hampton's account of what is relevantly wrong in criminal acts the problems are of three related kinds. First, it is not clear that a 'moral injury' occurs in every case of criminal wrong doing. An affluent and insured householder whose property is burgled does not feel that her moral value has been diminished;[6] her community does not see the robbery as evidence that this is so; and the burglar does not think himself of superior moral value in virtue of his profession (cf. Dolinko 1991: 554). Similarly, to use an example of Duff's, if a dropped purse is stolen it is hard to think that what is done wrong is appropriately captured in the language of moral injury (Duff 1996: 38).

---

[3] The thought that underpins Hampton's account here echoes Murphy's analysis of resentment and self-respect.

[4] Hampton's theory, thus, relates to the retributive intuition described at the end of Ch. 2 that the crime has brought about some 'tear' in the 'moral fabric' of human relations (in Hampton's theory, a distortion in relative apparent values) that needs to be undone through the punishment of the offender. In 'defeating' the offender the proper relation of crime and victim is restored.

[5] For criticisms see Duff 1990, 1996: 36–9; Dolinko 1991; Dare 1992; Marshall 1992; Slattery 1992; Golash 1994.

[6] That is not to say that the householder may not feel that her property and her moral standing have been violated. However, the recognition that the burglar failed to respect one's standing does not amount to 'damage to the realization of one's value' or to 'damage to the acknowledgement of one's value'.

It is, of course, open to Hampton to argue that all crimes contain an element of disregard for the value of the victim (assuming that even so-called 'victimless crimes' can be said to have the whole community as 'victim'). However, this raises a second problem with the account, which revolves around the allegation that Hampton has the account of wrongness backwards. It may be true, particularly for free-rider crimes, that what is done wrong is that the offender treats others with whom he co-operates as of lesser importance than himself (it is argued above that this is an important part of the correct understanding of such crimes), but for a serious crime such as murder this is not (or, not only) what matters. Murder does, of course, infringe the victim's rights, it permanently and completely damages the chances of the victim realizing his value, but it is because what the murderer does is wrong that it denies the value of the victim; the denial of value is not constitutive of its being wrong (Duff 1996: 37).

Hampton's mistake, which lies behind the two objections above, is that by isolating the message conveyed by some act as the crucial element in its wrongness, she makes the theory liable to the same charge as she levels at fair play theory; that the account of punishment is separated from the actual wrong done (cf. Dolinko 1991: 551–2). It is because of this that she finds the same wrong in all crimes, and because of this that she distorts what is wrong in (at least certain) crimes. A failed attempt to lynch a black man, because he is black, and the publication of a book that states that blacks are inferior to whites may both convey a message of unequal value—both inflict a 'moral injury'—but arguably the latter is not (in the relevant sense) wrong at all. Moreover, even if it is considered wrong, what constitutes its being so is surely not the same as in the case of attempted murder (Hampton 1992*b*: 1679; cf. Dolinko 1991: 551–2).

The second part of Hampton's account connects moral injury, retribution, and punishment. This, too, raises problems. If Hampton is right in what she believes about both wrong and the equal value of human beings then the criminal conveys in her actions a false assertion—that her victim has no value—and, as this is false, it might be thought that it is best ignored. Hampton calls on three related arguments to connect moral injuries and retribution: that morality is something for which we should care and its flouting evokes in those who do so care a critical attitude; that the message conveyed by the wrong action must be annulled, the worth of the victim reasserted, and the right moral relationship between the victim and offender restored; finally, that the damage done to those things necessary for the victim's value realization (his autonomy, bodily integrity, property, etc.) ought to be repaired.

These arguments are important, and each conveys an idea with which it is hard to disagree. However, in focusing on what is expressed by the crime and the annulling of that message (arguments one and two), Hampton invites the standard criticism of expressive theories that the denouncing of wrongdoing could take forms other than that of penal sanctions. Hampton's third argument might be taken to show why merely expressing in words, or in symbolic actions, that the victim is of value and that the actions of the wrongdoer were wrong is insufficient. The third argument is that, where possible, the offender (or possibly others) ought to compensate the victim. However, for reasons given above (in Chapter 2) this is normally thought to be something that is required in addition to punishment. Furthermore, insofar as the crimes in question are crimes that, say, undermine the victim's sense of self-worth or capacity to live an autonomous life (by, for example, making her afraid of going outside at night) it is hard to see what kind of compensation or restitution could be appropriate. As Hampton notes, sometimes an apology is all that is needed for the victim of some wrong to feel vindicated, to have his self-worth restored, but at other times there might be nothing that could possibly fully compensate the victim (Hampton 1992*b*: 1697–8).

The other two arguments for 'righting the wrong', are, as Hampton says, 'expressive'. The second argument is that without a retributive response the crime will be allowed to 'stand'. However, as with Murphy, this argument seems to presuppose what it is that it is meant to justify. If part of what it is for something to be a moral injury is that it calls forth an appropriate retributive response then the idea cannot help to justify that response (cf. Duff 1996: 38). Even granting the appropriateness of the retributive response, the difficulty remains the connection between the retributive response to wrongdoing and the infliction of punishment, especially of penal hard treatment. Given that what is at stake in these arguments is the denial of a 'message' conveyed by a wrong there seems no reason why the expression of the denial should not be verbal or symbolic rather than in the form of imposed suffering.

It is hard to discern Hampton's response to this problem, or even whether she would consider it a problem at all. In places she is dismissive of 'mere expression', declaring that wrongs cannot be undone by 'just a few idle remarks' (Hampton 1992*b*: 1686). In others, she is open to the thought that 'retribution can include more than punishment' (1992*b*: 1695). She considers both a biblical tale of the humiliation of an offender and the vindication of his victim through the manipulation of a parade and 'apologizing' and attempting to 'make it up' in ordinary life, and declares both to be appropriate illustrations of retribution in response to wrongdoing (1992*b*: 1695–6). The difficulty is that the account of retribution as the 'defeating' of the wrongdoer and the reassertion of the value of the victim suggests not only expressive or symbolic forms of response, but also a case by case approach. Hampton's abstraction from the wrong done and focus on the message of unequal value contained within the crime shifts attention to how the particular message can be nullified and, as she says, this may sometimes be achieved by an apology, sometimes by a parade, and sometimes by compensation. Of course, it is true that the reasserting of the moral value of the victims of serious crimes and the defeating of wrongdoers may, as a contingent matter of how we 'speak', take the form of penal hard treatment. Just as it happens to be true that we express love (among other things) with flowers, so it is true that we express serious moral criticism by imposing some kind of suffering on the offender. However, the infliction of suffering on another agent, even for a past wrong, is problematic and stands in need of justification; that this is how we express particularly serious criticism is what needs to be defended. Hampton's claim that the route to this justification lies in the need to respond to the message conveyed by the offender is an interesting one, but it falls significantly short of a full account in her work.

Perhaps the accusation of incompleteness is not something with which Hampton would disagree. She concludes her argument with the claim that retributivism is not the only value to be considered when designing a system of punishment. She declares herself a 'pluralist', claiming that 'punishment can also justifiably be used as a deterrent, or as a means of moral education' (1992*b*: 1700–1). Thus, she falls short of offering a fully retributive account of punishment. Unfortunately, Hampton provides no indication of how the different demands of a system of punishment are to be integrated, but given the weakness of the connection between the wrong done, the retributive response to that wrong, and the infliction of punishment in her account she is optimistic in thinking, as she does, that her theory establishes 'retribution to be the primary justification of punishment' (1992*b*: 1701 n. 65).

Hampton's theory, then, fails to justify the appropriateness of a retributive reaction to wrongdoing, and (even were it to do so) fails to connect that reaction to punishment. However, before leaving her account it is worth considering again her claim that the failure to punish a wrongdoer will allow the crime to 'stand', the criminal to go 'undefeated', and the victim to remain 'diminished'. This cannot be an argument directed to particular wrongdoers and their victims (and not only because it is an implausible account of what is at stake in many criminal wrongs). Most crimes go unpunished; the offender is never defeated and the moral value of the victim is not reasserted through the offender's suffering. That crimes go unsolved (indeed, unreported) and criminals go unpunished matters for various reasons, but not because the failure to punish leaves a situation in which what has been expressed by the crime remains yet to be annulled. Rather, the argument must be directed toward the criminal law as a whole. If the argument that human beings are of equal value can be validated then whatever else informs the construction of the law, it must be consistent with this claim.

Once the focus of the argument is correctly identified, Hampton's examples take on a different hue. Consider the case that she offers of a sentencing system 'that gives certain types of sexual offenders lighter sentences, on average, than those given to people who have been convicted of burglary' (1992*b*: 1692). What matters here is that what is expressed by the law is, at least arguably, that women have the same value as objects. The law reflects a sexist undervaluing of women. This is objectionable because a system of law must be just. It must not give lesser consideration to some because they are women or because they possess some other morally arbitrary feature. The equal value of human beings is important in this respect. However, this is a different argument from that which would sustain a claim that what underpins the content of the criminal law, from the prohibition of burglary to that of murder, is only that these acts all express a denial of the equal value of human beings. In some cases that seems too much, as in the affluent householder. In others, too little. The punishment of the rapist should not refer to the abstract wrong of failing to attend to the equal value of humanity, but to the actual wrong imposed on his particular victim. Hampton is misled by her examples, which concentrate on women and racially motivated crimes. These cases highlight the need for the criminal law to be just, and the failure of the law to respond adequately is informative. However, the wrong done by the rapist is not the same as the wrong done by the sexist sentencing system.

Murphy's and Hampton's accounts are interesting and instructive. In their analysis of retribution they offer a more adequate characterization than does fair play theory of the response to wrongdoing that retributive theories try to capture. They also point to an important claim: that to care about moral norms is to stand prepared to respond to and criticize those who knowingly flout them. However, they fail to show how this reaction justifies punishment and penal hard treatment. In attempting to link the retributive reaction and punishment Murphy relies once more on an abstract account of 'benefits and burdens' and Hampton on an equally abstract commitment to 'equality'. Where these theories are most instructive is in their focus on the communicative or expressive nature of the response to wrongdoing. What remains to be achieved is both an adequate account of this and of its connection to penal hard treatment. However, before looking to a full blown communicative account (in the work of Antony Duff) it is worth pausing to consider a theorist for whom the connection between the response to wrongdoing and the imposition of suffering is more direct, the legal philosopher Michael Moore.

## GUILTY UNTO DEATH

Like Murphy and Hampton, Moore looks to the wrong done and to the response to that wrong in his account of punishment. As noted above, Moore is robust in the claims that he wishes to make, holding that those with the authority to punish have not merely the right, but also the duty to do so (see Chapter 2 above). His argument is in four steps: (i) Certain particular judgements are reliable guides to valid moral claims.[7] (ii) Such particular judgements can be used in a theory-building procedure such as reflective equilibrium to reveal moral first principles (Moore 1992: 2509). Such principles, (iii) make sense of the particular judgements that we accept as valid (Moore 1997: 109). Finally, (iv) in the case of the first principle of desert there is reason to think that the state is justified in acting so as to ensure that the person 'who deserves it gets it'.[8]

To put some meat on this, consider the case of Steven Judy who 'on finding a woman with a flat tire, raped and murdered her and drowned her three small children, then said that he hadn't been "losing any sleep" over his crimes'.[9] On hearing of this, or observing it, a 'normal' reaction is that 'Steven Judy deserves to suffer for these acts'.[10] Assume that such a reaction

---

[7] Leaving aside, for the moment, what is meant by valid.

[8] Moore has developed his position over a number of years. The most important statement of his retributivism is Moore 1987, much of which reappears in Moore 1997. In reconstructing his argument I found Moore 1982 and 1992 (neither of which is greatly cannibalized in 1997) helpful. See also Moore 1993.

[9] Moore 1997: 98, quoting the US newspaper columnist Mike Royko (Royko 1981: sec. ii, 7)

[10] Moore (1997: 110) takes the claim, 'Steven Judy deserved to die for his murder of a mother and her three small children' as the relevant particular judgement. I have weakened this partially because I don't have that response and I am not convinced by Moore's argument that I should do so. More importantly, it is not necessary for the characterization of retributivism that follows.

is replicated whenever people are aware of significant moral wrongdoing (Moore presents a catalogue of heinous crimes as examples). Moore argues that such reactions are 'reliable' guides to moral features of the world (Moore 1992: 2509); 'good heuristic guides to moral truth' (Moore 1997: 135). The next two steps are made very quickly: 'We can justify a moral principle', he claims, 'by showing that it best accounts for those of our more particular judgements that we also believe to be true' (1997: 106). Such a method is not just a matter of 'fit between general principles and particular judgements', but can reveal first principles that 'can be justified only by showing that they imply, but are not implied by, both secondary principles and particular judgements that we accept as true' (1997: 169). These first principles are more than mere matters of coherence, of 'fit', because they do some 'explanatory work for us' (1997: 109). The conclusion of the argument is that what best accounts for the particular judgements revealed in the reactions to cases such as that of Judy—what makes sense of 'why it is that we have the strong emotional and cognitive responses to [such] stories' (1997: 109)—is a first principle of desert, the 'instance' of which relevant to these cases being the retributive principle: 'that offenders should be punished because, and only because, they have culpably done wrong' (1997: 188).

Moore's argument is one that appeals to many people perhaps because of its overlap with what is sometimes called 'common sense morality'. The idea is simply this: we (those possessed of common sense) know that offenders deserve to suffer. This claim is entailed by, and part of how we know and understand, a general principle of desert. The question is, can Moore do any better in justifying punishment than those who merely proclaim common sense? The reason to doubt that he can is that all four stages of the argument are open to question.

Moore's first claim is that certain particular judgements are reliable guides to certain moral features of the world. Take first the judgement that Steven Judy has done something wrong. This is correct according to most, if not all, moral theories. Thus, in this case, the observer's emotional response mirrors a valid moral claim. However, this does not ground a general claim that human emotions are a 'good heuristic guide to moral truth'. There are all too many examples of societies in which, for example, witnessing a rape evokes in some nothing more than titillation. Such a response fails to correlate to a valid moral claim.

There is a defence against this argument available to Moore. A society that promotes the idea of women as sex objects perverts the emotional responses of its members and thus makes them unreliable. Just as sometimes—in some environments—human sight is unreliable (for example, when in a hall of mirrors), so in some environments are moral responses distorted. There is a danger of circularity here: how the theorist knows which agents are reliable is likely to be determined by the degree and regularity of the agents' agreement with what is known to be right. However, if this is the case then there is no need for a heuristic guide to the truth, as it is knowledge of the truth that allows one to identify the guide.[11] Of course, it is possible that an agent who has proven in the past to be generally reliable might be thought to be a good guide in resolving further matters where there is no independent answer available. Such a thought is commonly offered in crude summary of Aristotle (what one ought to do is what a man of practical reason would think one ought to do). However, the man of practical reason judges how best to apply what he knows; he extends established principles to new particular cases. Aristotle's *phronemos* reacts to many and various particular situations involving women and slaves by thinking he ought to treat them differently from the way in which he treats other citizens. Asked to justify the practice of doing so, he is, on Moore's account, bound to say that this set of particular cases provide reliable guides to the moral truth of a principle of desert, the particular relevant instance of which is that women and slaves are less deserving than free men (cf. Dolinko 1991: 557–8; Moore 1997: 165–88).

Once the argument is extended (as Moore needs it to be) to the response that 'Steven Judy ought to suffer for his acts' matters becomes even more difficult. Of course, the above objection applies to this response just as it does to the claim that Judy has done wrong. If observers of Judy's acts have the response that Judy ought to suffer this is most plausibly explained not by the claim that Judy's act has some property of being 'deserving of imposed suffering' that supervenes on its natural properties (cf. Moore 1992), but by those observers having been brought up in a society in which culpable wrongdoing is thought to ground justified punishment. However, it is precisely this claim that Moore, and punishment theory, is trying to justify.[12] In addition to this, the response that Judy ought to suffer introduces a number of problems of its own.

---

[11] The problem might be thought to be that there is no obvious equivalent to the 'physical tests' that might be performed in the natural sciences to test the responses of humans. Thus, when one discovers that one's informant about some event was drunk when she witnessed it, one tends to consider her evidence unreliable. Note, however, that this is not always so. One might establish whether the informant was 'too drunk to be useful' by asking questions of her to which one already knows the answer.

[12] What lies behind the concern of punishment theorists is the spectre that the belief in the permissibility of imposing suffering on an agent for some past wrong is no better than

Moore wishes to build on the reaction that the culpable wrongdoer ought to suffer, but such a reaction is hardly common to all crimes. To borrow from Dolinko, an English driver who, early in the morning and with no one else around, momentarily forgets which side of the road she should be driving on when in the United States hardly evokes such a response (Dolinko 1991: 557). In reply Moore argues that even in such a case a moral wrong is committed and, although the reaction will be less intense (and this guides us to the truth that the traffic offender deserves less punishment) than in cases of rape and murder, it is nevertheless present. His focus on particularly heinous crimes, Moore says, is justified because these 'work our intuition pumps most vigorously' (Moore 1997: 185). If Moore's argument in relation to cases such as that of Judy was successful then he would work from the 'truth' of these particular judgements to a justified first principle that would then entail other particular judgements. However, Moore cannot use only heinous crimes to generate a general retributive first principle, one that is to be applied in all cases. The retributive principle that culpable wrongdoers deserve to suffer does not 'make sense' of the normal reaction to many minor crimes, for these do not evoke a retributive response.

Where crimes do evoke the response 'the perpetrator of this act ought to suffer', there are a number of reasons why its reliability might be questioned. First, such a reaction often does not survive further enquiry into the circumstances of the act or of the offender. Second, the observer might feel that she is in no position to judge the offender. Third, the observer might consider her retributive response a sign of her own moral depravity. Some emotional responses—envy, jealousy, and *Schadenfreude*, for example—are such that a morally sensitive agent will think less well of herself for their possession.

Moore is concerned to rebut these objections and his method in so doing is to ask the reader to engage in a thought experiment. The reader is to ask, 'What would [I] feel like if it were me who had intentionally smashed open the skull of a 23 year old woman with a claw hammer while she was asleep?' Moore's own answer is that he hopes that he would feel 'guilty unto death' (1997: 145).[13]

the belief that killing witches was a demand of God, or that slavery was in the interests of the 'backward' non-white peoples who were subjected to it. The reliability of the reaction that offenders deserve to suffer is no more guaranteed than the reliability of the reactions of slave owners when slavery was prevalent.

[13] The example here has switched from Steven Judy to Richard Herrin (who committed the act described in the text), but it makes no difference to the argument.

The point of the thought experiment is both to stop the reader backing down from the original judgement and to reduce the possibility of the judgement being corrupted. Judy, for example, Moore explains in an earlier article, had a horrific childhood during which he suffered great quantities of mental and physical abuse (Moore 1987). On learning of this readers might, if not endorse the common claim *tout comprendre c'est tout pardonner*, at least 'soften their judgements' (Moore 1997: 512). However, Moore claims that to do this is to treat those who do commit such crimes as different from oneself, as mere 'object[s]'. It is 'élitist and condescending', 'a refusal to admit that the rest of humanity shares with us that which makes us most distinctively human, our capacity to will and reason—and thus to be and to do evil' (1997: 148–9). Thus, the move to the personal addresses, in Moore's view, the problem of the withholding or weakening of the original retributive response because one would apply the judgement that one ought to suffer to oneself whatever one's background or claims to sympathy. It also addresses the problem of the reaction being thought corrupt as one is unlikely to think of oneself that one ought to suffer because of envy, jealousy, or *Schadenfreude*.

Moore's focus on guilt is interesting, and in conjunction with an understanding of wrongdoing as appropriately evoking criticism forms much of the basis of communicative accounts of punishment (examined below). However, it is not clear that it addresses the problems described above. First, although it is true that most, charged with answering the question put in the thought experiment, will hope that they would feel 'guilty unto death', none of the readers of this, or Moore's, book has either experienced the kinds of things that regularly punctuated Judy's early life or (perhaps) committed murder. It is important to Moore's argument that the data which he uses in 'theory building' are actual, but at best what he has is a set of hypothetical reactions. Most people hope that they would feel 'guilty unto death', but that is not to say that they do and thus the reaction cannot be reliable in the way Moore describes (cf. Duff 1996, 29). Second, the move to the personal does not explain why the immediate reaction 'Judy deserves to suffer for these acts' is a reliable guide to a moral truth, but some later reaction (on learning of the circumstances of Judy's life), for example, that 'Judy is undeserving of further suffering' is merely 'philosophically impure common sense' (Moore 1997: 512).[14] Finally, whilst the

---

[14] Mike Royko, Moore's favourite source of examples, is quoted by Murphy as writing, on returning home after covering the 1972 Democratic Convention in San Francisco, that 'it's great to be back in Chicago where people still know how to hate' (Murphy and Hampton 1988: 88). What this implies is clearly that some people (those outside of

move to the personal eliminates the worry that the response that another ought to suffer is motivated by some morally distasteful sentiments, it opens the possibility of other corrupting influences. Often people feel guilty for the wrong reasons and often for things for which they could not be held responsible. This is not just a phenomenon of the obsessive or the self-abasing. The driver of a car who is involved in an accident in which, through no fault of his, someone is killed may feel guilt and this may be what others expect of a 'decent human being'. However, this feeling of guilt is not a reliable guide to any truth that he deserves to suffer (Williams 1973: 207).

The details of Moore's account of retributive emotions are interesting, if unconvincing. More important is his failure successfully to resist the allegation that his argument 'rests ultimately on an appeal to unexplained intuition' (Duff 1996, 29). Moore thinks this an unjust description of his position, for he does not simply claim that a retributive first principle is true, but that it can be arrived at through the use of particular judgements that we know to be true. The difficulty is not that sometimes things that we think that we know to be true turn out to be false (after all, to explain that merely requires the claim that we can sometimes be mistaken, just as sometimes—as in a hall of mirrors—we are mistaken about what we think that we see), but that for his account not to beg the question he must show that the particular judgements that matter (that certain acts are wrong and that culpable wrongdoers deserve to suffer) reliably pick out some feature of the acts and actors themselves; some properties in the world (or that supervene on some properties in the world). Moore's argument that there are such properties follows the method of his argument for punishment: the only explanation that makes sense of our particular judgements is one that involves strong realist claims (Moore 1982: 1992).

However, this is just not so. The explanation of such judgements can be given entirely in terms of psychological facts about us.[15] In addition, even if one does think that some reference to an act having a moral property is the best explanation for the belief that the observer has about the act (one believes that Judy did something wrong because his acts had the property of wrongness), this does not mean that one need endorse the rest of Moore's theory. It is, for example, compatible with a contractualist under-

Chicago, or perhaps just those in San Francisco) fail to 'hate'. The retributive reaction that Moore takes to be widespread might not, after all, be nearly as common as he thinks. For some comments on responsibility and judgements of guilt see Norrie 1999.

[15] This is the argument offered by Gilbert Harman (1977, 6–9). It is criticized by, among others, Moore (1982, 1992) and Sturgeon (1984).

standing of wrong such that the property of wrongness which the act possesses is constituted by some kind of agreement as to some relevant rule under which the acts of rape and murder (in the stipulated circumstances) are wrong.[16]

The accusation that Moore's argument is circular, then, stems from the claim that agents have the particular responses that they have because they have been brought up in societies in which those reactions are deemed appropriate. Such reactions are validated not by being correctly connected to the world, but by being in accordance with local practices. When Huckleberry Finn, as he sees it, 'steals a nigger' he feels 'guilty unto death'. His reaction is sincere (it is also a first person reaction so it fits the demands of Moore's thought experiment), it maps onto what he, and the greater part of his community, believes to be true about moral wrong and about desert. Moore needs to show not merely that his account can accommodate such mistakes, but that it can explain the idea that Huck is making a *mistake*.[17] As Moore offers no independent reasons for thinking the retributive principle justified, the allegation that he adds nothing to the justification of retributivism holds.

## PUNISHMENT AS COMMUNICATION

Murphy and Hampton both direct attention to the appropriateness of resentment, and Moore to the appropriateness of guilt, in response to certain forms of wrongdoing. These ideas provide some link between the past act and the present, but none of these theorists has adequately transformed this link into an account of justified punishment. In *Trials and Punishments* (1986) and in a series of subsequent papers (1988, 1993, 1996, 1999, among others) Antony Duff has developed an account of punishment that aims to be both forward looking and retributive. Duff's argument is in two connected parts: first, that punishment communicates censure, and second, that penal hard treatment provides a vehicle for repentance. The heart of Duff's communicative account is described as follows:

there is surely nothing puzzling about the idea that wrongdoing deserves censure. An honest response to another's culpable wrongdoing—a response that respects and treats her as a responsible moral agent—is to criticize or censure that conduct

---

[16] I am grateful to Christian Piller for discussion of this point.
[17] I am grateful to Sue Mendus for suggesting this example.

... we may indeed sometimes think that we ought to censure her—that we owe it to those she wronged, to the values she flouted, and also to her, to censure her. So too, a society which declares certain kinds of conduct to be wrong, as criminal, can and should then censure those who nonetheless engage in such conduct . . . Censure addresses the wrongdoer as a responsible citizen; it is owed to him as an honest response to his crime; to his victims (if there are any), as expressive of a concern for their wronged status; and to the whole society, whose values the law claims to embody. (Duff 1999: 50)

As noted above, the idea that wrongdoing appropriately evokes a response of resentment and an expression of criticism is familiar and convincing. Not to feel, and in the appropriate circumstances to express, resentment and criticism is (as Murphy claims) to fail to act in a way consonant with self-respect and respect for one's own value and the values that the offender has flouted. Duff's account goes further than this. If someone unknown to an agent harms her deliberately, she may express her anger and resentment by giving voice to some abuse of the offender. She does not attempt in any full sense of the term to 'communicate' with the offending person, she merely expresses (vents) her resentment. What differentiates this from 'communication' is that the latter is a '*reciprocal* and *rational* activity*' (1999: 49). Duff's argument is that these features, which transform the account from an expressive theory to a communicative one, arise out of a proper understanding of the relationship between the state and its citizens (see Duff 1986).[18]

The important claim is that 'censure addresses the wrongdoer as a responsible citizen'. That is, insofar as the law (at least in part) expresses and incorporates the moral values of the community, and insofar as the members of that community are regarded as responsible agents, capable of acting in accordance with reasons, when the state gives voice to censure of an offending agent it owes it to that agent as (at least potentially) rational to express to the agent the reasons for his conduct being wrong and deserving of censure. In addition, it owes it to him to allow him the chance to defend and to account for his actions. The hope of those communicating censure is that the offender will come to appreciate the 'nature and implications of his crime' (Duff 1986: 245).

---

[18]  In a similar way the same features can arise between citizens. Although there are times when merely giving voice to anger or resentment is appropriate, between friends or in certain circumstances between rational people whatever their relationship, it is sometimes appropriate to give reasons for one's anger and to provide the opportunity for the other to respond.

Duff's argument, which extends to an understanding of the law and criminal process as a whole, is subtle and sophisticated. In arguing that an honest and non-manipulative expression of criticism between moral agents is an intrinsically related and appropriate response to wrongdoing he offers a compelling account of retributive censure. In differentiating it from manipulative attempts to alter the future behaviour of the offender (or of others) he strengthens his case for the retributive conception. Adult, moral agents feel cheated and manipulated by the rank sentimentalism of many films and novels and by arguments aimed not to persuade by reason, but to bypass reason by an appeal to the emotions, because these fail to respect their status as rational agents. However, although censure connects the past act of the agent and the current response of others, it remains to be shown that this analysis can be connected to the infliction of penal hard treatment by the state.

The connection of censure and penal hard treatment in Duff's argument is attempted through the idea of 'repentance' or 'penitence'. The difficulty for Duff is that the model of censure looks to be completed in the reasoned denunciation of the offender and his crime, having allowed him the opportunity to account for his acts. Duff has two arguments that connect censure and hard treatment. Both rest on the claim that in addition to the expression of resentment and denunciation, censure aims at bringing the censured to a proper understanding of his acts; it 'seeks to communicate to the offender, and to persuade her to understand and accept, the fact, nature, and implications of the wrong she has done' (Duff 1999: 52).

The first argument is that in order to bring about such understanding, penal hard treatment can be used 'to direct (to force) [the offender's] attention onto his crime' (Duff 1999: 51). However, this kind of 'coercive attention-getting' (von Hirsch 1999: 72) looks to be inconsistent with Duff's insistence that the state treat the offender as a (potentially) rational agent. If $A$ censures $B$ it is open to $B$ to ignore or disregard what is being said. This may itself be disrespectful, in that $B$ is failing to treat $A$ as even worthy of being heard, but this is only a further failing on $B$'s part. $A$ is not entitled to make $B$ suffer until $B$ agrees to listen. Indeed, the model that comes to mind is that of a parent who forces a child to remain in the room so as to hear why the child's behaviour is unacceptable, but if such coercion is justified it is only so because the child is not a full person, or perhaps because the parent's act is assumed to be for the child's good (it is paternalistic).

What, then, of Duff's second argument? This is that a correct understanding of what it is that he has done wrong will evoke in the offender a penitential response. Punishment provides a vehicle through which [the offender] can strengthen and deepen that repentant understanding of his wrongdoing, and express it to others: a vehicle, that is, both for the attempt at self-correction and self-reform that sincere repentance involves, and for the communication to others (to those he has wronged, to his fellow citizens) of that sincere repentance. (Duff 1999: 51)

In addition, through such penitential punishment 'the wrongdoer can reconcile himself with his fellow citizens, and restore himself to full membership of the community from which his wrongdoing threatened to exclude him' (Duff 1999: 51–2). It is this argument that provides Duff's account with its forward looking dimension. However, it is important to distinguish this from a consequentialist argument that punishment is justified because it brings about the reform of the offender. In the consequentialist theory, punishment has a merely instrumental role—if it is justified it is because of the contingent fact that it is the best means of reforming the offender—whereas for Duff punishment is internally related to the end of bringing the offender to a 'repentant understanding of her crime' (1999: 52).

Nevertheless, the introduction of repentance, and the aim of bringing the offender to a 'repentant understanding of her crime', must be approached cautiously. Censure, conceived of as a critical communication between agents, involves the giving of reasons in condemnation of an act and actor, with the opportunity for the condemned to answer. Now, it may be thought that a decent person, realizing that he has done wrong, will feel bad about himself, will wish perhaps to apologize and to make amends. It may even be that in certain cases he will take on some suffering or penance because he wishes to undergo some suffering to 'cleanse' himself, or because he wishes to display to others the sincerity of his remorse, or both, but it is crucial to this kind of penitential suffering that it is embraced voluntarily (cf. Baldwin 1999; von Hirsch 1999). The aim of censure might be said to be to bring about feelings of guilt and remorse in an offender (in that such feelings in part constitute what it is to have a correct understanding of the offence), but that is all. The provision of an opportunity to express this remorse through suffering is something different. It is as if *A*, having wronged *B* and been made to realize this through *B*'s censorious response, were to apologize to *B* and then ask *A*, 'what can I do to show you that I mean it?' *A* might be able to suggest something ('if you really mean it you would . . .'), but what is essential is that *B* undergoes the penance voluntarily.

Three different claims, then, need to be separated: (i) penal hard treatment is part of how censure is conveyed; (ii) penal hard treatment is a vehicle for the offender's repentance; (iii) penal hard treatment is a vehicle for the offender to display to others the sincerity of his repentance and thus to be reconciled with them. The first of these might, as was seen in the discussion of Hampton, be true. As a matter of fact the way in which certain societies express censure is in the form of imposed suffering. However, this makes the connection of punishment and repentance contingent (and, as noted above, hardly adds to a justification of imposing suffering). The difficulty with the second and third arguments is that in both cases it is central to the correct understanding of repentance that it is voluntarily embraced.

Duff is aware of this difficulty. Describing punishment as 'a kind of enforced apology', he separates out the formal aspect (the behaviour that 'conventionally bears a certain meaning') from the individual (the genuine expression, that cannot be forced, of the agent's remorse and repentance). Punishment, according to Duff, 'essentially involves the former aspect, and *aspires* to take on the latter' (Duff 1999: 83). However, this cannot be right. To borrow and adapt Dworkin's description of hypothetical contracts, 'an enforced apology is not simply a pale form of an actual apology; it is no apology at all' (cf. Dworkin 1989: 18). If, having communicated the reasons for the wrongness of the offender's conduct to him, having evoked in him a genuine understanding of the nature and quality of his wrongful acts— if, having censured him—the offender asks 'help me to atone for this' or 'what can I do to show I am sorry?' then there might perhaps be a case for there being a scale of recommended sufferings, but this is not an account of punishment as the imposition of suffering on an offender for an offence.[19]

The nature of Duff's attempt to connect his censure-based account of desert and punishment raises questions of a more general kind than whether he is successful. In particular, even if he could connect censure and punishment through the idea of a 'secular penance', would this provide an

---

[19] Duff at times comes very close to endorsing this reading. He writes that in punishment the offender 'is forced to hear the punitive message: but it must be up to him whether or not he accepts that message, and the *opportunity* for repentance and reconciliation which his punishment provides' (Duff 1999: 59, emphasis added). This is accurate as a description of his account, but it leaves it open why the offender must express repentance through suffering. Should the offender, having been censured, not wish to take the opportunity to repent through suffering then, as Duff makes clear, it is wrong to force him into a pretence of repentance. A successful punishment correctly conveys the accurate degree of censure to the offender. It cannot be part of its being successful as a punishment that the message is accepted. Even should the offender wish to repent and display his remorse there seems to be no reason why the only 'language' in which that can be done is in terms of suffering. Why should he not just apologize?

appropriate model for the contemporary liberal democratic state? The communicative model presupposes a community united by a shared set of values to which each member ought in some way to be oriented. The model must provide an answer to 'what' is to be said, and to 'why' what is said should matter to the offender. This raises a number of difficulties. First, about the source of these values. In multicultural, pluralist societies it might be asked 'whose norms?' and 'which values?' (Ivison 1999) are to provide the content of what is communicated in censure. Second, the communicative model raises the question of the grounds of these values. If the community is to be confident in censuring the offender, and is to have an account of the moral 'defect' (Duff 1996: 47–8) exhibited by the offender, then it must be able not merely to justify its moral norms and values, but also to explain the relationship of the offender to these norms in a way that is neither instrumental nor circular. That is, confronted with an agent whose reply to censure is, 'so, it's wrong, but what is that to me?' it must have an answer that is neither 'if you do wrong things we will punish you', nor 'it's not good to do wrong things' (Matravers 1999*a*). These worries underpin a more general concern: the modern democratic state is one in which the writ of the state is not thought to extend into the mind, motivation, and 'private life' of its citizens. It might be thought, therefore, that the message conveyed in censure ought to refer to the behaviour of the offender in terms of those 'public virtues' needed to maintain a stable public environment. In short, there is something in Duff's rich communicative account that is, to liberal ears, 'reminiscent of Maoist criticism and self-criticism sessions' (Sorell 1999: 25; cf. von Hirsch 1993: chs. 2 and 8, 1999; Narayan 1993).

These concerns cannot be addressed without investigating the justification of moral norms and their relationship to the state. If there is an account of justified moral norms and of moral motivation then there may be reason to think that these norms ought to be reflected in the laws and actions of the state. Nothing in that need deny the importance of individuality or autonomy. If not, then there may be reason to believe that the state should remain 'neutral' between accounts of morality and of moral motivation, or that what norms are embodied at the public level ought to be subject to discussion and negotiation between groups. Addressing questions such as these is the project of the next several chapters.

Duff's account, then, is problematic in two ways: it cannot justify the infliction of hard treatment and it presupposes the existence of a state as a unified moral community with a legitimate interest in the 'moral life' of its citizens (in bringing wrongdoers to redemption). A more limited communicative theory has been proposed by von Hirsch and Narayan (von Hirsch 1993; Narayan 1993) which retains the retributive idea of punishment as essentially involving the censuring of the offender, but which conceives of penal hard treatment as a prudential supplement to the moral appeal of the law. Von Hirsch endorses the communicative model, punishment essentially censures the offender and allows her the opportunity to response, but in explaining why such censure is conveyed in penal hard treatment von Hirsch appeals to a rationale of crime prevention. Such hard treatment provides a prudential reason to obey the law, it speaks to agents neither as 'angels' who are always capable of being effectively moved only by moral reasons nor as 'beasts' that only respond to coercion (von Hirsch 1999: 70).

This is an attractive theory. In maintaining the essential connection with censure it captures the idea that the offender deserves to be blamed and criticized and it emphasizes the importance of what is expressed in punishment. In justifying hard treatment as a prudential disincentive to wrong actions, it avoids the problem for fully communicative theories of how to integrate hard treatment. It also avoids giving the state an interest in the redemption of offenders. Finally, it proposes an account of penal hard treatment that does not divide society into 'us' and 'them' (the virtuous who obey the law for moral reasons and the vicious who need to be threatened with sanctions in order to secure their obedience). Rather, it treats all agents as fallible and sometimes in need of additional prudential reasons to do what they ought to do.[20] However, two problems remain to be addressed. First, in maintaining the rich element of censure this view must still presuppose a state modelled on a moral community with a rich set of shared values that appeal (even if not always decisively) to its citizens as moral agents. Second, some account is needed of how censure and penal hard treatment are to be integrated.

The first of these issues must be postponed until the investigation that follows of the nature of the state and of the values that inform it. The second also depends in part on the answer to those questions, because it depends upon the relationship of prudential and moral reason. Von Hirsch claims that censure regulates the implementation of a system of punishment designed both to convey censure and to deter wrongdoing. Indeed, it is an advantage of his account, he claims, that it delivers both ordinal and

---

[20] This is a familiar idea. It appears in the offers we make to ourselves in the form 'if I wash the car (or write this chapter) today then I will take myself to dine at my favourite restaurant' or, more coercively, 'if I fail to wash the car then I will not go to the party tonight'.

cardinal proportionality in sentencing. If the system of punishment is to convey censure (as well as deter crime) then it must relate the degree of punishment to the seriousness of the crime (ordinal proportionality). Furthermore, since penal hard treatment is meant to supplement the moral force of the law, the threat of hard treatment must not be so great as to 'drown out' or replace that moral appeal (thus providing some guidance in determining cardinal proportionality).[21]

One difficulty with von Hirsch's integration of censure and deterrence is that it is not clear quite what considerations are to tell in fixing cardinal proportionality. Von Hirsch has suggested that penalties should be ratcheted down until they reach a level at which homicide should carry a maximum sentence of five years, no other imprisonable offence a sentence of more than three years, and lesser offences should attract much more minor punishments (von Hirsch 1993: ch. 5; cf. Matravers 1999*b*). However, it is not clear exactly on what this is based. At the moment in the UK and USA there seems to be a widespread view that current levels of sentencing are too lax, and that punishments are not sufficiently 'serious'. What carries von Hirsch's argument is a claim about what sentencing level will be such as to 'become almost wholly coercive, and render largely meaningless the communicative content of the sanction' (von Hirsch 1999: 71). However, to know what this means requires an understanding of how von Hirsch thinks of the relation between moral and prudential reason. For some, like Duff, it is so important that the primary message be conveyed in moral terms that anything but the most minor of threats will be sufficient to condemn their use as failing to respect the rational agency of the potential offender. However, such minor sanctions may fail to have any significant deterrence effect (Duff 1996: 45, 1999: 55–6; Chapter 9 below). For others, it might be thought that, if the purpose of having sanctions is to deter those who find that moral reasons have insufficient weight to be decisive in their practical reasoning then there is no reason not to have fairly stiff penalties. After all, 'people who would not dream of stealing or assault never have to engage with the law by means of thoughts about the penalties; neither do those who entertain the idea but find it repellent independent of the penalties. For them the specification of the penalty in the law is idle' (Sorell 1999: 17). Those who do obey the law for reasons of fearing the sanctions, of course, are not acting as full moral agents on this account, but the worry would be if they had not had the opportunity to do so. Nothing in the prudential supplement view can support the claim that such an opportu-

---

[21] The idea of ordinal and cardinal proportionality is discussed below in Ch. 9.

nity is not extended to those who live in this kind of system independent of the scale of penalties.

## CONCLUSION

At the beginning of Chapter 2, in the discussion of retributivism, the problem is set out as being that punishment seemingly cannot do without its backward looking element. This is neither merely because of the need to avoid the worst excesses of consequentialist theory discussed in Chapter 1 nor because of the conceptual claim that punishment must be of an offender, although each of these is important. What retributivism seeks to capture is an intuition that wrongdoers deserve punishment. This can take the form of a claim just about the offender—this person deserves to suffer for this act—or about the state of affairs brought about by the offence—punishment is needed to restore the status quo, to annul or negate what was done—or both. The purpose of this and the last chapters is both to investigate the plausibility of attempts to articulate and defend these intuitions in a theory of punishment and to further the enquiry into the relationship of punishment and moral theory. None of the accounts examined has plausibly connected the past act and present suffering in these terms. However, although desert fails to link the past act and the justifiability of imposed present suffering, it can more successfully connect the past act and present censure. The difficulty is that censure is not punishment and, *pace* Duff, cannot ground imposing suffering on those who do not feel the need to repent of their wrongdoing in that particular way. It remains the case that there is no plausible solely retributive theory of punishment.

What, then, of the relationship of punishment and moral theory? Whatever its merits as a theory of punishment, fair play theory fails the test of relative independence. To be complete it needs an account of the structure of social relations. Moreover, the particular version of social relations that it requires to substantiate its characterizations of benefits and burdens undermines the retributive character of the theory and introduces a separate assurance account of punishment. Censure-based theories appear to stand at some distance from the rest of moral theory in that the claim that wrongdoing deserves censure can be made without recourse to the content of what is wrong. However, the claim that the state should engage in such censure of wrongdoing, and the operation of this theory, both require recourse to substantive moral theory. The state must be shown not only to be justified in adopting the role of censor, but also to have the ethical resources with which to speak. Moreover, censure falls short of justifying punishment. It needs to be supplemented by appeal to prudential considerations of crime prevention. Thus, it remains the task of the punishment theorist to show how these can be reconciled.

# 4

# The Scope of Impartial Justice

## INTRODUCTION

The purpose of the first three chapters is, in part, to examine a number of current approaches to punishment with a view to investigating their plausibility. As important, the argument attempts to establish that the justification of punishment can only be found within an account of what justifies the having of rules that threaten sanctions in response to non-compliance and that this question can only be answered through considering the nature of the rules themselves. Finally, the argument attempts to draw attention to those parts of the two main approaches to punishment that need to be retained in any convincing justification of the practice.

Given that what is needed is a theory of punishment grounded in a broader theory of morality or of justice, the purpose of the next three chapters is to examine recent theories of that kind. One reason for this should be clear. What is needed is an account of the rules that regulate social co-operation (and that threaten punishment) so it makes sense to look at the justification of such rules. In addition, there are reasons for this strategy that arise from the puzzle mentioned in the Introduction: in the last thirty or so years political philosophy has undergone a transformation driven initially by Rawls's enquiry into distributive justice. The literature on distributive justice continues to grow and the concept remains dominant in the discipline. Yet with very few exceptions (and those mostly in the fair play school) these developments have not been extended to retributive justice (see Chapter 2 n. 17), and distributive justice theorists themselves have, for the most part, not considered retributive questions. Over the course of the next two chapters it is argued that (i) impartialist accounts of distributive justice cannot simply avoid the problem of punishment (the question of retributive justice); and (ii) once the problem of punishment is introduced its examination reveals faults in the impartialist approach as a whole, whether it is aimed at the issue of distributive justice or that of retributive justice. Finally, (iii) it is argued that the failure of impartialist theory to extend itself into questions of punishment is no accident. This final claim emerges in part from the argument of Chapters 1–3, that punishment theory needs to be placed in a wider context if it is to be successful. The argument of this and the next chapter is that this context cannot be provided by impartialist theory, and that this is just as damaging to the impartialist account of distributive justice as it would be to any attempt to develop an impartialist theory of punishment. Punishment theory thus provides a clue to what is needed to rectify the difficulties revealed in impartialist theory, for what is needed in both cases is a 'moral context' and an accompanying account of motivation. Chapter 6 examines an attempt to construct just such a moral context, and together with elements of the argument of Chapters 4 and 5 lays the groundwork for the account of moral norms and of punishment that follows in Chapters 7, 8, and 9.

## CONSTRUCTIVISM

Constructivist accounts of justice of one kind or another have dominated the landscape of political theory since the 1971 publication of Rawls's *A Theory of Justice*.[1] Contemporary constructivism can be distinguished from its traditional Enlightenment ancestors, which explained how political authority could be made legitimate—why one should obey the sover-

---

[1] A word or two about terminology. I have chosen to use the term 'constructivism' rather than 'contractarianism' or 'contractualism' in an attempt to capture an approach to questions of justice (and other moral questions) that, whilst it may—and most often does—take the form of a social contract theory need not do so. In this I follow Brian Barry 1989 (see especially 259, 264–82; cf. Gauthier 1997; Rawls 1980). Gauthier prefers to call what I call below '*faux* constructivism', 'contractualism' (after Scanlon 1982), and to contrast this with 'contractarianism'. Although this terminology offers some advantages I have chosen not to employ it because of the widespread use of contractualism and contractarianism as synonyms (Scanlon uses the one, Rawls the other, Barry interchanges them). The prefix *faux* also has the advantage of indicating the apparent similarity of the two positions in the techniques they use.

For reasons to be discussed below, I take this to make very little difference, as few contemporary social contract theories are really contractarian. Indeed, the contrast drawn below between genuine and *faux* constructivism mirrors the contrast between theories that are usefully captured in the language of 'contract' and 'bargaining' and those that are not. Thus, even were one to use the terminology of contractarianism one would need subdivisions resembling those given below. (Rawls, of course, describes his own 'contractarian' theory as an example of 'Kantian Constructivism', see Rawls 1980; 1993: III/1, 89–99, 110–16, III/3, III/5).

eign—in terms of promise keeping. Both the terms, and moral force, of the traditional contract stemmed from an assumed background of natural law. Traditional contract theorists, in short, claimed that one ought to obey the sovereign because one had promised to do so; one had given one's word. However, as Hume put it, such theorists 'find [themselves] embarrassed, when it is asked, *why are we bound to keep our word?*' (Hume 1994: 197). Contemporary constructivism asks a different question and does not rely on the analogy with promise keeping. The question upon which it has focused has not been that of political obligation but that of justice. Its starting point is not with a historical account of the genesis of society but with the question of how we are to understand and (de)legitimize the norms which currently govern society. It is thus a reflective practice, requiring that the theorist distance herself from the practices and norms current in her society and question how they are to be understood (cf. Kymlicka 1991).

Brian Barry sets two conditions in defining constructivism:

First . . . there must be a theory to the effect that what comes out of a certain kind of situation is to count as just. 'What comes out' might be a principle, a rule, or a particular outcome. Justice can be predicated of any of these, and the point is that we can derive its justice from its having emerged from the situation. A 'situation' is specified by a description of the actors in it (including their knowledge and objectives) and the norms governing their pursuit of their objectives: what moves are to be legitimate. And the 'emergence' is to be a particular kind of emergence, namely the result of the actors in the situation pursuing their given objectives within the given constraints.

That is a necessary condition of a constructivist conception of justice but not a sufficient one. The second requirement is that the constructing is to be done by a theorist and not by the people in the situation themselves. (Barry 1989: 266)

Clearly this is a broad definition, sufficiently so that it might be thought that it obscures an important issue: whether constructivism offers a genuine mode of justification in moral and political philosophy. The point is that the status of 'what comes out' is related to how the 'situation' is characterized which in turn is related to the purpose and aspirations of the enquiry. For some, for example David Gauthier, if constructivism is to offer a genuine mode of justification then it must begin with minimal assumptions. The 'situation' must be populated by individuals each of whom 'from her own deliberative stance must judge the social norms, and the practices to which they give rise, as ones to which it would make sense for her to agree, were she and her fellows to have the opportunity to decide together on their terms of interaction' (Gauthier 1997: 133). Thus, 'the validity of social norms is understood to depend on and derive from . . . only those norms that all members can recognize as ones they would themselves accept given appropriate circumstances' (1997: 133). For Gauthier what this means is that the norms must be such as to be agreeable to 'rational individuals, each seeking to co-operate with her fellows in order to max- imize her own utility' (Gauthier 1984: 255).

What this brief characterization of Gauthier's theory captures is the thought that constructivism offers a genuine alternative to coherentist or intuitionist accounts. As its name suggests, the theory proposes that social or moral norms are to be constructed and, if the account is not to be ques- tion begging, the building blocks of the theory must themselves be non- moral. Beginning with individuals who seek their own advantage and with certain assumptions about the benefits of co-operation, Gauthier seeks to establish whether there are norms for the regulation of that co-operation to which each could rationally agree. The theory seeks to meet the demand that norms that constrain the individual's pursuit of self-interest must be justified to that individual and does so in a way that tries to find a justifi- cation for those norms that does not appeal to pre-existing moral commit- ments of any kind.[2]

An entirely different understanding of constructivism arises out of the writing of those such as John Rawls and Brian Barry for whom the purpose of the construction is primarily to express certain moral commitments. As Barry puts it, 'these theories start from the idea that the choosing situation must be characterized by features that somehow ensure that the choices made will (in some sense) take an equal account of the interests of all the parties' (Barry 1989, 269). Such theories are described below as *faux* con- structivist. This is because, whilst they have the structure of construc- tivism, they do not attempt to construct moral or social norms using non-moral building blocks. Instead, as noted by Kymlicka, *faux* construc- tivism uses its characterization of the situation 'in order to develop, rather than replace, traditional notions of moral obligation; . . . to express the inherent moral standing of persons, rather than to generate an artificial moral standing; . . . and to negate, rather than reflect, unequal bargaining power' (Kymlicka 1991: 191). In short, *faux* constructivism does not attempt to ground morality, but to explicate the content of a duty to treat others with equal consideration.

Given that *faux* constructivism builds on substantive moral commit- ments—uses such commitments to shape the 'situation'—can it sustain a

---

[2] Gauthier's theory, and the form and aspirations of constructivism, are discussed at length in Ch. 6.

claim to be a mode of moral justification rather than merely explication? Clearly, even if the answer to this question is yes, it will not be the kind of ground-up construction offered by Gauthier. This is not something denied by *faux* constructivists. For example, Barry is clear that,

once we admit that substantive intuitions have to go into the [situation] if we are to derive any definite implications, the case for saying constructivism is something different from intuitionism becomes weaker. But it still seems to me that there is a good case for saying that the construction is doing some real work provided what is put in is more general than what comes out. (Barry 1989: 275; cf. Rawls 1951)

The contrast drawn above between *faux* and genuine constructivism is a familiar one (see, amongst others, Barry 1989, 1995*a*; Barry and Matravers 1998*a*; Gauthier 1997; Kymlicka 1991), but is incompletely sketched above. The easiest way to add detail is to examine examples of the two approaches. However, in what remains of this chapter—although the subject (impartialist approaches to justice) is an exemplar of *faux* constructivist theorizing—the focus is not primarily on the method employed by impartialist writers, but on whether their theories can successfully articulate a justification of public rules. In the next chapter the strategy of impartialist theory in coping with certain kinds of rules is examined, as is the question of motivation. It is in the next chapter, then, that the idea of *faux* constructivism receives closest attention. Before that, more needs to be said about the problem of justice and about impartialist theory.

## THE PROBLEM OF JUSTICE

The impartialist theory of justice stems from a particular understanding of the problem of finding public rules to regulate the interactions of citizens of plural, modern, societies. Amongst 'the circumstances of justice' that Rawls identifies as providing both the conditions for, and the problem of, justice is that whilst social co-operation is both feasible and desirable it does not yield sufficient benefits to meet all the demands of those who are engaged in it. Most important, people have what Rawls calls their own 'plans of life' or 'conceptions of the good':

These plans, or conceptions of the good, lead them to have different ends and purposes, and to make conflicting claims on the natural and social resources available. Moreover, although the interests advanced by these plans are not assumed to be interests in the self, they are the interests of a self that regards its conception of the good as worthy of recognition and that advances claims in its behalf as deserving satisfaction. . . . I also suppose that men suffer from various shortcomings of knowledge, thought, and judgment. . . . As a consequence individuals not only have different plans of life but there exists a diversity of philosophical and religious belief, and of political and social doctrines. (Rawls 1971: 127)

This diversity of philosophical and religious belief (and of related political and social claims) is what Rawls calls 'the fact of pluralism'. This is an unfortunate phrase. The term 'pluralism' is not meant to denote a particular position on the source(s) of value, as in the writing of someone like Isaiah Berlin. Rather, what is meant is nothing more than that there are profound differences in the answers people give to the question of what is the nature of the good life. Different people possess distinct beliefs concerning what it is that makes life worth living, what it is that is of value in a human life, what is the source of such value, and so on. Normally, people possess such 'conceptions of the good' as adherents or members of distinct ethical traditions; religious, humanist, utilitarian, Kantian, or whatever (although this is not all there is to conceptions of the good). However, 'the fact' of such differences is not meant merely to refer to the existence of a multiplicity of such traditions, but to the reasonableness of disagreement between them on the question of the good.

Rawls claims that reason is insufficient to determine whether there are one or many sources of value and which, if any, conception of the good is the right one (Rawls 1993: 56–7). Given that reason cannot demonstrate the superiority or inferiority of any one conception of the good to any other, the reasonableness of pluralism describes a situation in which there is *profound, reasonable,* and *seemingly irresolvable* disagreement between people about the nature of the good life for persons. The problem of justice is, then, that of finding rules that can govern co-operation and determine the distribution of the benefits and burdens that result from it given agents who profoundly but reasonably disagree in their conceptions of the good (and subsequently in their social and political beliefs). As Brian Barry has put it, in contrast to the traditional question of morality, 'how ought one to live?', the question of justice is 'how are we to live together, given that we have different ideas about how to live?' (Barry 1995*a*: 77; emphasis suppressed).

## JUSTICE AS IMPARTIALITY[3]

The impartialist answer is deceptively simple. If what is needed is to find fair rules of co-operation given the reasonableness of pluralism then such rules must be justified independently of any reference to the truth, falsity, or validity of any particular (or group of) reasonable conception(s) of the good. At the heart of impartialist theory is the aspiration to what Will Kymlicka has called 'justificatory neutrality'. This is the idea that 'the state does not justify its actions by reference to some public ranking of the intrinsic value of different ways of life, for there is no public ranking to refer to' (Kymlicka 1989: 884). Another way of putting the same point is to say that the reasons that are appealed to in justifying the use of public power must be thin (that is, compatible with the demand of justificatory neutrality). So, in Rawls's original position the contractors are denied knowledge of their conceptions of the good in order to ensure that the two principles are fair. Their decision is informed only by a thin theory of the good and the metric of justice—primary social goods—is chosen precisely because it is rational to desire such goods no matter what else one desires (Rawls 1971: § 4, § 15, §§ 20–30). To a similar end, proposed rules of justice that can be rejected as unreasonable in Brian Barry's variation of T. M. Scanlon's contractualism include those that appeal for justification to a particular conception of the good (Barry 1995*a*: chs. 3, 6, 7).

Typically impartialist theories of justice are restricted in three related ways: First, the principles of justice apply only to what Rawls calls 'the basic structure of society' (1971: 7) or are what Barry calls 'second-order' (1995*a*: 194). What this means is that impartial reasoning is restricted in its application to the problem of justice as it affects public institutions that govern the manner of distribution of such things as income, wealth, and political rights (and to people only in relation to these things). It is not meant to be a guide to how to conduct one's personal life or a guide to how one ought to live in every aspect of one's life. Second, it follows from this that the principles that emerge from the application of impartialist reasoning are principles of justice not of morality as a whole. Quite how this

---

[3] Justice as impartiality is a term borrowed from Brian Barry (1989, 1995*a*). I take John Rawls's *A Theory of Justice* (1971) to be the exemplar of this approach and it is with this work and Barry's own *Justice as Impartiality* (1995*a*) that I shall be mostly concerned. Rawls's more recent work diverges from the impartialist ideal in a number of significant ways (for a discussion of early and late Rawls see, among many others, Brian Barry 1995*b*, David Estlund 1996, Mulhall and Swift 1996).

distinction is to be drawn is discussed below, for the moment it is enough to say that questions of justice are those that concern the basic structure of society and the distribution of the benefits and burdens of social co-operation. Third, the principles of justice apply only to the distributive and not to the retributive sphere.

These restrictions seem to follow from the characterization of the problem of justice as given above and they are hardly surprising given that the project is one of avoiding thick moral commitments. Constructing from reasons that do not presuppose any conception of what it is to lead a good life looks to be an unpromising route to a broad moral theory. As Russell Hardin puts it, 'clearly fairness is not a full moral theory in the way that utilitarianism is—presumably no one seriously holds that morality is merely a matter of fairness' (1998: 139).[4] Nevertheless, impartialist theorists correctly see themselves as engaged in an aspect of moral philosophy and even in Rawls's most avowedly political works he never distances himself from the claim that justice as fairness is a 'moral conception' (see, e.g., Rawls 1985: 223; 1993: 11, 175).

### The relationship of impartial justice and morality

Impartialist theory is concerned that the account of justice that it offers is not meant to replace morality. Justice is part of morality but it is neither the whole of, nor a substitute for, it. This suggests that the relationship of questions of justice to accounts of morality is simply that amongst the range of moral propositions will be a class that concern questions of justice. The impartialist theorist identifies this subset of moral propositions by their subject matter; they concern the distribution of the benefits and burdens of social co-operation and apply only to the basic structure of society. A theory of justice, then, aspires to give an account of the truth conditions of such propositions in a way that is compatible with the account of our reasoning about justice and our ordinary experience of justice. In addition, it aims to address the question of the agent's motivation to be just. Such an account supplements a given theory of morality by paying special attention to a particular class of moral sentences.

This seems perfectly reasonable. There is no reason to think that there cannot be distinct theories of piety, courage, or justice simply because all of these things have at one time or another been thought of as moral virtues.

---

[4] The limited scope of impartial norms and their relation to individuals' lives is the subject of intense debate. See especially Williams 1981 (on which see Barry 1995a; Mendus 1998).

However, what makes the impartialist position more difficult is the claim that the account of justice must aspire to justificatory neutrality. This puts into question the straightforward understanding of the relationship of moral theory and impartialist theories of justice as described above.

On an ordinary reading of the above it would seem that whereas a theory of morality would aspire to give an account of the propositions that it is morally good (other things being equal) to help an elderly person across a road that she desires to cross and that it is just to distribute the benefits and burdens of social co-operation in a given manner, a theory of justice concerns itself only with the latter.[5] However, the impartialist need for justificatory neutrality means that the types of reasons available to the agent in considering these two questions may not be of the same kind, and may even be incompatible. An agent may consider that it is morally right to help an elderly person across the road because the parable of the good Samaritan suggests that this is part of leading a life in emulation of the life of Christ (and this is the paradigm of a moral life). In such a case the agent may also have views about the just distribution of the benefits and burdens of social co-operation (views that appeal to reasons derived from a particular understanding of the Bible), but these are not reasons that are relevant when considering the question of justice. Rather, the agent is required to engage in different activities, reasoning from thick moral beliefs as a private individual (as a pursuer of a particular conception of the good), and from thin reasons as a citizen.[6]

It is this separation of the right from the good that is the distinguishing feature, and distinctive contribution, of justice as impartiality, and it is the stability of the distinction between reasons of justice and what might for the moment be called other moral reasons that is the concern of this chapter. In part this is a question of scope. For if it can be shown that there is a

[5] Consider, for example, a consequentialist who endorses 'utilitarianism as a public philosophy' (to borrow the title of Goodin 1995) and some form of indirect utilitarianism as a guide to everyday conduct. The reasoning engaged in by the agent *qua* citizen and *qua* private individual might be different, but both would be explicable by reference to the same consequentialist theory.

[6] Barry writes: 'Although utilitarianism and Thomism differ substantively at almost every point, they agree that justice and morality are cut from the same cloth. By this I mean that, within these theories, the relation between justice and morality is a simple one. In both cases, we start with a conception of the good that is to be achieved, as far as possible. We then assess potential rules of justice by their conduciveness to the achievement of that good. Principles of justice have a purely derivative status: they function as guides to the selection of the appropriate rules. . . . Impartial justice has to be conceived of as having a radically different status from this. We are looking for a free-standing notion of justice: one that is not subordinate to any conception of the good' (Barry 1995a: 76).

clear distinction between questions of justice and other moral questions then it would seem reasonable to maintain that there might be different sets of reasons appropriate to the different sets of questions. This is suggested by one reading of Rawls, especially of the works that followed *A Theory of Justice*, as well as by the restrictions placed on impartialist theories mentioned above. Rawls writes of a political conception of justice that it

is framed to apply solely to the basic structure of society, its main political, social, and economic institutions as a unified scheme of social cooperation; . . . it is presented independently of any wider comprehensive religious or philosophical doctrine; and . . . it is elaborated in terms of fundamental political ideas viewed as implicit in the public political culture of a democratic society. (Rawls 1993: 223)[7]

The political conception is nevertheless a 'moral' one. What Rawls means by this is that the content of the conception of justice 'is given by certain ideals, principles and standards; and that these norms articulate certain values, in this case political values' (1993: 11 n.).

This is not the place to offer a full-scale interpretation of *Political Liberalism*. A defensible reading of what is relevant for the moment is that Rawls's political conception is moral in that it builds on the two 'moral powers' he attributes to persons: the capacities for a sense of justice and for a conception of the good (see 1993: 19, 103–10). In relying on this conception of the person (or at least, this conception of the citizen in democratic societies) he does not commit himself to a comprehensive moral view because of the limited scope of the conception of the person invoked. Thus, attributing to the person a 'highest order interest' in the 'capacity to form, to revise, and rationally to pursue a conception of one's rational advantage or good' does not preclude Rawls arguing that the person will also hold 'a determinate conception of the good' which may be 'comprehensive' (1993: 19). That is, it may include 'conceptions of what is of value in human life, and ideals of personal character, . . . and much else that is to inform our conduct, and in the limit to our life as a whole' (1993: 13). Thus, the political conception is political in its scope, in what it applies to, and in appealing only to a limited, non-comprehensive, moral ideal of persons as free and equal: a moral ideal that is itself to be thought of as capturing political values; that is, as relevant when thinking of oneself and others as parti-

---

[7] It is worth pointing out that given a certain interpretation of the third feature (referring to ideas latent in the public political culture of a democratic society) these features of the political theory are shared by the original theory as presented in *A Theory of Justice*. On this 'defence of Rawls against Rawls' see Barry 1995*b*: esp. § II.

cipants in society conceived of as a co-operative venture for mutual advantage.

The plausibility of Rawls's theory need not detain the argument here; what is relevant for the moment is simply to get straight what impartialists understand to be the connections (or lack of them) between the reasons relevant to questions of justice and those relevant to other moral questions. Rawls's argument would seem to depend upon there being distinct, recognizable, political questions that are to be considered by people conceiving of themselves as citizens. This 'domain of the political' (Rawls 1989) is defined by Rawls in a number of places as covering only 'society's main political, social, and economic institutions, and how they fit together' (Rawls 1993: 11, see also 223–30). Rawls is clear that this leaves a great deal out: 'Many if not most political questions do not concern those fundamental matters, for example, much tax legislation and many laws regulating property; statutes protecting the environment and controlling pollution; establishing national parks . . . and laying aside funds for museums and the arts' (1993: 214). The relationship of Rawls's political, but still moral, conception of justice and comprehensive moral theories does, then, seem to be in part a matter of scope. Political questions, to which (impartial) public reason is addressed, are only those to do with constitutional essentials and are approached from the perspective of the individual as citizen.

For Barry, for reasons to be discussed below, the scope of impartial justice is limited more pragmatically. Where people or groups disagree about matters that might deleteriously affect their ability to live in accordance with their conception of the good justice has a role. Thus restrictions on religious worship and homosexuality are matters of justice whereas a restriction on one's ability to ride a motorcycle legally without protective headgear is not (Barry 1995*a*: 87; see pp. 114–17 below). Moreover, as questions of justice can mostly only be addressed at a fairly abstract level, impartialist theory is to be used in establishing basic constitutional provisions (see Barry 1995*a*: esp. ch. 4). Nevertheless, where Barry and Rawls agree is that when justice is being invoked it must be free from the taint of reasons that appeal to thick, comprehensive accounts of the good.

In what follows (in this and the next chapter) the plausibility and stability of the distinction between the thin theory of justice and comprehensive moral theories (between the individual reasoning as a citizen and reasoning as a holder of a distinct comprehensive conception of the good) is tested. The method is to look at the use of public power in areas that do not (at least not uncontroversially) involve questions of justice, thus tying the argument together with that of the previous chapters.

Such an approach to impartialist theory might seem misguided. If the areas to be examined are not in the domain of justice then it may seem that they can reveal little about theories of justice, especially theories that are carefully restricted in their scope. However, there are two reasons to think the method employed below appropriate. The first is that it is important to the liberal principle of legitimacy that the use of public power be publicly justifiable (see, for example, Rawls 1993: 137). Yet, public power is not merely (or, indeed, most often) exercised when questions of constitutional essentials are at stake. If a regime is to be legitimate, then, it must be that it can defend the use of public power in non-constitutional areas. This leads to the second reason for the approach that is taken below. Given that the use of public power must be publicly justified even in matters that are not, or at least not uncontroversially, matters of justice the nature of this justification must stand in some relation to the thin reasons invoked in considering constitutional essentials. There would seem to be three possibilities: (*a*) that all uses of public power can be described in the thin language of justice, a language that can then be applied directly; (*b*) that all uses of public power can be justified using normative resources that can be derived from the demands of justice, but without being restricted to the direct application of the language of justice; (*c*) that some uses of public power are to be justified in a different way from the way in which impartial reason justifies its use in cases of justice. However, if this is so then some account needs to be offered of the relationship of the two normative languages.

In what follows the argument proceeds largely without reference to any particular impartialist writer so it may be worth offering a preliminary summary of the problem. Impartial theories of justice depend upon separating the right from the good, reasons and questions of justice from other moral reasons and questions. This separation is necessary because the existence of reasonable disagreement about the good apparently precludes understanding justice in the traditional way; that is, as a moral virtue the content of which can be derived from a broader moral theory (including a theory of the good). The impartialist therefore attempts to establish the requirements of justice using a procedure framed by thin, public, political reasons. The idea that such a procedure can be established independently from thick considerations of the good gains plausibility from the restrictions on scope that impartialists place on their theories. The theory is meant only to apply in the domain of the political and thus appeals only to 'political' reasons. If successful the impartialist can fulfil an essential requirement of the liberal account of legitimacy: that the use of public power ought to be able to be publicly justified.

Yet if impartialist liberalism is committed to the public justifiability of the use of public power it is on the face of it odd that impartialists have had so little to say about, for example, the criminal law, a central feature of the use of public power in contemporary societies. Below various possible conceptions of non-justice rules that are compatible with impartialism (in accordance with the three possibilities mentioned above) are considered. To anticipate the argument in part: the difficulty for the impartialist is that, although public, some rules seems to contain an 'extra' normative element beyond justice, an element of wrongness. If the impartialist attempts to treat such rules in a reductionist manner by making them all a matter of justice, she is left with an implausible account of the public sphere. If she appeals to 'enriched' public reasons to account for the extra normative force of these public rules then the stability of the distinction of reasons of justice and other moral reasons is threatened. The difficulty is that the public domain cannot be adequately theorized using only public reason (reasons of right) unless public reason is enriched. However, if it is so enriched then the distinction between public reason and other moral reasons is destabilized.

## THE PUBLIC DOMAIN

The public domain contains numerous kinds of rules, from those that govern etiquette to those that criminalize certain activities. The argument below concerns those rules that are typically the subject of public power. This category cannot be clearly fixed, for (as John Stuart Mill among others is at pains to point out) public power takes many forms. It is important, then, to distinguish more clearly what is of interest in what follows.

Above it is claimed that impartialist theorists of justice focus on the rules that regulate the use of public power; on what might be called, borrowing from Hart (1994), *secondary* rules. That is, rules that establish the powers of legislation and adjudication and that create conditions that must be met for a rule to be valid. However, there are, of course, rules in the public domain—*primary* rules—that apply to individuals directly. Such rules may be aimed at mandating or prohibiting agents to or from doing certain things, or at enabling agents to do things. For example, rules concerning murder or rape prohibit these activities and those concerning the payment of taxes mandate certain behaviour (call these 'injunctive rules', as they issue injunctions) whereas rules that, for example, determine the conditions for the making of a valid contract or a valid will enable agents to do certain things. Typically rules of the first kind involve the threat of sanctions, rules of the second do not (although both involve the use of public power).[8]

The remainder of this chapter is concerned primarily with the understanding of injunctive rules that is available in impartialist theory. Such rules often invoke public power in its most explicit and visible forms (for example, in the criminal law). It is for this reason that the self-imposed restriction of impartialist theory to secondary rules does not fit with the claim that impartialist theory is centrally concerned with the question of the legitimacy of the use of public power. Even where the impartialist claims that her interest is only in the legitimacy of the use of public power in establishing, regulating, and maintaining the basic structure it is still possible to enquire into the relationship of this account of the use of public power and its use in maintaining and enforcing primary, injunctive rules.

Although in the argument that follows important parts are played by injunctive rules such as those prohibiting intentional killing and rape and the relationship of such rules to impartialist theory on the one hand and moral theory on the other, the argument is only tangentially related to debates in the philosophy of law, specifically the argument between natural law theory and legal positivism. The protagonists in that debate differ crucially on the *validity* conditions of law. A positivist such as Raz, for example, holds that the validity of a law is determined by some social fact, for example its having a particular source (see Raz 1985). Another, like Coleman, may hold the even weaker position that what characterizes legal positivism is adherence to two claims: (i) 'that it is not *necessary* in all legal systems that for a norm to be a legal norm it must possess moral value' and (ii) 'that what norms count as legal norms in any particular society is fundamentally a matter of *social conventions* (Coleman and Leiter 1996: 243). However, no positivist need (or does) deny that there is an extensive overlap between law and morality, perhaps even that where it is possible greater convergence between law and morality is desirable (Coleman and Leiter 1996). What is claimed below is that a full account of the place and nature

---

[8] Hans Kelsen (1992) argues that injunctive rules involve 'punitive' sanctions whereas enabling rules involve 'privative' sanctions. To understand what is meant by 'privative' sanctions consider someone who fails to make a valid contract and then when she thinks that the other party to the 'contract' has failed to honour his obligations with respect to the 'contract' appeals to the state. The power of the state to enforce contracts is only available (under normal circumstances) given that the contract is valid and thus the agent is, in the case described above, deprived of the use of the state.

of injunctive rules, such as those prohibiting intentional killing and rape, must include reference to the wrongness (and not merely the source or legal status) of such acts. This is compatible with the positivist denial that it is a necessary condition of the legal validity of a rule that it correctly incorporate some valid moral claim. Thus, what is primarily the subject of examination below is the understanding of moral norms that overlap and inform—whether or not they determine or validate—many legal rules.

## IMPARTIAL JUSTICE AND INJUNCTIVE RULES

Consider some fairly standard injunctive rules (usually incorporated in the criminal law): prohibitions on assault, murder, burglary, and so on. Of course, the normative discussions that go on around such rules involve, in part, matters of justice. Indeed, the criminal law is probably the area most closely associated in ordinary language with issues of justice. However, for the most part insofar as justice is relevant it is to the implementation of the criminal law. It is unjust to treat one offender differently from a relevantly similar other; it is unjust knowingly to punish someone who did not commit a crime; and it is unjust to alter evidence and to interfere with the ordinary running of a criminal trial. However, the claim that the laws against assault, murder, burglary, etc. are (only, or even primarily) there to prevent injustice and that what is wrong with murderers is only that they behave unjustly towards their victims twists ordinary language out of shape. The content of these laws expresses moral commitments that are not ordinarily captured in the language of justice.

That such rules are not normally treated as matters of justice would seem to fit well with the impartialist restriction on the scope of justice. The content of the criminal law seems to fall outside matters essential to the constitution even if the way in which that content is arrived at, and its formal shape,[9] do not. Nevertheless, the criminal law is an instance of the use of public power. What is more, it is often a paradigm case of the use of public power in upholding certain normative standards and values.

Of course, in some cases injunctive rules seek only to solve a coordination problem. There is no immediate, morally compelling reason to

---

[9] What I mean by 'formal shape' is that the criminal law is subject to restrictions and demands based on justice in addition to those that stem from an account of wrongness. For example, I take it that it is a requirement of justice that the criminal law offer 'equal protection' to all citizens (see the discussion of Hampton in Ch. 3 above).

decide one way or the other on an issue such as whether to drive on the left or right side of the road. However, an individual who recklessly and wilfully drives on the wrong side of a busy street is liable to condemnation not merely for breaking the rules, or for taking advantage of the self-restraint of others, but also for a moral failure to take seriously the claims of others. Similarly, a law prohibiting murder expresses a belief in the value of human life and the wrongness of taking such a life. The point is that some rules seem to 'pick out' a wrong action, the wrongness of which is recognized rather than created by the rule. In this sense prohibitions on murder and rape are not like prohibitions on parking in a restricted zone.[10]

The problem for the impartialist theorist is that in a society characterized by the reasonableness of pluralism there will be different views on the status and nature of the content of rules such as those prohibiting murder. Participants in most religions will regard this prohibition as capturing the wrongness of intentional homicide, where the nature of that wrongness is that it contravenes the law of (their) God; others might believe that the act of killing a person (without excusing conditions) has some mind-independent property of wrongness that can be intuited by human beings using some special moral sense; others that there are mind-dependent but nevertheless objective moral facts and that 'intentionally taking a human life is wrong' is one such; and so on. The question that arises is whether the public justification of the use of coercion by the state in pursuit of the maintaining and enforcing of such rules and in condemning and punishing those who transgress them can adequately characterize these types of rule whilst maintaining the commitment to impartiality when justifying the use of public power.

It might be thought that the question is being set up here in a manner so as to create difficulty for impartialist theory. By seeming to define certain injunctive rules as having a moral content and by asking questions about what is expressed by such rules, the assumption is made that such rules do have and express a particular moral content independent of their being just or otherwise. Given that the impartialist wishes to avoid talk of morality and to speak only of justice this is unfair. If the impartialist cannot explain these rules as they are characterized above then this shows merely that the characterization is wrong not that the impartialist is in trouble.

---

[10] The distinction between co-ordination rules and rules governing such things as murder can be characterized in a number of ways. For example, some people think that the former apply only to participants in a practice or only to those who have, in some sense, consented. Rules covering, for example, murder seem to have a wider scope and seem not to need the element of consent to be binding. The distinction is often drawn using the language of *mala prohibita* and *mala in se*.

However, this is not the position. Given that the impartialist allows that justice is not the whole of morality, that some injunctive rules appeal to an understanding of wrongness, and that such rules (typically) involve the exercise of public power, the impartialist must accept that there is a question as to the relationship of the use of power in these cases and the impartial restriction on public reason. The three possibilities for this relationship are given above—(*a*) that all uses of public power can be described in the thin language of justice; (*b*) that all uses of public power can be justified using normative resources that can be derived from the demands of justice, but without being restricted to the direct application of the language of justice; (*c*) that some uses of public power are to be justified in a different way from the way in which impartial reason justifies its use in cases of justice—and each is examined below.

## *All a matter of justice*[11]

One possible account of the relationship between questions of justice and what are called above other moral questions is to reduce the latter to the former: to treat all uses of public power, including its use in the criminal law, as concerning matters of justice to be justified directly by the thin reasons of impartialist theory. This is the argument found in the fair play theory of punishment and as it is the subject of detailed and critical consideration in Chapter 2 it can be quickly dismissed. The criticism of the theory made in Chapter 2, that it 'distorts the essential character of crime' (Duff 1996: 27), reflects precisely the concern of this chapter, that some prohibitions have a force that goes beyond the impartialist conception of questions of justice.

The fair play account would provide what is needed: a way to understand the use of public power in relation to all public norms such that it can appeal for justification, and can thus be made legitimate, by the account of justice. However, as demonstrated above, fair play theory is implausible and impartialists quite rightly distance themselves from it.[12] As they are

---

[11] The following three sections borrow from my discussions of moral reason and communicative accounts of punishment (1999*a*) and of the universalist aspirations of impartial theories of justice (2000*a*).

[12] See, for example, Barry 1996: 329: 'it would be eccentric to say that what makes murder or grievous bodily harm wrong is that they are unjust in virtue of their taking unfair advantage of the forbearance of others. Some philosophers have, admittedly, said this; but all that shows is that some people will say anything.' Fair play theorists seem to fall into that category of people who according to Hardin (quoted above on p. 104) think the 'unthinkable'—that morality is 'merely a matter of fairness'.

careful to distinguish questions of justice from other moral questions they have no reason to adopt an implausible theory simply to make all moral matters issues of justice.

## *The force of pedigree*

The idea that in a legitimate regime all uses of public power can be justified using normative resources that can be derived from the demands of justice, but without being restricted to the direct application of the language of justice, is suggested by Rawls's references to the political conception of justice being limited to constitutional essentials. One purpose of a constitution is to establish decision procedures through which decisions can be taken on such issues as, to borrow from Rawls, taxation and national parks. It is not, or not obviously, a matter of justice whether a certain area is designated a national park, or an area of special scientific interest, or whatever. It is a matter of justice that should this decision be taken by, say, a local referendum then people should not be disqualified from voting on the basis of their skin colour. A just constitution ensures that the mechanisms for arriving at certain decisions are just. The force of those decisions is that they have been arrived at in the right way. Rules, including injunctive rules, have the force of their pedigree.

The advantage of this argument is that it allows that the reasons invoked when a given policy is under discussion can be broader than the thin reasons of impartial justice. Yet the ultimate justification for the use of public power in implementing or maintaining the policy can appeal to the account of justice. Thus, in a debate over whether to spend some public money on a war memorial or a public park the proponents on each side can appeal to their own conceptions of the good; for example, to arguments about the value of honouring the society's dead and to those concerning the importance of public amenities. When a decision is taken by (for example) a democratically instituted legislature neither side need alter its opinion about how the money ought to have been spent in order to accept that the decision is just. Subsequently, in defending the building of the park to those who would rather have had a war memorial it does not need to be said that what makes the use of public power just is that the park is a better outcome, or a means to the creation of greater value in the world. All that needs to be said is that the arguments were heard and that the park won the day (cf. Barry 1995*a*: 145–52).

On this view, then, there is no public account of the use of public power beyond the scope of what is offered by impartial justice. Arguments about the rightness or wrongness of the park or the war memorial are relevant only to the making of the decision, but not to the rightness or wrongness of whatever decision is made. In the example given this is a plausible account of the use of public power. However, there are good reasons to doubt that the theory can be applied across the board. The problems are of two kinds: first, the decision as to what is a matter of justice directly and what is a matter for some, for example, preference aggregating procedure established by justice introduces considerations that appeal to questions beyond the scope of impartial theory. Second, the effective restriction of the public domain to matters of justice and matters the normative force of which is derived only from their having been decided correctly is implausible. There are issues that are essential to a correct understanding of the public domain, and the use of public power, that fall into neither of these categories.

Consider the first of these problems. The account given above has the following structure: certain matters concerning the distribution by the basic structure of the benefits and burdens of social co-operation are governed by principles of justice that are justificatorily neutral (and that appeal only to norms of justice as impartialists conceive of them). Subordinate matters, not concerning these essential questions, are to be decided in accordance with some decision procedure that is governed by impartial principles of justice (the procedure is understood through norms of justice, but the content of the decisions is not, once they are made, understood in terms of public norms of right and wrong). Decisions taken in the latter case must, of course, be compatible with the requirements of justice. To make this clearer consider the US constitution as an example. The US constitution consists in part of a series of secondary rules determining who should hold power and how decisions are to be made. It also stipulates that decisions made must be compatible with certain requirements such as that 'Congress shall make no law respecting the establishment of religion, or prohibiting the free exercise thereof . . .' (these from the First Amendment).

Thus, for example, were a popular referendum to outlaw referring to Jesus as the son of God this could be struck down on the grounds that, even were it to be correctly instituted by a legitimate decision procedure, it discriminates in an unjust way against those who hold a Christian conception of the good.[13] The direct application of justice must always trump even a just decision-making procedure where the outcome of the latter is in

---

[13] Of course, it could also be struck down as a restriction on freedom of speech (which is also guaranteed in the First Amendment).

conflict with the demands of the former. However, this means that assessing a primary rule regulating some activity requires establishing whether that activity is an essential part of some persons' reasonable conception of the good or whether it is 'just a preference'.

This is a well-worn problem, but its significance is great for a theory that tries to divide the public domain into direct and indirect applications of the language of justice. Barry, for example, discusses the issue using the cases of homosexual practices (which he considers as an essential part of a reasonable conception of the good that is held by some people and, thus, as protected by considerations of justice) and motorcycling without protective headgear (which he regards as 'just a preference' and, thus, as a matter for some public decision-making procedure). He asserts that 'in sharp contrast with bans on certain forms of religious worship or on homosexual activities, it is not plausible for people to say that their lives are going to be blighted—in relation to their own conception of the good—if they cannot . . . ride on a motorcycle without protective headgear' (Barry 1995*a*: 87).

There is no doubt that Barry's argument will seem to many to capture an important difference: a ban on homosexual activities is different from a rule that requires the wearing of protective headgear when riding a motorcycle. However, it is not so straightforward—the contrast is not as 'sharp'—as Barry makes out. First, Barry's judgement concerns the plausibility of a claim about what makes life valuable. In response to someone who believes that an essential part of the good life is the feeling of freedom that she finds uniquely in riding a motorcycle with the wind through her hair, who orients her life around this, meets like-minded people and, when not on her motorcycle, spends part of her time reading motorcycle magazines and learning about great motorcycle tourers, Barry asserts that this is not plausibly part of a conception of the good. There may be good reasons for Barry's judgement, although he gives none. This is not surprising, for Barry is making a judgement about the good and not about the right; a judgement of a kind that impartialist theorists are meant to eschew. Thus, even if there are good reasons for Barry's assertions about what is, and what is not, to count as a conception of the good these are reasons that are unavailable to him as a defender of an impartial theory.[14]

---

[14] Some judgements about what is to count as a conception of the good may be unavoidable if impartialist theory is to be at all plausible (cf. Rawls 1993: 59). Nevertheless, the suspicion remains that Barry has independent reasons for thinking the two cases different, and he resorts to judgements about what kind of thing can count as part of the content of a conception of the good in order to deliver what he, and no doubt many others, believe to be the right outcome.

Note, even the argument concerning homosexual practices can be challenged. After all, the idea that sexual identity and sexual practices are essential to (the living of) persons' conceptions of the good life is also a
judgement about the good, and also controversial.[15] The argument
between those who think sodomy a deviant preference and those who
think it essential to their living of a good life cannot be resolved using the
resources of impartial justice.[16]

It is argued above that considerations of justice are part of what motivates Jean Hampton's expressivist theory (see Chapter 3 above), and the failure of her theory is instructive here. Consider, for example, a society that
chooses through some democratic procedure not to allow rules against
such things as assault, battery, and rape to apply to incidents between married couples. There is, as Hampton points out, an important consideration
of justice here. A society committed to justice as fairness ought to treat
people equally and assuming that in this instance marriage is not relevant
in distinguishing between cases, a society that makes the above decision
fails to extend equal protection—equal treatment—to some.

However, two points need to be noticed about this. First, it is an alleged
advantage of the restriction of the scope of impartial justice that it leaves
many everyday decisions to the democratic sphere and, thus, does not
overcomplicate the issue of what is to be the subject of the legitimate use of
public power in the sphere of justice (see, for example, Barry 1995*a*: 92). If
the argument concerning motorcycle crash helmets above is right, this will
not be the case. Indeed, surely the threat is that many lobby groups faced
with the prospect of defeat at the polls will turn their demands into claims
about what is essential to their 'way of life' or into claims of 'equal treatment', thus moving the debate to the level of justice. Moreover, it is argued

[15] Cf. Michel Foucault's claim, made in the first volume of his *The History of Sexuality*,
that 'as defined by the ancient civil or canonical codes, sodomy was a category of forbidden
acts; their perpetrator was nothing more than the juridical subject of them. The nineteenth-
century homosexual became a personage, a past, a case history, and a childhood, in addition to being a type of life, a life form, and a morphology . . . The sodomite had been a
temporary aberration; the homosexual was now a species' (Foucault 1978: 43).
[16] Certainly if one extends the argument to individual sexual practices the argument
becomes very controversial. A law against sodomy or one against oral sex (both of which
exist in some states of the USA) is not the same as a 'law against homosexuality' (although
a restriction on sodomy may have a more significant impact on homosexuals than on heterosexuals). There is surely something odd about thinking that a law against male–female
sodomy (such as exists in the UK) is fundamentally different from a law against male–male
sodomy because the latter will 'blight' the lives of some 'in relation to their own conception
of the good' whereas the former only restricts the opportunity of some to indulge their preferences.

above that such a move cannot be countered using the resources available in a theory dedicated to justificatory neutrality.[17]

Second, as is pointed out above in relation to Hampton's argument, this is not all that can, or should, be said about a society that does not have the resources in public reason to say more than that the failure to protect the married in these instances is unjust. The analysis in terms of justice misdescribes and distorts at least part of the issue. The issue of whether some policy is fair—whether it discriminates against some more than others or will affect some more than others where this could be avoided—is important, but it is not the only issue. What is also needed is an account of the wrongness of certain actions, and the importance in the light of their wrongness of their public recognition as such. Without this the understanding of these rules will not only be distorted, but there will be no plausible public account of what it is that ought to motivate people to obey such injunctive rules. On the pedigree argument given above all that could be said of a prohibition against, for example, murder is that it is a prohibition that was correctly instituted. The motivational appeal of this would presumably have to be to the importance of adhering to decisions taken by an appropriate and just decision-making body. However, this is absurd. When defending the prohibition of murder it is true neither that the complete account of the justified use of public power involved in such a prohibition is contained within the claim that the rule was correctly instituted by a legitimate legislature nor that the understanding of the motivational force of this prohibition lies in its being so instituted. The prohibition of murder and the condemnation of murderers have a moral force that goes beyond that provided by pedigree.

The difficulty for the impartialist, as noted above, is that the nature of this moral force will be the subject of reasonable disagreement between members of the society who hold different conceptions of the good. An individual's belief about what makes murder wrong and whether, and if so how, murder being wrong should provide a reason not to do it will depend on the individual's view of the source and nature of moral value. This, of course, the impartialist takes to be the subject of reasonable disagreement. The difficulty, then, is explaining the moral force of certain parts of these non-justice injunctive rules whilst respecting the reasonableness of pluralism.

---

[17] In addition to the examples given above, consider the apparently straightforward case of religious freedom. All manner of primary rules, for example those governing the use of hallucinogenic drugs or the handling of dangerous snakes, can be challenged as restrictions on religious freedom. Indeed, the phenomenon of groups converting their claims into the language of justice and right appears already well established.

One way of avoiding the disagreement that underpins the reasonableness of pluralism is to leave aside deep questions of the nature of the wrong involved in, say, murder and concentrate instead on the surface of moral argument. It is a reasonable assumption that there will be widespread agreement that murder is wrong even in conditions of disagreement about why it is so. This opens up the possibility that the rule expresses and gains normative force from this agreement. Everyone has reasons to believe that murder is wrong, but their reasons are different. The existence of the reasons is nevertheless important and adds normative force to the prohibition of murder. The rule against murder prohibits a wrong action, and those who murder can be condemned for doing wrong.

This would seem to be an accurate description of the current practices of law in pluralist countries. Moreover it seems to provide an account of the relationship of justice and other moral questions that involve the use of public power. To continue with the example, the rule prohibiting murder has the force of having been correctly instituted and, when invoked, of being justly implemented, but it has additional normative force because it reflects a widespread moral conclusion.

As noted above, this account is probably close to the way in which the criminal law in pluralist societies actually works. However, it suffers from three defects. First, it is clear that even where there is surface agreement on certain moral conclusions this consensus is too much on the surface to be helpful in determining the content of injunctive rules. Agreement that deliberately and voluntarily killing another person 'with malice aforethought' is wrong is not the same as agreement about what constitutes voluntariness, killing, and forethought. Such agreement also does not extend to what difference it would make if the victim consented or requested to be killed, or if the attempt to kill failed.[18] These are important matters and, once again, each person's view on these things will be profoundly affected by the ethical tradition to which she belongs and by the conception of the good that she holds. In short, there is insufficient agreement even on the surface of moral argument.

Second, although the existence of a shared belief in the wrongness of an act can add some normative force to the prohibition on murder it does not add enough, at least for those who think that the sanctions of the law have as (at least) one function the expressing of moral condemnation to an offender who is in principle capable of understanding why that condemnation should

---

[18] I am grateful to Antony Duff for this point. It is discussed also in Matravers 1999*a*: 115.

matter to him. The expressing to the offender that what he has done is wrong, but that the public authority holds no official view on why it is that what he has done is wrong, leaves out something significant.

Third, and most important, there is surely something wrong with an argument that makes a significant part of the normative force of the prohibition of murder contingent on there being agreement amongst the citizens that murder is wrong. As it stands, the argument is that once a rule against murder is correctly instituted it claims some additional normative force from the existence of agreement that murder is wrong. However, note that the extra normative force of wrongness is not created by the agreement. Nobody need hold that what makes something wrong is that people agree about its being so. Rather, the agreement reflects only that differing views on what is wrong coincide on the matter of whether murder is wrong.

An additional difficulty for the impartialist theorist in adopting this account is that in order to establish that, for example, an injunctive rule prohibiting rape is a requirement of justice the impartialist must draw on the fact that justice requires that citizens ought to enjoy equal treatment. However, the relevant feature of equal treatment in the matter of rape must refer to features of rape—such as the harm that it inflicts—that are more appropriately captured in the language of wrongness. It is because it does harm to its victims, a harm comparable to other harms such as are done in assault, battery, murder, and the like, that equality and justice require that rape be subject to an injunctive rule. Agreement plays no part in this. The situation would not change were it to be the case that in a given society there was no agreement about the wrongness of rape.

The existence of a shared moral conclusion—for example, that killing for pleasure is wrong—is not helpful in understanding that part of the public domain that is not covered by considerations of justice. Such shared conclusions could incorporate claims that are (held by impartialists to be) incompatible with requirements of justice, for example that homosexuality is wrong. In such cases it is not merely that an injunctive rule prohibiting homosexual practices would be unjust that informs the judgement that such a rule is illegitimate. Rather, the shared conclusion about the wrongness of such practices must be the subject of critical attention. Similarly, the failure to agree on the wrongfulness of, for example, rape does not mean that an injunctive rule can only be understood in terms of justice. Indeed, for it to be so understood reasons must be appealed to that concern what it is that makes rape wrong. Finally, the construction of injunctive rules that refer to the wrongfulness and not only the injustice of certain acts needs to be supplemented by an account of motivation. The argument above would leave the public domain only with rules of justice that happen to coincide with shared moral conclusions, but with an account of motivation only in terms of justice. This does not advance the argument beyond the claim of pedigree, and, as is pointed out above, the motivating force of an injunctive rule prohibiting, for example, murder cannot merely be that the rule emerged from some just decision-making procedure.[19]

The argument that the construction of all public rules can be either all a matter of justice, or all derived from considerations of justice, fails. This is hardly surprising and might be thought not to be a challenge to impartialist theorists who, as noted above, are careful to circumscribe the scope of their theories very narrowly. In addition, impartialist theorists need sometimes to appeal to considerations that normally lie beyond impartial, second-order justice. It is not plausible to claim that what can be criticized about a society that treats sexual assault as on a par with littering offences is only that it fails to extend to the victims of such assault sufficient protection of those capacities essential to living in accordance with their chosen conceptions of the good. What is the legitimate subject of criticism is rather that the society has made an error about the wrongfulness of rape; a mistake that perhaps (additionally) reflects the failure of that society to take seriously the egalitarian claims of the sexes. What is needed, then, is an account of what are called above other moral reasons and of their relation to impartial justice.

## CONSTRUCTIVISM AND WRONG-MAKING PROPERTIES

Impartialists wish to separate the right from the good; reasons of justice from other moral reasons. By doing so they believe that they can offer an account of the legitimate use of public power: public power used in core constitutional matters is legitimate when it can be justified using public reason—reasons of justice—and thus when its use can be accepted by all reasonable citizens. In many sub-constitutional cases the justification of

---

[19] It is important to distinguish the argument in this section from the sophisticated non-cognitivist meta-ethical positions espoused by writers such as Simon Blackburn (1993, 1998) and Alan Gibbard (1990). The argument here is that certain injunctive rules can gain support from agreement on the surface of moral argument. This is not the same as the meta-ethical claim that there are only first-order moral propositions. Such an argument would, of course, contravene the impartialist commitment to avoiding claims of a meta-ethical kind.

the use of public power can appeal to those justified decision-making procedures established by the constitution. However, prohibitions of such things as murder and rape appear to require something different. At least in part, such prohibitions express normative judgements whose authority goes beyond that which is transmitted by just procedures. They are understood in terms of wrongdoing not, or not only, injustice.

That the public domain contains injunctions and duties that go beyond the demands of justice is not something that impartialist writers deny. Rawls, for example, carefully distinguishes between the domains of distributive and of retributive justice. Whereas for Rawls distributive justice involves fairness and reciprocity and distributive inequalities are designed as 'a scheme of taxes and burdens designed to put a price on certain forms of conduct and in this way to guide men's conduct' for the greatest benefit of the least advantaged, he claims that 'the purpose of the criminal law is to uphold basic natural duties, those which forbid us to injure other persons in their life and limb, or to deprive them of their liberty or property' (all quotations from Rawls 1971: 314–15). However, the existence of this domain of natural duties, and of the use of public power in enforcing those duties, raises the question of how this domain and the reasons associated with it stand in relation to, on the one hand, public reasons of justice and, on the other, to non-public reasons attached to particular conceptions of the good. It has already been noted that there will be disagreement between conceptions of the good about the nature and source of such natural duties even where there is agreement about their essential demands.

It might be thought that there is an obvious route for the impartialist to take here; one that need not be so circuitously arrived at. What is needed is a thin account of wrongness to accompany the thin account of justice (both within the domain of 'the right'). This should not be difficult for the impartialist theory of justice is founded in part on an account of people's interests. This account is used in a particular way when considering matters of justice, but can be used in other ways when looking at other questions. The interests of the person *qua* citizen underpin the account of justice. Interpreted differently her interests can justify the use of public power in pursuit of matters other than those that are essential to the constitution.[20]

---

[20] It is argued above that the requirement of equal treatment can be used to show the injustice of societies that do not take seriously certain kinds of (for example, abusive) acts only given an account of the interests of each person. Given this, it is reasonable to think that impartialists are committed to a connection between the account of interests given in the distributive sphere and that which might be utilized in a broader account of wrong.

Consider, for example, the following argument: *qua* citizen the Rawlsian individual has a highest-order interest in her capacity to choose, revise, and pursue a plan of life. Whatever this plan may be, Rawls alleges, she has an interest in her access to primary goods: that is, her access to primary social goods such as 'rights and liberties, powers and opportunities, income and wealth' and to primary natural goods such as 'health and vigor, intelligence and imagination'. Rawls's theory (notoriously[21]) concerns only the fair distribution of primary social goods for such goods are 'at the disposition of society' whereas primary natural goods 'are not so directly under its control' (all quotations from Rawls 1971: 62). Of course, a citizen's rights, including his right to life, are part of the package of primary social goods and, thus, a murderous attack is, in part, an injustice: a failure on the part of the murderer to respect a right that the victim can fairly claim. However (as noted above), Rawls is explicit that this is not the whole story. Individuals have natural duties that include the duty not to harm or injure one another (1971: § 19). Natural duties, Rawls argues, whilst part of the concept of right, 'obtain between all as equal moral persons' (1971: 115). The thought is this: from an assumption of equal moral worth and a thin account of the person and of her interests two kinds of prohibitions and two normative languages arise. One revolves around fairness and justice, the other around harm and wrong. The relationship between them is that they both arise from, first, an account of interests and, second, the claim that the selves that possess those interests have equal moral standing.

If this is the manner in which the impartialist is to incorporate the idea of wrong relevant to the discussion above then the question of the relationship of this and the public reasons of justice as given in impartialist theory arises. A clue to this relationship is given in Rawls's discussion of constructivism in *Political Liberalism*. Constructivism, Rawls argues, is not committed to the claim that 'the facts that are relevant in practical reasoning and judgment are constructed'. Rather, it makes use of non-constructed facts that are 'relevant for political reasoning'. Amongst those are facts that 'are cited in giving reasons why an action or institution is, say, right or wrong, or just or unjust. These facts are the so-called right-and-wrong-making characteristics' (Rawls 1993: 121). The reference to right-and-wrong-making characteristics is crucial. To borrow an example from Scanlon (who is cited by Rawls as sharing this view, see 1993: 121 n. 30),

---

[21] 'Notoriously' because Rawls's use of primary social goods eliminates the possibility that it is just to distribute more resources to some on the grounds that they possess some natural characteristic that disadvantages them in the conversion of resources into welfare (for example the disabled).

the act of killing someone for pleasure possesses some 'wrong-making property' (Scanlon 1982: 118).[22] Note, the property possessed is not the property of 'wrongness' and thus the description avoids Mackie type criticisms of positing 'queer' intrinsically action-guiding properties (see Mackie 1977; Rawls 1993: 123 n. 30; Scanlon 1982: 118, 1999). Rather, the act of killing for pleasure possesses properties that make it 'wrong-making'. In the absence of the constructivist procedure this moral feature of the act is, in a sense, inert. It has no motivational or justificatory force without the constructivist procedure through which such properties or characteristics become reasons in moral argument and reasons for action. As Rawls puts it, constructivism provides 'a framework of reasoning within which to identify the facts that are relevant from the appropriate point of view and to determine their weight as reasons' (Rawls 1993: 122).

It is worth noting that the above account puts back together the public accounts of justice and injustice, right and wrong. If this is right, then it is necessary to distinguish between justice broadly and narrowly conceived.[23] Broadly conceived, justice includes that which would normally be covered by the terms right and wrong (and much else). Thus, murder and rape have wrong-making properties that would be 'picked out' by a constructivist procedure and insofar as the products of the constructivist procedure are referred to in the language of justice these things are unjust. This is a broad sense of justice that covers everything that emerges from the constructivist procedure. Some subset of what emerges concerns questions of the distribution of the benefits and burdens of social co-operation by the institutions of the basic structure of society and this is a matter of justice narrowly conceived. Thus, murder and rape, in addition to being wrong (broadly unjust), may also be narrowly unjust in that they violate a principle of equal liberty (cf. Barry 1998: 215).

Thus, although the principles of distributive justice (justice narrowly conceived) continue to be limited in the ways described above, the separa-

---

[22] Scanlon's use of 'property' seems to me to be clearer than Rawls's choice of 'characteristic', but nothing seems to hang on the choice of word.

[23] I borrow these terms from Barry 'Sustainability and Intergenerational Justice', n.d.: 2–4. Cf. Barry 1998: 215 where he writes: 'the conception of justice with which I am working is a broad one which includes everything that Scanlon would include in the sphere of wrongness and a lot more besides'. This does not affect the claims made earlier about the separation of the right and the good and the restrictions placed on the account of justice. Barry grants that there is a narrower concept of justice, the one employed earlier in the chapter. He employs the broader sense of justice to cover all those things that could be subject to the Scanlonian formula. His inclusion of matters of right and wrong, of harm, etc. in the account of justice will, I think, surprise some readers of *Justice as Impartiality*. He does not consider whether this broad concept of justice restricts his impartialism.

tion of the spheres of justice and of wrongness is dissolved (at least in the public domain). For example, the people in Rawls's original position choose principles of justice that identify 'facts' that are to count as reasons in arguments about the distribution by the basic structure of the benefits and burdens of social co-operation and that assign weight to those reasons. Similarly, they determine 'natural duties' that also identify, and assign weight to, facts that are to count as reasons beyond the distributive sphere. Thus, the agent considering whether to help the old person across the road (in the example given at the beginning of this chapter) might consider that he would be wrong not to do so as he has a natural duty of mutual aid that is grounded in the same procedure as grounds the principles of distributive justice.

The challenge posed for the impartialist towards the beginning of this chapter is to offer an account of a certain part of the public domain, a part in which public power is exercised, that revolves around questions that are not normally, or uncontroversially, thought of as matters of justice. On the account given in this section, the public domain is characterized, in part, by rules of justice that appeal to reasons that in turn are constructed from relevant facts, including the 'circumstances of justice', and that regulate the distribution by the basic structure of society of the benefits and burdens of social co-operation. Given the reasonableness of pluralism, the constructivist procedure assigns no weight to claims based on particular comprehensive conceptions of the good, but does give weight to the account given in a 'thin' theory of the good. The public domain is also characterized by rules relating to natural duties—relating to acts that are more normally understood as right or wrong—that also appeal to certain features of persons and the world that they inhabit. Together, these constitute a complete understanding of the public domain that is nevertheless not comprehensive in the Rawlsian sense that what is contained within this understanding does not inform all aspects of a person's life, provide ideals of personal character, etc. It would seem, then, that the impartialist has the resources to meet the challenge. However, what is required of impartialist theory is not merely an account of the public domain, but one that is compatible with the aspiration to justificatory neutrality that underpins and drives the impartialist project. The question of whether the account given in this section is neutral in the specified sense is a complex one. It brings to the fore the issue of the status of the account and the structure of *faux* constructivism. It is this that is taken up in the next chapter.

# 5

# Impartial Justice, Motivation, and Punishment

## INTRODUCTION

At the end of the last chapter the skeleton of an argument was offered in an attempt to show how impartialist theorists of justice can cope with the need to give an account of rules within the public domain that involve the use of public power, but which are not matters of justice narrowly conceived. The strategy involves the construction of a public account of natural duties—of right and wrong—that mirrors the account of distributive justice. Returning to Barry's characterization of constructivism: the actors in the 'situation' determine rules beyond those of distributive justice using 'facts' that are morally relevant. These facts, and the shape of the situation, need not be identical to those that are used in choosing principles of distributive justice, and the weight that is given to certain facts that are relevant to both need not be the same. Nevertheless, the relationship of the accounts of justice and of wrongness is clear. In both cases, the appeal is to a constructivist procedure and to a 'public' or 'political' account of the facts that are relevant in moral argument.

In this chapter this argument is given further explication. Initially, the concern is with the relationship of the public account of wrong and individuals' comprehensive conceptions of the good. However, the point of this is to bring the argument back to the fundamental structure of *faux* constructivist theories with a view to investigating that structure and its relation to questions of motivation and, ultimately, of punishment.

## JUSTICE BROADLY CONCEIVED AND COMPREHENSIVE CONCEPTIONS OF THE GOOD

Consider again the example from Chapter 4 of the agent who is moved to help an elderly person across the road. In the account of justice broadly conceived it is pointed out that this agent now has reasons from within the impartialist constructivist account to think it right to help the elderly person. These reasons do not conflict with, and are not of a different kind from, the reasons that she has to believe it her duty to uphold the principles of justice, or those for thinking the content of the principles correct. However, the point of the example when initially introduced at the beginning of Chapter 4 was to illustrate that an agent who believes that she has a duty to help because to do so is part of what God has established as a morally worthy life will find that her reasons for doing what she believes right (*qua* individual believer) are not reasons that are relevant to questions of justice; they cannot be part of public reason. The question to be discussed now is how the individual's reasons—related to the individual's belief in one or other comprehensive conception of the good—stand in relation to the expanded understanding of the public domain that results from the inclusion of natural duties and considerations of right and wrong. The compatibility of the account of justice broadly conceived with the demand of justificatory neutrality can be investigated by looking at the status of the account; its scope; and its foundations.

### The status of justice broadly conceived

A natural way to interpret the account of justice broadly conceived would be to follow Scanlon's account of the core of morality—of what Scanlon calls 'what we owe to each other'—given that it is to this account that both Rawls and Barry are deeply indebted (see Scanlon 1982, 1992, 1999; for their endorsement of Scanlon's approach to questions of right and wrong, see Barry 1998: 214;[1] Rawls 1993: 121–4). However, Scanlon offers an

---

[1] It is not clear to me whether Barry fully endorses Scanlon's position, and thus whether his position is similar to that of Rawls. Barry endorses much of the above, including the claim that 'killing for pleasure' is a 'wrong-making property' (indeed, he quotes the example from Scanlon 1982). However, he goes on to claim, 'so long as the contracting parties have a healthy dislike of the prospect of dying a violent death (a dislike that strongly outweighs the desire to be free to kill other people at will), they cannot reasonably reject a rule outlawing murder' (Barry 1998: 214). Barry is keen to avoid the criticism of Scanlon's theory (offered by Judith Jarvis Thomson 1990: 30 n. 19 and repeated to Barry by Simon Caney

alternative account of the nature of morality to those given by convention-alists, certain kinds of relativists (see Scanlon 1999: ch. 8), and realists (including, for example, those whose view on the nature of morality is derived from a belief in God). Clearly, this is not something that impar-tialist writers can endorse if the use of public power is to be justificatorily neutral. Scanlon's is an argument about what kind of thing morality (or that part of morality concerned with what we owe each other) is, and that is not territory on which the impartialist can tread for it involves the denial of the claims of rival accounts as to the nature and source of moral rules.[2] Instead, the impartialist must treat the construction of a broad account of justice as the construction of a public account to be endorsed by reasonable citizens when thinking as citizens. Just as justice narrowly conceived—the principles of distributive justice—is free standing, so it must be with prin-ciples of justice broadly conceived.

Towards the beginning of Chapter 4 it was suggested that the demand that the individual reason differently *qua* believer and *qua* citizen is made easier by the restriction of the scope of justice to questions of the distribu-tion by the basic structure of the benefits and burdens of social co-operation. However, once attention is turned to justice broadly conceived this argument appears to be under strain.

## The scope of justice broadly conceived

The extension of the public construction of rules to govern how we are to live together into areas beyond distributive justice has a number of advan-tages for impartialist theory. Chief among these is that it allows the impar-tialist to offer an account of the public domain and the use of public power in the many and varied areas that lie beyond the narrow realm of distribu-tive justice. Once this is established it is possible for the impartialist to account for particular uses of public power in a way that is far more plau-

---

1998: 95) that it gets the relationship between reasonable rejection and wrongness back to front. That is, he wishes to avoid the claim that 'torturing babies is immoral *because* reas-onable people would reject it' (Barry 1998: 214, responding to an example from Thomson via Caney). Barry rightly claims that Scanlon is not committed to such a view. Nevertheless, I am unsure whether Barry would agree with the use to which the constructivist procedure is put above. Scanlon's own reply to Thomson's objection is that his formula is 'intended as an account of what it is for an act to be wrong. What *makes* an act wrong are the properties that would make any principle that allow it one that it would be reasonable to reject (in this case, the needless suffering and death of the baby)' (Scanlon 1999: 391 n. 21).

[2] It is worth emphasizing that impartialist theories must not merely remain justificator-ily neutral with respect to the content of moral reasons, but also with respect to the nature and source of such reasons.

sible than if she restricts herself only to the language of justice (narrowly conceived) and only to considerations of fairness.

One obvious conceptual tool to be deployed here is harm. The wrong-making property of killing for pleasure can be unpacked in terms of the harm done to the victim, and a so-called 'positive harm principle'—an act being harmful is a prima-facie reason for deploying public power to prohibit or prevent it—is used by Barry as a principle of justice as impartiality (Barry 1995*a*: § 14). For Barry, the category of harmful acts is captured in the thought that such acts are 'deleterious from the point of view of a very wide range of conceptions of the good' (1995*a*: 88), which he later fills out in other terms by citing those things denial of the possession of which would be harmful. These are:

security against the deliberate infliction of injury and death by other people, and the provision of sanitation, portable water, shelter and heat (as required by climate), and medical care . . . a supply of food adequate to provide for normal growth, work at full capacity, enjoyment of leisure, pregnancy and childrearing. (Barry 1996: 332)

Before considering this, it is worth pausing to comment on how much work this argument can be put to within impartialist theory.[3] A great many policy proposals, ranging far wider than the discussion of injunctive rules of the kind that have brought the argument to this point, could be subject to question given the need not to do harm. As a consequence of this such matters become issues of justice and not issues for some decision-making procedure established by just rules. This is significant, not least because as the scope of impartial justice broadens the question of what weight is assigned to different reasons becomes both more important and more difficult to determine in a manner compatible with justificatory neutrality.

An additional use to which the argument from harm can be put is in its negative form. Mill's harm principle is, of course, a negative principle; the use of public power is not justified unless it is directed to the prevention of harm (and not always then). This, as Barry notes, relies too heavily on a conception of human good as autonomy to be a theorem of justice as impartiality (Barry 1995*a*: § 14). Nevertheless, using the harm principle in its negative form allows the impartialist to escape some of the more absurd implications of using only the test of whether a proposal will 'blight' for some the living of their conception of the good to decide whether it is just.

---

[3] I have discussed the use of the argument from harm to declare unreasonable approaches to justice such as Robert Nozick's 'entitlement theory' (1974) in Matravers 1998: 117–18.

For example, in Chapter 4 above, it is noted that distinguishing between restrictions on certain sexual practices on grounds of the intimacy of the connection between those practices and the living of some conception of the good might, for example, lead to the odd conclusion that the same act has a different status in justice when it is performed by heterosexuals and by homosexuals (see Chapter 4 n. 16). The argument is far more plausible if, instead, it is put in the form that in neither case (that is, applied to homosexuals or heterosexuals) can such a restriction be justified on grounds of preventing harm. Thus, in the absence of any other available justification (that is, a justification available from within public reason)[4] in neither case is the restriction justified.

The pressure on justificatory neutrality from broadening the scope of justice comes from the need to define and weight those interests that are to be counted as relevant in the construction of rules of co-operation. In Rawls's account of distributive justice the people in the original position have available general facts about, for example, economics, politics, and sociology (Rawls 1971: 137–8) and they know that the circumstances of justice obtain (see Chapter 4 above). In addition, in choosing principles of justice they refer to the 'thin theory of the good'. That is, they take it as given that people prefer more rather than fewer primary social goods and that people have highest order interests in choosing, revising, and pursuing their conceptions of the good and in the development of their sense of justice.

Focus, for the moment, on the idea of primary social goods. These, as noted in Chapter 4, are 'rights and liberties, opportunities and powers, income and wealth' (Rawls 1971: 92), and a sense of self-respect (1971: § 67). This list is determined by two considerations: primary social goods are things 'that a rational man wants whatever else he wants' (1971: 92), and they reflect a 'social division of responsibility' between the institutions of the basic structure and citizens (see Rawls 1982*a*: esp. 168–70). That is, in addition to being things on which there could be general agreement as to their desirability, they are things which it is reasonable to expect to be matters for the public domain; for distribution by the institutions of the basic structure.[5] Having thus established the distribuand, principles of distributive justice can be chosen that reflect certain 'facts', where the process

---

[4] The possibility of there being another kind of justification for the restriction follows from the rejection of the negative harm principle as a theorem of impartial justice.

[5] For a discussion of the significance of the second requirement of primary social goods—that they are things which it is reasonable to expect to be subject to distribution by the basic structure—see Scanlon 1999: 243–5.

of choosing principles is a process of assigning weight to these facts as reasons. Amongst these are, of course, facts about the world (the objective circumstances of justice) and about people (the subjective circumstances). The construction of the situation, and the reasoning engaged in by the people in the situation, is designed to weed out those facts that are arbitrary from a moral point of view.

Clearly, in considering justice broadly conceived many of the same facts will be relevant to the construction. Others, such as that humans can feel pain, that they are vulnerable to attack, and so on, will play a more significant part in the deliberation. Lists of the features of agents and the world in which they live that shape the nature of morality are common to a wide variety of philosophers, and clearly the quotation given from Barry above is part of another contribution.[6] The difficulty arises in the construction of rules of justice that are consonant with the aspiration of justificatory neutrality. In part, such a difficulty should be expected for what many moral systems have in common is that they are attempts to deal with many (or all) of the conditions described by Rawls as the circumstances of justice. What separates them is the different significance they give to certain features. Agreeing on the significance of a given fact in moral argument, then, is likely to raise the question of whether the procedure privileges (or discounts) a particular view of human excellence.

Consider some examples. A feature of human agents on which there is likely to be agreement is that they are capable of feeling offended. However, the significance of offence is different amongst different cultures and between conceptions of the good. Given that there is also likely to be disagreement about the significance of human beings' expressive powers, the relative weight of considerations of offence and of freedom of expression may be a subject of legitimate disagreement.[7] Perhaps more significantly,

---

[6] Hart, for example, offers the following 'simple truisms' about human beings and the world that they encounter in part as an explanation of the similarity between systems of law and of morality (both attempt to address these facts). He acknowledges both Hobbes and Hume in their formulation. Human beings: desire security, but are vulnerable to attack and to harm by others; are approximately equal in their talents, abilities, and vulnerabilities and thus all can benefit from systems of restraint and co-operation; act mostly out of self-interest (or, cannot be relied on to act altruistically) and, therefore, cannot be relied upon to sustain co-operative practices that require their restraining the pursuit of their self-interest; encounter a world in which there are scarce resources; are fallible and do not possess perfect information; are not always capable of controlling their behaviour on the basis of the understanding and knowledge that they do have (Hart 1994: 190–3).

[7] Brian Barry argues, in relation to the issue of abortion, that where an 'issue cannot be pre-empted by an appeal to justice' justice had better 'abandon the field' (1998: 208–11). As he does not think this the case for the examples given in the text this should not affect the

many practices belonging to different conceptions of the good involve deprivations and suffering, often in the pursuit of some form of spiritual purity. Disputes over the significance of human vulnerability may range from those for whom a life of total security is a life without point or inter-est—such a view may be taken by those who endorse a martial conception of the good or by those for whom phrases of the 'better to live one day as a lion than a thousand as a mouse' sort have a particular resonance—to those who believe that the ability to suffer is a gift from God, and those for whom some act is sanctioned (or even demanded) as part of living a good life which, perhaps incidentally, involves the deliberate infliction of suffer-ing.

Into this last category fall perhaps the most difficult—certainly the most discussed—cases, the most extreme of which are such things as female gen-ital mutilation, widow immolation, and so on. These involve the infliction of damage on the subject's body in ways which in another context would no doubt be considered, even by those who endorse the practices them-selves, as harmful. The difficulty is that in context they are thought by some not merely to be not harmful, but to be in the interests of those who undergo these ordeals. Using public power to prohibit such acts appears partial; it seems to deny the validity of the beliefs which underpin these practices. However, the impartialist would appear to have a response. Given that even those who approve of such practices would accept that the deliberate infliction of pain or death is in general harmful, and given that they can only defend such practices with reference to a particular compre-hensive conception of the good, they cannot deny that such practices can be prohibited by a justificatorily neutral state. Thus, although the outcome is not consequentially neutral (the demands of these groups are cut back further than the demands of less extreme groups), the use of public power is not justified by appeal to some conception of the good (cf. Barry 1995*a*: 75–9).

This argument captures the spirit of impartialism. Those who wish to 'veto' the use of public power must be able to justify their so doing on grounds that can be expressed in public reason. Those whose defence of their traditional practices appeals to rich, comprehensive, conceptions of the good cannot expect such arguments to be convincing to others.

argument. If, for example, differences over the weighting of different interests are reason-able, it may be that the impartialist could employ this strategy and leave the matter to indi-vidual discretion or some just decision-making procedure. However, this would limit the role of justice in an unacceptable manner, and would profoundly change the approach impartialists would have to take to the question of the legitimacy of the use of public power.

Prohibitions of deliberate killing or maiming can be justified by appeal to public reason, to 'thin' facts about human flourishing to which all agree; exceptions to those prohibitions to make space for genital mutilation or widow immolation cannot be so justified.

However, given that impartialists wish to respect the diversity inherent in the reasonableness of pluralism, this argument appears to miss an important point about the possibility of similar acts having different meanings in different cultures and between different conceptions of the good.[8] Whilst all might agree that the painful mutilation of bodily parts is in general harmful and can justly be prohibited, it is not clear that those whose traditional practices involve such things as cliterodectamy accept that it is captured by this description. This is not to say that there are no 'facts of the matter'. Assume that cliterodectamy is painful, risky, and imposes long-term suffering on a normal subject. These are 'facts', for sure, but the point of the constructivist procedure is to assign weight to these facts as reasons (initially, to convert some facts about human physiology into claims about 'harm'). No number of facts about physiology can compel the conclusion that the practice is harmful and ought to be prohibited. This is a moral claim, one that requires that these facts be fitted together with a notion of how a human life goes well (or, at least, how it goes badly).

Of course, the impartialist claims to have access to such an account in the agreed, thin theory of the good. However, the 'thinness' of this account is brought into question in cases such as these. This point is made clearer by considering how the argument appears to the proponents of some traditional practice that involves the deliberate infliction of suffering. The impartialist theorist claims that an act that involves the deliberate infliction of suffering is generally harmful and on that basis can be prohibited and public power can legitimately be used to prevent such acts occurring. The 'traditionalist' claims that some given act does involve suffering, but this is not harmful (indeed, it is beneficial), and it would be illegitimate to use public power to prevent it. It is a different kind of act in the context from some mere deliberate infliction of harm. The impartialist's response is that the account of the act in which it is beneficial and not harmful is an account that appeals to some controversial, comprehensive, conception of the good and, thus, is inadmissible in the constructivist procedure. The impartialist, that is, claims that whilst what the traditionalist says may be true, it cannot be justified to others who disagree.

---

[8] This kind of argument is commonly associated with communitarian writers, particularly Michael Walzer (see Walzer 1983), although for the purposes of the argument given in the text it is not necessary to endorse the use to which Walzer puts the point.

The admission by the impartialist that what is believed by the tradition-alist may be true, and that questions of its truth or validity are not the basis for judgement about the use of public power, may come as scant consola-tion to the traditionalist, but for the moment consider the further objec-tion of the traditionalist that there is an account of the good which is being privileged here, one in which bodily integrity is not only interpreted a par-ticular way, but is given priority over other interests (such as the ability to live without shame). The point is this: the impartialist claim that all—or almost all—would agree that human beings are capable of suffering and that the deliberate infliction of suffering is in general deleterious does not fix what is to count as the infliction of harm and, thus, what is to count as a legitimate basis for the use of public power. This requires agreement not merely on certain 'facts', but on their significance and the impartialist claim that there is such agreement is unsustainable.[9]

It is in part the extension of the scope of justice that undermines the jus-tificatory neutrality of the account. Extending the scope from justice nar-rowly conceived to questions of right and wrong, specifically to questions of harm, means that the impartialist needs an agreed account of human interests, and their ranking, that goes beyond the interests relevant to dis-tributive justice on which impartialist theory has focused. The more that is needed in the construction of the situation and in determining the decision procedures of the agents located in the situation, the less plausible the claim of thinness. It is perhaps for this reason that impartialists have focused on distributive justice. However, the argument of this and the last chapter is that impartialists need the broader account of justice in consid-ering the use of public power both for completeness and because in many instances it is the broader account that is most plausible in defending, or in denying the legitimacy of, the use of public power.[10]

The problem highlighted by the extension of justice beyond the distrib-utive sphere concerns the assumptions that go into the construction of the

---

[9] Scanlon's account, which has a similar structure, does not depend on finding agree-ment between people whilst avoiding reference to the truth, validity, plausibility, etc. of par-ticular conceptions of the good. Rather, in Scanlon's account the construction of rules of 'what we owe to each other' has available the full repertoire of 'best available reasons' (cf. Matravers 2000*b*).

[10] In defending his position against quasi-perfectionist criticisms, Barry writes, 'suppose that people did all agree on a number of things being good. This would still not get us very far unless they also agreed on the relative priority to be attached to these good things. In the absence of this kind of agreement, nothing of an action guiding kind can be said to follow from propositions such as those advanced by my critics to the effect that everybody could reasonably agree such-and-such is a good thing' (1998: 230). Quite so.

'situation' in impartialist theory. It is argued in the next section that this is part of a more significant problem with the structure of the impartialist account, whether limited to the distributive sphere or not.

## The foundations of justice broadly conceived

Recall (from Chapter 4) that justice as impartiality uses the idea of the contract in order to determine the content of the duty to treat others as equals. The shape of the 'situation' is determined by a pre-contractual moral commitment to the equality of agents.[11] Moreover, the nature of the situation and the rationality of the parties located within it reflects commitments concerning what is to count as morally relevant and what morally arbitrary. The point of the contract is, in Rawls's words, to make the argument 'vivid' (Rawls 1971: 18) and to 'say that a certain conception of justice would be chosen in the original position is equivalent to saying that rational deliberation satisfying certain conditions and restrictions would reach a certain conclusion' (1971: 138). In part, the argument concerning harm above aims to show that as the scope of justice increases the chances of finding an account that is compatible with the demand of justificatory neutrality of what is morally arbitrary and what morally relevant, and of the weight that is to be assigned to those things that are relevant, decreases.

Whereas the focus of the argument so far has been the claim of justificatory neutrality, the remainder of the chapter is concerned more with the nature of impartialist justice; its accounts of motivation and of punishment. After all, whether justificatorily neutral or not, the impartialist offers an account of wrong and of the kind of injunctive rules that are discussed in Chapter 4 that is worth taking seriously. To do this it is necessary to return to the *faux* constructivist structure of justice as impartiality.

If the purpose of the construction is to 'make vivid' an argument or, at best, to boil down general commitments to specific principles, a question arises as to the status of what goes into the construction. This is an important question because it determines the limit of what such a constructivist procedure seeks to establish and because it has a profound effect on what account of motivation is needed. Moreover, the relationship of what goes into the construction and the motivation of those who are to be regulated by the principles that result from it significantly effects the understanding of the place of coercion and of punishment in the theory.

---

[11] An interpretation of Rawls's recent work that is consistent with this claim is offered below.

The most general, and significant, premiss of justice as impartiality is the claim of the fundamental equality of agents (for the moment whether persons or citizens). It is this that makes the constructivism of impartialist theories a *faux* constructivism, for the moral claims that are generated by it stem from this premiss. In what follows a number of ways of understanding this premiss and their associated accounts of motivation are examined. In part, the strategy employed is to consider the place of coercion and punishment in *faux* constructivist theory. The argument is that the assumption of equality, and the *faux* nature of the construction, mean that the principles of justice that emerge from the situation take the form of alien restrictions on the pursuit of the individual's good. The threat, and imposition, of sanctions is required to close the gap between the principles of justice and agents' reasons for action. This gives rise to an inadequate account of punishment (the structure of which must replicate the failed structure of one or other of the theories examined in the first three chapters above).

## THE PREMISS OF EQUALITY AND THE QUESTION OF MOTIVATION

One way to interpret the claim of equality that underpins *faux* constructivist theories is as a premiss for which no further argument can be given. Brian Barry endorses this, stating, 'I do not know of any way of providing a justification for the premise of fundamental equality: its status is that of an axiom' (Barry n.d.: 6). Barry is not afraid to put this to work. In responding to theories that link individuals' claims to the protection of justice to their contribution to a reciprocal scheme of co-operation, he argues that 'justice as impartiality, in contrast, makes the basis of justice reside in our common humanity. Human beings can make a claim to fundamental equality of moral status'. Moreover, lest there be any doubt of the importance of this commitment in defining the *faux* constructivist 'situation', the passage continues, 'and that notion is instantiated in a situation for choosing principles of justice that embodies the values of freedom and equality' (Barry 1998: 222–3).

At its most robust, then, the equality premiss is a claim about the moral equality of human beings that has the status of an axiom. The principles of justice that emerge from the situation provide (more) detail about what is required of moral agents in their treatment of one another. The claim to justificatory neutrality applies to the explication of the equality claim, not to the claim itself. That is, it would be unjust to understand what it is to treat another as an equal in terms that appeal to a particular conception of the good. Those who simply deny that human beings have equal status and thus reject the *faux* constructivist procedure stand outside the theory and their complaint that the procedure is not impartial is of a different kind from that of groups who accept that human beings are equal, but whose interpretation of this they believe to be illegitimately discounted by the impartialist.

For the moment put to one side the issue of whether to treat the equality premiss thus is to forgo confronting the question of justification, and consequently is to ensure that *faux* constructivists and constructivists will talk past one another (an issue discussed in Chapter 6 below). Focus, instead, on the question of motivation. If the moral obligation to treat others as equals is given then this raises a question of how moral obligations connect to the motivation of agents. What precludes an agent from accepting the account of justice, but denying that rules of justice have any significance for him? This is not a psychological question about what does, in fact, motivate agents to behave in one way or another. Rather, it is a question of what one has reason to do. Moral propositions are in part propositions about what one has reason to do or not to do.

In addressing the question of motivation, Barry posits an 'agreement motive' that, he says, 'plays a central role in contemporary arguments for justice as impartiality in all its forms' (Barry 1995*a*: 165). This motive is 'the desire to live in a society whose members all freely accept its rules of justice and its major institutions' (1995*a*: 164). In the Scanlonian variant that Barry favours, the account of motivation is as follows: 'the source of motivation that is directly triggered by the belief that an action is wrong is the desire to be able to justify one's actions to others [who are similarly motivated] on grounds they could not reasonably reject' (Scanlon 1982: 117; but see n. 12 below). Although the reference to 'directly triggered' muddies the water somewhat, Barry is an externalist (cf. Barry 1989: 8). That an action is just or unjust provides a reason for the agent to perform or not to perform it only given an additional desire; the desire to be able to justify her actions to similarly motivated others on grounds that they could not reasonably reject. In this context 'directly triggered' simply means that it is recognizing that something is just that provides direction for the agent's actions given the desire to be just.

As it stands this is simply a psychological claim—people either do or do not possess the relevant desire—and in its absence it is not clear what kind of criticism, if any, is appropriate. Even the claim that most people do in fact possess this desire—a claim that both Barry and Scanlon make (Barry 1995*a*: § 26; Scanlon 1982: 117)—falls short of addressing the issue raised by persons who do not give this desire priority over other desires (for example, over the desire to advance their good). It is clear that many people, much of the time, fail to act justly. They may feel bad about this, and this may be because they believe that they ought to give priority to the demands of justice and not to their desire for greater personal advancement, but the account given has no explanation of why such people ought to feel bad. At worst they have behaved irrationally by not doing what they most want to do, but this is surely the wrong kind of criticism for it puts the desire to act justly on a par with other desires and simply stipulates that, contrary to the way most people act at least some of the time, it is always a stronger desire. However, what must be sought is an account of why the motivation triggered by the recognition that something is just is of a different kind, not a different strength, from other desires.[12]

Before considering such an account, it is worth pausing to examine the stability of a society based on the above and the role of coercion and sanctions within it. Barry makes much of the problem of stability in the theory of justice as mutual advantage, which he considers to be the main rival to justice as impartiality. In brief, the argument is that mutual advantage theories posit agents who are motivated by self-interest and thus the motivation to defect from the agreement is continuous with the motivation to enter the agreement. Given this, Barry argues that 'a self-interested person will comply with the terms of agreement to co-operate only when the probability of being found out and penalized is high enough to make cheating a bad bet' (Barry 1998: 216) and that no such system of penalties is feasible. This is not merely a matter of there not being enough policemen who are reliable. It is also a consequence of the failure of justice as mutual advantage to be able to make sense of the moral condemnation of offenders and their subsequent remorse, as against mere penalties that invoke regret at being caught or at having miscalculated what would best further one's self-interest (cf. Barry 1995*a*: 34–7, Chapter 6 below). If the characterization of justice as mutual advantage is accurate then this is surely right; no society that relies solely on prudential sanctions will be stable.

---

[12] It is worth noting that Scanlon has changed his position on motivation in response to worries of the kind expressed above. He says in the introduction to *What We Owe To Each Other* (1999) that the account of motivation in terms of desire 'proved untenable' when pressed about whether 'a person who lacked this desire would have any reason to avoid acting wrongly, and to explain how I would account for the fact that lacking this desire is a particularly serious fault' (Scanlon 1999: 7).

However, it is not clear that a theory of justice as impartiality that relies on the simple desire-based account of moral motivation given above is in a better position than its mutual advantage competitor. Those who give priority to their own interests over their desire to act justly similarly need to be deterred from so doing if the society is to be stable, but there is no scope for moral communication in punishment or for any confidence that the offender will be, or can be brought to be, remorseful.[13] In order for that to be achieved what is needed is an account of the moral fault of the offender in not giving priority to the demands of justice. That is, what is needed is a more sophisticated account of motivation.

## Fair play and reciprocity

The above account gives justice as impartiality a structure in which the demands of justice are derived from an axiom of the fundamental equality of human beings, but in which these demands appear to lack any connection to the agents who are to be regulated by them. The attempt to fill this 'gap'[14] is made using a desire, but this fails to meet the challenge of explaining the nature of the fault of not having the desire, or of not giving it priority. It might appear that one possibility would be to appeal to considerations of fair play. As each agent participates in the social structure, and benefits from it, the failure to act in accordance with its demands is a failure to play fair (or, in other terms, a failure to meet the demands of reciprocity). Moreover, as the regulations that govern the structure instantiate a moral claim of the equality of agents, fair play theory in this instance may be able to account for the moral nature of the condemnation of free-riders, which it is alleged in Chapter 2 is missing from those fair play accounts that are disconnected from some constructivist base.

[13] If it is assumed that the desire to act from the priority of justice will be effective in motivating those agents who possess it only in circumstances in which they are reasonably sure that others will also comply then the threat of penal sanctions in response to non-compliance will have an 'assurance role' in a society regulated by justice as impartiality. The advantage that justice as impartiality has over justice as mutual advantage is, according to Barry, that whereas in justice as mutual advantage the motivation to defect is continuous with the concern for mutual advantage, in justice as impartiality the principles of justice are grounded in fairness and the motivation appealed to is the desire to be fair (see n. 15 below). However, this advantage is only realized if people not only have a desire to be fair, but give that desire regulative priority. By basing the account of motivation on such a desire, justice as impartiality leaves itself without the resources to criticize or evoke remorse in someone whose desire to be fair does not have such priority.

[14] I borrow this term from G. A. Cohen's review of Thomas Nagel's *Equality and Partiality* (Cohen 1992). Nagel discusses the problem of moral motivation in terms of 'personal' and 'impersonal' standpoints (Nagel 1991).

The difficulty is that as long as the structure of the theory remains the same, the motivation to play fair takes the place of—or is perhaps just a variant of—the desire to be able to justify one's actions to others (similarly motivated) on grounds that those others could not reasonably reject. An agent who lacks the desire to play fair, or who fails to give it priority in his dealings with others, presents the same problem as the agent who lacks the Scanlonian desire given above. The apparent difference between the two accounts lies in the evocation of reciprocity in fair play theory. The agent has benefited from co-operation and this connects the agent and the scheme of rules that regulate and make it possible. However, this cannot simply be wheeled in at this point. After all, there is no actual contract, or actual promise, in the *faux* constructivist account. If the reciprocal element in fair play theory is to do any work what must be explained is the place of reciprocity in the reasoning of the agent.

Although Barry cites John Rawls's *A Theory of Justice* as an exemplar of impartialist theorizing in both volumes of his *Treatise on Social Justice* (1989, 1995a) part of the point of the first volume of the *Treatise, Theories of Justice*, is to make clear that Rawls unsuccessfully combines elements of both justice as impartiality and justice as mutual advantage. The crucial claim shared by Rawls and a justice as mutual advantage theorist such as David Gauthier is that justice is a product of co-operation for mutual advantage. Of course, although they share this claim, what separates Rawls and Gauthier is that Rawls stipulates that the principles of distribution must be determined from a position of fundamental equality; from behind the veil of ignorance. This gives rise to tensions in the Rawlsian account that are arguably not found in Gauthier's theory, which does not impose any such moralized restrictions, and that are not found in Barry's account, which rejects the claim that is held in common between Rawls and Gauthier (see Barry 1989: parts ii and iii, Barry 1998: 217).

Rawls's reasons for combining constructivist and *faux* constructivist elements in his account are linked to his trying to develop an adequate account of motivation. However, in what might be called its pure form, justice as impartiality eschews any reference to mutual advantage. Whereas in justice as mutual advantage the starting point is with fully informed individuals who enter into co-operation for mutual advantage and who, thus, enter into bargaining in which they try to further their interests relative to some non-agreement point, the *faux* constructivism of justice as impartiality does not give any role to the non-agreement point and thus gives no role to bargaining (Barry 1998: 225). Instead, the baseline is given by the fundamental equality of agents and their entitlements are to be established by the principles that emerge from a fair situation (in which—and, of course, here Rawls falls squarely in the impartialist camp—there is no bargaining, but simply the representation of a process of reasoning from certain premises and restrictions to a certain outcome). Reciprocity, then, plays no part in the foundations of pure justice as impartiality.[15]

The absence of considerations of reciprocity from the impartialist theory is obscured by the metaphor of the 'contract', in other words, by the constructivist appearance of *faux* constructivism. These metaphors have traditionally suggested both a method for agreeing on principles of justice and a means of explaining moral motivation. The agent, standing back from her commitments and asking what principles should guide her behaviour, conceives of herself in a state of nature and asks what she would agree to in co-operation with others. However, as Dworkin famously put it, 'a hypothetical contract is not simply a pale form of an actual contract; it is no contract at all' (Dworkin 1989: 18). The metaphor of the contract suggests a motivational link between the demands of justice and the agents whose co-operation is to be regulated by them, but whatever is implied by this language, this is not, as is made clear above, the structure of *faux* constructivist theories. In *faux* constructivism, the role of the construction is simply to represent an argument from certain premises to certain conclusions given certain restrictions. It is this that means that there is nothing to tie persons to the principles of justice, which emerge as moral commands derived from a foundational claim of equality. Even if the agent accepts the *faux* constructivist account of what justice demands, there is nothing in the procedure that gives the agent reason to accord priority to these demands. The invocation to play fair may give content or direction to those who desire to do only what can be justified to others, but it cannot provide a reason to adopt, and give priority to, that desire.

---

[15] In *Justice as Impartiality* Barry writes that justice as mutual advantage and justice as impartiality are distinguishable by looking at their underlying game theoretic structure. The former has the structure of a prisoner's dilemma and the latter of an assurance game (1995*a*: 51). However, describing both in game theoretic terms threatens to hide the most significant difference between the two approaches. The game theoretic structure of justice as mutual advantage applies both to the derivation and justification of the content of justice and to the analysis of the motivation of the parties. Game theory is not relevant to the derivation and justification of the content of justice in theories of justice as impartiality. Moreover, the use of the assurance game is relevant to the question of motivation only if it is assumed that the desire to be able to justify one's actions to others similarly motivated will be less effective in motivating those who possess it in circumstances where few people possess it. In short, for justice as mutual advantage theorists, in the absence of agreement there is no justice. For justice as impartiality theorists, justice is given independently of agreement.

It might be thought that the place of reciprocity in *faux* constructivism is revealed in the demand that the principles be publicly justifiable. If principles of justice are, for example, the product of a Scanlonian procedure of asking what could not be rejected by agents who are motivated to find terms on which they can live together with other agents similarly motivated then reciprocity finds a home in the last clause. However, it must be remembered that the construction is, in Barry's words, 'to be done by a theorist' (see Chapter 4 above). Rules of justice, then, depend on what could reasonably be justified to entirely hypothetical others. They are not the product of co-operation.

Where reciprocity does play a role, then, is in the account of the desire to be just that is deployed by *faux* constructivists to fill the gap between the demands of justice and the agent. In a society in which many people are free-riding on the restraint of others, or in which it is believed that this is the case, the desire to be just is unlikely to be strong. This is an important point, but it is important to recognize that it is also a contingent claim about what motivates people. The demands of justice apply to individuals in such a society, it is only that they are unlikely to be obeyed. The contrast with constructivism is stark. For the constructivist, in the absence of agreement there is no justice (see n. 15 above).

The problem of what reasons people have (once the veil of ignorance is lifted, so to speak) to give priority to the demands of justice has motivated a great deal of Rawls's recent, and not so recent, work. In the remainder of the chapter the focus is on that work. This is not a matter of Rawls exegesis for its own sake. Over the last thirty years, Rawls has canvassed, and often combined, a number of arguments concerning motivation. In looking to his work, then, the purpose is to examine a number of different possible positions. For this reason, too, the arguments that Rawls deployed in 1971, some of which he has subsequently retracted, are given their place in the discussion. In short, Rawls offers two kinds of argument. In the first, he attempts to show that there is reason to give priority to justice. In the second, he tries to dissolve the conflict between the demands of justice and the pursuit of individual interest.

## THE SEARCH FOR CONGRUENCE[16]

In part iii of *A Theory of Justice* Rawls offers a preliminary account of 'goodness as fairness'. Chapter 8 largely considers moral psychology and the ways in which agents acquire the motivation to give priority to the demands of justice. In chapter 9, as the book reaches its conclusion, Rawls states that 'it remains to be shown that [the] disposition to take up and to be guided by the standpoint of justice accords with the individual's good' (Rawls 1971: 567). Rawls is not concerned with the project of justifying morality to an egoist. Rather, he assumes that each individual possesses a sense of justice and a conception of the good. Each, then, can assess the institutions of the basic structure, the actions she performs or is called upon to perform, and her plan of life using criteria both of justice and of goodness. 'The question of congruence', as Rawls puts it, 'is whether these two families of criteria fit together' (1971: 567).

Rawls is concerned with this question because he takes it to be essential to the (right kind of) stability of a well-ordered society. On the face of it, this concern might seem unnecessary, for as Rawls himself says, 'being the sorts of persons they are, the members of a well-ordered society desire more than anything to act justly and fulfilling this desire is part of their good' (1971: 569). Nevertheless, the problem of congruence arises given that an agent might not give priority to the demands of justice, but instead might treat the desire to be just as merely another desire to be weighed in the balance when deciding how to act. Just persons must give a 'regulative' (1971: 570) place to the demands of justice, and only if they do so will the well-ordered society achieve stability for the right reasons.

Rawls offers three kinds of reasons that support congruence. First, our failing to act justly will have costs for those we care about and 'wanting to be fair with our friends and wanting to give justice to those we care for is as much part of these affections as the desire to be with them and to feel sad at their loss'. Moreover, 'in a well-ordered society these bonds extend rather widely' (1971: 570–1). Second, 'it follows from the Aristotelian Principle

---

[16] In writing this section I have drawn on work done at the LSE at a time when Brian Barry was working on similar questions and at York when Susan Mendus was doing the same. I am grateful to both of them for many conversations about the twists and turns of Rawls's argument in the closing pages of *A Theory of Justice*. I have also drawn on Barry's subsequent article (1995*b*) and Susan Mendus's later paper (1999). In this section the focus is largely on Rawls's argument for congruence as given in the Kantian interpretation. Much of what Rawls says in chapters 8 and 9 of *A Theory of Justice* can be used in the construction of another account, which is examined briefly below.

(and its companion effect), that participating in the life of a well-ordered society is a great good' (1971: 571).[17] Third, there is the Kantian interpretation: 'acting justly is something we want to do as free and equal rational beings. The desire to act justly and the desire to express our nature as free moral persons turn out to specify what is practically speaking the same desire' (1971: 572).

Describing these as the 'chief reasons . . . for maintaining one's sense of justice' (1971: 572), Rawls considers the question of whether they are (together or separately) 'decisive'. It is clear that the argument that guarantees decisiveness, and secures congruence, is given by the Kantian interpretation. This requires some interpretation for, if the 'desire to act justly' and the 'desire to express our nature as free moral persons' are 'practically . . . the same' and the problem is that the first desire is not final (decisive), then the second, Kantian desire can only add to the argument if the Kantian 'desire to express our nature as free moral persons' necessarily is (or ought to be) a final, decisive, desire. If this is right then the Kantian element in *A Theory of Justice* is much more than an interpretation, it is a metaphysical claim about the nature of persons that explains the reason agents have to give priority to the demands of justice. Rawls certainly gives considerable textual evidence for this interpretation. He states that 'the desire to express our nature as a free and equal rational being can be fulfilled only by acting on the principles of right and justice as having first priority. . . . it is acting from this precedence that expresses our freedom from contingency and happenstance' (1971: 574).[18]

Of course, the problem with invoking the Kantian argument to account for stability is that it involves a commitment to a particular, comprehensive conception of human flourishing, and such a commitment is incompatible with the justificatory neutrality that motivates the theory. Thus the Kantian interpretation is an unacceptable basis for stability in a well-ordered society, and it is clear from Rawls's recent work that his commitment to the Kantian interpretation in addressing the problem of stability is a cause of his dissatisfaction with *A Theory of Justice*, which he now

---

[17] 'The Aristotelian Principle is as follows: other things equal, human beings enjoy the exercise of their realized capacities (their innate or trained abilities), and this enjoyment increases the more the capacity is realized, or the greater its complexity' (Rawls 1971: 426).

[18] Cf. Rawls 1971: 575: 'We cannot . . . express our nature by following a plan that views the sense of justice as but one desire to be weighed against others. For this sentiment reveals what the person is, and to compromise it is not to achieve for the self free reign but to give way to the contingencies and accidents of the world'. Other passages on 574 and 476 support the interpretation given in the text (cf. Barry 1995b: 886–7). The passage quoted in the text is understood differently by Mendus (1999).

describes as invoking a 'comprehensive philosophical doctrine' (Rawls 1993: p. xviii).

However, Rawls's commitment to a characterization of persons as realizing their true natures in giving priority to the demands of justice is not straightforward. Even given the Kantian claims that he makes, Rawls admits that there will be 'those who find that being disposed to act justly is not a good for them' (Rawls 1971: 576). For such people 'it is, of course, true that in their case just arrangements do not fully answer to their nature, and therefore, other things equal, they will be less happy than they would be if they could affirm their sense of justice' (1971: 576). Given Rawls's attitude to the arbitrariness of both genetic and social factors it might be expected that such people would be entitled to compensation or special consideration. However, this is not the case. Rawls concludes the passage just quoted by stating: 'but here one can only say: their nature is their misfortune.'

This has interesting implications for the place of punishment in *A Theory of Justice*. Those whose natures are such that they cannot affirm their sense of justice will have to be coerced. However the integrity of the two principles eases the moral burden on those who are going to have to coerce them (cf. Honig 1993: 137–48; Barry 1995*b*: 888). 'Requiring [those who cannot affirm their sense of justice] to comply', Rawls says, 'is not treating these persons unjustly' because 'having agreed to the [two] principles . . . it is rational to authorize the measures needed to maintain just institutions' (Rawls 1971: 575). Thus, punishment is morally worry free for those doing the punishing even if 'there are many' people unable to affirm their sense of justice. Of course, in such circumstances 'the forces making for stability are weaker' and 'penal devices will play a much larger role in the social system' (1971: 576).

These are difficult passages. Rawls's position is that the argument for the two principles is free standing. Those who reject this argument, then, are to be engaged with using the resources of the first two parts of *A Theory of Justice*. Those who accept the argument for the two principles must accept that even in a well-ordered society there will be a need for penal devices to assure the participants in the society that others are 'doing their bit' (an argument that Rawls makes explicitly, see 1971: 240). Those who accept the argument for the two principles, but whose conception of the good precludes congruence, are liable to punishment. However, this does not explain why Rawls holds these people responsible for their inability to affirm their sense of justice, and thus is unconcerned for their suffering (as a result of a feature of themselves that might be taken to be arbitrary from a moral point of view). The question is, why is criminality different from, say, indolence?

Bonnie Honig argues that the difference between indolence and criminality lies in the Kantian reading of Rawls. Criminality is different, argues Honig, because whilst our talents, abilities, and liabilities are contingent parts of us, our ability to 'affirm our sense of justice' reveals who we are and is thus subject to a 'brute' notion of desert:

> The mesmerizing pull of desert is not finally overcome by Rawls's critique; it returns to haunt justice as fairness when Rawls reaches for antecedent moral worth (or unworthiness) to account for the presence of criminality in a just regime and to justify its punishment. In so doing, he relies on desert to serve its traditional function: it explains the inexplicable, it makes sense of evil and justifies our dealing harshly with it. . . . Rawls, because he does not acknowledge desert's return, makes no provisions for its engagement. (Honig 1993: 131)

Honig's interpretation can claim some textual support from one passage of *A Theory of Justice*, discussed below, but in general her appeal to preinstitutional desert gains little support from the text. Honig is right to think that Rawls differentiates between agents' talents etc. and their capacity to regulate and revise their ends in light of the demands of justice, but wrong to think that this reveals something in particular about Rawls's account of punishment, or about his views on things 'evil' or 'inexplicable'. In the passages cited above from the closing passages of *A Theory of Justice* there is no mention of desert or of a retributive account of punishment. Punishment is explicitly referred to as needed to 'maintain . . . the principles of justice' (Rawls 1971: 576). What explains Rawls holding those who cannot affirm their sense of justice responsible is not that this is part of some pre-institutional commitment to desert, which would inform the construction of a desert-based system of punishment. Rather, these people are held responsible in accordance with Rawls's account of 'legitimate expectations'. Rawls argues that once the rules of justice are up and running persons must revise their choices of ends so that their ends are compatible with their legitimate expectations. 'Citizens (as individuals) and associations accept . . . responsibility for revising and adjusting their ends and aspirations . . . this . . . relies on the capacity of persons to assume responsibility for their ends and to moderate the claims they make on their social institutions in accordance with the use of primary goods' (Rawls 1982*a*: 170).[19]

---

[19] Cf. Rawls 1971: 31: 'In justice as fairness . . . persons . . . agree . . . to conform their conceptions of their good to what the principles of justice require, or at least not to press

Rawls's reasons for holding people responsible for their conceptions of the good are complicated. In part, he must do so if he is to generate a resource-based theory from a starting point in which both the social and genetic features of persons are held to be morally arbitrary (cf. Barry 1991*a*). However, his view also follows from his commitment to the congruence of justice and individuals' goods. For, if the agent's reasons for acting in accordance with the demands of justice must be congruent with her interpretation of what advances her good then, given that the demands of justice are fixed in the first part of the theory, the agent must revise her idea of her good in accordance with those demands.[20]

An inability to adapt one's ends in light of the demands of justice will mean that the demands of justice appear to frustrate those ends, and the agent who is so unable will thus be 'less happy' than he would be were he to change his ends. Moreover, if he acts in ways contrary to justice then he may be subject to penal sanctions. Nevertheless, such an agent does not suffer because he deserves to do so—because suffering is an appropriate response to his moral unworthiness as revealed in his failure to give regulative priority to justice—rather, he is liable to what he, and others, legitimately expect given that the principles of justice are public and the demands of justice are known. His nature is his *misfortune*; *pace* Honig, it is of no interest whether it is his *fault*.[21]

What, then, of Rawls's other comments on punishment in *A Theory of Justice*, and specifically the passage that supports Honig's interpretation? As described above, Rawls's account of punishment is consistent with his post-institutional approach to legitimate expectations. Penal sanctions are justified by appeal to the assurance problem (Rawls 1971: § 38), and are

claims which directly violate them. . . . The principles of right, and so of justice, put limits on which satisfactions have value; they impose restrictions on what are reasonable conceptions of one's good'. In fairness to Honig, Rawls goes on to say, 'thus certain initial bounds are placed upon what is good and what forms of character are morally worthy' (1971: 32). However, it is clear from the context that Rawls has in mind the exclusion of those who deny the equality of persons on which the priority of the right over the good is based.

[20] Barry is especially critical of Rawls's argument. Barry's argument is that if an agent desires something as part of her good ('a trip around the world'), but the resources to which she is justly entitled do not allow the satisfaction of this desire, then Rawls is committed to the view that she should revise her ideas of what is in her good (rather than simply believing that whilst such a trip would be good, it is not compatible with the demands of justice). Barry's view is that this is a *reductio* of Rawls's position (Barry 1995*b*: 888–9).

[21] The account given in this and the preceding paragraphs offers, I think, the best account of Rawls's comments on penal sanctions on p. 576 of *A Theory of Justice*. That is not to say that the account is plausible or that it is consistent with the rest of Rawls's book. Whether Rawls's account of the responsibility agents have for their ends is consistent with the argument of ch. 2 of *A Theory of Justice* is a complex question not addressed here.

'needed to maintain just institutions' (1971: 576). As Rawls writes, 'even under reasonably ideal conditions, it is hard to imagine . . . a successful income tax scheme on a voluntary basis. . . . The existence of effective penal machinery serves as men's security to one another' (1971: 240). However, as noted in Chapter 4, Rawls also specifically eschews the comparison between distributive and retributive justice and, crucially, does so in a section on the place of moral desert in the theory. Rawls states:

No doubt some may still contend that distributive shares should match moral worth. . . [and] . . .this opinion may arise from thinking of distributive justice as somehow the opposite of retributive justice. . . . The purpose of the criminal law is to uphold basic natural duties, those which forbid us to injure other persons in their life and limb, or to deprive them of their liberty and property. . . . [It is] not simply a scheme of taxes and burdens designed to put a price on certain forms of conduct and in this way to guide men's conduct for mutual advantage. It would be far better if the acts proscribed by penal statutes were never done. Thus a propensity to commit such acts is a mark of bad character, and in a just society legal punishments will only fall upon those who display these faults. (1971: 314–15)

Samuel Scheffler argues that this passage should not detain the careful reader of *A Theory of Justice*. Rawls's view of retributive justice, he writes, 'is not developed at any length and plays virtually no role in the overall argument of the book'. Moreover, 'it is dubiously consistent with his account of distributive justice'. Scheffler's conclusion is that it is 'a small and insufficiently motivated departure from the general attitude toward desert that dominates [Rawls's] work' (Scheffler 1992: 306 n.). However, even if this particular passage reveals nothing significant about Rawls's theory, its appearance should not be that surprising. Rawls's comments on punishment when in relation to the need for assurance given that there will be individuals who fail to give justice priority do not pose any such interpretative problems. In the above passage Rawls is concerned not with the need for assurance—with tax evasion or the failure to accord the demands of distributive justice their place—but with wrongs of a different sort. In relation to these—the doing of injuries, or the taking of an agent's property, or his freedom—Rawls, as Honig rightly argues, reaches for another kind of account.

The difficulty is that so long as the premiss of moral equality is simply given, and the argument from the Kantian interpretation unavailable, the demands of justice appear as restrictions on agents' pursuits of their self-interest. The threat of punishment fills the gap left when the desire to act justly is not effective. If so, then punishment must take the form of either a device for deterring would-be offenders (changing the calculation of interest) and for assuring those whose desire to act justly is effective only when they believe others to be doing so too, or it must be given some independent, retributive justification. In the troublesome passage from *A Theory of Justice*, Rawls, who for the most part endorses the assurance account appears to realize its limitations and appeal to a retributive theory. The argument of the first three chapters above is that neither of these accounts of punishment is (or could be) successful. In the case of retributive theories their failure is ensured by the problem that also afflicts *faux* constructivist accounts; the separation of the rules that govern individuals from the account of motivation and that of the justification of the threat of sanctions against those who would disobey the rules.

## THE TURN TO THE POLITICAL

Rawls's dissatisfaction with the account of stability offered in part iii of *A Theory of Justice*, and reactions to that work, have prompted him to reconsider the theory in a series of papers and in his 1993 book *Political Liberalism*. It is interesting that although the focus of that book is on the problem of stability, the issue of punishment and the place of penal sanctions receives even less attention than it does in *A Theory of Justice*. It is possible to discern two reasons for this and both are instructive. First, whereas in the earlier work Rawls was concerned with stability in a general sense, in *Political Liberalism* his interest is, for the most part, specifically in the issue of whether the demands of justice can be compatible with those reasonable comprehensive conceptions of the good that exist in the well-ordered society. Second, and even more significant, Rawls's changes to his theory mean that he is no longer as sanguine as he once was about the place of punishment within it.

The shift in Rawls's argument is demonstrated by his changed attitude to the role of penal sanctions. As discussed above, in *A Theory of Justice* Rawls argues that those people who find that they cannot give a regulative place to the demands of justice will need to be threatened with penal sanctions. 'Where there are many' such people, 'penal devices will play a much larger role in the social system' (Rawls 1971: 576, quoted above). However, such people do not threaten the reasonableness of the demands of justice. In *Political Liberalism*, Rawls takes a different approach. In addressing the compatibility of the demands of justice and citizens' reasonable comprehensive conceptions of the good, Rawls now argues that the demands of

justice must be able to be endorsed from within each reasonable conception of the good. This profoundly changes the problem of stability and the
part penal sanctions play in securing it:

The problem of stability is not that of bringing others who reject a conception to
share it, or to act in accordance with it, by workable sanctions, if necessary . . .
Rather justice as fairness is not reasonable in the first place unless in a suitable way
it can win its support by addressing each citizen's reason, as explained within its
own framework. (Rawls 1993: 143)[22]

*Political Liberalism* diverges in a number of ways from Rawls's earlier
work, but it is not necessary to examine all of these, or to consider the independent merits of the later work. The argument above is that Rawls's
attempt to bring together the demands of justice and the interests of those
who are to be regulated by them fails because it relies on a controversial,
Kantian, conception of the person. The place of punishment in the theory
is to secure stability by coercing those who do not give regulative priority
to the demands of justice so as to assure those whose motivation to do so is
dependent for its effectiveness on the belief that others are not free-riding.
Rawls's recent argument is designed to remove one, according to Rawls the
most significant, cause of instability in a well-ordered society. If the principles of justice are capable of winning support from within each reasonable comprehensive conception of the good—if they form the core of an
overlapping consensus (see Rawls 1993: Lecture IV)—then one cause of
instability is removed. Whether principles of justice as fairness (especially
principles of justice broadly conceived) can form the basis of such a consensus is an open question.[23]
    Even if it were the case that the demands of justice could find support
from within each of the reasonable conceptions of the good in society, this
does not provide the basis of an account of the place of punishment.

---

[22] Although Rawls, in a footnote at the end of this passage, explicitly connects this to the
two stages of the argument in *A Theory of Justice*, the argument has changed. Although, in
the earlier work, the principles chosen in the original position had also to pass 'the strains
of commitment' test—that is, the people in the original position 'cannot enter into agreements that may have consequences they cannot accept. They will avoid those that they can
adhere to only with great difficulty. . . . Moreover, when we enter an agreement we must be
able to honor it even should the worst possibilities prove to be the case. Otherwise we have
not acted in good faith. Thus the parties must weigh with care whether they will be able to
stick by their commitment in all circumstances' (Rawls 1971: 176)—this is deployed as an
argument against the demand of utilitarianism 'that some should forgo advantages for the
sake of the greater good of the whole' (1971: 178). It does not challenge the place of penal
sanctions as described in the text above.
[23] Although the argument above concerning the justificatory neutrality of justice
broadly conceived provides reasons to think that finding such a consensus is unlikely.

Punishment is a public matter, and its justification and implementation must appeal to public reasons. What is needed, then, is a public account of the 'fault' of failing to give priority to the demands of justice and of the justification of penal sanctions. As noted, Rawls says little about this in *Political Liberalism*, but his account of the motivation of citizens provides the context in which it can be discussed.

Rawls's argument depends on a conception of reasonable citizens as ready 'to propose and to abide by fair terms of co-operation' (Rawls 1993: 86). Although given more emphasis in *Political Liberalism*, the 'political conception of the person' and its associated 'ideal of citizenship' (1993: 87) has its roots in Rawls's early work.[24] In sum,

i) besides a capacity for a conception of the good, citizens have a capacity to acquire conceptions of justice and fairness and a desire to act as these conceptions require; ii) when they believe that institutions or social practices are just, or fair . . . they are ready and willing to do their part in those arrangements provided they have reasonable assurance that others will also do their part; iii) if other persons with evident intention strive to do their part in just or fair arrangements, citizens tend to develop trust and confidence in them; iv) this trust and confidence becomes stronger and more complete as the success of co-operative arrangements is sustained over a long time; and v) the same is true as the basic institutions framed to secure our fundamental interests (the basic rights and liberties) are more firmly and willingly recognized. (1993: 86)

As noted above, this idea of citizenship is found in Rawls's early work (although it must sometimes be disentangled from the Kantian interpretation). It is, in part, a psychological account of motivation, but it is also an ideal. It offers, therefore, the possibility of an account of the failure to act as a just citizen (and in (ii) above, the basis of an assurance justification of punishment). However, as with its predecessor, it is not clear what kind of fault it is not to give priority to the demands of justice; not to be an ideal citizen. Those who organize in the well-ordered society can see the need for penal sanctions to solve an assurance problem, but this is not an adequate account of punishment and, more than that, it reveals a fault in the account of motivation. Again, it seems that the theory is without an account of what reason the agent has to endorse the demands of justice as regulative of his

---

[24] Reviewing Rawls's *Collected Papers* (1999), Jeremy Waldron comments that 'the leitmotif of Rawls's work has been the idea of well-ordered society' (1999: 3). I think this is right. In particular, Rawls's work is driven by a belief in the possibility of free and equal citizens motivated by a concern to live on fair terms with one another. It is this idea that is developed below with reference to both 'early' and 'late' Rawls.

good; what reason he has to conceive of himself and his ends in accordance with the ideal of citizenship.

Clearly, for reasons discussed above, Rawls cannot appeal to the agent's true nature as a Kantian being (or any other true nature). Instead, Rawls's argument depends on the recognition of the 'good of political life . . . the good of free and equal citizens recognizing the duty of civility to one another' (Rawls 1998: 616). This can be interpreted in a way that offers an alternative vision of Rawls's project, one which may perhaps not resolve the problem of motivation, but which is none the less suggestive of how that problem might be addressed.

### The ideal of a social union[25]

The argument thus far is that justice as impartiality, because of its *faux* constructivist structure, delivers judgements about the content of justice that are derived from an assumption of the fundamental equality of agents.[26] A reflective agent concerned to theorize his relations with others encounters the demands of justice as external restrictions on the pursuit of his good. This gap between the agent and the demands of justice cannot be filled using a conception of human flourishing, because of the need for impartial theory to be impartial, but is, instead, filled by a desire to be just.[27] The result is inadequate because, when challenged, the *faux* constructivist cannot give an account of the failure to have the requisite desire. This is revealed in the resulting account of punishment in which, at best, punishment plays the role of deterring those who would act unjustly and reassuring those who would act justly. However, Rawls's great political good suggests a different idea of what it is to reflect on one's relations with others. The appeal is to an idea of reciprocity that is different from that found in the game theoretic structure of justice as mutual advantage.

Rawls's argument can be presented as an attempt not to solve the problem of motivation, but to dissolve it by showing that the demands of jus-

---

[25] 'The idea of a social union' is taken from Rawls 1971: § 79. It is worth emphasizing that what is presented here is an extension, not an interpretation, of Rawls's argument.

[26] In the case of the later Rawls this assumption takes the form of the 'liberal principle of legitimacy': 'our exercise of political power is fully proper only when it is exercised in accordance with a constitution the essentials of which all citizens as free and equal may reasonably be expected to endorse in the light of principles and ideals acceptable to their common human reason' (Rawls 1993: 137).

[27] Although, of course, the argument of the earlier parts of this chapter is that some account of human flourishing (albeit one that need not be comprehensive) is needed if impartialists are adequately to theorize the public domain.

tice do not conflict with the interests of actual citizens. In other terms, rather than address the self-reflective agent who distances herself from her social ties and considers whether she has reason to co-operate with others on terms that do not treat those others as of only instrumental value to the realization of her good, Rawls can be interpreted as addressing a just agent engaged in the pursuit of self-understanding. An already just agent, reflecting on her relations with others, understands that together with others she is part of the creation of something that she and others together value: the construction of a social union in which 'the members all freely accept its rules of justice and its major institutions' (Barry 1995*a*: 164, quoted above as part of the 'agreement motive').

Although as a psychological picture, and as an ideal of a social union, this has much to commend it—and the brief argument of this section will be drawn on in the presentation of a constructivist theory in Chapters 7 and 8—the argument can appeal only to those agents whose understanding of (at least part of)[28] their own good is such as to be advanced in an ideal of a social union of equal recognition. No doubt, participation in such a society will increase the chances of citizens thinking of themselves in this way (see points (iii), (iv), and (v) in the quotation from Rawls given above). However, the questions of what it is not to do so, and what can be said to commend such an alignment of the individual's good with that of the whole, remain unanswered.

The claim made in Chapter 4 is that in order adequately to theorize the public domain the *faux* constructivist must have an account of wrong (or, of justice broadly conceived). Such an account is available in the construction of rules that appeal to certain 'facts' that are used in determining the shape and outcome of the initial situation. However, this cannot be done in a way that is compatible with the aspiration of impartialist theory to justificatory neutrality. Rather, the account needs agreement on the relevance and weighting of the facts that are to inform the account of wrong. An argument as to how such an account might be generated from within a genuine constructivism is offered below. Does this mean that impartialists insofar as they try to incorporate the account of wrong are genuinely constructivist? No, because the account that they offer begins with an extra-constructivist premiss of the fundamental equal worth of agents. The result is that the demands of justice are disconnected from the personal perspective adopted by the agent and appear to him as alien restrictions on the pur-

---

[28] Of course, the good realized here is only a political good. As such it addresses the reason of persons thinking of themselves as citizens and is non-comprehensive.

suit of his good. Coercion is thus needed to close the gap between morality and self-interest.

The next chapter turns to a genuine constructivist account in an attempt to ground morality in self-interest and thus to show without question that morality can be commended to each individual as rational. The argument is that rational self-interest alone is not sufficient to give a foundation to morality. Nevertheless, if an adequate account of motivation and of punishment is to be found then moral norms must be connected to an account of individual interests. This idea is pursued, using resources borrowed from both the impartialist and mutual advantage approaches in the final chapters, 7–9.

# 6

# Justice as Mutual Advantage

## INTRODUCTION

Whereas impartialist theorists build in a commitment to the fundamental equality of persons and use the social contract 'to express the inherent moral standing of persons . . . [and] . . . to negate, rather than reflect, unequal bargaining power' (Kymlicka 1991: 191; quoted above, Chapter 4) the position with which this chapter is concerned attempts something altogether more ambitious; to derive moral principles from mutual agreement. David Gauthier characterizes the project thus:

Morals by Agreement is an attempt to challenge Nietzsche's prescient remark, 'As the will to truth . . . gains self-consciousness . . . morality will gradually perish'. It is an attempt to write moral theory for adults, for persons who live consciously in a post-anthropomorphic, post-theocentric, post-technocratic world. It is an attempt to allay the fear, or suspicion, or hope, that without a foundation in objective value or objective reason, in sympathy or in sociality, the moral enterprise must fail. (David Gauthier 1988*b*: 385)

This chapter, then, examines an attempt at a genuine constructivism to be contrasted with the *faux* constructivism of impartialists such as Rawls and Barry.[1]

## JUSTICE AS MUTUAL ADVANTAGE

Constructivist theories of justice as mutual advantage begin with the standard model of asking what rational people, characterized in a certain way and placed in a certain situation, would agree to by way of rules (if any) to govern their co-operation (if any). However, unlike *faux* constructivists there is no attempt to build equality and impartiality into the choosing

---

[1] A similar contrast is drawn in Gauthier 1997 (see Ch. 4 n. 1 above).

situation, for to do that is to beg the question by presupposing the moral norms that are supposed to be justified by the agreement. Justice as mutual advantage begins with fully informed individuals who are not motivated to justify their actions to others similarly motivated, but rather who are driven to pursue their own self-interest. It is more ambitious, then, because it is an attempt to ground moral principles given the disenchanted state of the world. As Gauthier describes it, he is 'committed to showing why an individual, reasoning from non-moral premises, would accept the constraints of morality on his choices' (Gauthier 1986: 5). The argument of this chapter is, in part, that Gauthier cannot show that there are rationally compelling reasons such that 'reasoning from non-moral premises' the amoralist can be brought to adopt the 'constraints of morality'. However, in this and the succeeding chapters, it is argued that it is not necessary to show this in order to meet Nietzsche's challenge. The fear that 'the moral enterprise must fail' can be met without having to show that there are rationally compelling reasons for the amoralist to be moral, or so it is argued below.

## Co-operative rules

The first question to be addressed is why rational self-interested beings should think there to be a need for rules of justice. The reasons are similar to those given by Rawls in describing the circumstances of justice (see Chapter 4): the world is such that co-operative endeavours can yield mutual advantage, but there is also sufficient scarcity to ensure disagreement over the correct distribution of the product of co-operation. Given, then, that individual agents consider entering co-operation for mutual advantage, a familiar problem arises. If each agent is motivated by the pursuit of maximal individual self-interest then sub-optimal outcomes might result for reasons that are now well known thanks to the prisoner's dilemma.[2] As Gauthier describes it in a later essay, 'the key idea is that in

---

[2] The prisoner's dilemma is described by Gauthier as follows: 'Fred and Ed have committed (the District Attorney is certain) a serious crime, but some of the evidence needed to ensure a conviction is, unfortunately, inadmissible in the court . . . She is, however, holding Fred and Ed, and has been able to prevent them from being in a position to communicate one with the other. She has booked them on a lesser, although still serious, charge, and she is confident that she can secure their conviction for it. She then calls, separately, on Fred and Ed, telling each the same tale and making each the same offer. 'Confess the error of your ways—and the crime you have committed', she says, 'and if your former partner does not confess, then I shall convince the jury that you are a reformed man and your ex-partner evil incarnate; the judge will sentence you to a year and him to ten. Do not confess, and if your

many situations, if each person chooses what, given the choices of others, would maximize his expected utility, then the outcome would be mutually disadvantageous in comparison with some alternative—everyone could do better' (Gauthier 1991: 22–3).

In such situations an optimal outcome can be reached by each person agreeing to constrain the pursuit of her immediate individual self-interest; that is, through co-operation. However, a problem arises most colourfully expressed by Hobbes's Foole:[3] although it might be rational for an agent to agree to practices of mutual constraint on the direct pursuit of self-interest, 'it is rational to follow such practices only when doing so directly conduces to her maximal preference fulfilment' (Gauthier 1991: 24). In short, because the motivation to defect from agreement is continuous with the motivation to enter the agreement, the rational agent should, it seems, defect and free-ride whenever there are gains associated with doing so and the possibility arises. However, the knowledge that this is the case deters rational agents from making agreements in the first place.

For Gauthier, to meet the challenge of Hobbes's Foole it is necessary to explain how rational persons can commit themselves to mutually constraining agreements. This is to transform agreed rules of co-operation into morals by agreement. The feature of moral rules that Gauthier takes as central is their 'imperatival force'; the fact that they command independent of immediate self-interest. Thus,

the principles forming the object of agreement are those that [an agent] would have accepted *ex ante* in bargaining with his fellows, had he found himself among them in a context initially devoid of moral constraint. Why need he accept, *ex post*

---

partner does, then you may infer your fate. And should neither of you choose to confess, then I shall bring you to trial on this other matter, and you may count on two years.' 'But what', says Fred (or Ed), 'if we both confess?' 'Then', says the District Attorney, 'I shall let justice take its natural course with you—it's a serious crime so I should estimate five years', and without further ado she leaves Ed (or Fred) to solitary reflection.

Both are quite single-mindedly interested in minimizing their time behind bars, and so both represent the situation in this simple way: . . . "If he confesses, then I had better confess—otherwise I'm in for ten years. If he doesn't confess, then if I confess I'm out in a year. So whatever he does, I should confess" ' (Gauthier 1986: 79–80). Both, therefore, confess, and receive five years. This is, of course, a sub-optimal outcome. If neither confessed they would be back on the streets in two.

[3] 'The Foole hath sayd in his heart, there is no such thing as Justice; and sometimes also with his tongue; seriously alleaging, that every mans conservation, and contentment, being committed to his own care, there could be no reason, why every man might not do what he thought conduced thereunto: and therefore also to make, or not make; keep, or not keep Covenants, was not against Reason when it conduced to ones benefit' (Hobbes 1991: ch. 15, 101).

in his actual situation, these principles as constraining his choices? A theory of morals by agreement must answer this question. (Gauthier 1986: 9)[4]

### Straightforward and constrained maximization

According to Gauthier Hobbes's Foole makes two related errors:

First, he fails to understand that real acceptance of such moral practices as assisting one's fellows, or keeping one's promises, or telling the truth is possible only among those who are disposed to comply with them. If my disposition to comply extends only so far as my interests or concerns at the time of performance, then you will be the real fool if you interact with me in ways that demand a more rigorous compliance. . . . The Foole's second error, following on his first, should be clear; he fails to recognize that in plausible circumstances, persons who are genuinely disposed to a more rigorous compliance with moral practices then would follow from their interests at the time of performance can expect to do better than those who are not so disposed. For the former, constrained-maximizers . . . will be welcome partners in mutually advantageous cooperation, in which each relies on the voluntary adherence of the others, from which the latter, straightforward maximizers, will be excluded. (Gauthier 1991: 24–5)

In brief (the argument is discussed more fully below), Gauthier's argument depends on a claim that the parties to possible co-operative agreements have motivations that are 'translucent' (neither opaque nor transparent). That is, they can tell of one another with less than 'certainty' but more than 'mere guesswork' (Gauthier 1986: 174) whether they are disposed to keep their agreements when others are expected also to do so, even where defection promises the greater pay-off (that is, whether they are disposed to 'constrained maximization') or whether they are disposed to maximize their pay-offs, even where that requires defecting from some agreement (that is, whether they are disposed to 'straightforward maximization'). Given translucency, constrained maximizers (CMs) will only enter into agreement with others who they think are also CMs, and not with those they suspect of being straightforward maximizers (SMs). SMs will, of course, be unlikely to enter into agreements with one another. Thus, far greater possibilities for mutually advantageous co-operation can be had by adopting the disposition of constrained maximization and Gauthier claims that it is, therefore, rational to do so.

[4] The question of how agents can trust one another to keep agreements is, of course, not regarded as a problem only for the theory of morals by agreement. Consider Nietzsche's question: 'To breed an animal capable of promising—isn't that just the paradoxical task which nature has set herself with mankind, the peculiar problem of mankind?' (Nietzsche 1956: ii/1, quoted in Hollis 1998: 23).

Gauthier's claim that adopting the disposition of constrained maximization is rational depends on his changing the question from one about the rationality of compliance to one that concerns the rationality of having the disposition to comply. Gauthier's argument is that the straightforward conception of practical rationality is 'self-defeating' and 'it is surely mistaken to treat rational deliberation as self-defeating, if a non-self-defeating account is available' (Gauthier 1994: 702). The point being that straightforward maximization will fail to further the agent's goals all things considered (cf. Margaret Moore 1993: 84; Velleman 1997).

The argument for adopting the disposition of constrained maximization is meant to demonstrate the rationality of being disposed to comply and, thus, of compliance. However, this is not yet enough to ground moral rules, as for that the rules must have some property of fairness or impersonality. The final element of Gauthier's theory requires the inspection of two further features: the baseline from which the agreement is made and the nature of the bargain.

## The baseline and the bargain

If the argument for constrained maximization demonstrates the rationality of being disposed to enter and comply with agreements, the argument that the rules that govern the co-operation that results are moral depends upon showing that they are more than merely rules of co-operation. Consider first the baseline from which agreements are made. Clearly Gauthier cannot build fundamental equality into the baseline (by, for example, insisting that people come to the agreement behind a veil of ignorance). Instead he must show that rational self-interested individuals would accept a non-coercive baseline. He has two arguments in defence of such a claim.

The first is that agreements based on an initial position which itself is a product of coercion (of force or fraud) are inherently unstable. In the parable of the slaves (Gauthier 1986: 190–1) a group of masters decide to offer a deal to their slaves in which the masters agree to free the slaves in return for the latter becoming their willing servants. The proposal has all the appearance of mutual advantage (the slaves gain their freedom and a wage greater than the sum previously spent on keeping them alive. The masters can save on the costs of coercion and will benefit from the enhanced productivity of non-coerced labour). Moreover, one of the masters has understood enough of *Morals by Agreement* to convince his colleagues that as it is rational to keep agreements they can be sure that things will turn out just as they predict. Of course things don't turn out that way. As soon as the slaves are emancipated they defect from the agreement and demand its renegotiation from the new baseline. Although coercion made the initial bargain rational, in the absence of coercion the co-operation to which the ex-slaves can rationally agree is not plausibly one based on the previous power relations (Gauthier 1986: 195). The point is this: given that agreements made from a coercive baseline are likely to be unstable, and that there are gains to be had from successful and stable co-operation, it is irrational to attempt to benefit from force or fraud in the establishing of the baseline.

Gauthier's second argument is that it is irrational for others to bargain with those who have gained from 'predatory' behaviour (those who enter the agreement with the benefits of force or fraud amongst their bargaining counters). Even where there is immediate advantage to such a bargain it is irrational to agree because if one shows oneself to be willing to co-operate from an unfair baseline then, given the translucency of one's dispositions, this will invite future partners in co-operation to 'engage in predatory and coercive activities as a prelude to bargaining' (Gauthier 1986: 195). Given that others will not bargain with those who engage in predatory behaviour such behaviour is irrational, for the predator is less likely to be included in future co-operation. It is better to bargain from a fair starting point than it is to try to gain the advantages of an unfair baseline, but be excluded from future co-operative ventures.

These two arguments are meant to establish that rational, self-interested agents will accept a non-coercive baseline and not attempt to exploit opportunities for the use of force or fraud to improve their initial bargaining position. That leaves one remaining element of Gauthier's account to consider; the bargaining itself. In *Morals by Agreement* Gauthier developed a bargaining solution, 'the principle of minimax relative concession' (Gauthier 1986: ch. 5). The idea was that each agent attempts to secure agreement whilst minimizing the maximum relative concession that he needs to offer. However, Gauthier has since renounced his allegiance to this solution and now endorses something similar to the traditional Nash solution (for a discussion of this see Sugden 1993a: 15–17). In fact, the precise nature of the solution does not matter a great deal to the overall argument as Gauthier himself admits (see Gauthier 1986: 146). The important features of the argument are that there is a unique solution to bargaining games acceptable to rational players by virtue of their rationality (in this sense the solution is impersonal),[5] and that what each player gets from the

---

[5] This claim has been challenged by Robert Sugden 1991, 1993b.

bargain will reflect her contribution. These, then, are the key elements of justice as mutual advantage. In *Morals by Agreement* Gauthier tries to give a rational justification for co-operative rules that are binding (that a rational agent will be disposed to follow), fair, and impersonal.

Critics of justice as mutual advantage in general and of Gauthier in particular have tended to allege two kinds of faults: first, that whatever justice as mutual advantage might be, it is not a theory of justice or of morality; second, that it is internally flawed such that it cannot deliver what it promises. The following sections examine each of these in turn.

## IS IT JUSTICE?

Will Kymlicka, in his review of the social contract tradition in ethics, suggests that justice as mutual advantage might not be an alternative moral theory, but a theory of an alternative morality (Kymlicka 1991: 190–1). Kymlicka is not simply playing with words. He makes it clear in another work (Kymlicka 1990: 7) that he thinks a way of testing the validity of a moral theory is to assess the conclusions it offers against our considered moral convictions.[6] It is on this test that Kymlicka and many others think justice as mutual advantage fails. There are two often cited problems: the exclusion of those with whom no one has reason to co-operate, and the link between the rules that govern the distribution of the social product and parties' initial bargaining positions.

The first problem can be brought to light by considering the plight of non-human animals, children, and the seriously disabled. A number of moral theorists might accept that non-human animals have no moral status (independent of their relationship to human beings), and that children have only the potential for moral status. However, few would be comfortable writing, as Gauthier does, that 'animals, the unborn, the congenitally handicapped and defective, fall beyond the pale of a morality tied to mutuality' (Gauthier 1986: 268). A number of people think this a *reductio* of justice as mutual advantage; a theory of morality simply cannot be right if it denies moral standing to the severely disabled.[7]

---

[6] Kymlicka writes, 'the ultimate test of a theory of justice is that it cohere with, and help illuminate, our considered convictions of justice. . . . I do not believe there is any other plausible way of proceeding' (1990: 7).

[7] Jean Hampton, for example, writes that 'Hobbesian moral theory gives us no reason to respect those with whom we have no need of cooperating, or those whom we are strong

There is a short and a long version of the answer that justice as mutual advantage theorists can offer to these kinds of attacks. The short version is given by Gauthier in *Morals by Agreement*: 'if the reader is tempted to object to some part of this view, on the ground that his moral intuitions are violated, then he should ask what weight such an objection can have, if morality is to fit within the domain of rational choice' (Gauthier 1986: 269; see also 1986: 8).[8] Such a seemingly cavalier attitude to ordinary moral intuitions and the bluntness with which he states the position of those 'beyond the pale' have done little to assuage the doubts of those unconvinced by the moral credentials of justice as mutual advantage and sometimes of Gauthier himself.[9]

However, if one considers the nature of justice as mutual advantage and of constructivism then it is apparent that these criticisms are much less damaging than they might at first appear (or at least that they are misdirected). The long version of the reply is that constructivists (including mutual advantage theorists) begin by confronting the disturbing thought that morality is a mere fetish (or worse, a confidence trick); unjustified and unjustifiable. Moreover, the account of its nature that is most widely accepted (that it is the creation of some divinity) is discredited as anything but an error theory. To draw a crude contrast, the *faux* constructivist begins with many moral principles and tries to sort out those for which something can be said from those for which there is nothing to be said. The genuine constructivist begins from the assumption that there are no justified moral principles except those that emerge from the construction (in the case of Gauthier, those that emerge from agreement for mutual advantage). Viewed from this constructivist perspective each and every moral principle that can be shown to be justified is a reason for celebration. Of course, it would be, in some sense, easier if the result of the construction was everything one would want from a moral theory (although note that each per-

enough to dominate, such as old people, or the handicapped, or retarded children whom we do not want to rear, or people from other societies with whom we have no interest in trading. . . . this shows that Hobbesian moral contractarianism fails in a very serious way to capture the nature of morality. *Regardless* of whether or not one can engage in beneficial cooperative interactions with another, our moral intuitions push us to assent to the idea that one owes that person respectful treatment simply in virtue of the fact that he or she just is a *person*. It seems to be a feature of our moral life that we regard a human being, whether or not she is instrumentally valuable, as always intrinsically valuable' (Hampton 1991*b*: 48–9). See also Barry 1995*a*: § 7, 1998.

⁸ Of course, typically opponents of Gauthier do not think that morality is 'to fit within the domain of rational choice'.

⁹ Brian Barry has unfavourably compared the 'moral reflexes' of Gauthier to those of 'the man who fell to earth' (Barry 1996: 369).

son will think that ideally the construction should yield principles coextensive with her own moral convictions) and where this is not the case one might regret that a rationally defensible morality does not extend as far as one's moral convictions.[10]

*Faux* constructivists take certain things as given (equality, the intrinsic value of persons, etc.) and thus can use as a test of a moral theory whether it accords with these givens. Finding that a morality tied to mutuality results in conclusions that are not coextensive with (their) ordinary moral convictions they therefore conclude that justice as mutual advantage is not a theory of morality. In contrast, constructivists think that a theory of morality must explain the imperatival force of impersonal norms. Insofar as such norms are congruent with our considered convictions we have reason to be pleased, but the test for the theory is not that this is the case. For this reason constructivists are likely to think that the proponents of justice as impartiality and other *faux* constructivists are not offering a theory of morality at all, but merely an account of a set of coherent beliefs that remain ungrounded. Just as the ten commandments tell one what (not) to do if one believes in a Christian god (of a kind), impartialists consider what (not) to do if one believes in a particular account of the fundamental equal moral worth of human beings, but neither of these is (on the constructivist account) a *theory* of morality.

Of course, nothing said so far in this section constitutes a defence of justice as mutual advantage (or of constructivism). It is plausible to maintain that it is a legitimate test of a moral theory to ask how well it captures and reflects ordinary moral experience. The point is just to show that *faux* constructivists and constructivists, despite their apparent similarities, have profoundly different views of what needs to be done and on the place of moral intuitions in the project. To criticize constructivist theories, then, it is not enough simply to show that their conclusions are not coextensive with some set of moral intuitions. First it must be shown that the capturing of moral experience is the correct hurdle over which a moral theory must pass.

Similar remarks apply to one version of the second criticism of justice as mutual advantage; that it establishes rules that reflect initial bargaining positions. The issue is this: if the motivation to co-operate on terms established by agreed rules is mutual advantage then each person must do better than she would in the absence of co-operation. Those with very little to

---

[10] Of course, it would be odd to regret giving up false beliefs. However, it is not odd to wish that the beliefs that one does have, and with which one is comfortable, should on examination turn out to be true.

offer—who would fare badly in the notional pre-contractual state—who enter into co-operation with those better endowed with natural talents and abilities will find that the terms of agreement reflect this unequal bargaining strength. Even from a baseline that excludes fraud and coercion the terms of agreement will not be equal, rather they will reflect the unequal contributions made to the products of co-operation by the contracting parties.[11]

Gauthier, far from seeming embarrassed about this, claims it as an advantage of his theory. Replying to a contrast between Rawls and himself drawn in favour of Rawls by Percy Lehning on the question of whether justice corrects or reflects contingent natural and social features of the contractors (features which Lehning takes to be morally arbitrary), Gauthier writes, 'this contrast precedes Lehning's claim that I have missed an important element of justice. But for me, this contrast reveals what is central to a view of justice grounded in rational choice—that it does transmit natural inequalities into society' (Gauthier 1993*b*: 181; see also Gauthier 1998: 126). Gauthier's defence of this (for Rawlsians especially) rather startling claim is important for what follows. Continuing directly on from the above passage he writes: 'social institutions that failed to do this would not be rationally acceptable in failing to recognize the separateness of persons.' Gauthier's argument is that the benefits of co-operation ought to reflect the contributions made by the parties to that co-operation. Any pattern of distribution in favour of the less well off (or those with nothing to contribute) would, he claims, require a 'unilateral sacrifice' on the part of the better off and such sacrifices cannot be demanded by justice. Indeed, that justice cannot ask 'too much' of agents by asking that they accept that they do less well just so that others can do better is, Gauthier rightly claims, something that is common to both justice as impartiality and justice as mutual advantage (see Gauthier 1998: 125–6).

Gauthier's argument appeals to a deep-seated notion of desert, that justice is relative to contribution. The difficulty is that the notion of a 'sacrifice', or of what is to count as a 'contribution' the benefits of which might legitimately be claimed by the contributor, is one of the things that is at issue between the impartialist and mutual advantage accounts. If those better endowed with natural abilities and talents have no claim on the benefits of those abilities and talents then distributing the benefits of co-operation in accordance with the difference principle (for example) is not 'sacrificing'

---

[11] Robert Goodin argues that those with greater initial endowments are also in a position to hold out for longer (risking getting no agreement at all) and so can extract concessions from those who cannot afford to lose the chance of agreement (Goodin 1993).

the better endowed. Thus, to claim, as Gauthier does, that an egalitarian principle of justice fails to respect 'the separateness of persons' first requires that one show that the account of just claims—in the relevant sense, the account of the person—endorsed by the egalitarian theory is itself flawed (cf. Barry 1998: 223–4).[12] The question of 'sacrifice' (whether of non-contributors or of the most talented), then, is merely an instance of the larger debate between the two approaches as to what can legitimately be claimed by the person. It is not, then, a 'knock down' argument for either side. Nevertheless, Gauthier's position on what may be legitimately extracted from co-operation is both complex and revealing. It is discussed below. However, before pursuing this it is worth examining the second set of criticisms of justice as mutual advantage: those that take the project seriously, but find the theory to be incomplete.

## MUTUAL ADVANTAGE, STABILITY, AND PUNISHMENT

There is a significant literature on *Morals by Agreement*.[13] The intention in what follows is to concentrate on the broad structure of justice as mutual advantage, taking it for granted that some of the more technical problems can be solved. The question is whether justice as mutual advantage is the right approach. Having examined arguments that the theory fails to capture our considered convictions about morality it is now worth considering criticisms of a different sort; those that allege that justice as mutual advantage cannot deliver the rational grounding of stable moral norms that it promises.

Brian Barry alleges that justice as mutual advantage cannot deliver stable norms, both because the agreement must be subject to constant renegotiation as and when the relative bargaining power of the contracting parties changes, and because it cannot overcome the problem of free-riders. Justice as mutual advantage, he argues, delivers agreements (if it delivers them at all) which 'are no more than truces', the component rules

[12] Of course, the same applies to impartialist theorists who wish to argue that Gauthier's exclusion of non-contributors, and his account of justice as relative to contribution, undermines justice as mutual advantage. Barry's criticism that Gauthier 'comprehensively begs the question' in mounting the 'separateness of persons' defence (Barry 1998: 223) applies equally to Barry's initial argument that Gauthier is prepared to ignore those who cannot contribute to the co-operative enterprise.

[13] Many of the best papers on Gauthier's theory are collected in Gauthier and Sugden 1993; Paul, Miller, and Paul 1988; and Vallentyne 1991*b*. See also Velleman 1997.

of which resemble legal sanctions without any moral element (Barry 1995*a*: 39; Chapter 5 above). Barry questions the very intelligibility of the idea that there 'could be such a thing as moral sanctions in a society of self-interested people' (1995*a*: 36). Barry makes his point by considering the role of moral condemnation: imagine that a rational, self-interested agent defects on an agreement and is discovered. The agent may regret having done so either because there are legal sanctions (she is put in prison) or because she is excluded from future co-operation having been revealed as an SM but, as Barry says, 'regret is not remorse' (1995*a*: 36). There seems to be something significant missing from the moral universe of justice as mutual advantage.[14]

It would seem, then, that the view justice as mutual advantage must take of sanctions is one in which they play a purely instrumental role. If all rules are legal rules and we accept that rational agents will be tempted to defect given the fundamental motivation of pursuing self-interest that is attributed to them, then it would seem rational to agree to a system of sanctions as a system of taxes on certain conduct (cf. Rawls 1971: 215; Chapter 5 above) aimed to deter the performance of some acts and to contribute to the condition of sufficient security. The threat of sanctions, then, merely changes the expected pay-offs so as to dissolve the prisoner's dilemma.

The impact on the understanding of punishment of conceiving of rules and sanctions in such a way would be great (as noted above in relation to aspects of fair play theory). The problem is that what is missing is a recognizably moral (and not necessarily legal) element. The fabric of any advanced society is largely maintained not by laws, but by self-restraint, and by social approbation and opprobrium. In the implausible world of a society based on Barry's vision of justice as mutual advantage the scope of the law would have to be at least as wide as that employed by the more 'totalizing' of totalitarian regimes. This is because, without effective moral sanctions—that is without sanctions that appeal to the moral (rather than merely the prudential) reason of an offending agent—the society would have to rely only on legal sanctions. Even Hobbes recognized that this was not sustainable, arguing that men 'need to be diligently, and truly taught; because [civil society] cannot be maintained by . . . terrour of legal punishment' (Hobbes 1991, part ii, ch. 30, 337). In short, if 'terrour of legal punishment' has to carry the entire burden of ensuring co-operation then it will have to be truly capable of inducing terror. Considering that a ra-

---

[14] This argument is deployed above in relation to the adoption by fair play theory of a crude mutual advantage contract theory, see Ch.2 above.

tional agent will calculate the degree of terror he should feel based in part on the likelihood of conviction it also means that there is likely to be distortion in the normal proportionality of seriousness of offence and size of sanction as where the chances of apprehension are low the size of the threatened punishment needs to be great, as it does where temptation is strong.[15] Of course, it is difficult to say what will sorely tempt an agent of the kind envisaged in this account of justice as mutual advantage. It may still be that people contracting on the basis of this vision of mutual advantage may wish the penalties for crimes against the person to be more severe than for crimes against property (given that they fear the greater harm of crimes against the person), but it is still likely that the penalty for crimes against property (and minor offences such as motoring offences) would have to be severe and relatively more severe when compared with the penalties for crimes such as murder (the punishment for which would not need to be ratcheted up as much).

Barry's argument is compelling as an attack on one version of mutual advantage. If each agent reasons as an SM and sticks to her agreements only when it is in her immediate self-interest to do so (a calculation that will include any potential costs of defection) then the theory is not a theory of morality (it does not deliver norms which meet the criteria of fairness, impersonality, and imperatival force). Moreover, a world in which such norms predominate will not be stable both because of the status of each agreement as a 'truce' and because the provision of the condition of sufficient security is unlikely. However, these damning arguments apply to a version of justice as mutual advantage that has little in common with Gauthier's account. To be threatened by these attacks it must be shown that justice as mutual advantage cannot account, as Gauthier thinks it can, for the transformation of the norms and of the agent from rules of cooperation addressed to individuals who pursue only their immediate self-interest to moral norms addressed to agents disposed to constrain their behaviour in accordance with such norms.

---

[15] As J. F. Stephen put it, 'surely it is at the moment when temptation to crime is strongest that the law should speak most clearly and emphatically to the contrary' (Stephen 1883: ii., 107). Cf. Bentham: 'The strength of the temptation (*ceteris paribus*) is as the profit of the offence: the quantum of the punishment must rise with the profit of the offence: *ceteris paribus*, it must therefore rise with the strength of the temptation' (Bentham 1970: ch. 16, § 9). There are countervailing considerations, even on a strict deterrence account of punishment (see Ch. 9 below).

## CONSTRAINED MAXIMIZATION RECONSIDERED

Gauthier has written that he thinks constrained maximization 'the most fruitful idea in *Morals by Agreement*' (1993*b*: 185). It is certainly not hard to see why he should think it central. Without constrained maximization the theory is vulnerable to the devastating critique that it cannot overcome the prisoner's dilemma which lies at the heart of the derivation of justice as mutual advantage. The idea of constrained maximization is a difficult one. One way in which to begin to unravel it is to compare a CM with a well-informed and prudent SM.

Imagine an agent who is good at disguising his dispositions in a setting in which the number of other agents with whom co-operation is feasible is small. The circumstances are such that the agent realizes that taking his long-term utility and possible future offers of co-operation into account it is rational for him for the most part not to defect on agreements, and to constrain the pursuit of his immediate self-interest in accordance with the norms of agreement. He is an SM; one who takes a long-term view (an LSM). Such an agent may have all the appearance of a CM but he is not one. He is not correctly disposed, he is just aware of the long-term benefits of being thought a reliable co-operator. What, then, is the difference between the LSM and the CM?

Gauthier states that 'the constrained maximizer does not reason more effectively about how to maximize her utility, *but reasons in a different way*' (1986: 170; emphasis added).[16] This is a very important claim and one that justice as mutual advantage needs if it is even to be considered as a moral theory. The theorist of justice as mutual advantage must be able to find space for distinctively moral rather than merely prudential reasons. Gauthier's analysis of how the CM reasons differently from the SM serves as an example of what must be achieved by a theory of morality born out of agreement for mutual advantage. Gauthier writes:

The constrained maximizer considers (i) whether the outcome, should everyone do so [base their action on a joint strategy], be nearly fair and optimal, and (ii)

---

[16] Elsewhere Gauthier states, 'the agent who takes her reasons for acting exclusively and directly from her utilities is an amoral agent. She pursues her concerns . . . without constraint. In her behaviour she may indeed conform perfectly to the demands of some moral code. But her conformity can only be a matter of preference; were she to suppose that she had some reason, either for preferring to conform to the code or for conforming whether or not she preferred, then she would not be taking her reasons exclusively and directly from her utilities' (Gauthier 1993*b*: 188).

whether the outcome she realistically expects should she do so affords her greater utility than universal non-co-operation. If both of these conditions are satisfied she bases her action on the joint strategy. The straightforward maximizer considers simply whether the outcome he realistically expects should he base his action on the joint strategy affords him greater utility than the outcome he would expect were he to act on any alternative strategy . . . Only if this condition is satisfied does he base his action on the joint strategy. (Gauthier 1986: 170)

The crucial claim is that the CM does not consider the option of defecting in comparing possible outcomes. Rather, given a prediction that others will co-operate, the CM asks only whether the outcome is 'nearly fair and optimal' and better than having no co-operation at all. Put more forthrightly elsewhere, 'the theory of justice as mutual advantage characterises a just man as one who takes the justice of an action to provide a motivating reason for performing it' (Gauthier 1998: 121; cf. Gauthier 1986: 328). It is this leap from rational, self-interested beings to moral agents disposed to do what is just, simply because it is just, that must be made.

If justice as mutual advantage is to retain the starting point of rational (where this means utility maximizing), non-tuist[17] agents and provide a rational grounding for moral norms and moral agency then it must be shown that adopting the disposition of constrained maximization is rational. Gauthier's argument is, as noted above, that it is rational to become a CM because the assumption of translucency means that more opportunities for mutually advantageous co-operation will be offered to CMs than to SMs (or LSMs). This is because, given certain plausible conditions, it is only rational to enter into co-operation with CMs. Of course, it is only rational if (i) there are a sufficient number of other CMs in the community and (ii) the probability is fairly high that one will be able to judge others' motivations correctly and that others will with similar probability be able to detect one's own (that is, if the assumption of translucency holds).

Although one might wonder just how the threshold of CMs was ever reached (given the irrationality of becoming a CM in a world of SMs), this problem can be put to one side. Perhaps it is fortunate that people believed in the past in a god (of one sort or another) and thus irrationally disposed themselves to constrained maximization. Focus instead on the assumption of translucency. Although it is surely not unreasonable to think that most people's motivations are neither opaque nor transparent the degree to which they are translucent is likely to vary widely. One problem with

[17] A non-tuist 'takes no interest in the interests of those with whom he interacts. His utility function, measuring his preferences, is strictly independent of the utility functions of those whom he affects' (Gauthier 1986: 311; for further discussion see Ch. 7 below).

Gauthier's theory is that the choice he offers is so limited and so stark: SM or CM. However, there are many other possible positions (for an array of these see Smith 1991). Not all deceivers are out-and-out sociopaths. Some will keep to a proportion of agreements and sucker their victims into believing that they are trustworthy by being so some of the time or by not fully exploiting the possible advantages of defection. The appearance of honesty is not all that difficult to attain if one is sufficiently skilled and disciplined.

In short, the CM gains from co-operation, but if it is assumed that in certain instances of co-operation he could gain more from defecting then it would seem that the SM must do better. This is false only if the SM has fewer opportunities for co-operation (having been recognized for what he is and excluded from co-operation). However, a rational, disciplined, and skilled deceiver avoids exclusion and so gains the advantages of co-operation and, in some cases, of defection. Even if one is inclined to think that only a few people are sufficiently skilled at deceit, so that Gauthier can avoid this problem—or at least discount its threatening the threshold of CMs needed to make adopting the disposition of the constrained maximizer rational for others less skilled—there is a still less dramatic example than that of the clever, occasional deceiver that needs to be considered.

Consider, a reserved maximizer (RM):

A reserved maximizer has exactly the disposition of a constrained maximizer, except that he will violate a requirement of a cooperative scheme whenever he has the opportunity to win a jackpot. He will take opportunities to make very great gains in utility, when the probability of detection is very low. For example, unlike a constrained maximizer, he may steal the money from a lost wallet, provided enough money is involved and provided he is quite sure he was not observed finding the wallet. (Copp 1991: 221)

Copp argues that 'a person might do better as a reserved maximizer than as a constrained maximizer' (1991: 221). Moreover, the power of the translucency assumption to rescue Gauthier's position is greatly weakened in this case. The argument is that it is rational for an agent to adopt the disposition to keep agreements except in certain very restricted circumstances. The RM defects only when the gain is great and the risk of detection very small. Is it plausible to assume that such a person will be excluded from co-operative opportunities because his disposition is not that of the constrained maximizer?

The answer to this question depends upon the view taken of how motivational dispositions are detected. If it is assumed that for the most part people judge one another in the light of their acts (and their reputation as it is formed by their acts) then there is very little chance that the reserved maximizer will be detected. It is part of the definition of the reserved maximizer that she behaves as a constrained maximizer except in circumstances in which it is very unlikely that other people will be able to detect her defection. However, if this is how people's motivations are translucent then the LSM would also remain undetected or at least would ensure that the payoff from his defections was always greater than the total loss of benefit from being excluded from future co-operative opportunities. Perhaps, then, the nature of translucency is different. Rather than translucency being based on actions giving rise to judgements about reliability, what might be translucent is the actual disposition to reason independent of immediate self-interest.

Consider again the quotation from Gauthier given above that the CM 'reasons in a different way' from the SM and, therefore, also from the LSM or RM. The LSM and RM still consider whether defecting will pay, they just ordinarily decide that it won't (the RM doesn't bother to consider the question of defecting except in certain very restricted circumstances). Is it possible that it is this that gives the game away to CMs and allows them more often than not to detect SMs, LSMs and RMs, thus (given a certain threshold of CMs) making the adopting of those dispositions irrational? This is clearly what is needed, but it is difficult to see how it can be the case. The capacity to consider immediate self-interest must always be retained, even by the CM, because of the possibility that the CM will mistakenly enter co-operation with, or find himself surrounded by, SMs. Under these circumstances the CM is rational, as Gauthier admits, to act as an SM. In short, becoming a CM does not involve a moral transformation such that the idea of defecting from agreements becomes a 'moral incapacity' (to borrow the title of Williams 1993), or such that the agent values being just for its own sake in all circumstances. Even CMs view the norms of agreement as constraints. At most, constrained maximization involves being disposed not to consider the pay-off from defection when co-operating with another CM. In other circumstances the CM must act as an SM. However, given this it is very difficult to grant that the claim that agents will be able to detect with sufficient regularity the difference between an LSM, RM, and CM even if they can detect crude SMs.[18]

---

[18] The structure of Gauthier's theory is similar to that of rule-utilitarianism and has the same drawbacks. A rule-utilitarian can plausibly claim that the rule 'keep your promises' (subject to normal excusing conditions) is justified in that it better promotes utility in comparison with any other rule or having no rule. However, an agent aware of the goal of

The focus has been on one reason why it might be doubted that it is rational for a utility maximizing non-tuist to adopt the disposition of constrained maximization.[19] Although there is no reason to think the idea of constrained maximization useless (cf. Binmore 1993: 131, 133), there are good reasons to believe that Gauthier cannot defend the rationality of adopting constrained maximization given the thin, utility maximizing notion of rationality that he endorses. The problem is, in essence, that Gauthier cannot convincingly argue that it is rational for the CM to understand the norms of co-operation as anything other than constraints that, where possible and where the costs are not too high, it is rational to avoid. The gap between self-interest and morality is narrowed, if Gauthier is right in his belief that defection doesn't often pay in the long run, but not overcome.

In places Gauthier hints at a different interpretation of what it is for the CM to 'reason in a different way' (and of how the CM comes to do so); an interpretation in which self-interest and morality are brought together. It is worth considering this, if for no other reason than to establish what a convincing constructivist account of morality must achieve.

## CONSTRAINED MAXIMIZATION AND LIFE-PLANS

Consider the example of the RM once again. The RM, where the pay-off is great and the risk of detection small, will renege on agreement. The example given by Copp is of someone who will steal money from a lost wallet when he is sure that no one has seen him find the wallet. Copp's point is that, given the understanding that the agent has of his good, there is nothing in Gauthier's account that could show his behaviour to be irrational (unless it is granted that even the RM would be spotted for a fraud and deprived of co-operative opportunities). If the CM is to be a moral agent,

---

utility promotion nevertheless has recourse to direct utilitarian reasoning and, in certain circumstances, will be obliged to break the rule (see Ch. 1 above). The status of the rule cannot be 'embedded' in the reasoning of the agent. Similarly, Gauthier cannot (and needs not to) argue that the CM internalizes the demands of agreement so that she is predisposed to comply with rational agreements no matter what. However, once the agent recognizes that her disposition to constrained maximization is only rational because it promotes her interests, she has available the thought that in certain circumstances the 'master goal' of promoting her interests might be better promoted by straightforward maximization.

[19] There are others. See e.g. Copp 1991; Hollis 1993; Kraus and Coleman 1991; Margaret Moore 1993: ch. 4; Sayre-McCord 1991; Smith 1991.

what needs to be explained is the agent's response that stealing the money would be incompatible with his self-understanding. The agent, on such a revised account, does not view his overall good as constrained by a norm that he would much rather avoid, but rather understands his good as furthered through the norms of co-operation. There is, then, no conflict between the agent's understanding of his good and the demands of morality. What constrained maximization must somehow achieve is what Martin Hollis has claimed to be 'untenable': the disposition of constrained maximization must be both 'constitutive and regulative, with the value of morality consisting both in the constitutive fact that moral agents do not have a further goal thus served and in the regulative claim that the further goal of maximising utility will be best served thereby' (Hollis 1993: 51).

As noted above, Gauthier has hinted at developing his theory in this direction. Far from thinking Hollis's criticism fatal, he thinks that this dual role of constrained maximization must be embraced. In a number of recent papers (1993*a*, 1993*b*, 1997: 1998) Gauthier has pursued the exchange of 'life plans' or what the agent 'judges good' for 'maximizing utility' in his theory.[20] Although he thinks that this 'leaves the basic structure of the theory unchanged' (Gauthier 1998: 122), the consequences for the aspirations of his account, rather than for its structure, may be more significant. Gauthier writes:

Constrained maximization creates a space for moral reasons. Whether moral reasons actually fill that space, or some part of it, depends on an agent's circumstances and concerns. The key idea is that the interaction with her fellows made possible by social institutions and practices that express a double mutuality—of agreement and of advantage—is a constitutive and core element in the agent's overarching life-plan. For then the constraints that those institutions and practices impose . . . will fall among those considerations that the agent takes from her life-plan as reasons for acting. (Gauthier 1993*b*: 188)

Above, it was noted that Gauthier's project of 'allaying the fear' that the moral enterprise must fail need not take the form of showing the rational, utility maximizing non-tuist that she has reason to adopt the constraints of

---

[20] Arguably many of Gauthier's recent reflections on the nature of his theory were prefigured in the final (and, to a lesser extent, also in the penultimate) chapter of *Morals by Agreement*. Nevertheless, the changes in Gauthier's theory have been marked. The original version of the contractarian test was that 'the principles of justice are those principles for making social decisions or choices to which rational individuals, each seeking to co-operate with her fellows in order to maximize her own utility, would agree' (Gauthier 1984: 255), whereas he now argues that the test is that agreement to the constraints of society must 'advance what one judges good'. A change to which Gauthier himself draws attention (Gauthier 1998: 121–2).

morality. Gauthier's recent arguments suggest that he now thinks the same. His project now, he says, is to address 'those persons whose overarching life-plans make them welcome participants in society' and whose life plans 'constitutively incorporate . . . a concern with interactions that reflect [just] terms, and so make . . . social participation itself an aim or objective' (1993*b*: 189). In other terms, the argument of *Morals by Agreement* is to be directed towards those with a 'sense of justice' (1993*a*).

If this is the right approach for the constructivist project, it must, of course, avoid the *faux* constructivist trap of positing moral reasons that are independent of prudential reasons. It must avoid opening up a gap between persons and moral norms. The difficulty demonstrated above in the analysis of Gauthier is that if moral reasons cannot be given a distinct regulative place in the agent's reasons then they lack the necessary imperatival force. When it comes to the crunch the agent has reason to treat moral reasons as simply instrumentally valuable and thus as dispensable. *Faux* constructivists simply posit a realm of moral reasons and are left closing the gap between this realm and the agents that it is meant to govern with unsatisfactory accounts of coercion and of motivation. Gauthier's original attempt to eradicate this gap by grounding moral reasons in prudential ones fails because he cannot explain the rationality of giving a regulative place to moral reasons when these conflict with the demands of self-interest. However, Gauthier's more recent work suggests a different route, one in which constrained maximization takes the form of part of a regulative life plan; a way of understanding oneself and one's good. As such the theory might initially be taken to be an explication of what it means to be a moral being—a being who takes the justice of an act to be a reason to do it just because it is just—rather than a justification of morality 'from the ground up'. It might as a result be taken to be a form of *faux* constructivism. In what follows, it is aimed to show that there is a form of constructivism that is not *faux* and that will answer Nietzsche's challenge, but will fall short of Gauthier's original aspiration of a justification of morality that could be offered to a rational egoist.

The argument that follows in some ways develops Gauthier's (and Rawls's) idea of social institutions as expressing a 'double mutuality of agreement and of advantage'. It addresses agents who have an understanding of themselves as united together with others in a co-operative scheme through which each understands her good. Whilst it retains the constructivist claim that justice is a product of co-operation, it is a product of agreement between persons for whom co-operation is, as Albert Weale puts it, 'a condition for individual advantage rather than a derivative from it' (Weale

1993: 92). However, before finally leaving Gauthier's account, it is worth briefly examining one further argument that he offers that can be taken to support such a move.

## EXCURSUS ON DISTRIBUTIVE JUSTICE

As noted above, Gauthier claims that the fact that the terms of agreement reflect the inequalities of agents' initial starting points is an advantage of his theory (see Gauthier 1986: esp. 254; 1998: § 7; p. 164 above). However as Albert Weale (1993) and others have pointed out, Gauthier allows the taxation of factor rent.[21] The discussion is framed in reference to the (ice) hockey player Wayne Gretzky (see Gauthier 1986: 272–6). Gretzky is a very good player and the result of his appearing in games is that stadia fill to capacity whereas in his absence they remain unfilled. He is thus able to command a very high salary, far higher than the total cost (including opportunity cost) to him of playing. The difference between what he can command in salary and what would be needed to ensure that he plays is factor rent. It could, as Gauthier points out, be subject to a 100 per cent tax and Gretzky would still play hockey.

However, imposing such a tax would be, as Weale and Sugden point out (Weale 1993; Sugden 1993*a*), incompatible with Gauthier's account of the just outcome of bargaining. Gauthier's argument, remember, is that it is the result of rational bargaining (and an admirable result at that) that each person's claim on the social product is equal to his marginal contribution. Gretzky's marginal contribution to the surplus realized is very large as without him there would be a greatly reduced product, whereas each spectator contributes virtually nothing at the margin as without that spectator all the others would nevertheless be able to watch Gretzky play hockey (Sugden 1993*a*: 13). How then does Gauthier justify taxing Gretzky?

The answer lies in an implicit appeal to Gretzky's good fortune (and, by extension, to its therefore being undeserved). After all, the value of factor rent is created by its relation to other factors; it does not inhere in the

---

[21] Rent is the difference between the return on some good and the cost of supply. Factor rent occurs because of the scarcity of a particular factor in relation to others (the value lies in its scarcity) such that the factor commands a greater return than would be needed to ensure its supply in the market (the difference between the two being factor rent).

factor itself.[22] Although it appears that Gretzky has a right to exploit his natural talents, to 'use them as he pleases' (Gauthier 1986: 273) and enjoy the resulting power he has in the market, Gauthier argues that:

Society may be considered as a single co-operative enterprise. The benefit represented by factor rent is part of the surplus afforded by that enterprise, for it arises only in social interaction. . . . Each person, as a contributor to social interaction, shares in the production of the benefit represented by factor rent. . . . The right to use one's capacities . . . does not entail a right to receive factor rent, but only a right to share, with others, in the surplus represented by such rent. In so far as this surplus takes the form of a single, transferable good, each member of society is entitled to an equal portion of it. (Gauthier 1986: 274)

As Sugden quips, this is 'a passage that could almost have been written by Rawls' (Sugden 1993*a*: 12).

Although Gauthier warns against thinking that the right to equal shares of factor rent has significant redistributive consequences, the importance of this passage lies not so much in its significance for income distribution as in the conception of society that underpins it. This is not a conception of a market society of atomized individuals, but rather of society as what Weale (borrowing from Rawls) calls a 'social union' (Weale 1993; Rawls 1971: § 79).

The point is this: even if it is true that Gretzky is fortunate in controlling a scarce product desired by others (the ability to play ice hockey well would not have been of much value in numerous other times and places), Gretzky's marginal contribution to the surplus still entitles him on Gauthier's official theory to the factor rent that he commands. However, if Gauthier's account is reinterpreted in the manner suggested by Weale then a very different argument emerges. The realization of rent is only possible given co-operation. Co-operation is dependent on (among other things) the condition of sufficient security holding which, in turn, is dependent on social institutions (using that term to denote systems of norms, legal systems, mechanisms of moral education, etc.). Insofar as such institutions are maintained and flourish only through individuals constraining the pursuit of their self-interest then each co-operating individual can be regarded as an equal co-creator of the institutions that make co-operation possible and so as entitled to a share of the product of that co-operation.

---

[22] As Gauthier puts it, 'the recipient of rent benefits from the scarcity of the factor she controls—a scarcity which is of course entirely accidental from her standpoint, since it depends, not on the intrinsic nature of the factors, but on the relation between them and the factors controlled by others' (Gauthier 1986: 98).

## CONCLUSION

*Faux* constructivists assume as a premiss that individuals are of equal moral worth and use the techniques of constructivism to explicate what is demanded by such equality. This opens up a gap between the personal perspective and the demands of justice. Rawls, who is acutely aware of this problem, tries various arguments to close this gap, but none is satisfactory. However, there is, it is suggested above, a possible extension of Rawls's thoughts that would tie the individual to the community and the rules that govern it through the idea of the good of participation in a society of a particular kind. Gauthier sets himself a more ambitious task: 'to show . . . why an individual, reasoning from non-moral premises, would accept the constraints of morality on his choices' (Gauthier 1986: 5, quoted above), which he takes to be necessary to respond to 'Nietzsche's challenge'. The project is to close the gap between the personal perspective and morality by deriving morality from self-interest. The argument of this chapter is that Gauthier fails in his project, but that this need not mean that there is no response to Nietzsche's challenge. Finally, Gauthier, like Rawls, hints at a different understanding of his own argument, one in which the project is to address someone located in a particular kind of society who understands himself and his good in relation to that society. However, the development of this idea must proceed cautiously, for if it is to be used to respond to Nietzsche's challenge it must not take the form of a *faux* constructivism.

# 7

# Self-Interest and
# the Commitment to Morality

## INTRODUCTION

The two standard approaches to distributive justice differ fundamentally in
what they take to be the central aim of political philosophy and thus in
their approaches to the questions being considered here. *Faux* constructivists build in a commitment to the fundamental equal moral worth of
agents. This introduces a gap between the individual and the moral standpoints. From the individual perspective the demand for impartiality
appears as alien and serving only to frustrate the fulfilment of the agent's
good.[1] Impartialist theorists are thus forced to depend on importing an
account of moral motivation. This gap is replicated in the account impartialists give of coercion, for the theory commits them to the view that
morality is individually binding on a given agent independent of any agreement by others to adhere likewise to moral norms. A separate justification,
then, has to be found for coercion, either in bridging the motivation gap
for everyone's advantage (i.e. in consequentialism) or in some mystical retributivism.

The theory of justice as mutual advantage attempts the more ambitious
project of deriving moral norms from self-interest, thus uniting the two
perspectives. However, the transformation that is needed in the agent to
explain the imperatival force of moral norms—in which the agent
endorses herself as a moral being and, in so doing, converts the norms of
co-operation into moral norms—is not satisfactorily accounted for by the
thin accounts of rationality and of agents' goods that are posited as the
building blocks of the mutual advantage project. Justice as mutual advantage, too, must endorse the use of coercion to deter agents from free-

[1] For a good introduction to these perspectives and to the problems they give rise to, see
Nagel 1986, and Nagel 1991: Introduction.

riding. Once again the role of coercion is to fill the gap left when moral norms appear as alien restrictions on the pursuit of self-interest (cf. Charvet 1995: 153).

These conclusions may come as little surprise to many people. There is a widespread assumption that as contractarianism captures a conception of society as a co-operative venture regulated by moral norms the only possible form of agreement over the use of coercion will be one that is made to ensure that free-riders are deterred. On both accounts (impartialist and mutual advantage) it will sometimes be the case that an agent is tempted to give priority to the demands of self-interest rather than to those of morality and, given the problem that each agent pursuing her self-interest independently gives rise to sub-optimal social outcomes, it is rational to agree to a system of coercion to change the prudential calculation and make the unrestrained pursuit of self-interest less tempting.[2]

However, there is another tradition in social contract theory, one represented more by Rousseau than by Locke or Hobbes. In this tradition the construction that creates moral norms is such that the will to coerce is implicit in the will to create or endorse the norms in the first place. The function of coercion in Rousseau's *Social Contract* is not (only) to deter potential free-riders, but also to assist the offending agent in realizing his true will. In addition, it is part of the function of punishment to repair the damage done to the social harmony of the general will caused by the agent's mistaken pursuit of his narrow self-interest. Coercion is justified in that in being coerced the agent is, in the famous phrase, 'forced to be free' (Rousseau 1968: book i, ch. 7).[3] Of course, no liberal or right-minded late twentieth-century political theorist would claim to be able to justify Rousseau's claims in full and nor is Rousseau's work genuinely constructivist. However, the point is just to establish that there is a different tradition in social contract theory, one in which the relationship of coercion to the construction of norms (or to the system by which norms are adopted) is far more intimate than is suggested by the 'deterrence' reading of contract theory given above.[4]

---

[2] This is the idea appealed to by some fair play theorists (see Ch. 2 above).

[3] A similar argument appears in Hegel's *The Philosophy of Right* (Hegel 1991: §§ 99–104).

[4] Rousseau is an interesting figure in the analysis of social justice offered above. Rousseau's agents undergo a transformation (a 'great change') to become moral beings in submitting themselves to, and participating in the discovery of, the general will (see Rousseau 1968, especially chs. 6 and 8). The reasons for action that the agent accepts before and after immersion in the general will are meant to be different. Gauthier's account would seem to require a similar transformation.

A constructivist account of morality, then, has one main aim and a number of subsidiary concerns. The central goal is to establish a grounding of morality that can overcome the separation of the personal and moral perspectives. In uniting these perspectives it is additionally hoped that it can be shown that the rationale of coercion is implicit in the construction of the norms themselves and so not dependent on some supplementary argument from deterrence, fairness, or 'celestial mechanics'. This is the argument offered below; an argument that owes much to John Charvet's *The Idea of an Ethical Community* (Charvet 1995).

Although the aspirations of constructivism are substantial there is one sense in which the claims that a constructivist theory can make are rather modest. For in arguing that morality is possible only as the form given to the norms which govern the co-operation of a community of rational self-reflective agents, the constructivist is committed to the view that the precise content of the moral norms of a community is a subject for the agreement of the co-operating members of that community. Thus, the analysis of the content of morality that can be undertaken in the abstract is necessarily limited to identifying the general claims that must find embodiment in the practices of such a community.[5]

## WHERE TO BEGIN?

If the goal of constructivism is to address the question of what grounds morality, its method is to begin with an individual self-reflective agent concerned to answer the question, 'Given that I have value for myself what is the nature of my relations with others?' This, of course, is just another version of Gauthier's 'contractarian test'. Yet in Chapter 6, it is argued that Gauthier's project fails. The constructivist theory described in what follows, then, must distinguish itself from the Gauthierian project. This is done, in part, by focusing not on the idea of rationality, but on the goods that the co-operating agents pursue. As described at the end of Chapter 6, Gauthier at times commits himself to a view of agents' goods in which social interaction is a condition of formulating a plausible account of individual advantage and not a product of it. It is claimed below that the development of this, and cognate, ideas can underwrite a constructivist account of morality sufficient to meet Nietzsche's challenge.

[5] A similar claim is made by Scanlon in relation to his contractualist theory in the final chapter, 'Relativism', of his *What We Owe to Each Other* (1999).

However, a constructivist theory must also distinguish itself from its *faux* counterparts. The question given above may seem to achieve this. In claiming value for herself, the agent does not claim objective value. She does not claim value in herself (by virtue of some feature such as her humanity) and is thus not committed to the recognition of the value of others (who possess that feature). To assume the objective stance would be to beg the question of how to justify morality; it would be to adopt the position of *faux* constructivism.[6] However, although the initial claim made on behalf of the agent reflects only the value the agent claims for herself, in addressing the question of the agent's relations with others there remain *faux* constructivist routes that must be avoided. As noted above, the constructivist theory developed below looks to a characterization of agents' goods to give an account of the moral norms that are to govern co-operation. Yet, such a theory must avoid grounding moral rules and motivation in contingent affective ties such as sympathy. A theory of morality must aim at showing that moral behaviour is not simply a fetish, possessed by some people with particular affective ties. Moreover, such contingency cannot be overcome within a constructivist framework by defining certain affective ties not as contingent preferences, but as essential features of persons (cf. Gauthier 1993b: 189). Having to avoid an objective interpretation of the initial claim and having also to avoid grounding morality in affective ties, whether contingent or essential, thus places restrictions on the construction of an answer to the question posed at the beginning of this section.

If the question of the relations of agents each of whom claims subjective value is to give rise to a theory of morality, the constructivist must not only determine the content of any norms governing those relations, but also the nature and degree of their motivational force. If these norms are to be understood as moral rather than as mere terms of co-operation, the constructivist must give an account of the criteria for distinctively moral propositions and show that the terms of agreement meet them.

Although there is a sense, then, in which in a constructivist theory 'the constructing is to be done by a theorist' (Barry 1989: 266; quoted above, Chapter 4), it is done from the perspective of an agent reflecting on his

---

[6] Alan Gewirth's argument that the claim agents make of the value of freedom and well-being for themselves commits them to recognizing the claims to freedom and well-being of others mistakes the subjective form of the initial claim for the objective form (Gewirth 1978). Gewirth's argument has been criticized in a number of places. A good summary of both the original argument and its weakness can be found in Margaret Moore 1993: ch. 2. On the subjective and objective formulations of the initial question see Charvet 1981: 157–61, 1995.

commitments, interests, etc. Any answers must, then, take the form of answers for such an agent (cf. Williams 1985: ch. 1). The agent putting into question his relationship with others is to be understood as a self-conscious social being possessed of language who is already a member of a community. He stands back from his social ties and questions the norms and practices of the community of which he is a member. It is important to note that the agent is already engaged in social interaction; he is reflecting on the moral commitments that he has, and asking whether it is rational to acquire commitments that he does not already recognize, and to maintain and cultivate those that he does.

Such a question is only available to a self-conscious individual able to distance herself from the community that formed her. An individual formed without social interaction (should one exist) could not take up this question not only because, *ex hypothesi*, questions of her relations with others would not occur, but also because she would be incapable of determining her good as a self-conscious rational being without either language or standards of rationality both of which are socially engendered; she would not in fact be a self-conscious rational being. Likewise the individual, even if brought up in a society, has to be capable of formulating the question (of her relation with others); of achieving the necessary distance between self and community.

The absence of an external authority distinguishes the theory presented here from the classical contractarianism of Locke and, less explicitly, of Hobbes and Rousseau. The achieving of distance between the agent and the community distinguishes it from some recent communitarian thought.[7] In the past (and perhaps in certain very simple societies), either the gap between the individual and moral perspectives was insufficient for the individual to question the norms and practices of the community—her identification with the community was, in Hegel's term, 'naïve'[8]—or the

---

[7] Something like the claim that the individual cannot escape his community so as to reflect upon it is often, and perhaps rightly, the interpretation given to the 'embedded self' arguments of some communitarians (most notably Sandel 1982; see e.g. 150). If the claim is this strong we surely have good reason to reject it. As Kymlicka puts it, Sandel 'violat[es] our deepest self-understandings . . . We do not consider ourselves trapped by our present attachments, incapable of judging the worth of the goals we inherited or ourselves chose earlier' (Kymlicka 1990: 213). However, it is a matter of reasonable dispute whether Sandel or other leading communitarians (Taylor, MacIntyre, and Walzer), really make so strong a claim.

[8] See esp. Hegel 1977: §§ 464–76; also Hegel 1974: vol. i. As Allen Wood puts it: 'until the rise of the subversive idea of subjective freedom in fifth-century Athens, the distinction between different interests, as something that might be mutually opposed, was not a natural one to draw for people living in the naïve harmony of Greek culture' (Wood 1990: 57).

source of authority for the community's norms and practices was posited in an external authority, a god. In the former case the motivation problem does not arise.[9] In the latter, it can be overcome by arguing that the agent as possessor of an immortal soul has good reason to be moral if some account is offered of the relationship of the soul and the source of value (for example, that they share the same nature), and of the chance of posthumous rewards and punishments. However, if the problem is as Gauthier describes it, that we moderns live in a 'post-anthropomorphic, post-theocentric' world (Gauthier 1988*b*: 385), then there is no recourse to god, to an enchanted world, or to authoritative norms of community.

The use of the device of the reflective agent wondering what the nature of her relationship is with others attracts a great deal of criticism especially when it is combined with an answer that takes the form of asking what one would agree to in a hypothetical situation, as it will be here. The criticisms take two forms. For some the whole idea of separating oneself off from the social conditions in which one has developed is incoherent. For others the hypothetical device is at best redundant and at worst misleading. The second of these criticisms is considered below, but not the first. This is not because the first is regarded as unimportant, but because it fails to challenge the possibility of the kind of enquiry of which this book is one example. There are any number of works on the debate between 'liberals' and 'communitarians', and the current enquiry has nothing original to add to the defence of the idea that the type of reflective question asked above is both possible and meaningful.[10] However, it is worth emphasizing that the question posed above is put by an already socialized being who reflects on commitments that she already has. Standing back from oneself and one's attachments and asking 'why is keeping one's promises right?' and 'even if it is right what is that to me?' requires neither that one become a *tabula rasa* nor that one engage in some superhuman effort of self-induced amnesia.

Emphasizing the already socialized nature of the agent questioning her relations with others allows one further methodological point to be made.

---

[9] It seems to me fantastic to suggest that any society (past or present) could be so monistic as to eradicate the individual perspective. Rather, the motivation problem does not arise because when conflicts between individual interest and the interests of the community occur the agent gives precedence to the community. If this is a goal of communitarianism—and the suspicion must be that it is more often imputed to communitarians by critics than expressed by communitarians themselves—we have good reason to reject it, for the outcome would be a society of unreflective moral cripples.

[10] The literature on the liberal/communitarian debate is extensive. Good summaries can be found in Caney 1992, Gutmann 1985, Kymlicka 1990: ch. 6, Mulhall and Swift 1996, Taylor 1989*b*, Walzer 1990.

It was noted above (Chapter 4), that one way to characterize the difference between constructivism and *faux* constructivism is that the former aims to justify morality and the latter to explicate what is demanded by a commitment to the fundamental equal moral worth of persons. A genuine constructivist theory must, as noted in relation to the subjective form of the question given above, do more than engage in this kind of explicatory work. However, there is a different sense of explication to which the constructivist theory developed here appeals. What is primarily at issue is the existence of norms that engage the agent with imperatival force. If the regulative place of such norms can be explained in such a way as to show that it is reasonable for an agent to endorse this regulative role of moral reasons— indeed it can be recommended to the agent that she do so—then this, it is argued below, is sufficient to meet the challenge to which constructivism is put.[11] This will not be a justification in the sense traditionally associated with constructivism, an answer to the rational egoist who asks 'why ought I be moral?', but that is not to say that it cannot be conceived of a justification of morality at all. Explanations can sometimes serve as justifications. The difference, then, between the explicatory project of *faux* constructivism and the project undertaken here is that the former seeks to unpack a particular substantive moral commitment whereas the latter seeks to understand and explain the place of moral norms in practical reason. Of course, in pursuing the latter there are, as already noted, *faux* constructivist dangers.

So, the question is, 'Given that I have value for myself what is the nature of my relations with others?' To answer this, it is necessary first to consider the perspective of the individual.

### The personal perspective

Constructivism attempts to overcome the separation of the personal and moral perspectives without 'smuggling in' substantive moral assumptions. It posits a socialized agent standing back from her commitments and asking whether she has reason to endorse, cultivate, and maintain those commitments that she has, or whether she has reason to renounce those commitments and, perhaps, adopt new ones. What does it mean to stand back from one's commitments? If constructivism is to avoid the charge of begging the question the agent must, in the first instance, try to shed the organizing forms of reason through which she is used to living her life.

---

[11] Nagel pursues a similar strategy in *The Possibility of Altruism* (1970: see esp. 5).

Initially, then, she must think of herself as a mere psycho-physical organism possessing certain latent and actual capacities and desires. Although it is difficult to conceive of a person in this way it is possible to conceive of a human being living in an 'immediate' way, acting without reflection (in a manner unregulated by reason) on the desires that she has at any given moment. The first question, then, is whether it can be shown that such a being has reason to endorse any of the substantive regulating forms of reason that the constructivist theorist puts into question.

It might be thought that there is at least one principle that the agent ought to accept: the instrumental principle that the agent 'take the means to his ends'. This looks straightforward. Given that the agent desires certain things, it makes sense to endorse a principle that ensures the organization of his activities so as best to realize his desires. However, making this step is considerably less straightforward than it might appear. This is because for the instrumental principle to have any normative bite the agent must conceive of himself as having a reason to flourish, in the first instance to realize his desires as effectively as possible. However, this is not merely an extension of any original desire. In short, if what is really at issue is a principle of prudence, to organize one's activities so as best to realize one's ends, then the agent must commit himself to a conception of his flourishing and to his doing so. This point is made, in a different context, by Christine Korsgaard. As she puts it, 'the instrumental principle says nothing about our ends, so it is completely unequipped to say either that we ought to desire our overall good or that we ought to prefer it to more immediate or local satisfactions' (Korsgaard 1997: 231; cf. Charvet 1995: ch. 4).

Given that the agent in question is conceived of as having shed those aspects of her self-understanding owed to her social formation, the question is whether the agent has reason to adopt a regulative prudential principle designed to allow her best to realize her overall good. Of course, given that the agent is conceived of at this stage as a separate asocial individual the account of her good must similarly be from an asocial perspective. The account that meets this requirement must, then, be in terms of those goods that promote the individual's well-being given the kind of psycho-physical organism that she is; goods such as food, water, shelter, and the freedom to gain access to these (cf. Charvet 1995: 79). The adoption of prudence as a regulative principle allows the agent to organize the pursuit of her good in the most effective way. Moreover, if the agent can rightfully think of herself as having an interest in the realization of her good as a single psycho-physical organism extended over time, then a still richer prudential principle will be needed to regulate the agent's pursuit of her good. However, this is not to answer the constructivist question, which is whether the self-reflective agent, standing back from the regulative principles in accordance with which she lives her life, has reason to endorse (maintain, or adopt) a prudential principle as a higher-order regulative principle. What can the constructivist say, as it were, to recommend such a course?

In the first instance, of course, what recommends the adoption of prudence is that it better allows the agent to flourish. It ensures the more successful pursuit of those things that the agent, given the kind of being that she is, has reason to value. However, this is not all that can be said. In addition, the constructivist can appeal to what Rawls calls the 'Aristotelian Principle'. It will be recalled from Chapter 5 that this says that 'other things equal, human beings enjoy the exercise of their realized capacities (their innate or trained abilities), and their enjoyment increases the more the capacity is realized, or the greater its complexity' (Rawls 1971: 426, see also 426 n. 20). Although it is not always true that, to use Rawls's example, someone who can play both chess and checkers (draughts) well will invariably prefer to play chess (sometimes the simple pleasures are the best), the constructivist can hold out to the agent the possibility of organizing the pursuit of his good through a regulative principle, and this is to take control of (an aspect of) one's life; to live by a law that one gives oneself.

The trouble is, of course, that these recommendations speak to the agent insofar as she commits herself to a conception of herself as a being of a particular kind and to a related account of her flourishing, and the constructivist cannot claim that any such commitment is commanded by reason, or by anything else (cf. Charvet 1995: 79–80). Insofar as the agent makes the commitment to understand herself and her good this way, the constructivist can claim that the agent has reason to endorse (maintain or adopt) the regulative role of prudential reason. The commitment that the agent has to prudence can, then, be partially underwritten by reason, but nothing more. Thus, confronted by an agent who insists that the constructivist must show that there is a decisive reason why an asocial individual, committed to living unreflectively—or indeed to not living at all—ought to adopt prudence as an organizing form through which to live his life, the constructivist must accept that this cannot be done. However, that is surely not a reasonable demand. To meet the challenge that prudence is, in some sense, a fool's strategy (or a perverse confidence trick performed by the weak and uncertain on those who would seize the day) the argument above is enough.

Already, then, the constructivist theorist must accept a degree of contingency in the grounding of regulative norms through which the agent conducts herself. Reason itself cannot command that the agent commit herself to flourishing as a being with particular interests and capacities. However, there are reasons why an agent would endorse a regulative role for prudential reason, and these are surely sufficient to convince the agent reflecting on the nature of her good (who is already a social agent) that the commitment involved in endorsing this conception of herself, in taking control of her desires through the regulative use of prudential reason, is a reasonable one. At its weakest, the claim might be understood in terms of the negative question put by the agent reflecting from a subjective stance: 'Do I have reason to renounce the commitment that I have to prudential reason?' The answer to this question, given by the constructivist theorist on behalf of the agent reflecting on her good, is 'no'.

## Entering co-operation

If the agent endorses her commitment to her own flourishing through prudential reason, the first question of her relations to others is whether it is in her interests to enter co-operation at all. Given the very thin conception of interests to which the agent can appeal this question takes the form of asking whether her access to the goods of food, shelter, etc. that she needs to flourish as a separate being is more secure, and whether the goods themselves are likely to be more plentiful, in co-operation than would be the case if she acted alone. It is a condition of the agent endorsing the will to co-operate that there must be a 'pay-off' in terms of access to these goods. Fortunately it is clear for most people in most societies that the co-operative surplus is, as Rawls and Gauthier agree, very great, although not sufficiently so for there to be no questions of its proper distribution.

However, the agent's self-interest cannot be adequately understood in these narrowly individualistic terms. The agent, taking the reflective stance, realizes that her flourishing depends upon the co-operation of others in that it is only insofar as there is mutual recognition of terms of co-operation to govern interaction that co-operation and the co-operative surplus can be realized. The agent has reason to will the existence of terms of co-operation through which the co-operative surplus and her self-interest is served, and in doing so her self-interest becomes tied to the interests of her co-contractors. This is because in willing the existence of terms of co-operation she wills the existence of terms which are to the benefit of all the co-operating members, for if organizing the pursuit of their good through the terms of co-operation were not in others' interests they would have no reason to co-operate. This, then, provides the idea of a common good through which the self-interest of each is aligned with that of every other. However, the terms of co-operation are not moral terms. The agent's self-interest merely coincides with the self-interest of other agents; each views the terms as a necessary means to the realization of her ends. The constructivist theory has advanced no further than a society of straightforward maximizers.

To be clear, the idea of agents coming from the personal perspective to will terms of co-operation can be contrasted with the Lockean (and Nozickean) idea of individuals coming to the contract as possessors of absolute rights and the ensuing problem of finding a mechanism through which to mediate the claims of each individual with respect to those rights (Locke 1988; Nozick 1974). The Lockean account cannot overcome the problem that when conflicts arise between rights holders in the use of their rights each has a well-grounded claim in his possession of absolute and natural rights. Any mediation of those rights claims through a collective determination of the content of the rights undermines the individualist core of the Lockean theory. If the external account of rights as guaranteed by a god, or derived from transcendental reason, is rejected then the terms which govern co-operation must be grounded solely in the wills of the contractors; each has reason to will the existence of terms of co-operation and to understand her self-interest as tied to the maintenance of these terms. This is the theory that is being developed here.

However, the better realization of the agent's non-social interests is only one condition for moral co-operation because whilst it provides a good reason for the individual to co-operate, it provides good reason to enter co-operation on the best terms available, and if this is the case then the community could only organize around co-operative (prudential) principles of mutual advantage. The idea that the agent's self-interest is tied to the interests of others through the existence of terms of co-operation is insufficient to ground morality, therefore, because each is tied to the terms of co-operation only by self-interest. The relationship of the agent and the terms of co-operation is a contingent and instrumental one. That is to say, the terms of co-operation lack imperatival force.

## BEYOND SELF-INTEREST

The view of morality that will be defended here is, as has already been noted, that moral constraints are those that could be justified to agents in a hypothetical choosing situation in which each stands back from her commitments and claims value for herself, and in which each attempts to advance her good.[12] If the theory is to make the step from self-interest to morality it must be able to overcome the gap between the agent and the terms of co-operation and explain the latter's imperatival force. The theorist constructing on behalf of the agent reflecting on the commitments that she has must explain why the agent should accept the content of some or all of those commitments and endorse the regulative priority that she gives to them. Moral constraints are terms of co-operation, but they cannot just be that.

Thus, in the remainder of this chapter (and into the next) the concern will be largely with the feature of imperatival force. The project is to show how each agent can incorporate adherence to the terms of fair co-operation into her idea of the good, and give them priority over the direct pursuit of her self-interest. Rather than conceive of her self-interest as fundamentally at odds with the demands of co-operation, then, the moral agent (as developed below) understands herself as a co-operative being and conceives of her self-interest mediated by co-operative norms. To borrow from the title of Charvet's book, an 'ethical community' (Charvet 1995) is a co-operative endeavour for mutual advantage, but it is also a community of agents each of whom conceives of his individual flourishing as connected to the flourishing of the others through the sharing of a set of norms to which each gives imperatival force. Thus, it is this feature, above all, that demands explanation.

To recall, the agent, reflecting on the commitments that she has, begins by endorsing prudential reason as a way of organizing her life so as to flourish in strictly individual terms. She realizes that co-operation—and, therefore, norms of co-operation—is necessary if she is to flourish and therefore wills such terms and general adherence to them. However, she has reason to will (i) terms of co-operation that favour herself and (ii) that everyone else should adhere to the terms of the agreement whilst allowing that she free-ride. The constructivist must provide additional reasons for the agent to endorse the priority of the co-operative norms over the narrow pursuit of self-interest, thus showing to the agent that she does not have reason to

---

[12] The hypothetical choosing situation, then, is not some imaginary meeting place nor an account of the way that co-operation could have come about without the contravention of any agent's rights or rationality. Rather, all that is meant is that a reflective standpoint is adopted in which the agent considers the nature of her relations with others given that she has value for herself. I describe it as a hypothetical choosing situation because this reflective process is to be undertaken by a theorist rather than by each agent.

renounce the moral life, but rather that she should endorse it and take responsibility for the living of it.

The constructivist can appeal here to the arguments to which Gauthier appeals: that agents have translucent dispositions and that constrained maximizers will flourish because they will be offered opportunities for co-operation which straightforward maximizers will be denied. These arguments, as noted above, have some force, but not enough to explain what constructivism must explain; the integration of the personal and moral perspectives. The reasons given by Gauthier as to why the agent should adopt the disposition of constrained maximization are insufficient to explain this integration and so cannot give an account of why an agent should commit herself to morality as a regulative ideal. The rational non-tuist concerned to maximize her utility cannot recognize the imperatival force of moral norms, but can only sometimes treat the norms of co-operation as if they have such force in order to maximize her utility.

Gauthier's arguments provide some reasons why the agent will not try to enforce terms that reflect force and fraud (even if they do reflect unequal bargaining strength), and why the agent may not find it rational to free-ride. However, as long as Gauthier cannot adequately explain how distinctively moral reasons become relevant to the agent this cannot be an adequate theory of morality and it will be possible to show (as was demonstrated in the previous chapter) that under certain circumstances it is rational to use force and fraud, and to free-ride.

## An existential commitment

What is needed is for the agent to conceive of his interests as aligned with the interests of others, not merely in the sense that each accepts that there are prudential reasons for participation in a common enterprise of co-operation, but also in the sense that each agent comes to view every other participating agent as a being of equal value to himself and comes to think of his flourishing as tied together with the flourishing of those others. The difference is between the agent viewing others as necessary co-participants in co-operation whose existence is merely useful to him and his viewing others as the source of valid claims, as beings to whom equal respect is owed.

If the reasons Gauthier gives are insufficient to show the rationality of such a dispositional change is there any more that can be said? John Charvet presents the decision to accept the regulative priority of moral reasons as analogous to the step taken when the agent endorses the regulative role of prudential reason; that is, as a decision for which there are some (very good) reasons but which is not fully underwritten by reason:

The gap between reason and [the] authority [of moral norms] has to be filled by an existential commitment of the individual to pursue his good through the moral life . . . This is evidently no blind and irrational leap in the dark. The reasons for making the commitment are evident for everyone to see, and the ability to sustain it will already have been developed in each normal person. (Charvet 1995: 172)

Although the choice is 'ungrounded', then, it is not 'irrational' (Charvet 1995: 172).

The analogy with the endorsing of prudential reason is clear. In that case reason cannot bridge the gap between the pursuit of desires as they occur and without regard for future states of affairs, and the living of life, conceiving of one's individual good, from the perspective of prudential reason. However, it was argued above that there are many good reasons why the agent should choose to endorse herself as prudentially rational; reasons accessible to the desire-driven but self-conscious agent. Certainly these reasons are 'evident' and 'the ability to sustain' such a commitment will be present in any normal being brought up in conditions that are not characterized by dreadful uncertainty.[13]

In the case of morality, the reasons that at least partly underwrite the commitment—the existential leap—are related to the agent in more complex ways than was the case with prudence. What is being demanded of the agent in the jump from prudential to moral reason is very great. One is to conceive of one's good as realized through the living of a moral life, through the organizing of the pursuit of one's self-interest in accordance with the demands of impartial norms. This is to accept reasons of a different kind. The prudential attitude is to see co-operation and the rules of co-operation as necessary means to the realization of one's ends. To endorse oneself as a moral being is to alter the conception of one's ends. Rather than understand one's ends as those of a separate, asocial being, and as better secured through co-operation, one must understand one's ends as the ends of a co-operative being. One's flourishing is thus not merely contingently aligned with the flourishing of the whole, but necessarily connected to it.

---

[13] Clearly if one is brought up in conditions such that one has good reason to doubt that one will be alive tomorrow, or that resources available today will still be available tomorrow, one will be unlikely to have developed prudential reason as a regulative desire. That is not to say that prudential reason has no place (since any plausible account of prudential reason will include discounting for uncertainty and in these conditions the rate of discount could be 100%). It is to say that the agent's ability to endorse prudential reasons as regulative might be undermined.

Given that the commitment to morality is very demanding what are the reasons that could, at least partially, underwrite it? If constructivism is to bridge the gap between self-interest and morality it must be that the agent can reasonably understand her good as advanced through co-operation. Charvet's argument, like Gauthier's, depends on the individual realizing that stable co-operation is only possible insofar as each co-operator commits himself to the regulative priority of moral reasons, albeit that Charvet, unlike Gauthier, is aware that reason is insufficient to ground such a commitment (Charvet 1995: ch. 8). However, as long as the agent's understanding of her good is strictly in terms of her individual interests, the reasons that she has for committing to the regulative priority of morality will be undermined by the possibility of her taking up an 'intermediate' position between outright straightforward maximization and morality. If this is the case it would seem that reasons to do with stable and secure access to a co-operative surplus cannot contribute to the closing of the gap between the personal and moral perspectives for such reasons can underwrite long-term straightforward or reserved maximization. That is not to say that an agent, reflecting on the benefits of stable, moral co-operation and realizing that this is made possible by the joint commitment of all to the moral life, is unreasonable in making the existential commitment to pursue his good through such a life. The point of the idea of commitment is, after all, that it goes beyond what can be commanded by reason. However, the personal perspective so far adopted does not contribute much to the underwriting of such a commitment. Whilst morality must serve self-interest, self-interest as conceived of so far does not recommend morality.

It will be remembered that there was an additional reason for the agent to endorse the regulative role of prudential reason: the Aristotelian Principle. Can this add to the reasonableness of making the commitment to the moral life? It is, of course, true that the organization of the pursuit of one's good through authoritative moral norms does meet the requirements of the Aristotelian Principle, for it represents an additional (and higher) level in a hierarchy of reasons. The agent in organizing his life first in accordance with prudential and then moral reason takes command of his life and takes responsibility for shaping a particular kind of life (this is developed below). However, there are many conflicting 'ideals' of a good life, many of which are repugnant and the Aristotelian Principle alone cannot distinguish them. A person may adopt as a highest good the goal of inflicting the most suffering on other human beings or of being able to remember the value of pi to more decimal places than anyone else. Such a person may live her life in a single-minded, self-disciplined way, extending and developing her latent talents and organizing her desires in the light of this conception of the good. Yet the first of these activities is morally repulsive and the second morally neutral (cf. Charvet 1995: 170–1).

What is needed is a commitment to the moral life and given that this choice cannot be fully underwritten by reason it must have the characteristics Charvet ascribes to it. However, Charvet, like Gauthier, believes that the decision is not 'blind' or 'irrational' because of reasons of stability and of access to the goods of social co-operation. It has been argued above that these reasons can underwrite a prudential attitude to the norms of co-operation and that they, therefore, fail to speak to the rational, self-interested non-tuist as reasons to conceive of herself as a moral being. That is, as a being whose flourishing is to be understood as realized through organizing her life in accordance with the regulative priority of moral norms. The full weight of the final step to morality, then, must be borne by the existential choice.

However, it is argued below that the weight borne by the commitment to morality can be reduced by a careful examination of the personal perspective. The assumptions of rationality and self-interest are foundational and provide the basic building blocks of constructivist theory. The condition to be questioned then is the assumption of non-tuism.

Before turning to the assumption of non-tuism, it is worth sketching what a commitment to morality entails, should such a commitment be a reasonable one to make. What is envisaged is that the agent endorses the priority of moral norms over the pursuit of narrow self-interest. That is, she understands herself as, together with others, creating (or taking responsibility for) the authority of moral rules. To do this is to align one's good with others so that one understands the pursuit of one's good in a manner mediated by the demands of morality. Of course, in doing so one realizes that each contractor can only reasonably make the commitment to live the moral life if the terms of agreement are acceptable to each. The advantages of stable co-operation in which the norms of co-operation are endowed by every participant with imperatival force are only available if those terms could be freely accepted by every participant. Thus, to take up morality is to recognize one's co-participants as of equal status, 'equally valuable founders of the moral order' (Charvet 1995: 172), or, as Gauthier puts it,

The just person views her fellows, not as instruments that she may use in advancing her own ends, but as partners in a cooperative enterprise each of whom is due a share of its benefits. . . . seeing them as rational deliberators, she determines their due in interaction by appealing to what would be the outcome of their joint deliberation about the terms of interaction. In other words she supposes that what is due a rational deliberator from interaction is what he would agree to voluntarily but subject to his recognition that everyone involved in the interaction also agree. In this way she gives determinate content to the idea that from the standpoint of justice persons are valued as ends in themselves. (Gauthier 1993*c*: 206)

The point is, of course, that the constructivist generates impartiality—the commitment to view others as ends in themselves—from the commitment to conceive of oneself with others as the 'founders' of the moral community. It is not an external requirement that must be reflected in the agreement.

Finally, in committing himself to morality, the agent (as noted above) extends his latent powers in accordance with the Aristotelian Principle. In subjecting his desires, passions, feelings, and so on to the regulation of prudence and morality, the agent gives himself a sense of self that is beyond that which belongs to a being that merely responds to these things. The agent, to repeat Rousseau's phrase, lives by a law that he gives to himself. This idea provides another interpretation of those Kantian passages of Rawls cited in Chapter 5. In taking control of her life and organizing it in accordance with the demands of prudential and moral reasons, the agent frees herself from 'contingency and happenstance' (cf. Charvet 1995: ch. 4; Korsgaard 1997: 247; Mendus 1999: 68–73).

However, the argument is getting ahead of itself. Above it was promised that a re-examination of the assumption of non-tuism would reduce the burden of the existential commitment, and it is time to turn to that investigation.

## THE ASSUMPTION OF NON-TUISM

A non-tuist 'takes no interest in the interests of those with whom he interacts. His utility function, measuring his preferences, is strictly independent of the utility functions of those whom he affects' (Gauthier 1986: 311). Non-tuism is a concept first introduced in economics (see Wicksteed 1993: i. 180; cf. Gauthier 1986: 87) and its usefulness in economic theory is not hard to determine. A perfectly competitive market is premised on the relations of discrete suppliers and consumers who individually own and consume factors of production, goods, and services. If producers and consumers take an interest in the interests of those with whom they interact the free market of economic theory will be distorted. Although similar comments apply to rational choice theory, in which the non-tuist assumption is equally common and equally useful, non-tuism has a less obvious role in both *faux* constructivist and constructivist political theory.

Rawls adopts a stronger version of non-tuism than the one given above as a stylized assumption about the motivations of people in the original position; they are 'conceived as not taking an interest in one another's interests' (Rawls 1971: 13), but he makes it clear that this is just a simplifying assumption and not a description of actual people. In fact, the assumption is necessary to remove the possibility that the adoption of the difference principle is put into doubt by problems related to envy. As the argument for the difference principle can be made independent of the contract the assumption of mutual disinterest is revealed as an (in this case, slightly unfortunate)[14] assumption required to get the hypothetical choosing situation (the original position) to deliver the right answer.

Nevertheless, even if the assumption of non-tuism plays no significant role in *faux* constructivist theory, its importance to economics and rational choice theory should make the constructivist theorist cautious about tinkering with it. Both Charvet and Gauthier assume non-tuism in their constructivist theories, yet both deny that it is a realistic assumption to make of real people. Why then do they think it essential to the motivation of people in the construction? The reason is that both worry that to allow the possibility of tuistic motivations will render the justification of morality dependent on the contingent affective dispositions of agents. The worry is that if morality is grounded on certain affective states it is hard to resist the conclusion that it is binding only on those who possess such traits. Charvet and Gauthier, like Kant[15] and (to an extent) Rawls, think that moral constraints must hold independent of our affective ties.

What the constructivist desires, then, is an account of morality that can generate, or build on, people's affective capacity for morality, but this must be distinguished from an affective morality:

---

[14] The assumption of mutual disinterest is unfortunate because, like the assumption of risk aversion, it is needed for the original position to generate the two principles. However, neither assumption meets the condition of being a 'restriction' that people would think 'reasonable to impose' when considering the question of justice (on this see Barry 1989: 1995*a*).

[15] Gauthier explicitly draws the connection with Kant. He writes: 'For we agree with Kant that moral constraints must apply whatever preferences individuals happen to have' (1986: 100). Note, this is incompatible with the assumption that individuals do have preferences of a particular kind (that is, non-tuist preferences).

The capacity for an affective morality does not pre-suppose any prior conception of morality. It is simply the capacity to be constrained in one's asocial pursuits by concerns for others; it is identified as moral in that it introduces constraints, not in that it motivates one to adhere to constraints that one already recognizes. An affective capacity for morality . . . introduces no constraints, but disposes one emotionally and motivationally to adhere to constraints previously and independently accepted. (Gauthier 1986: 328)

Yet constructivism, if it is to succeed as a moral theory, must account for the individual aligning his interests with others in a common good—a co-operative scheme for which morality is the organizing form—through the adoption of fair and impersonal norms as regulative of the pursuit of self-interest. As Gauthier says,

economic man [a self-interested non-tuist] lacks the capacity to be truly the just man. He understands the arguments for moral constraint, but he regards such constraint as an evil from which he would be free. Given the opportunity to use morality as an instrument of domination, he unhesitatingly does so, because his concern with morality is purely an instrumental one, and his goals to which morality is instrumental are asocial. (1986: 328)

Although in the final chapter of *Morals by Agreement*, 'The Liberal Individual', Gauthier thinks that he can show how morals by agreement are 'more than the morals of economic man', he continues to maintain that they have a 'non-tuistic rationale [such that] their constraints bind rationally' (1986: 328).

However, Peter Vallentyne has questioned why it is that Gauthier and Rawls adopt mutual unconcern as a characteristic of their bargaining agents when both admit that it is a counter-factual assumption; real people are not (for the most part) non-tuists. Recall that the reason for the assumption of non-tuism is to avoid grounding morality on certain contingent (specifically, altruistic) affective ties. Gauthier writes 'moral constraints must apply in the absence of other-directed interests, indeed they must apply whatever preferences individuals may happen to have' (1986: 100). However, this argument admits of two interpretations. Vallentyne distinguishes them as follows:

On the strong view (the one held by Kant), the existential quantifier over constraints comes first: there are (particular) rational constraints on conduct that apply no matter what people's desires are like. On the weak view, the universal quantifier over preferences comes first: no matter what people's preferences are like, there are (some sort or other of) rational constraints on conduct. (Vallentyne 1991a: 72)

It is clear that constructivists (thus, Charvet and Gauthier) cannot hold the strong view because this would be to accept that there are constraints on conduct that are rationally binding independently of whether they contribute to the satisfaction of people's preferences. However, the weak view not only makes the assumption of non-tuism unnecessary, but, given the nature of the constructivist attempt to derive rules from the agreement of people unconstrained by artificial restrictions on which of their preferences are to count, actually renders the non-tuist assumption incoherent. As Vallentyne puts it,

But on the weaker reading, there is no need to *assume* that we are mutually unconcerned. On the weak reading, the important point to make is that *the existence* of constraints on conduct does not depend on the nature of our preferences (and, in particular, it does not depend on the existence of altruistic preferences). One need not establish that the *content* of these constraints is independent of what our actual preferences are like. Indeed, if these constraints are to be rationally grounded, and if one accepts (as Gauthier does) the instrumental conception of rationality, then the exact content of the constraints (determining which actions satisfy the constraints) must depend on people's actual (reflective) preferences. The counterfactual assumption of mutual unconcern, therefore, undermines the rationality of the constraints that would be agreed upon. (1991*a*: 73)

Although the claim that non-tuism has no role in constructivist theory is straightforward, Vallentyne's point needs to be unpacked carefully. The constructivist project, as Gauthier conceives it, is to show the existence of rationally justified constraints on the pursuit of self-interest. The existence of these constraints must not depend on people having particular preferences (for example, their being altruistic). The project is one of trying to show that even if people are strictly self-interested it is rational for them to conform with the demands of morality. However, this project requires that the constructivist make no assumptions about people's preferences, for the whole point is to show that no matter what people's preferences are like there exist rationally justified constraints on the manner in which they should pursue those preferences. The second point that Vallentyne makes in the quotation above is that the constructivist is also committed to defending the content of particular constraints as rationally justified. However, given that the test deployed by Gauthier is whether the constraints could be justified to each agent given that each is concerned to advance her good, the assumption of non-tuism is also inappropriate here. What it is rational for the agent to agree to depends on the agent's actual (reflective) preferences.

If the first project is to show that no matter what people's preferences there are rationally justified constraints on the pursuit of self-interest then even if the assumption of non-tuism is inappropriate one can understand what the constructivist is trying to do in adopting it. The point, surely, is to deal with the most difficult case: if the non-tuist can be shown to have reason to constrain the pursuit of his self-interest (in a way that can be plausibly interpreted as in accordance with moral constraints) then the argument is won. However, it is noted above that this is not the constructivist project that is being pursued here. To meet Nietzsche's challenge it is not necessary, and nor is it possible, to show that rationality alone can generate moral norms such that the rational egoist can be shown that he ought to constrain the pursuit of his self-interest in accordance with such norms. Rather, the constructivist project as it is understood here is to understand the place of moral reasons in the practical reason of a socialized agent reflecting on her commitments. Of course, if her commitment to morality is thereby revealed as entirely irrational, or as a commitment the nature of which is, in some sense, non-rational, then the agent can reasonably reject it. However, if, as in the case of the demands of prudential reason, the agent can be shown that there are good, if non-decisive, reasons for endorsing and maintaining her commitment then that will be taken to be enough to show that morality is neither a fetish nor a confidence trick.

Nevertheless, constructivism, even as it is conceived of here, is committed to showing the existence of constraints on conduct that can be partially underwritten by reason. Even if the assumption of non-tuism is inappropriate here, this argument cannot be converted by sleight of hand into the argument that such constraints are grounded in the affective ties that people actually have for one another. It would hardly be a triumph for the constructivist to show that some people have reason to behave well towards those others for whom, for example, they happen to feel sympathy.

Vallentyne's division of the constructivist argument into the projects of showing that whatever people's preferences there exist some constraints on conduct and of showing what content such constraints have obscures an important point. If the agent is committed to his flourishing, to his best realizing his overall good, then there are some constraints on the agent if what is first imagined is an agent who is entirely driven by his most immediate and strongest desire. Such an agent has, it is argued above, reason to endorse norms of prudential rationality and, what is more, has reason to constrain the direct pursuit of his self-interest in co-operation with others. In this sense, the LSM and RM do obey constraints on the pursuit of their self-interest. What is currently at stake is the status of such constraints. As it stands, the agent conceives of them as constraints, as 'an evil from which he would be free'. This, of course, is not the case for the reflective agent when considering prudential norms. Such an agent may sometimes be tempted by immediate desires, but by incorporating prudence as a higher-order regulative principle he accepts that prudence offers the best means through which to pursue his overall good; he does not see it as imposing alien and regrettable restrictions on the pursuit of that good. If constructivism is to succeed it must similarly show that reason can underwrite the incorporation of the constraints of co-operation as such a regulative principle. This is an argument not so much about the existence of constraints as about their status.

The argument that follows is that dropping the assumption of non-tuism and paying attention to the goods valued by co-operating agents provides a basis from which to argue that the commitment to the moral life can be understood as supported by good reasons, and as neither a fetish nor a confidence trick. Moreover, this is not to reduce the theory to an affective account, for it is not an assumption about people's goods that grounds the constraints. The constraints are not a product of contingent preferences.[16] The point is this: morality is to be understood as the organizing form of a community created by the commitment of each to live together with others on moral terms. In asking whether she should make such a commitment, the agent must be able to conceive of herself as an independent (for otherwise the question would be meaningless). However, the conception of herself as an independent need not—indeed, cannot— be maintained as the only perspective from which the question of whether to make the commitment to morality can be asked. From the stance of an independent, if this is what the agent's idea of her good happens to be, the commitment to give regulative priority to the constraints of co-operation represents a great step; one which narrow self-interest cannot commend. However, once the assumption of non-tuism is relinquished, the agent may be able to appeal to considerations of her good that provide reasons that will underwrite the moral commitment. What follows is an attempt to show that there are such reasons to which the constructivist theorist can appeal without the theory depending on the merely contingent; on affective ties that agents happen to have.

---

[16] Constructivist theory cannot succeed entirely in meeting the requirement of even the weak view (because the existence of any rational constraints—even those of prudential rationality—requires an assumption that the person possess certain minimal desires related to her flourishing), but it can meet the relevant demand of showing that the existence of some constraints is not dependent 'on the existence of altruistic preferences'.

## THE PROBLEM OF RECIPROCITY

Towards the end of the section on prudential reason, the agent reflecting on the question 'what is the nature of my relations with others, given that I have value for myself?' is considered as formulating the first part of the enquiry in the negative question 'given that I organize the pursuit of my interests, and understand those interests, through the application of prudential reason, have I cause to renounce the role of prudential reason and to give myself up to the unregulated pursuit of desires?' The analogous question that the already socialized and moral agent asks concerns whether she has reason to renounce the moral norms through which she regulates her conduct. Of course, there is a difference between asking what one has reason to renounce and what one has reason to endorse or adopt, but nevertheless pursuing this negative question might offer an insight into the reasons that the agent might have for affirming (rather than merely not renouncing) his understanding of his good as mediated through the demands of morality.[17] Indeed, in his discussion of non-tuism and affective morality Gauthier hints at such a way of viewing things:

We may distinguish the pure non-tuist, whose affections cannot be engaged except by his own concerns, from the person who demands a non-tuistic rationale for constraint, but whose affections may then be engaged by constraints so justified. *She does not allow herself to be disadvantaged or worsened* by historic concerns, but she does not seek to take advantage of or better herself in relation to others by seeking to circumvent constraints non-historically justified. (Gauthier 1986: 329, emphasis added)

Of course, if constructivist theory is to do any work at all it cannot be sufficient just to show that an agent with a desire to live a moral life might just as well not renounce morality, for such a result would hardly be surprising. However, as suggested above, an enquiry into the kinds of reasons relevant to deciding whether to renounce morality as a highest-order regulative ideal might provide assistance in analysing the arguments that can be offered on behalf of the moral life in general. Of course, those reasons will not be sufficient to show that it is irrational for an immoral, non-moral, or even moral agent to refuse to adopt (or endorse) the moral life, but they

---

[17] This idea first emerged during a meeting of the Political Theory Workshop at the University of York and I am especially grateful to the participants (many or all of whom are acknowledged at the beginning of this book) and to Sue Mendus for subsequent written comments.

may be such as to show that at least there are some good, if non-decisive, reasons that underwrite the commitment to the moral life.

The point of the personal perspective from which the regulative role of prudential reason is adopted is to capture the authority of self-interest in constructivist theory. The personal perspective encourages the agent to consider the question of his relations to others from the view of what those relations do for him. However, this would seem to be at the heart of the failure of Gauthier's theory to give an account of 'moral' rather than 'economic' man, for it seems to leave no room for anything other than an instrumental attitude to the norms of co-operation. Concentrating still on the imperatival force of moral norms, the problem would seem to be this: the moral agent, reflecting on the commitments that she has, can ask whether these commitments lead her to be taken advantage of. However, this thought seems destined to place the agent on a slippery slope towards an instrumental view of all constraints (and of other people). Nevertheless, despite the danger of the slippery slope, the constructivist is committed to a conception of moral relations as being underpinned by reciprocity. Morality is the product of co-operation between agents each of whom claims value for herself. If such co-operation is to be reasonable, then, it must further the good of those who engage in it. Before considering the regulative role of moral norms, it is worth considering in more detail the idea of reciprocity.

The place of reciprocity in human interaction will be more or less explicit depending on the nature of the relationship. In a contract between strangers, for example, the reciprocal nature of the deal is explicit and provides a complete account. One agent contracts to do $x$ for another in return for the other doing $y$. In other relations the place of reciprocity is not so obvious. Consider relations of friendship: some philosophers, notably Michael Sandel and others to whom the label communitarian is often given, argue that it is inappropriate and damaging to talk of questions of justice—or relations of reciprocity—between friends. Once the language of justice is introduced it tends to dominate or replace other kinds of virtues, such as loyalty and love. The argument is often put that, for example, to invite one's friend to dinner only because one feels a duty to repay an invitation is to mistake the nature of friendship. Similarly, to go out to dinner with someone who is your friend, but then to think that it is important and just that one divide the bill scrupulously so as to ensure that each person pays for exactly what she has eaten, is also to invoke a language that is inappropriate to friendship.

This objection to the use of the concept of reciprocity in analysing all, or most, human relations is intuitively attractive. Most people would find a couple who invariably divided up household tasks equally because they regarded doing so as just (so that some acts, such as doing the washing up when it is the other's turn because one knows the other to be tired, become acts of injustice) as having missed something important about the relative importance of love and justice in being a couple. However, imagine that two friends go out for a meal one day each week. They always split the bill equally and neither is particularly short of money. Having to pay half the bill is not a serious inconvenience for either party. However, one person invariably orders the most expensive items from the menu while the other tends to think that he can eat just as well choosing cheaper things. It is surely plausible to imagine that the one person might say, 'I like my friend, and think of him as my friend, but it irritates me that he never suggests paying more of the bill when he always orders more expensive dishes.' Although clearly if this person went on also to order expensive dishes just so as to get back at the other we would say that relations of friendship no longer obtained, it does not seem to be the case that the invocation of justice in the irritated thought expressed is unreasonable, inappropriate, or destructive of the relationship of friendship. Jean Hampton makes a similar argument for a woman who is taken for granted by her family (Hampton 1991*b*: 54). In such a case, the woman having the thought that she is taken for granted (and expressing this thought in terms of reciprocity) surely does not immediately negate the relations of love that (*ex hypothesi*) characterize the family, it just reveals the ubiquity of relations of reciprocity in human relationships.

In all these cases the invocation of justice, the appeal to a fair distribution of benefits and burdens, perhaps reveals a failure of the relationship—the friend ought to realize that he always eats the more expensive items and offer to pay more; the husband and children ought to appreciate the woman and offer to share some of the household chores, etc. (but see below and n. 19)—and further breakdown might result in the domination of concerns of justice and the marginalizing, or disappearance, of the other virtues, but this is not inevitable. Most importantly, it is not the case that the appeal to justice does not make sense or is an appeal to something that must be imported into the relationship. Rather, reciprocity lies buried deep within all these relationships, perhaps beneath every human relationship (characterized by any and every virtue) that is not paternalistic or supererogatory.

The worry about the destructive effect of the language of reciprocity is that it seems to focus the agent's attention on her self-interest and place those with whom she co-operates and the rules that govern that co-operation in a relation to the agent such that they have only instrumental value. If human relations are at some level relations of reciprocity and there is a concern that those ties and commitments that go beyond self-interest and regulate our conduct appear to be the debris of an anthropomorphic or theological age, then the agent, realizing that her relations are underpinned by reciprocity, seems left with only the rationale of the economic individual. The allegation is that as constructivism encourages the agent to consider her relevant relations as, in part, underpinned by reciprocity, the constructivist cannot avoid establishing only a prudential or instrumental relationship between the individual and the norms of co-operation.

However, the situation is more complicated than this analysis allows for and the slippery slope can be avoided. Return to the agent who is reflecting on his commitments. Such an agent is required to consider whether maintaining those commitments advances his good. It is argued above that he has good (but not decisive) reasons to endorse the constraints of prudential rationality. The question then posed by the constructivist is, 'Does the agent have reason to endorse morality as a regulative ideal?' The answer is, 'Yes, if and only if, doing so serves the agent's good.' The allegation is that this stance inevitably leads to an instrumental view of co-operation and of other co-operators. However, critics of constructivism interpret 'good' as self-interest and, given the assumption of non-tuism, self-interest as self-concern. By doing so they provide themselves with the ammunition to allege that it is inconceivable that the agent should commit herself to a moral life, and they are encouraged in this interpretation by the insistence of constructivists on the assumption of non-tuism.

Recall the example of Fred and his co-waiters from Chapter 2. In the discussion of that example it was alleged that the fair play account could not make sense of the idea that Fred's co-participants—those with whom he had a reciprocal arrangement—did not envy him for his actions or wish to be like him (only more successful). Rather, they resented his actions and were disappointed that Fred should have tried to cheat them. The notion of reciprocity that lies beneath a plausible account of this tale cannot be the notion that fuels the arguments of the critics of constructivism or that which fuels Barry's critique of justice as mutual advantage (discussed in Chapter 6 above). How then is it to be understood? The crucial claim is that the agreement to which Fred and the other waiters had come created a common good, one which is given an organizing form by the norms of co-operation. Each, then, pursues his flourishing through those norms and conceives of his good as best realized through adherence to the norms that create and sustain the group. Such norms are, then, in Hollis's terms both regulative and (at least in part) constitutive of the agents' goods. Thus, when Fred's associates discover his cheating and call on the language of fairness and justice, they do not destroy or corrupt the shared enterprise. The allegation is that Fred, by his failure to adhere to the shared norms, has indicated that when he asked himself, 'what is in it for me?' he came to an answer that appealed only to his interests as a separate being. Of course, such a question and answer must be available to Fred, but the task of constructivism is to show that there are good reasons why, when he asks the question, he should give a different answer; an answer that appeals to an understanding of his good as aligned with that of others in the co-operative enterprise. The point here is just that if constructivism is successful in fulfilling this task then it can appeal to an idea of reciprocity that is far removed from that which underpins the allegation of the 'slippery slope'.[18]

Thus, the task of the argument below is to show that there are reasons that can underwrite the commitment that the agent makes to align his good together with others in a co-operative enterprise that is created and sustained by that commitment as made by each of the co-operating parties, and that is given an organizing form by the norms to which each would agree. Moreover, although it is argued above that the assumption of non-tuism is not part of this project, the argument must nevertheless avoid collapsing into either an affective theory or into a *faux* constructivist account. The moral motive is less than a dictate of rationality, but must be more than a merely contingent preference.

---

[18] I am grateful to Sue Mendus for discussion of these ideas and for a memo, 'Does Harpic Destroy Gauthier?'. Her ideas cast light on the example (taken from Hampton above) in which a wife feels taken for granted. The wife, in appealing to reciprocity and in alleging injustice, is not corrupting the relationship that she has with her family through the invocation of this language for her complaint is that her family do not do their bit, not for her in return for her having done what is agreed, but for sustaining the common good from which all benefit. In appealing to justice, the wife does not slide down the slippery slope of 'economic' reasoning, rather she alleges that such (inappropriate) reasoning is what is engaged in by those who free-ride.

# 8

# A Constructivist Theory of Moral Norms

## INTRODUCTION

The constructivist poses the question, 'Does the agent have reason to endorse morality as a regulative ideal?' and the answer is, 'Yes, if, and only if, doing so serves the agent's good.' This secures the authority of self-interest, but in so doing opens up the question of whether the constructivist can explain the imperatival force of moral norms. What is posited is a social agent standing back from, and reflecting on, her relations with others in light of her initial claim to value for herself. Assuming that the agent possesses certain minimal desires to flourish, the constructivist argument is that the agent has reason to understand her good as best pursued through the norms of prudential rationality. Further, the agent has reason to enter co-operation with others and reason, therefore, to regulate her behaviour in accordance with the demands of co-operation. However, from this starting point it would seem that the agent must take an instrumental attitude to co-operation and to those with whom she co-operates. The rules and norms of co-operation are, it would seem, restrictions on the agent's pursuit of her good. If so, at best the constructivist can ground mere compliance with norms of co-operation.

At the end of the last chapter it was argued that the gap between self-interest and morality was made artificially wide in constructivist theory by the assumption of non-tuism, and that such an assumption was unjustified. Moreover, it was argued that as there are no decisive reasons for an agent to accept the priority of moral norms, the agent had to make an existential commitment to the moral life. Whilst the advantages of participation in a stable system of co-operation are great, the misplaced assumption that the agent must have non-tuistic preferences means that (on that account) the commitment to morality must carry great weight. However, given that the assumption of non-tuism has no place in the theory, further consideration of the personal perspective is necessary. Thus, the first parts of this chapter are largely concerned with reflections on the goods that persons have reason to seek.

Before that one possible objection to the whole way of proceeding needs to be flagged. This is the argument that if the aspiration of constructivism is to ground moral constraints in non-contingent features of agents then it cannot rely on the goods that people happen to seek. Unless constructivism wishes to endorse certain goods, for example the good of friendship, as essential parts of human nature (which, of course, it does not), it must regard any preferences that people have for particular kinds of life as mere contingent features of those people. To do otherwise would be to deny the account of the self that the constructivist invokes, as being able to stand independent of its ends. In short, if the question is interpreted as, 'given the kind of life that I value, have I reason to affirm the regulative priority of moral constraints?', then this seems to sell short the foundational aspirations of constructivism. Surely, the constructivist should pose the initial question, 'is it in my interests to continue to value the kind of life that I value?'

This is a serious challenge because the separation of the self and its ends is essential to the whole reflective standpoint endorsed by constructivism. However, this standpoint is adopted by the constructivist theorist who is called upon to theorize about what reflective agents have reason to do and not to do. Without some account of what the agent has reason to pursue, the constructivist theorist could say nothing. So, for example, in the case of prudential reason the theorist posits that the agent has reason to pursue the goods of life, food, liberty, and so on, and, from this, goes on to argue that the agent has reason to pursue these goods in accordance with the demands of prudential reason. Of course, the constructivist avoids making essentialist claims, or claims on behalf of the external authority of transcendental reason, God, or whatever. Nothing, including the dictates of reason, commands the agent to understand his flourishing in the manner posited, nor to seek to flourish. None the less, there is nothing incomprehensible nor incoherent in the constructivist theorizing from the perspective of a particular account of human flourishing. Moreover, there are many good reasons that at least partially underwrite the commitment to prudence.

Nevertheless, there is a danger of begging the question in extending the account beyond that of the separate individual. However, the constructivist has no choice (and thus must find a way to avoid the danger). Whilst the perspective of the independent must be retained as one possible account of the good that the reflective agent might seek, the constructivist cannot assume that this is true of all agents. Thus, what is needed is some general account of the goods that, given the type of beings that they are, agents have reason to seek. This, it is argued below, is not to rely on what actual agents happen to prefer. Nor is it to deny the possibility of the separation of the self and the goods that it pursues.

Of course, the conception of the self as being separable from its ends does not require that the agent is imagined to be able to question every commitment that she has at one and the same time. Rather what is supposed is that the agent is capable of putting into question any given commitment in the sense that she can imagine what it would be to be otherwise (not to have that commitment or to have some other commitment). Consider, for example, an agent who carefully puts aside a certain amount of her income each month so as to build up savings for her old age. Such an agent might ask the question, 'have I reason to renounce this careful life?' On reflection she might find that, given that she is risk averse and that she desires to have a comfortable retirement, she does not have reason to do so. Of course, it might also be the case that she comes to the opposite conclusion. This might be for a number of reasons. For example, she may realize that far from putting money aside to ensure her comfort she was in fact doing it to ensure that she had something to leave to her children. She may now believe that she has no reason to do this, perhaps because her children have revealed themselves to be ungrateful and money grabbing. Alternatively she might have discovered that one of the beliefs on which her decision was based—the belief that she would live to retirement—is false. In fact, tests show that she will die within a year. If the same question is asked of the agent (does she have reason to renounce her careful life?), but at the same time all knowledge of all her values and beliefs is disregarded, it is clear that the question becomes meaningless. An agent who knows nothing of herself cannot answer questions about what she has best reason to do.

Those who think that going beyond the perspective of the non-tuist is a mistake might be motivated by a more general concern: that by doing this constructivism is liable to collapse into an affective morality. This, too, is a serious challenge. However, before considering it, it is necessary to see whether anything can be said about the personal perspective that goes beyond that which has been said about the pursuit of life, food, shelter, and so on. The defence against the charge of being an affective theory is taken up after that.

## A 'KIND OF LIFE'

Rawls characterizes a determinate conception of the good thus:

A conception of the good normally consists of a more or less determinate set of final ends, that is, ends we want to realize for their own sake, as well as attachments to other persons and loyalties to various groups and associations. . . . We also connect with such a conception a view of our relation to the world—religious, philosophical, and moral—by reference to which the value and significance of our ends and attachments are understood. (Rawls 1993: 19–20; see also 1993: 74, 81)

Rawls carefully distinguishes the choice of ends from the understanding of value that informs that choice and makes it clear that both are to be thought of as constitutive parts of agents' conceptions of the good. This is important, as the apparent implausibility of the constructivist project might be, in part, a consequence of the focus of both mutual advantage theorists and their critics on too narrow a conception of agents' ends.

An agent may pursue athletic glory: for example, the project of becoming the world's fastest sprinter. The critic of constructivism alleges that such an agent, when confronted by constraints on the pursuit of this end, must (given that she views those constraints from the individual perspective advanced by the constructivist) conceive of them as alien restrictions on her and try, when possible, to flout them so as more directly to pursue her end. However, pursuing an end of becoming the world's fastest sprinter because one has dedicated one's life to extending one's abilities, and because one thinks the imposition of discipline that is required is an expression of one's capacity to shape one's own life, and so on, is different from pursuing the end of running fastest over a given distance in order to win a gold medal or to make money. Someone dedicated to an athletic life does not advance her good by cheating even though she may be more successful than she otherwise would be.[1]

Of course, many people do not commit themselves to one easily identifiable kind of life in the sense that there is one thing and one thing only the pursuit of which regulates, and gives sense and meaning to, their lives. In addition, few, if any, people commit themselves to one kind of life for the duration of their lives. As Rawls puts it (in a passage that continues on

[1] Similar reflections inform Alasdair MacIntyre's analysis of practices and internal and external goods (see MacIntyre 1984: ch. 14). Society's reactions to these different projects also mirror ideas of worthwhileness. Our reaction to Carl Lewis is very different from our reaction to Ben Johnson, although the latter ran faster.

directly from the quotation given above), 'persons' conceptions of the good are not fixed but form and develop as they mature, and may change more or less radically over the course of a life' (1993: 20). This is important because whilst it may be true that someone is committed, say, to Mill's harm principle as his rule-of-thumb when thinking about his and others' lives, that is hardly a complete picture. Persons' lives are neither so simple nor so static. For many people what it means to have a conception of the good is to have ends that they think it worthwhile to pursue and a mixed set of values that inform that pursuit. Thus one might think that one wishes to be an honest person (among other things), but not think that honesty is such an overriding virtue so that when considering one's role as a father (and the pursuit of the goal of being a good father) one thinks that one is obliged to tell one's young child that Father Christmas does not exist or that the child's braces do, in fact, make her look ugly.

Not only is one's conception of the good liable to change over time, but there is a link between the choices that one makes and one's future understanding of one's good. It is absurd to think that someone who aspires to be a philosopher as an undergraduate has a 'philosophic' conception of the good (whatever that might be), but it is not absurd to think that the same person, having forgone various benefits that she could have had from pursuing different ends and having dedicated a great part of her life to doing philosophy, comes to understand and think of herself and her ends from the perspective of a philosopher. Understanding one's life is surely in part a process of understanding how one's later choices have been shaped not merely by some commitment to a set of given values, but to the way in which one has made earlier choices (including those that incorporate one's values into one's life).[2]

Understanding an agent's good, then, is not solely a matter of considering what the agent wants, but rather of grasping how she understands the pursuit of what she wants in the light of the kind of life that she thinks worthwhile. Of course, this is doubted by those who think that what is good is the pursuit of something that is objectively valuable. However, given the anti-realist premiss of the argument this is not a position that can be endorsed by the constructivist. The problem with such anti-realism is that it seems to leave the constructivist with nothing general to say about agents' goods. However, this is not the case.

---

[2] This point is made forcefully in both MacIntyre's analysis of what it is to give narrative unity to one's life (1984: ch. 15), and in Mendus's account of moral motivation in Rawls (1999).

*Choosing well*

In his impressive study of the modern advanced economies, *The Market Experience*, Robert Lane distinguishes between 'ego-syntonic' and 'ego-alien' choices:

Ego-syntonic or authentic choices (1) are congruent with the most stable and firmly held *beliefs* of the individual; (2) are resonant with and satisfy the individual's long term *interests*; (3) express the individual's deepest and most keenly felt *emotions*; and (4) serve the individual's dominant *values*. *Ego-alien* choices lack these properties. (Lane 1991: 551)

This analysis can usefully be applied to the choice of kinds of life or conceptions of the good. Lane claims, with the support of psychological surveys, that ego-alien choices do not satisfy the agent in the sense that they do not contribute to her well-being. Of course, this thought is hardly original. As the language in which it is couched suggests it is present in Freud, and it also has a long history in political philosophy. Both Plato and Marx thought that people were prone to making wrong decisions when choosing their ends. What Plato, Marx, and (to an extent) Freud have in common is an essentialist story about the 'true' ends of human agency and, thus, the pursuit of wrong ends is something that can be easily identified. Constructivism, of course, does not have that luxury. Nevertheless, what is striking about Lane's characterization of ego-syntonic choices is the degree to which they depend upon socially influenced features of the agent, such as her beliefs and values. From this analysis it is possible to make some remarks about how agents come to their good. These can be divided into comments on the role of worthwhileness and self-esteem and on necessarily social goods such as friendship and love.

The links between an agent's well-being, her self-esteem, socially constituted ideas of worthwhileness, and such things as occupational satisfaction are complex and multifarious. Amongst the conditions of ego-syntonic choices are that the agent makes choices congruent with her beliefs, interests, and values. The degree to which these things are determined by particular characteristics of the agent, by other, general, features of human beings, and by social factors is (currently) impossible to determine. Nevertheless, the claim that all three of these factors are socially influenced is uncontroversial. Moreover, ideas of what constitutes a worthwhile life are intimately connected to social understandings. This is something that Charles Taylor makes a great deal of in his discussion of 'value frameworks' (see e.g. Taylor 1989*a*: part i) and is also to be found in the MacIntyrean idea of a 'practice' as has already been noted. At its simplest the point is just that when, say, Socrates considers what is a worthwhile life he comes to a different conclusion from that arrived at by Achilles, and this is not wholly due to differences in their psychological make-ups. Of course, Socrates comes to a conclusion about what is worthwhile that is not wholly in accordance with the prevalent ideas of worthwhileness in fifth-century BC Athens.[3] Socrates does this in part in response to the Delphic Oracle's statement that he is the wisest amongst men, and also because he feels compelled to do so by some kind of inner voice, his *dæmon*. Insofar as this is interpreted as providing some objective validation of worthwhileness the matter is of little interest. Nevertheless, Socrates' idea of what constitutes a worthwhile life is not uninfluenced by his being an Athenian of the time, as his reasons for not appealing for banishment, or escaping from his death sentence, make clear (Plato 1969).

Why is this important? It matters because under circumstances in which agents have as part of their good feelings of satisfaction, choosing lives which are thought to be worthwhile and which fit with agents' perceptions of their value is an important part of agents advancing their goods. A related point is that what one perceives as one's particular skills is also, in part, influenced by social factors. Developing and valuing particular skills is a matter of how those skills fit into a vision of one's place in a particular social environment. Thus, the development of, say, ball-handling skills is regarded in a significantly different way from the way in which such skills were regarded a hundred years ago. Today, professional sports offer a source of both income and social status. In short, individuals reflecting on the aspects of themselves that they value, and that are sources of satisfaction for them, will be influenced in their thoughts by the circumstances— including social circumstances—in which they live.

These arguments—from ideas of worthwhileness and of skill development—come together in occupational choice. Of course, different occupations attract different social assessments of worthwhileness, but this does not mean that people engaged in occupations which are not socially valued are necessarily less satisfied in what they do. Rather, what matters is the 'fit' between the agent's skills and their occupation. In what can be seen as an extension of the Aristotelian Principle, the claim is that an occupation that is challenging and that correlates to the agent's abilities provides greater

---

[3] It is put to Socrates in the *Republic* that Socrates ought to have grown up and put aside the childish concern with philosophy in order to take up an occupation more suitable to a man's estate.

satisfaction than is accrued where this fit is missing.[4] There is also evidence that a bad fit can lead to a vicious circle: 'research has found that self-confident people tend to choose tasks with an appropriate level of difficulty; those with low self-confidence choose tasks that are either too easy or too difficult' (Lane 1991: 553). Finally, occupational choice and 'fit' are not to be thought of as assessed in some kind of time-slice. People develop in their careers and the fit between occupation, skills, and personality normally develops and improves (from an adequate starting point) with time (Lane 1991: 554 ff.).[5]

The role of necessarily social goods in satisfaction is also important. Ego-syntonic choices are in accordance with the agent's emotions. Here 'emotions' is to be taken very broadly. It is not only meant to mark that an agent may have particular characteristics, like risk aversion, but also that one choice of kind of life is influenced by the effect that has on certain emotional states. There are some goods—notably friendship and love—that can only be realized by agents who are not entirely self-concerned. If John loves Jane and expresses the thought that her happiness makes him happy, he does not mean that he is happy that Jane is happy because it gives him pleasurable feelings. As philosophers sensitive to the nature of friendship remind us, the nature of true friendship requires that one align one's relevant interests with those of one's friend in the construction of a common interest: 'In loving another person, I cease to think exclusively in terms of my own interests and their consonance or conflict with the interests of the person I love. Rather, I acknowledge an additional set of interests which are "ours" and which may, in turn, inform my understanding of what constitutes my own interest' (Mendus 1999: 67). The significance of friendship and love for human well-being is hard to overestimate. They are sources of

---

[4] See Lane 1991: esp. part v and the citations therein.

[5] Consider the following from David Gauthier: 'Now I can sketch very abstractly part of the fit between individuals and society that would be required in an agreement among rational contributors on their terms of interaction ... The society must be structured that, first, for each normal person, there is a range of social roles effectively available, each of which demands a productive contribution from its holder, and rewards the holder appropriately to her marginal contribution to the joint social product. Second, each of these roles must be compatible with a set of life plans, any of which could in normal circumstances be chosen by and satisfyingly pursued by someone occupying the role, and having at her disposal that share of the joint social product which rewards effective occupancy. If a role is to be effectively available to an individual, then it must be suited to her capacities, and she must have had the opportunity to develop and train them. And if the pursuit of plans is to be satisfying, then it must be suited to her motivations and affections, and she must have had the opportunity to educate them' (Gauthier 1997: 138–9). (See also below n. 26, and Ch. 9 below.)

enormous satisfaction and this of course is not incompatible with the fact that they can also be sources of great pain. They require, and build upon, the agent's capacity to align her interests with the interests of some other(s) in a common project.

Finally, all these factors will influence an agent's self-esteem. As noted above, considerations of self-esteem affect choice of occupation and activity. Self-esteem is also affected by such things as one's reputation with others, the evaluation of oneself against one's ideas of worthwhileness, and so on. Of course, this can be harmful to an agent's well-being if the agent makes impossible comparisons with others (cf. Nozick 1974: 239–46), in the sense that, for example, anorexia (an illness that is commonly associated with low self-esteem) in young women in developed Western countries is (controversially) linked to these women comparing themselves unfavourably with the super-slim models paraded in fashion magazines and on the television. Whatever the truth of this, the claim that self-esteem is linked to socially influenced ideas of worthwhileness (albeit in complex ways) can hardly be controversial. This is important given the connections that there are between self-esteem and occupational choice as well as between self-esteem and satisfaction. Recent, albeit inconclusive, research suggests that the very capacity of human beings to feel happy may be linked to self-esteem through the occurrence of the chemical seratonin.[6]

The remarks made in this section are unlike those that normally characterize discussions of conceptions of the good. References to occupational choice and to such things as brain seratonin levels are not the normal stuff of political philosophy. This is in part because discussions of conceptions of the good often form part of considerations of the problems raised by pluralism and this encourages a characterization of conceptions of the good on a grand scale. The fact of pluralism, after all, refers to such things as the conflict between Christianity and Islam or that between Christian sects. Moreover, the conclusions that can be drawn from this section are limited. What is being argued for is not an objective account of value nor is it a claim that people do in fact invariably choose life plans in accordance with the analysis given above.[7] It is also not the case that the goods of self-esteem and satisfaction are directly linked to being moral. After all, the

[6] Research on baboons, whose social structures are similar to those of humans, suggests that seratonin levels are linked to self-respect. Seratonin is a chemical in the brain linked to 'happy feelings' (it is the chemical on which Prozac and other SSRI anti-depressants work).

[7] Part of Lane's point is that many people (in developed capitalist economies) consistently fail to do so, which (to put it crudely) is why we are all so unhappy.

range of an agent's friends and loved ones is likely to be considerably more narrow than is the scope of morality. Finally, it is not being argued that a person will always think that her life goes better in circumstances where she pursues a good that is held up in the society to which she belongs as worthwhile. As some of the women in Betty Friedan's *The Feminine Mystique* (1965) make clear, having all that society teaches one to want (a nice house, a husband, children, etc.) is not always the path to well-being.[8]

## THE MORAL COMMUNITY

Given this list of all the things that this discussion does not show, how, then, does it relate to the search for reasons that will partly underwrite the agent's commitment to organize the pursuit of his good together with others through moral norms? Recall, the argument is that the moral community is constructed by the commitment of each to live together with others giving priority to the terms of co-operation, which themselves must be such that all can freely agree to them. If the constructivist project is to have any meaning the agent must be able to conceive of his interests independently of others and ask whether he has reason to renounce co-operation and take up the stance of an independent. Fortunately, from such a stance the agent will understand that he has very good reasons to engage in co-operation with others. Indeed, he has good reasons to will a system of stable co-operation. Unfortunately, as a being concerned only with his separate interests, there are no rationally compelling reasons to make the commitment to the terms of co-operation as binding on the pursuit of his narrow self-interest; to align his good together with that of his co-contractors in a moral community. The theory, therefore, accepts that this step must be made by an existential commitment of the agent.

Given this contingency at the heart of the justification of morality, it is apparent that the constructivist theory developed here cannot provide

---

[8] Similarly, one of the points of Lane's analysis is that the pursuit of money and other goods that are highly valued by the market is often undertaken by agents trying to compensate for their failure to realize more satisfying goods (Lane 1991: 553–6; cf. Singer 1997: ch. 10). Of those whose major life concern is the accumulation of money Lane's conclusion is to endorse Carin Rubenstein's finding that they are 'least likely to be involved in a satisfactory love relationship. They also tend to be sexually unsatisfied, report worsening health, and almost half of them are troubled by constant worry, anxiety and loneliness. They are dissatisfied with their jobs and feel that they earn less than they deserve' (Rubenstein 1981, quoted in Lane 1991: 555). This may cheer up any British academics reading this book.

rationally compelling reasons for the agent to be moral. If, therefore, it is thought that the answer to Nietzsche's challenge requires that the egoist (or anyone else) be shown that there is a decisive account, grounded in rationality, of why one ought to be moral, then the theory cannot answer this challenge. But, meeting Nietzsche's challenge does not require this. As described, the challenge is to show that morality is not groundless, to allay the 'fear, or suspicion, or hope . . . that the moral enterprise must fail' unless it is grounded in 'objective value or objective reason, in sympathy or in sociality' (Gauthier, quoted above in Chapter 6). The account developed here aims to explain the place of moral reasons as authoritative and in so doing make it clear that morality is neither a fetish nor a confidence trick. Moreover, it aims to do this without relying on 'objective value or objective reason' or 'sympathy'. It cannot do without sociality of a kind, but for reasons discussed below that should not be a challenge to its credentials to be able to meet the 'fear, or suspicion, or hope' that there is nothing to be said for morality (and plenty to be said against it).

The discussion above is relevant to this aim. For the constructivist theorist, theorizing on behalf of an agent who stands back from his commitments can appeal to the social nature that is characteristic of human beings' construction, and pursuit, of their goods. The arguments above link the agent's flourishing to her participation in certain kinds of social enterprises. Moreover, her understanding of that flourishing is informed by this participation. Of course, the constructivist must be wary here of accepting uncritically the particular preferences that agents have. This danger is discussed below. However, this does not exclude the constructivist from appealing to general features of human flourishing that depend upon participation in a society of the right kind. In most agents, the will to participate and the commitment to give priority to the norms of co-operation will already have been developed. Standing back from this commitment, the agent asks whether the possession of this will can be understood as a dictate of rationality. The answer to this question is 'no'. However, this does not mean that the will to co-operate is a mistake and nor does it mean that it is simply a fetish or a preference that the agent happens to have and could just as well do without. The question the constructivist theorist seeks to answer is whether there are reasons that can, at least partially, underwrite a commitment to morality on the part of a self-reflective agent who has stood back from her particular commitments. The answer to this question is that there are. These reasons are not such that anyone who fails to make such a commitment has made a mistake. Nevertheless, the advantages of participation in a stable society of the right kind are very great.

The error is to think that endorsing oneself as a moral being *must* be a mistake, for the agent could get everything that she wants from society without paying for it in terms of the burdens of constraining the pursuit of her self-interest in accordance with society's demands. This is an error because what the agent wants need not be understood in terms only of the goods pursued by separate individuals. To retain the perspective of the separate individual in conceiving of one's overall good, even where for prudential reasons one subsequently behaves in accordance with the demands of morality, is not to make the moral commitment; not to be a moral being. With morality, as with love, to treat it as instrumentally valuable is to gain some of what it offers—and perhaps all of what one wants—but not all, for, as Rawls has it, 'there is no such thing as loving while being ready to consider whether to love, just like that' (Rawls 1971: 573; cf. Mendus 1999).

If the constructivist theory is accepted and agents endorse their commitment to live together with others in a moral community, the constructivist must hope that the community becomes self-sustaining as its members come to value their participation in its creation and maintenance. If so, then each will come to think of the good of participation in a community in which each aligns his good together with the others and in which each commits to live in accordance with principles that all can accept as a very great good, in the realization of which each agent understands himself to be both beneficiary and benefactor.

These phrases echo Rawls on the good of a well-ordered society and Gauthier on the importance of reciprocity. That is not accidental, for the description of the moral community—or in Rawls's case the 'great political good' of a well-ordered political society—is something on which Rawls and Gauthier have much in common. Consider just one passage from part iii of Rawls's *A Theory of Justice*:

Given the social nature of humankind, the fact that our potentialities and inclinations far surpass what can be expressed in any one life, we depend on the cooperative endeavors of others not only for the means of well-being but to bring to fruition our latent powers. And with a certain success all around, each enjoys the greater richness and diversity of the collective activity. Yet to share fully in this life we must acknowledge the principles of its regulative conception, and this means that we must affirm our sentiment of justice. To appreciate something as ours, we must have a certain allegiance to it. What binds a society in one social union is the mutual recognition and acceptance of the principles of justice. (Rawls 1971: 571; cf. Gauthier 1986: 336, 1993c, 1997)[9]

---

[9] Rawls's recent work, which extols the great good of a political society in which each citizen is prepared to offer and abide by reasons that every other can accept in the light of the

The constructivist theory offered here differs from Rawls's account in that it is the commitment of agents to live together with others on moral terms that creates the moral community. Thus, the principles of justice are not acknowledged in, but are the product of, agreement. This, of course, reflects the crucial difference between the two approaches. The constructivist generates the condition of equality from the agreement whereas for Rawls the agreement merely expresses what is demanded given an assumption of fundamental equality. This matters, for it means that the constructivist can retain the perspective of self-interest and unite it with the moral perspective. In the constructivist theory, the construction creates moral norms that bind only insofar as each person commits himself to the community that instantiates the agreement. Such a commitment is conditional on the agent reasonably expecting that he will do better if he organizes and understands the pursuit of his good in accordance with the demands of morality. Thus, the agent's commitment is also conditional on the reciprocal commitment of others. One cannot commit oneself to live through moral norms constructed by the will of all in the absence of others making that commitment.

The arguments above attempt, albeit briefly, to build on the claim that the constructivist must not deal only in the goods that agents could be said to have given the assumption of non-tuism, and recognize that agents characteristically have complex systems of preferences. In addition, the claim is made that insofar as agents seek satisfaction and well-being, they will be influenced in their choice of goods by social factors including the social understanding of the goods that they seek.

These points are familiar from what is known as the communitarian literature. That the value of goods is in part a factor of social understanding and that persons value what their actions express, and are recognized by

burdens of judgement (Rawls 1993), seems also to be very close to the notion of a moral community developed here (albeit that the route to this community taken by the two accounts is very different).

To be clear, I am not claiming that Rawls would endorse the theory offered here. However, appreciating that there is a richer sense of reciprocity at work here, one that incorporates the simple sense of mutual advantage, but goes beyond it in also appealing to the fact that each contributes to the great political good of a well-ordered society his willingness to offer and abide by reasons that all can accept and each benefits from his fellows' willingness to do the same, allows one to understand better Rawls's claim that he is a reciprocity theorist. Rawls describes himself thus in response to Brian Barry's argument that *A Theory of Justice* contains an incoherent mix of justice as mutual advantage and justice as impartiality. Barry denies that justice as reciprocity is a viable option and it is somewhat perplexing that Rawls associates himself with this school without much comment (Rawls 1993: 16–17). However, if the notion of reciprocity to which Rawls appeals is not the same as the notion which Barry criticizes then this puzzle is dissolved.

others as expressing, are things that should hardly come as a surprise to any reflective being. Similarly, that one's good can be advanced through the flourishing of another or of an association of which one is a member (without this being reduced to valuing the feelings of pleasure that one gets as a result) is a familiar thought. However, this association with communitarianism ought to make the constructivist wary. The point, after all, is to stand back from one's commitments and to question them critically. Given that these arguments have been used in partially underwriting the commitment to morality, the constructivist theory must come under a suspicion of building on the merely contingent; of constructing only an affective theory (or of making essentialist claims about human nature). The form of constructivism defended here is distinguished from its *faux* constructivist counterparts above. Below, it is defended from the allegations of essentialism and of being merely an affective theory.

## AFFECTIVE MORALITY AND AN AFFECTIVE CAPACITY FOR MORALITY[10]

In Chapter 7 above, after citing Vallentyne's argument to show that the assumption of non-tuism had no place in constructivist theory, it was commented that the reason non-tuism was an attractive starting point for the constructivist was because it made the theory immune to allegations that it built on the merely contingent or on claims of the true nature of human flourishing. However, it was also pointed out that constructivism must incorporate a certain degree of contingency. Even in the case of prudence, the best the constructivist theorist can do is offer reasons that will partially underwrite a commitment by the agent to a particular account of flourishing and to the will to flourish in accordance with that account. Nevertheless, it might be argued that what was assumed there—that agents have reason to seek food, shelter, and so on, and the freedom to gain access to these—was sufficiently minimal not to be troublesome. By contrast, in the argument above the account of what agents have reason to pursue goes well beyond what can be said to be needed by the human physical organism.

The danger is identified by Korsgaard. Having shown that the 'economic theory' that prides itself on being 'merely instrumental' must give an

---

[10] These terms are taken from Gauthier 1986: 328. The passage in which they occur is quoted in full on p. 196 above and in part below.

account of the ends that it is worth pursuing, she continues 'the fans of morality could just as well stipulate that what we "really want" are things consistent with love and respect for everybody, and then they too could claim that we don't need to go beyond instrumental rationality. Nothing is gained by such devices' (Korsgaard 1997: 231). Now, the argument pursued above does not depend on claims about what people really want, if that is taken to be either an argument about human nature or about the 'real content' of people's preferences no matter what the expressed content. An agent who refuses to commit himself to the moral life cannot thereby be said to have made a mistake about his nature or about the content of his preferences.[11] However, the allegation may be that the argument does depend on people happening to care about morality. In the end, then, morality is just a fetish. If this is true then the theory would be an affective theory for, to borrow from Gauthier, it would introduce constraints based on concern for others rather than, as an affective capacity for morality does, dispose one to adhere to constraints that are independently grounded (Gauthier 1986: 328, quoted above in Chapter 7).

The constructivist theorist can surely deny that this is straightforwardly the case. The constraints on self-interest are generated by the demands of stable co-operation. Morality is the organizing form of a community of persons who together commit themselves to give the terms of co-operation priority over the pursuit of their narrow self-interest. The basis of the constructivist argument is that reasons can be given that will partially underwrite that commitment and show it to be neither a fetish nor a confidence trick. Thus, the agent who commits himself to live on moral terms in one sense recognizes constraints that exist independently of his commitment. Yet taken together it is her commitment together with that of others that grounds the imperatival force of those constraints; that grounds their being moral constraints.[12] To this degree, then, the constructivist must accept that there is a degree of contingency built into the theory. Were no one to understand her good as realized through moral co-operation then such co-operation would not exist. However, once such co-operation exists then those who stand back from their commitment to it and ask whether they have reason to endorse or renounce that commitment can be given reasons (albeit non-decisive ones) to choose the former.

[11] He may have made a mistake about the 'facts of the matter'. This is discussed below.
[12] Thus, although the advantages of stable co-operation ground some constraints these are not moral for they lack imperatival force. The status of the constraints as moral, then, is a product of the commitment of the participants to make them so. Given that this commitment is not a dictate of reason, the theory must accept a degree of contingency.

Nevertheless, this partial acceptance of the contingency allegation ought not to be understood as committing the constructivist theorist to building on what persons actually want; constructing justice as it were for each person from that person's utility function. This would be to fail to put distance between the agent and the commitments that she has. The argument given above attempts to make general claims about what people have reason to seek. These claims are, to repeat, not aimed at unpacking either a true human nature or an empirically accurate account of what people do seek. The point is just this: the criticism of *faux* constructivists made in Chapters 4 and 5 is that an unbridgeable gap is opened up between the personal and moral perspectives because of their positing of the equal moral value of all persons without giving an account of the source of that value and thus of the relationship between the fulfilment of each agent and the agent acting in accordance with morality, a gap that *faux* constructivists deal with by trying to eliminate the personal perspective. In genuine constructivism the authority of self-interest does not disappear in the move to morality. The moral community is nothing other than a community of people who agree to align their flourishing together with that of others through co-operation. Their doing so is (and remains) conditional on co-operation advancing their (reflective) goods. Entry into the moral community must meet the condition that the agent furthers her ends through living the moral life. In order for the possibility of renouncing morality to be a real one the agent must have available an account of her ends as an independent. However, the argument cannot be limited to that account. Given this, there are reasons that can at least partially underwrite the agent endorsing her commitment to morality. But, crucially, this is not to say that the commitment to morality is only reasonable for those who have the moral life as an end.

## THE SCOPE OF CONSTRUCTIVISM

If this is the constructivist account of morality then questions arise as to whether it can meet the demands of being a moral theory. Is it fair and is its scope broad enough? Such questions compare the content of a constructivist morality with some set of current moral convictions. As already noted, critics of theories of 'morality tied to mutuality' allege that such theories cannot generate genuinely moral norms. Specifically, they cannot avoid the elimination from the scope of morality of those with nothing to contribute.

Before engaging with this challenge it may be useful to recall the description of the constructivist account of the moral community. The moral community is bounded by co-operation for mutual advantage. What distinguishes a moral community from a mere community of co-operators is the understanding that each agent has of the relationship between her good and that of the whole. Endorsing oneself as a being regulated by morality means endorsing the hierarchically superior place of moral reasons over those of narrow self-interest (Charvet 1995: 173). Impartiality emerges from the reflective standpoint because if each participant is to make the commitment to morality then the terms on which that commitment is made must be freely acceptable to all. Thus, each agent understands herself not as an independent, pursuing her good constrained by alien restrictions, but as a co-operating member of the community. As such her understanding of her good is already mediated by the norms of co-operation. These norms are understood then as the product of each contractor's will to conceive of herself as a being of a particular kind, one committed to living a moral life. Like the constrained maximizer, the moral person is not disposed to view morality as instrumental to the pursuit of self-interest, but rather understands herself as pursuing her self-interest together with others in a moral community created and bound together by nothing but the contractors' will to co-operate together through the pursuit of their goods in accordance with impartial norms of co-operation. The moral life is a 'kind of life' and thus the conception of morality being offered in this account resembles in many ways those offered in so-called virtue ethics.[13]

The constructivist theory as it is understood here is not an attempt to generate morality from nothing; from some hypothetical or actual state of nature. It is not an attempt to show to the committed egoist that there are rationally compelling reasons to adopt the moral life. Rather, it is the attempt to understand what we already have; societies of people co-operating for mutual advantage, bound to a lesser or greater extent by the rules that govern that co-operation. The constructivist takes the stance of an agent, already socialized and language bearing, who reflects on the nature of her relations with others given her claim to subjective value. Clearly what is not being argued for is that constructivism provides the

---

[13] The conception of moral norms used in this account ensures that a satisfactory theory of such norms will resemble a virtue ethics. See, for example, the quotation given above from Gauthier contrasting 'economic man' and the 'truly just man'. The description 'truly just' is of the man (the quality of his dispositions) not of the acts he performs. It is this that Gauthier tries to capture in his moving from assessing the rationality of acts to assessing the rationality of dispositions.

correct account of how people in the past understood—and in the present understand—their relations. What is being presented is an account of how we should now understand our relations to others given that we have entered the post-theocentric, post-anthropomorphic world for which Nietzsche was such an eloquent harbinger.

Therefore, insofar as the constructivist makes use of the language of a contract and speaks of a hypothetical agent on whose behalf the reflective process is undertaken this is not meant to invoke the idea that society was formed through the commitment of people to come together for mutual advantage, understanding themselves as of subjective value, and bound together by nothing other than their common commitment to a set of norms governing their co-operation. The constructivist reflects from the perspective of someone already involved in co-operation who realizes that the traditional justification for the rules and norms that govern her society is grounded in beliefs that she no longer regards as plausible. The use of the notion of agreement is meant to illustrate two things: first, that the justification of moral norms must be found in the justification that could be given to each agent who claims value for herself, rather than by appeal to some external source of value. Second, the language of contract is meant to capture the importance of reciprocity. The commitment of each agent to co-operation and morality is intimately connected to the commitment of every other.

The community of contractors, then, as a moral community is grounded in nothing other than the collective wills of its members to organize in pursuit of their common good, and morality is the organizing form through which this is achieved (cf. Charvet 1995: ch. 8). Of course, insofar as the norms of the community, language, and standards of rationality are socially engendered the contractors must recognize that they owe a debt as the people that they are to the community: just as they are co-creators of it so they are co-created by it.

Given this conception of morality there are two senses in which it is conditional. First, it is dependent on the reciprocal agreement of each to endorse himself as a participant in the moral community. Second it is conditional on the ability of participation to satisfy the demand that one is not worse off relative to the non-existence of co-operation.[14]

Thus, one limit on the scope of morality is that those who choose not to commit to morality, but who choose instead to pursue their goods as inde-

---

[14] As with the constrained maximizer the agent compares co-operation with the absence of co-operation (not with free-riding).

pendents, stand outside of moral relations. How they are treated cannot be a moral matter. However, an agent committed to living a moral life as part of the community, but who fails to live up to the ideal—who gives way to the temptation to free-ride in a given instance—is not in the position of the agent who chooses independence. Instead, such a person is a candidate for punishment. However, this is a matter for the next chapter.

Having given a sketch of the moral community it is time to turn to the criticisms and questions given above. Take first the allegation that constructivism cannot generate moral norms sufficiently close to those of 'common sense' morality. Specifically, the claim that its scope is too narrow.

## 'Beyond the pale'

Those convinced of the failure of justice as mutual advantage to deliver conclusions coextensive with ordinary notions of morality may level similar criticisms at the constructivist theory developed here to those that are directed at Gauthier's *Morals by Agreement*. In Chapter 6 it was pointed out that critics of justice as mutual advantage allege that it fails as a moral theory because it cannot include within its ambit those who have nothing to contribute. So, for example, Brian Barry argues that anyone who cannot understand that it is morally wrong deliberately to poison a river, the water from which is drunk by people in the next village with whom one has no co-operative relations (and no interest in future co-operation), has morally pathological views (Barry 1996: 369).

This criticism cannot be rebutted in a way that will satisfy some, perhaps most, critics. A constructivist theory that tries to integrate prudential and moral reasons results in an account in which those who cannot contribute to co-operation can reasonably be excluded from the protection of morality. If what is required is an account of the intrinsic value of human beings (or of all sentient creatures) so that wherever such beings make an appearance matters of morality arise then this is obviously not the kind of demand that the constructivist can meet.

As is pointed out above (in Chapter 6) the position of the critic is somewhat undermined by the fact that each critic will think the constructivist theory flawed because it does not generate conclusions coextensive with his own moral convictions. No doubt in past years people with strong convictions wrote in similar terms about all sorts of things. Barry, for example, does not think that full moral status can be extended to non-human animals and there are, as a consequence, people who would cast doubt on his moral sensibilities. The point is that the argument is about whether our moral convictions can be given some basis in reason. Although there are respectable arguments in defence of the claim that this enterprise is doomed, the mere assertion of (one interpretation of) the moral equality of all human beings combined with the claim that anyone who disagrees is obviously pathological is not one of them.

Moreover, the constructivist can also appeal to the argument often employed by utilitarians: that moral convictions are as they are because of the way the world is. In constructed examples in which the world is presented as a very different place (for example in which neighbouring villages could not benefit from co-operation) such convictions become much less reliable. Perhaps if the world was such that co-operation was not widespread and advantageous the critics of constructivism would not have the response that they have to the poisoning of the water. In short, if co-operation and security were significantly less common than they are now it is a plausible assumption that people would have very different moral convictions.

Nevertheless, there is a serious challenge to be met. Although the absence of a realm of moral injunctions that stands independent of the construction—injunctions to which all can appeal as constituting binding moral rules—should hardly bother the constructivist, this is no reason for the constructivist to fail to show the true scope of the theory. If in so doing the account becomes more plausible as an account of morality for those whose test of such a theory is its capturing our moral experience then so much the better. There are two different arguments that need to be considered. First, what might be called the 'ducking' argument. This amounts to the claim that, as it turns out, more people contribute and so stand within the protection of morality than might be thought. Second, people may extend the protection of morality towards those to whom they owe no moral duties.

Of course, in appealing to the ducking argument, the constructivist might be thought to have missed the point of the criticism. If the constructivist cannot condemn the poisoning of the water supply in the above example, the critic alleges, then it does not matter whether it is a plausible assumption that there are two villages linked by a common water supply and that the good of those who live in the villages could not be advanced by co-operation. Even if those upstream realized that there were advantages to co-operation and stopped poisoning the water supply, this would not meet the critic's demand that they stop poisoning the water for the right reason. The trouble is, of course, that this is just for the critic to repeat the demand that the account recognize the fundamental equality of human beings. All the constructivist can do is argue that co-operation grounds the only available reasons. If co-operation extends widely this will mean that the outcome of the theory is more in accordance with the convictions of the theory's critics. If not, not.

David Gauthier provides ammunition to the critics of constructivism with his comment, quoted above, that the scope of morality does not include 'animals, the unborn, the congenitally handicapped and defective' (Gauthier 1986: 268). This sentence has given widespread currency to the view that the disabled *tout court* as well as the helpless, the old, and the poor will be excluded from the protection of justice in the moral community envisaged by the constructivist. However, there is no reason to jump to this conclusion. Many people who are severely disabled contribute enormously to the good of the community and there is no reason to believe that they could be forced to do so given their inability to fight their corner. How a community comes to value certain things and, thus, how people in a community come to measure advances in their good is, as has been already indicated, a complex matter. It is an odd feature of contemporary political philosophy—perhaps perpetuated by references to the baseline of any agreement being a 'state of nature'—that bargaining power is somehow thought still to relate to an individual's capacity to engage in physical fights with others or to survive in the wild by picking apples off trees and gathering acorns.[15]

In sum, when it comes to the characteristic examples used by critics of justice as mutual advantage—those with nothing to contribute because of some incapacity—some of these will indeed fall 'beyond the pale' of morality. It should not be assumed too quickly that there are many such people as the whole notion of what it is to contribute is far more complex than it is often thought to be. However, another type of example that might be thought to be more accurate in its assessment of the possibilities of co-operation builds on the allegation that constructivism legitimizes the exploitation of the poor and weak by the rich and strong. Here the compelling examples refer to such problems as the street urchins in the cities of, say, Brazil and the relations of the first and third worlds.

Consider the following scenario. The affluent and powerful in a community decide to separate themselves from the wider community both geographically and economically because of population pressures, poverty,

[15] Of course, as already noted, this ducking argument is unlikely to satisfy those critics who think that, for example, the disabled ought not to have to be re-characterized as useful in order to qualify for moral status.

and the fear of crime. They set up in so-called 'gated communities' protected by private security. They eat in restaurants and shop in shops within such communities or in equally protected malls that lie beyond the outskirts of the city. Having been convinced of the virtues of constructivist theory, they commit to live together on moral terms. However, as they believe themselves to have no co-operative relations with the poor (nor interests in future co-operation), they think of their actions towards the poor as being neither moral nor immoral, but merely amoral. Furthermore, reasoning that they are less well off than they could be because, say, tourism is affected by the existence of street urchins and beggars, they set up hit squads the members of which spend their time killing street dwellers in campaigns of 'urban cleansing'.

Such a scenario is not far from reality in some countries and less extreme versions could be told of places such as the UK and the USA, although, of course, the situation is seldom exactly as described in relation to co-operation. The affluent employ the less affluent, for example as domestic servants, and also benefit from the existence of the poor as a pool of unemployed labour.[16] Nevertheless, the example is particularly troubling for the constructivist because the affluent seem to be using the very reasoning that is commended by constructivism.[17] However, there is one part of the argument that must be unpacked. This is the claim that the rich have no co-operative relations (or interests in co-operation) with the poor; that street urchins have nothing, nor could have anything, to contribute. This claim is revealed to be false by the very reasoning of the affluent, who realize that they have an interest in the street urchins stopping their activities so that tourists will not be dissuaded from coming to the country. The point is that the there are not only what might be called positive reasons for co-operation.

In Gauthier's parable of the masters and the slaves (Gauthier 1986: 190–1) the masters offer a change of status to the slaves because they realize that those who are currently slaves will work better as free men, and that the costs of wages will be less than the costs of policing enslavement (see

---

[16] 'Let us suppose . . . that an efficient capitalist society requires a certain non-trivial level of unemployment. It may then seem obvious that some persons will be unemployed through no fault of their own. The joint social product would be lessened if they were added to the numbers of the employed. And so their presence in society is not a net cost to their fellows . . . they would be treated unjustly if their unemployment is made the excuse for denying them a reasonable share of the joint social product' (Gauthier 1997: 137).

[17] It is scant consolation that this suggests that the constructivist account does not violate everyone's moral convictions. Indeed, phenomenologically, it seems to have a great deal going for it.

Chapter 6 above). Similarly, the costs of gated communities, employing private security forces, leaving the inner cities to decay, and creating out of them no-go areas, and of the creation of an underclass who (in the case described, accurately) feel themselves to be excluded from, and thus not restricted by, the laws of the community are very great. As the United States is discovering, using the criminal justice system as an alternative to dealing with problems of race is an expensive business. In sum, the choice is not between the possible surplus from restricted co-operation and the possible surplus from co-operation between all. Rather, the comparison must be between open co-operation and the co-operative surplus of restricted co-operation less the resources necessary to secure that co-operation from the independents created by the restriction. In addition, there is the loss of productive labour, some or many of whom may possess valuable talents and skills, as well as the loss of tax revenue that would be secured by extending employment.

However, the critic might allege that the methods of separation and control mentioned above are costly because they are, albeit in a very limited way, still restricted by normal legal and moral codes. Gated communities need to be policed and, indeed, 'gated' because of the presence of threatening elements. Eradicating those who threaten is expensive because it needs to be done in secret, and so on. It might be alleged that a genuine constructivist society would throw off the fetters of unjustified morality, denounce their own moral scruples using the recommended error theory, and use open and inexpensive force to eradicate all those in society who are thought not to be overall net contributors.

Such an argument, like that used by anti-utilitarians to argue that the ideal utilitarian society is one run by all-powerful 'Government House' officials who secretly manipulate people and circumstances so as to maximize utility, is absurd. No one ought seriously to entertain the thought that they can better advance their good in a society in which the government has unregulated power to eradicate perceived socially undesirable elements, in which the death penalty is imposed without recourse to appeal for all crimes, and so on. It might be true of people in a 'Brave New World' that they are happy and their good is advanced by being under total control, but the point is that the citizens of Brave New World are not us, and their goods are not our goods.

The importance of considering the security costs of restricted co-operation is perhaps most apparent in the case of first and third world relations. On the face of it the affluent first world has little reason to regard its relations with the third in anything other than an instrumental way and, thus, little reason not to (continue to) exploit the third world. However, if the first world offers terms of agreement that are exploitative and if it excludes the possibility of first–third world relations being conceived of through agreed terms then it must accept that its relations with the countries of the third world are nothing but prudential truces. Such agreements will be unstable and the third world will reasonably use whatever bargaining power it has to secure the best deal for itself. Thus, under conditions in which the countries of the first world act as straightforward maximizers in their dealings with those of the third, the latter have good reason to unite in fair co-operation and to exclude first world countries from future mutually advantageous opportunities. In addition, in the absence of normal bargaining strength, but in the presence of current exploitation, the third world has reason to adopt whatever means are available to it to correct the situation. Where *faux* constructivists and constructivists can agree is that the threat of suitcase nuclear devices, of massive movements of populations, of non-compliance with non-proliferation and trade treaties of various kinds, and the increasing ability of people to perpetrate huge financial frauds in countries with unregulated markets given the globalization of finance, are serious prudential reasons for the first world to consider the claims of the third.[18]

Such prudential reasons can, as has been stressed above, only ground a restrained, but nevertheless instrumental, view of the relations between co-operators. Of course, once this is accepted the constructivist has a starting point from which to advocate the commitment to morality. In principle, at least, the commitment to live together with others on terms that all can accept is limited only by the extent of co-operation for mutual advantage and the assurance problem (the commitment of each being conditional on the commitment of every other). However, certain features of international relations make the constructivist argument more difficult. First, and most important, is the absence of a reliable mechanism for deterring free-riding and providing the conditions of stability needed for co-operative relations to flourish. Second, what is considered above is the relations of agents who do, in fact, align their interests together with those of others in a moral community. This condition seems to be missing in international relations. Even ties of sympathy are weaker between people who are geographically separated, ethnically different, who face dissimilar problems, and so on. In

---

[18] In a piece on international justice on which Barry and I collaborated (Barry and Matravers 1998*b*) we conclude that the advance of the science of small nuclear weapons provides an example of a good (prudential) reason for the first world to reconsider its relations with the third.

the absence of a genuine global co-operative community and of the feelings and associations that would accompany this, there may be little possibility of establishing moral relations between co-operating societies.

For some the answers to these questions of scope will be a *reductio* of constructivism. The challenge for people who think this is to show how it is that moral relations obtain between groups of people who have no inter-action and who do not have as part of their good the good of those on the opposing side (cf. Gauthier 1993c: 186). Nevertheless, the constructivist theorist ought not to make light of the consequences of her theory. However, that said, it is also true that there is more to human relations than relations of morality. On the constructivist account, the scope of morality is narrow, not merely in the sense that it only applies to beings who have reason to co-operate, but also in the sense that it only applies to those kinds of relations. Morality concerns only what Scanlon calls 'what we owe to each other' (Scanlon 1999). There are, as Scanlon recognizes, other aspects to human relations and other virtues, such as loyalty, generosity, kindness, humility, and so on. Of course, these virtues are not on the constructivist account part of morality, and an account of them would need also to be constructed. But, there is no reason to think that this could not be done, and, indeed, the fact that they are not moral—that they do not bind with imperatival force—may mean that their construction can appeal to wider considerations. However, this is a project for another time.[19]

### Constructivism and pluralism

Before concluding this already long chapter it is worth considering another way in which the scope of morality is thought by some people to be restricted. In so doing the discussion will return to the question of whether the constructivist theory must endorse any set of norms to which people actually give allegiance and by which they might define their good. People do not in general kill those that they recognize as other human beings in an organized way and on a grand scale whilst thinking self-consciously that the only justification for their doing so is that they want what the others

---

[19] Scanlon, who argues for a narrow understanding of (the central core of) morality as 'what we owe to each other', writes about an example that involves the question of whether it is right or wrong to rescue some people that 'failing to rescue such people would be inhu-mane even if it were not actually wrong' (Scanlon 1999: 238). If it is possible to construct non-moral standards of judgement (and there is no reason why it should not be) then this might allow for the judgement that those who torture cats, coerce the disabled and the weak, etc. do things that are sadistic, cruel, callous, and so on, even if they do not do things that are immoral.

have. The justification for such things as genocide or systematic exploitation is seldom, if ever, a self-consciously resourcist one on the part of those carrying out the killing or exploitation. Rather, those people who pursue practices of genocide or exploitation often try to establish that those who suffer are subhuman, or to show that those inflicting the suffering are doing so in the name of progress (of one sort or another), or that there is some pre-existing right of the genocidal or exploitative community to the lives, resources, or both of their opponents. Thus, the settlers in the USA often appealed to their role in bringing Christianity to the new world, or to their role in advancing progress. Those who overthrew the tsars and whose successors systematically exploited and terrorized their own people as well as the peoples of Central and Eastern Europe did so in the belief that they were part of the unfolding of history, undermining capital on behalf of the proletariat. Many members of the extreme right in South Africa believed that God had created blacks differently from whites and for the specific purpose of serving whites. What links these claims is that there are no good reasons to think them true.

Imagine a community that organizes around the pursuit of national glory. The nation is defined in ethnic terms. Within this community certain types and ways of life are held up as ideal. Also, certain types and ways of life are condemned as corrupting and as treacherous. The community organizes around the pursuit of national purity, excludes from co-operation all those who do not fit the ideal, and regards itself as having no moral relations with these others. People in this community know that they will have to pay higher taxes because their society needs defending; that they will lose the contributions of all the non-pure (who may include members of valuable professions such as doctors); that their society is unlikely to be stable, and so on. However, *ex hypothesi*, they are prepared to pay these costs because they have committed themselves to conceptions of the good which have as constitutive parts living in a 'pure' environment and promoting that purity.

There is a less and a more extreme version of this example. The less extreme version is this: the people who wish to remain pure wish to do so for reasons to do with, say, the protection of their culture and their way of life. They do not regard others as corrupt in themselves, just as corrupting. They wish to live separately and to have nothing to do with outside influences. This is not because they think that they know the truth about the world, or the best way to live, but just because as a matter of fact the thing that each of them values is a life of a particular kind; one threatened by exposure to others, or impossible to achieve when living amongst others.

They realize that there are likely costs to this action, but they are prepared to pay them to advance their good. In such a scenario the constructivist theory must conclude that there are no moral ties between this group and the co-operative communities that surround them. Given that they separate themselves from all other communities they are not bound to interact on moral terms with those communities. Of course, such a complete separation on grounds such as these is very unlikely and the constructivist can argue that they have reason to pursue mutually advantageous co-operation with others in pursuit of goods that they have reason to value.

The more extreme version is this: the community organizes around certain ethnic and national lines and regards others as corrupt in themselves. It promotes views of the others as parasites and cancers and it systematically engages in their eradication. Insofar as there are any people within the group who deviate from what is prescribed as living a valuable way of life these people are also eradicated. What the extreme version shares in common with the examples given above is that the beliefs that underpin the actions of those who exploit and kill are based on beliefs about value that the constructivist denies. Whilst the pursuit of some ends by some people might be incompatible with community membership—a woman dedicated to seducing as many men in her life as is possible cannot join and remain a member of a convent—no ends or persons are corrupt in themselves. Insofar as arguments such as these have appeared in history they have been premissed on beliefs such as that, for example, Jews or Gypsies are evil; that they sacrifice, or eat, children; that Jews are in league with communists to secure world domination; and so forth. These examples, then, raise the question of the constructivist response to communities that organize around values and ends where the understanding of the source, nature, and content of those values is based on a (or a set of) false belief(s).

For the constructivist a community that organizes its collective life independently from the rest of humanity in order that the members of the community might best achieve their ends raises few conceptual problems if the members of that community share a subjectivist understanding of their ends and engage with one another in co-operation voluntarily. Where problems arise is where the community has an incorrect understanding of its own nature and of the norms and rules that govern it. For example, the community organizes around a belief in the existence of some supernatural entity. Insofar as the community has rules and norms that could be given a constructivist justification one might say that they are bound by moral rules the correct nature of which they do not understand. However, if amongst the rules there is the injunction to sacrifice a virgin each morning then this is not a defensible moral claim. Such a rule could not be given a constructivist rationale. Constructivism cannot be employed to engage in the reinterpretative justification of communities who organize around the pursuit of ends valued because of false beliefs. At best, it can offer a justification for some norms and rules that might be thought by those whom they govern to have a different, external, grounding.

It might be thought that this has little to do with the argument about the scope of constructivist morality, but this is not the case. The challenge is that the organizing form given to a community might be a set of rules that include, as in the example, the sacrificing of (some) virgins. Moreover, the community may be such that all its members, including those who are to be sacrificed, identify with these rules. They take these rules to advance their good and commit themselves to living in accordance with them. How can constructivism avoid endorsing this community as having met the requirements of the theory? How can it declare such a rule 'indefensible'?

The answer appeals to the critical distance that must be achieved between the agent and her commitments. The constructivist theorist cannot say that agents have reason to organize around any principles except those that are freely acceptable to all from the general perspective of an agent who is standing back from his commitments, is informed, and is rational. After all, the constructivist theorist is developing an account of what persons have reason to do and not to do. This means that the constructivist is not in the position of having to agree that the virgin-sacrificing community is an ideal manifestation of constructivist reasoning. Instead its norms and rules have no rational justification and the members of the community have reason to renounce their commitments to them.

This argument is important because the constructivist position is often presented by its critics as legitimizing the destruction or exploitation of some groups by others on some or other ideological grounds. This taints constructivism by association with the likes of Nazis or homophobes. Such an association is unfounded. The constructivist theory can be shown to be unable to condemn as immoral, say, the destruction of one group of solitary beings by another such group. This is, as noted above, not to be made light of even if in the real world it can for the most part be ducked. However, the constructivist cannot be shown to underwrite with reason beliefs that there are no good reasons to hold (cf. Gauthier 1998: 134–5).

It should be clear from this that the constructivist position developed here denies the reasonableness of pluralism as this is understood by impartialists. It also denies Barry's (and others') contention that no judgements about the good can be held with sufficient certainty to legitimize using them in the justification of the use of public power. The constructivist has an account of the source of value and of how moral value is constructed, one that she does not think to be on a par with other accounts (see Charvet 1995: ch. 1; Gauthier 1986: ch. 2). Of course, it is true that there are a variety of different conceptions of the good in the world and that many people are deeply committed to accounts of the good that are connected to claims of objective value. It is also true that even agreement on the constructivist account of value does not foreclose dispute about the nature of the good life for human beings. Indeed, quite the reverse. Freedom from the constraints of choosing between a number of historically endorsed conceptions of the good will lead—and has led—to a flourishing of a multiplicity of ideas about what is a satisfying and valuable human life.

This second type of pluralism is easily accommodated by the constructivist. All that can be generated by the constructivist account are general and highly abstract demands that must find instantiation in particular communities with particular traditions in particular circumstances. There are many social practices and institutions that will be such that they could be given a constructivist rationale (cf. Scanlon 1999: Chapter 8; Chapter 9 below).

For those who hold a conception of the good grounded in objective value or objective reason the constructivist society need not be an inhospitable place. The constructivist, unlike his *faux* counterpart, cannot pretend that the justification of the use of public power does not appeal to a particular account of value and thus does not deny the truth of other accounts. It does both. However, if the argument of Chapters 4 and 5 above is right, the *faux* constructivist must do the same. In standing back from their commitments and asking whether they have reason to endorse the moral life, the contracting parties ask themselves what they have best reason to do in the light of the ends that they have reason to seek. The constructivist cannot endorse the claim that what people have best reason to seek are things that they understand as being good because of commitments from which they have not distanced themselves and which are grounded in accounts of value that the constructivist explicitly denies are valid.

However, this does not mean that the constructivist community need be an impossible environment for the many who have commitments to, say, religious beliefs of one kind or another. In constructing impartial rules to govern co-operation the contractors have reason to endorse the liberal rights of freedom of association, belief, etc. Moreover, given the importance of these rights they have reason to embed them in a manner that protects citizens from intrusive interference even where that interference has majority support. Of course, the foundations for these rights lie in the need for agreed rules to which each can reasonably give a commitment of the kind described above, rather than in a command to respect persons by respecting their beliefs. Nevertheless, they provide a degree of space in which those who wish to pursue their plans of life may do so (subject, of course, to their not infringing the rights of others). Finally, those who would wish that their society reflect some or other of their beliefs can advocate that it should do so subject only to the condition that whatever practice they are advocating could be given a constructivist rationale. There are many practices in given societies that are compatible with the demands of constructivism that also coincide with various religious beliefs. That said, the public justification of such practices, should one be called for, is not that they are so compatible (or that they are commanded by some or other god), but that they could be agreed to (or are compatible with what could be agreed to) by contracting parties in the constructivist 'situation'.

## COMMITTING TO THE MORAL LIFE

The argument above has proceeded swiftly. The presentation has largely been in terms of a choice between endorsing a full commitment to the moral life and a life unregulated by the norms of the co-operative community to which one belongs. However, as was noted above in criticism of Gauthier, these are not the only two options. One might, for example, take up the stance of the reserved maximizer. Why, it might be asked, is not this the best choice for the agent? There is, of course, no rationally decisive argument for why it should not be. The constructivist community can coerce such a person to ensure that he keeps his contracts, but it cannot show him that his choice is an irrational one. However, the constructivist can argue that there are reasons that partially underwrite the commitment to morality and can try to show the person the attractiveness of a moral life. What should not be taken to be the case is that the reserved maximizer has managed to achieve all that the genuinely moral person achieves, without paying any of the costs. This is the misunderstanding that plagues fair play theory, and the last two chapters have been dedicated to showing that it *is* a misunderstanding. Conversely, then, the moral person does not fall foul of some confidence trick in committing himself to morality.

Of course, this does not mean that the moral person will always, and without effort, act in accordance with the demands of morality. To take up the standpoint of morality is to accept the priority of moral norms, it is to accept their 'hierarchical supremacy . . . over narrow self-interest' (Charvet 1995: 173). Narrow self-interest is not obliterated in this account and the moral agent may be tempted to free-ride on others in its pursuit. Fred's behaviour in the example given in Chapter 2 is not inexplicable. It reveals either that Fred thought of himself as pursuing his separate good and of the co-operative enterprise as instrumentally useful in the pursuit of that good, or that he failed to live up to the demands of the co-operative enterprise that he had incorporated into his own good. In the latter case, nevertheless, Fred benefits in terms of his narrow self-interest (or would do so if he were not caught). However, given that he is a moral being he fails to live in accordance with the demands of reasons that he accepts as having imperatival force. The moral commitment is a commitment to understand one's good, and to pursue that good, in a particular way. Thus, if there are reasons to endorse this commitment then there are reasons to maintain it even where the pay-offs of free-riding are great.

The moral agent described here has much in common with the description Gauthier gives of the constrained maximizer. Having committed himself to the moral life, he accepts the priority of moral norms over narrow self-interest and he does not think himself foolish for his choice.[20] The crucial difference lies in the route taken to this account. Gauthier believes that constrained maximization can be rationally justified to the non-tuist 'economic' agent. The argument here is that this cannot be done. Instead the agent must make an existential commitment to the moral life. This can be defended as partially underwritten by reason in conditions in which each agent is able to think of himself as better off through making the commitment. For this to be so it must be the case that the agent's commitment to morality is made together with others.

Moreover, whilst constructive morality is not an affective morality it is one which hopes to, and which must, attract the affections of those covered by it. In committing oneself to morality, more likely in endorsing oneself as a moral being, one recognizes the demand to treat one's co-participants in accordance with terms that all can freely accept as authoritative over the pursuit of narrow self-interest. This may build on affective states such as sympathy, and on the agent's desire to appear to others (and to herself) as

---

[20] Although, of course, insofar as Gauthier identifies the CM with the 'economic man' who thinks of moral constraints as 'evils of which he would be free' his account and the one developed here differ.

# 9

# The Moral Community, Justified Coercion, and Punishment

## INTRODUCTION

The commitment to a moral life is made by an agent who reflects upon her relations with others given that she claims value for herself. The making of this commitment is conditional on its being the case that by doing so she advances her good. The argument of the previous two chapters is that this is not a matter of moral co-operation advancing the goods of self-concern, but of its advancing much wider goods that people have reason to pursue. It might be thought that this amounts to answering the age-old philosophical question 'why should I be moral?' with the reply 'because that is what you want'. If so, this is both implausible and simplistic not least because if being moral were part of the good of human beings then conflicts between self-interest and morality would not occur and the problem would not have the philosophical pedigree that it has. However, this is not the argument that is on offer. Although it is part of the current project to close the gap between prudential and moral reasons, this is not to claim that moral reasons simply subsume prudential ones, or that making the commitment to a moral life is merely a matter of recognizing what is really in one's good.

An agent who reflects on his relations with others and comes to endorse morality as regulative of his life embraces a framework for understanding what he has reason to do. Just as an agent who reflects on his own flourishing as a particular kind of organism with interests extended over time embraces prudential reason as providing a framework through which he is to understand the pursuit of his good, so with moral reasons. The agent extends his capacity to take control of his life, and gives to his life a unity through endorsing the regulative role of prudential and moral reasons. He forms and shapes his life in accordance with his understanding of the kind of person that he is and by doing so he, in Rawls's words, expresses his freedom from 'contingency and happenstance'. It is in this sense that one can talk of the agent developing his autonomy, for in resisting the impulse of immediate desire and shaping his life in accordance with his conception of the good, and in understanding his doing so not as an act of obedience to some external authority, but as a matter of his own commitment to a particular kind of life, the agent takes responsibility for his life and extends his capacity for self-government.

The realization that one is responsible, together with others, for the maintenance of morality and the moral community through one's own will to live together with others on moral terms (rather than in response to the will of some external authority) places a great burden on both the agent and the community. This is because committing oneself to a regulative role for prudential and moral reason does not, of course, remove the presence of immediate desires and the temptation to satisfy them. As the language of 'commitment' suggests, the endorsing of morality is a matter of will and this is something that must be maintained by the agent in the face of, especially, the immediate pay-offs to be had by free-riding on others. The responsibility of the community is not merely in the maintenance of the condition of sufficient security and in the education of future citizens, but also in reinforcing the choice of the moral life on the part of its citizens. These roles, of the community as creator of the person and vice versa, have considerable implications for the understanding of coercion and of punishment.


## THE CONDITION OF SUFFICIENT SECURITY

The commitment to endorse oneself as a moral being is related to others making a similar commitment in two ways. First, the development of one's conception of the good is affected by the nature of the community in which one lives. In a dog-eat-dog world one will develop a sense of one's own good that is not connected to the good of others and will regard others as threats to one's welfare. Second, one's commitment to live together with others on moral terms can only be reasonable in conditions where others, too, make that commitment. As noted in the previous chapter, acting morally carries with it the danger that others will take advantage of one's restraint. In a world in which this is likely the connection between being moral and advancing one's good is likely to be severed.

This is a version of an assurance problem, or as noted above, what Hobbes called the problem of providing the condition of 'sufficient security' (Hobbes 1991: part i, ch. 15, 110). Hobbes recognizes this as the fundamental problem of the state of nature, and as the reason for the individual to authorize the 'common power' (the 'sovereign') without whom Hobbes believes the condition is unlikely to be satisfied.[1] Hobbes also recognizes that so long as others are not willing to solve this problem by transferring their rights to a common authority, no individual can be bound (by reason), to do so:

> For as long as every man holdeth this Right, of doing any thing he liketh; so long are all men in the condition of Warre. But if other men will not lay down their Right, as well as he; then there is no Reason for any one, to devest himselfe of his: For that were to expose himselfe to Prey, (which no man is bound to) rather than to dispose himselfe to Peace. (1991: part i, ch. 14, 92)

It is likewise recognized by a more modern theorist of justice, John Rawls:

> The assurance problem . . . is to assure the cooperating parties that the common agreement is being carried out. Each person's willingness to contribute is contingent upon the contribution of the others. Therefore to maintain public confidence in the scheme that is superior from everyone's point of view, or better anyway than the situation that would obtain in its absence, some device for administering fines and penalties must be established. (Rawls 1971: 270)[2]

Of course, the difference between the constructivist theory advocated here and that of Rawls and other *faux* constructivists is that *faux* constructivists have as a premiss the equal moral worth of all human beings. The ethical injunctions that emerge from their hypothetical choosing situations, then,

---

[1] Hobbes 1991: esp. part i, chs. 13–16, 86–115. For an interpretation of Hobbes based very much on the assurance problem see Barry 1968. 'Contracts, Hobbes tells us, are only conditionally beneficial; it only pays me to do my part given that you do yours as well. Therefore, it is not obligatory for one party to perform his part if he has a "reasonable suspicion" that the other party will fail to do his. The key is trust; in the absence of a "common power" over the contracting parties, the larger the element of trust involved, the less chance there is that a contract will create an obligation to perform' (Barry 1968: 123).

[2] Cf. Kant 1991: 307–8. Kant argues that 'No one is bound to refrain from encroaching on what the other possesses if the other gives him no equal assurance that he will observe the same restraint toward him. No one, therefore, need wait until he has learned from bitter experience of the other's contrary disposition; for what should bind him to wait till he has suffered a loss before he becomes prudent . . .?' Kant's position on what follows from this for the nature of wrongness is made difficult because of his separation of what it is to wrong someone and what it is to do wrong. He makes it clear that in a state 'of lawless freedom' men cannot wrong one another, although they do wrong by not resolving the assurance problem and thus leaving the state of nature. In a note to 307 he goes further and says that someone who 'breaks [an] agreement cannot complain of being wronged if his opponent plays the same trick on him when he can', although they both 'do wrong in the highest degree'.

hold independently of the construction. As such the construction is left doing little work and the assurance problem is reduced to a matter of under what conditions people will, in fact, be motivated to do their duty (see Chapter 5 above). For the constructivist that some act is a person's duty is dependent on the condition of sufficient security obtaining.

An agent who, for one reason or another, refuses to enter the co-operative community—who rejects the norms of co-operation as regulative of his way of life—is separated from the community and moral relations between him and the community do not exist (cf. Kant 1991: 307–8). In such a situation a 'state of nature' relationship between that individual and others holds. Where such an individual threatens the co-operative enterprise (or any member thereof), coercion and force may very well be required to restrain that individual. This is simply the protection of one's property and self (or the community's protecting of itself and its property) against an alien and, thus, there is no legal analogue in punishment. Such a situation is unlikely if the community is just, or nearly just, given that under consideration is an already socialized agent reflecting on his relations with others. Where the community itself is not just, of course, the agent may realize that he has no reasonable choice but to act as an independent (see pp. 265–67 below). For the most part, therefore, the questions of coercion and punishment will be discussed as directed against individuals who do claim membership of the community and thus who do have, in what might be a primitive form, a moral will.

An agent who accepts an understanding of herself as a moral being, as someone who understands her interests as tied together with that of others in fair co-operation for mutual advantage, and yet who free-rides on others is in a different situation from that of the independent. The act of free-riding represents an attack on the very foundation of the community, and it is argued below that through censure and sanctions the community expresses its abhorrence for such action. This is because given that the community is grounded in nothing other than the wills of its citizens to co-operate on terms on which they would agree when reflecting on their relations with others from a position of subjective value, and that it is this agreement, and action in accordance with it, that gives the terms their binding nature as moral principles, the community cannot tolerate free-riding. To admit free-riding would be to undermine the conditions of trust that must hold between persons if the moral community is to continue. If the free-rider is tolerated, individuals will have reason to suspect that their willingness to give priority to the demands of morality is leading them to be taken advantage of. Each, as Hobbes predicts, will thus make the preemptive move of breaking his commitment to morality and the 'warre . . . of every man against every man' (Hobbes 1991: ch. 13, 88) threatens. Moreover, not to differentiate between free-riders and other members of the community would destroy the identification of the personal and moral perspectives by breaking the connection between the individual's flourishing and the flourishing of the community; the individual could satisfy her narrow self-interest without regulating the pursuit of that self-interest in accordance with the terms of co-operation. In this sense, the formation in the individual of a sense of himself as a member of the community is accompanied by a will to coerce others who claim the benefits of membership without at the same time regulating the pursuit of their self-interest in accordance with the principles governing co-operation. This will likewise applies to himself should he turn out to be the free-rider.

In reflecting on her relations with others, then, the constructivist agent understands that she is responsible with others for the maintenance of the moral community. Her endorsing of herself as a moral being depends upon her understanding her self-interest as tied together with that of others through co-operation and the framework of rules and norms that regulates that co-operation. She has reason to renounce her commitment to morality if it does not advance her good. This may be because she is treated unjustly by the community and does not enjoy her share of the social surplus, or because her conception of the good is incompatible with membership. In addition, her commitment is tied to that of others. If others act towards her as exploiters and free-riders then moral co-operation does not obtain. The very act of commitment, then, is an act which renounces free-riding. The agent has good reason to embrace a system that deters free-riding to ensure the condition of sufficient security; to reinforce the tie between self-interest and moral co-operation; and to secure her interests against invasion by others.

The establishment and maintenance of the condition of sufficient security is essential if the moral community is to hold together. In its absence the agent reflecting on her relations with others will have no reason to endorse morality as regulative of her pursuit of her self-interest. The necessary tie between prudential and moral reasons will have been lost. However, although providing sufficient security is an essential part of understanding the coercive nature of the rules and norms of moral co-operation it is not the whole story. For, if securing sufficient security were the sole concern of agents considering the coercive nature of the agreed norms and rules that govern their co-operation the account would fall foul of the usual criticisms aimed at deterrence-based theories of punishment. It would make sense for sanctions to target those acts of free-riding that are most common and where the threat of sanctions is most effective. In addition, sufficient security depends only on the beliefs of the participants. It is a matter of assuring public confidence. In this sense the truth or otherwise of the efficacy of sanctions is only relevant insofar as it affects the beliefs of the population. It would be compatible with an assurance problem justification of punishment for punishment to be inflicted on innocents who are generally believed to be guilty, or for it to be inflicted on only some offenders. Rawls, for example, admits the possibility of some kind of deception in his brief answer to the assurance problem (although it fails to recur when he comes to discuss the role of sanctions in greater depth). He argues that in order to meet the challenge of the assurance problem, 'some device for administering fines and penalties must be established'; his conclusion, however, is that 'it is here that the mere existence of an effective sovereign, or *even the general belief* in his efficacy, has a crucial role' (Rawls 1971: 270; emphasis added).

However, this account of coercion and sanctions overlooks the interests of those to whom social institutions must be justified. To invoke the contract metaphor, people choosing the terms of agreement through which they will live together in moral co-operation would impose side constraints on those public institutions designed to maintain the condition of sufficient security. They will not accept institutions that can punish innocents or impose disproportionate punishments.

Nevertheless, such side constraints would not rule out a lottery, for example, in which only one in every three offenders was punished. A social institution of this kind might be sufficient to satisfy the condition of sufficient security (whether it would or not, of course, depends upon the conditions prevailing in the particular society). Note the proposal is not that those to be punished should be picked out at random and the evidence against them fabricated. That would not be acceptable to those choosing rules for their community. Rather the lottery being considered is one in which only those who have failed to act in accordance with the requirements of the rules of the community are eligible for selection. The argument is that an agent reflecting on his relations with others will agree to those relations being governed by rules that have a coercive element. In so doing, the agent agrees that should he fail then he will be the subject of the threatened sanctions. If the only reason for the agent's agreement is to deter free-riding and thus create or maintain the condition of sufficient security then it would make sense for the agent to agree only to that imposition of sanctions necessary to achieve that end. Amongst the people whose actions justify the imposition of sanctions only some will have to suffer. All get what they want, the condition of sufficient security, and those who are liable to suffer sanctions get a decreased chance of actually having to do so.

It is argued below that no such system will meet the constructivist test because the condition of sufficient security is not the sole concern of the reflective agent considering the nature of the norms and rules that govern his co-operation with others and theirs with him. However, insofar as the provision of sufficient security is a crucial component of the theory to be defended one objection needs to be addressed. If the use of coercive sanctions is justified by their contributing to the condition of sufficient security then how does this account differ from those accounts that are criticized above, for coercion would seem to be once again bridging the gap between prudential and moral reasons? However, this is not the case. In *faux* constructivist theory moral constraints exist independent of the agent and seem to the agent to be restrictions imposed from some source that is disconnected from her will. The threat of sanctions is necessary to close the gap between prudential and moral reasons. In simple accounts of utilitarianism, similarly, the agent is motivated to do that act which will best serve her utility, which is not necessarily the same as the act that will best promote aggregate utility. The threat of sanctions attempts to alter the initial calculation of what will maximize individual utility. In justice as mutual advantage, and in constructivist accounts more broadly, the argument is different. In such accounts morality is a product of agents' wills, specifically their will to live together bound by moral norms. The making of this commitment is contingent on others doing the same, and each agent in making it commits herself also to the sanctioning of those who fail to conform, including herself should she so fail. Coercion and sanctions, then, play an important role in the theory. They ensure that the condition of sufficient security holds so that agents can rationally make the commitment to morality and they find their grounding in the very same will as the will that makes co-operative norms moral. The coercive nature of the norms that govern co-operation is not some 'extra' applied to them to make them stick, but is implicit in their very nature as moral.

Nevertheless, what has been accounted for so far is nothing but the place of coercion in the construction of morality. For this to be an account of punishment in a moral community there is much more that needs to be said.

## JUSTIFIED COERCION AND 'MORAL' PUNISHMENT

Providing the condition of sufficient security, then, is the primary justification for the threat of 'hard treatment'.[3] However, justifying a system of punishment requires more than simply justifying coercion. Why should the agent reflecting on the terms of agreement not merely consider the assurance problem and agree to treat agents simply as prudential calculators who need to be deterred from free-riding and assured that others will be so deterred? The reason is that in agreeing to coerce and sanction people only to satisfy the condition of sufficient security she would be agreeing to treating the contractors (including herself) as only capable of responding to prudential incentives and disincentives rather than as beings capable of responding to moral argument. This is incompatible with the very foundation of morality offered by constructivism, which lies in the reflective will of each to commit herself to the priority of moral reasons. In agreeing to a system of threats and sanctions, the co-operating members have reason to agree to a system that addresses those who live under its jurisdiction as moral agents; as co-creators of the moral community; as entitled to equal consideration; and as potentially possessed of the moral will to live with others on moral terms.[4] A constructivist system of justified threats and sanctions appeals to this will, it addresses the offender as a moral being, and ultimately it is justifiable to the offender *qua* moral being as emanating from her own commitment. That is, the threat of sanctions cannot take the form of a mere appeal to the agent as a prudentially rational being—it cannot simply increase the price of certain actions—instead it must address the agent as a potentially moral being, as someone who has, in this instance, failed to live up to her commitment to live with others on moral terms.[5]

---

[3] 'Hard treatment' is a term of art denoting the imposition of suffering or deprivation as against education or therapy. I argue below that there may be conditions in which the other functions of punishment—moral expression and moral education—require hard treatment. Hard treatment is distinguished from the expressivist elements of punishment by Feinberg who admits that although the two elements are intertwined they can be separated for the purposes of analysis: 'we can conceive of ritualistic condemnation unaccompanied by any *further* hard treatment, and of inflictions and deprivations which, because of different symbolic conventions, have no reprobative force' (Feinberg 1965: 98).

[4] This raises the question (discussed below) of how such a commitment is compatible with the use of threats to impose hard treatment on offenders.

[5] As in the examples of the wife and her ungrateful family and of Fred and his associates, discussed in Ch. 7 above, the offender reveals in his actions that he has acted in response to his own narrow self-interest. The moral community must not respond in these same terms,

While this gives a moral dimension to coercion by linking it to the agreement to co-operate on moral terms, it does not, in itself, transform coercion into punishment. Punishment (as it is of concern here) is a legal response to wrongdoing and nothing said so far commits the community to giving the terms of co-operation a legal form. In smaller societies in which each person is known to every other, the role of law and penal sanctions, as against positive morality and social sanctions, might be very limited. Elsworth Faris, for example, tells of a primitive society in which the mere fact of being reprimanded by a small, weak, old woman is enough to cause extreme remorse and a desire to offer reparations in a brutal warrior who has offended against the tribal code (Faris 1914: 58; cf. Tunick 1992*a*: 78; von Hirsch 1985: 53, 1990: 278). This raises the larger question of the relatively indeterminate nature of the terms of co-operation as these can be established by a constructivist theorist. The demands of a constructivist morality are abstract requirements that must find embodiment in the positive law and positive morality of any moral community. Clearly, the constructivist cannot foretell how any given community will give specific content to them when resolving each issue that arises in regulating co-operation. To recall an example from earlier, although some determinate form must be given to the right to travel freely with respect to road use (at the most basic level there has to be an agreement as to which side of the road to drive on), such decisions can be left to an agreed decision-making procedure.[6]

This restriction on the scope of constructivist theory is perhaps less significant than it might seem. As with all constructivist theories (and social contract theories more generally including *faux* constructivists) the theorist is not attempting to construct an ideal code *de novo*, or anything resembling a comprehensive constitutional code in the Benthamite sense. Rather, constructivism offers a way of understanding the moral norms that govern a community. Of course, a correct understanding may require that some norms are altered, some enhanced, and others dismissed, but it remains true that constructivist moral theory is primarily addressed to understanding the grounds of the norms that govern persons' lives. As noted above, in small

---

by altering the pay-offs in such a calculation, but rather must, in its actions and words remind the offender that what grounds the community of which he claims membership is a commitment to the authority of moral reasons over those of narrow self-interest. It can hardly do this by resorting to the very reasoning that it is condemning in the offender.

[6] Given the principle of equality and the idea of agency, the form given to this decision-making procedure must be one of democracy. In smaller societies there seems to be no reason not to endorse some form of direct democracy. In larger, more complex societies, the contractors have reason to agree to a form of representative democracy accompanied by stringent checks and balances.

close-knit societies social norms and sanctions may be all that is needed. However, for the purpose of this argument it will be assumed that the assurance problem gives rise to the need for some hard treatment, and that the form given for the imposition of this hard treatment is legal; that is, the language of 'offender', 'punishment', etc. will be used in the argument that follows.

The argument that follows is that the contracting parties have reason to endorse an account of punishment that has a number of elements. First, there is the assurance problem, the precise response to which will depend upon the circumstances of the society. Second, there is the function of expressing the abhorrence the community feels for free-riders. Finally, linked to this second function, there is the role of law as a moral educator, as reinforcing the community's values and the injunction to be moral, and as a creator of the citizens that the community needs for its continued flourishing. Each of these must be considered carefully as each is controversial and combining them is difficult. In particular the idea of wrongness must be given content not least so as to explain how judgements of degrees of wrongness can be made in an account that is underpinned by the idea of reciprocity.

Providing the condition of sufficient security is the primary reason for imposing hard treatment. This means that part of the general justifying aim of punishment is preventive.[7] While such a rationale has traditionally been avoided by expressivist and educative theorists of punishment it fits well with the fact that the whole penality system seems to reflect what Andrew von Hirsch calls 'a preventive design'. 'When the state criminalizes conduct, it issues a legal threat: Such conduct is proscribed and violation will result in the imposition of specific penalties. This threat surely has *something* to do with inducing citizens to refrain from the proscribed conduct' (von Hirsch 1990: 275–6).[8]

---

[7] 'Preventive' is meant to include the functions of deterring others, deterring the offender, and preventing the offender from committing crimes during his punishment. In short, attempting to prevent the occurrence of future crimes.

[8] A similar point is made by John Charvet in relation to punishment as criticism: 'The purpose of having a rule is to secure the general realization of the conduct it prescribes. Therefore the existence of rules presupposes the possibility of affecting people's future actions. It is in this context that criticism operates, for it would indeed be meaningless and futile to criticize people for their actions, if such criticism never did or ever could have an effect on their future conduct. But since criticism is only relevant where rules exist, and since rules exist only where it is possible to affect people's actions by means of the rules, criticism is assured of having such general effects. Thus criticism does always in part look forward to the future actions of the rule-breaker and the other members of the community, as the Utilitarians have always insisted that punishment must' (Charvet 1966: 578; cf. Primoratz 1989*b*: 70–1).

Of course, the extent and nature of the hard treatment necessary to solve the assurance problem will depend upon the society (cf. von Hirsch 1985: 53, 1990: 275, 278). This is something recognized by thinkers as diverse as Hegel and Nietzsche.[9] It is conceivable that in small societies in which the communal bonds are extremely strong, hard treatment could be replaced by, say, public stigmatization. Likewise, it is conceivable that a society could be so unstable as to need extremely harsh penalties to solve the assurance problem. This raises a difficulty for the account of punishment being advocated here—a tension between the need for hard treatment to solve the assurance problem and the degree of punishment needed to express censure—which needs serious consideration. However, this is a problem that cannot be addressed until after the expressivist elements in the account have been considered.[10]

## PUNISHMENT AS CENSURE

Given the nature of the moral community as envisaged by the constructivist theory developed above, free-riding strikes at its heart by denying the necessary connection between self-interest and the regulating of the pursuit of self-interest in accordance with the terms of co-operation. When the individual commits an offence against those terms she, as Hegel insisted, harms not just her victim but also the community of which she is a part. The first function served in censuring the offender, then, is in reaffirming the principles against which the criminal has offended. As Igor Primoratz puts it, in language deliberately reminiscent of Hegel: 'in expressing emphatic condemnation of the crime committed, punishment *vindicates* the law which has been broken, *reaffirms* the right which has been violated, and *demonstrates* that the misdeed was indeed a crime' (Primoratz 1989a:

---

[9] 'The . . . magnitude [of the crime] varies, however, according to the *condition* of civil society, and this is the justification both for attaching the death penalty to a theft of a few pence or of a turnip, and for imposing a lenient punishment for a theft of a hundred and more times these amounts' (Hegel 1991: § 218R, see also § 218, § 218A).

'The "creditor" always becomes more humane to the extent that he has grown richer . . . It is not unthinkable that a society might attain such a consciousness of power that it could allow itself the noblest luxury possible to it—letting those who harm it go unpunished. What are my parasites to me? It might say. May they live and prosper: I am strong enough for that!' (Nietzsche 1956: 72).

[10] Similarly, there is a tension between the use of hard treatment and the requirement to address agents as responsible beings. This is discussed below.

196). This recalls the claim made, in trying to understand what was missing from fair play theory, that what was absent was an account of how the offender's action had torn at the moral fabric of the community, and that this called for some response (see Chapter 2 above).

In censuring the offender the community not only reaffirms the rights established by the agreement, and the identity of the personal and moral perspectives that underlies that agreement, but also treats the offender as a responsible agent. Thus, to return to Duff's argument discussed above in Chapter 3: the commitment made by the reflective agent to the moral life is a commitment to recognize others as equal moral beings, not merely as entities with which co-operation is sometimes valuable in the pursuit of one's separate ends. Recognizing the other as a moral being involves recognizing the appropriateness of censure in response to wrongdoing. Moreover, on the theory offered here, censure includes the claim that the agent, as a co-operator and in offending against the terms of co-operation, is offending against her own will to co-operate on moral terms; a will which must include the denial of the appropriateness of free-riding.

It might be objected that the offender could hardly be said to have the will to co-operate on moral terms given that she is an offender; she has manifestly not co-operated on such terms. However, this is to commit the mistake of thinking that someone who free-rides in a particular instance rejects co-operation and morality *tout court*. The community, in censuring, appeals to the agent as a responsible being who has demonstrated, in a myriad other ways, her commitment to co-operation on moral terms. It takes her at her word when she claims membership of, and benefits from, the community, and in punishing her when she fails to live up to its requirements it reminds her of her responsibility and commitment to the moral life. Censure is, in this sense, retributive not consequentialist: 'it is *because* we share certain moral standards that a response is required that recognizes both the conduct's wrongfulness and the actor's fault' (von Hirsch 1990: 272).[11] Duff is, therefore, right in emphasizing the important way in which condemnation is part of a discourse, 'a moral discussion' in which a 'challenge' is made to 'respond to this moral charge' (Duff 1986: 48; Chapter 3 above).

It is important to note the role of censure in the account of punishment as against that of the assurance problem in the account of coercion. If the community were to coerce the offender in a manner that was morally neu-

---

[11]  This view of the role of blame is vital in Duff's 'penitence' account (see Duff 1986: esp. 47–54, and ch. 9; also 1988, 1999; Ch. 3 above) and it appears in some version also in Primoratz 1989*a*; Hampton 1984; and Morris 1981 (but see Duff 1977).

tral it might well satisfy the demands of the assurance problem, but it would fail on two vital counts. First, it would not be addressing the offender as a moral being; it would not offer the offender a moral reason why he ought not behave in the manner that he has, it would merely offer him a prudential reason why it is in his self-interest not to do so in the future. Second, and interconnected, it would not affirm the moral status of the terms of co-operation. That is, it would not affirm their status as authoritatively binding on the pursuit of self-interest. Rather they would be affirmed merely as means to the better fulfilment of one's immediate self-interest; means that can be evaluated on a case by case basis in the light of this. In treating the offender as merely a prudential calculator, and in offering penalties as a scheme of taxes to alter the calculation, the community represents its norms as only prudential and this undermines the understanding of those norms that makes morality and the moral community possible.

Does it follow from the above account, then, that the 'offender wills her own punishment'? Not if this is interpreted as the crude claim that the justification of punishing some particular offender is that the offender willed his own punishment. The argument is rather that, from a reflective standpoint, each agent has reason to commit to morality only if the condition of sufficient security obtains. In making this commitment, each agent endorses the place of moral reasons as hierarchically superior to those of narrow self-interest on the condition that *every other does so too*. Implicit in this mutual commitment to the moral life is the will to coerce free-riders. Thus, a moral agent who has succumbed to temptation ought to be able, from the stance of a reflective agent, to will the system of punishment that now threatens to punish him. This is an idea that is often viewed scornfully,[12] and it brings into focus the difficult question of the role of consent in constructivist theory.

The agent, taking up the reflective stance, asks whether maintaining and cultivating herself as a moral character and rejecting the immediate and unconstrained pursuit of self-interest advances her good. Constructivism gives an account of those reasons that should incline the agent to answer this question in the affirmative. However, the idea of consent implied in this account is not a once and for all commitment to 'obey the state' or 'enter the contract', but a continual, hermeneutical, process in which the agent affirms her status as a moral character through self-creative reflection and action (cf. Taylor 1985: chs. 1, 2, 4).

---

[12] See, for example, Honderich 1984: 219–27, esp. 226.

The most common objection to any account that involves the offender willing his own punishment revolves around the claim that some—perhaps most—people have never deliberately thought of themselves separated from their commitments, considering their relations with others from an initial standpoint of subjective value. They have never 'chosen' to affirm themselves as moral characters and it is, thus, mistaken to speak of people having willed anything. Such a criticism is not plausibly levelled at the model of consent offered above. People in relatively just societies[13] do reflect on moral issues every day, and do ask themselves whether, for example, they want to be the kinds of persons who are dishonest, or greedy, or who lie and steal. They do ask whether they ought to try to avoid paying their taxes and in thinking about this question they are profoundly affected by thoughts about whether the system is just and whether others are getting away with not doing their share; whether by being moral they are being taken for a ride.

Thus, censure aimed at involving the agent in a discussion, aimed at the agent as a rational, responsible being, is not consequentialist. Although the aim is, in part, to try to get the agent to reflect on the wrongfulness of his actions, even if the community were sure that the agent would not do so it would still be justified in addressing him as an agent (so long, that is, as he fulfilled certain requirements of being responsible, and that he did not completely renounce the moral life), because he is capable of understanding that his actions have evoked the disapproval of others, even if he finds that such disapproval carries no weight with him.[14]

In a sense then, what is being defended is the idea that persons in a relatively just society face a choice of one of three options, a choice which they both think about and express in their actions. An agent may renounce cooperation and live as an independent. She may endorse co-operation and the authority of morality. Finally, she may adopt an attitude of constrain-

---

[13] How all of this is affected by a background of injustice is discussed below.

[14] See on this Duff 1986: 266; von Hirsch 1990: 274; Primoratz 1989*a*: 195–6. Primoratz argues that Duff's account of censure is consequentialist. Von Hirsch challenges this on grounds similar to those offered here although he thinks that 'Duff seems to lay himself open to this charge' (von Hirsch 1990: 274 n. 48). *Pace* von Hirsch, I think Duff holds that no agent is conceptually incapable of redemption (if she were she would not qualify as an agent), independent of how empirically likely redemption is. This is not only compatible with the account of blame offered throughout *Trials and Punishments*, but is also explicitly stated in the passage cited by von Hirsch; Duff says 'to talk thus of "the good that is in him" is not to make some psychological claim to the effect that he 'really' cares for the values which he flouts: it is rather to combine the conceptual claim that every moral agent has the capacity or potential for moral development and reform, with the moral claim that we should never give up hope of bringing him to actualise that potential' (Duff 1986: 266).

ing the pursuit of her self-interest only when it pays to do so and choose not to do so when she can free-ride. However, this final option is inconsistent with membership of a moral community and part of the function of punishment is, thus, to confront the agent with her behaviour and ask her either to declare herself an independent, someone not free to enjoy the advantages of co-operation, or to endorse her membership of the moral community and her understanding of herself as a co-operative being governed by moral norms.

Thus, punishment must express to the offender the full force of the understanding of morality as grounded in the wills of the members of the community. Punishment must say to the agent, 'you, and you alone, are responsible for your commitment to be moral (albeit that we can try to help you in making that commitment)'. It can, therefore, deepen the agent's understanding of morality and lead to her becoming a fully morally autonomous being; that is, a being who takes full responsibility for her moral commitment.[15] This brings the argument to the role of punishment as a moral educator.

## PUNISHMENT AS A MORAL EDUCATOR

Punishment in reaffirming the terms of agreement, in declaring the criminal action wrong, contributes to the moral education of the contractors (cf. Hampton 1984) and reinforces the injunction to be moral. In large modern societies, in which the traditional spheres through which moral education occurred have either disappeared or been discredited, law has an important role in setting the tone of the society. Law is a form through which to inculcate as well as to enforce moral injunctions, and penal sanctions, likewise, share this role. This is not to say that law can replace social morality; law is by its very nature cumbersome and general, and many of its commands are inapplicable to children (because they do not qualify as agents), who are the most obvious candidates for moral education. Nonetheless, the moral tone of society is dependent upon the law as the most important and visible instance of the terms of agreement through which persons agree to live together in a moral community. This is not to say, of course, that the law ought to enshrine and enforce every piece of

---

[15] This idea, that in accepting his punishment the agent deepens his understanding of himself, is vital to Hegel's account of punishment (see Hegel 1991: §§ 90–104).

traditional morality.[16] It is to say that the law ought to enshrine and enforce those justified moral injunctions (which are best enshrined in a positive law, rather than a positive morality) which would emerge from the reflective agreement of agents committed to a system of co-operation and to a principle of equality.

This is an instance of the idea that just as the moral community is created by the agreement of its members to co-operate on moral terms, it is also the case that the community is the creator of its members. It is through living in the community that the agent comes to flourish as a self-conscious, rational being. Further, the concrete form given to the abstract constructivist injunctions are given by the community, and it is these concrete rules that form and shape each agent's dispositions. Insofar as the community is challenging the agent to affirm the moral life, punishment has an important role reinforcing the community's standards and values.

The educative function of punishment is, then, tied to the expressive. The community expresses its abhorrence at the offender's action and reaffirms the choice that each agent must make between independence and membership. In thus excluding the option of partial or reserved compliance punishment also takes on an educative role. It forces the agent's attention onto the choice that confronts him, and it promotes the choice of moral co-operation by presenting the offender with the reasons that have been given above for the wisdom of this choice.

Punishment, then, while serving the assurance problem also has an element of censure; an expressive element.[17] Thus, although Michael Davis's criticism of expressive theories—that punishment is more than merely censuring—is correct, what *must* be recognized is that it is also censuring (see Davis 1991; von Hirsch 1990: 270). In choosing a system of punishment that involves all of these elements the contracting parties recognize the nature of their commitment to morality and their susceptibility to the temptations of narrow self-interest (cf. von Hirsch 1993: chs. 1 and 2).

However, having established this 'two-pronged rationale' (von Hirsch 1990: 278; Chapter 3 above) of hard treatment and censure, the question arises as to how these elements are to be integrated in one account. To answer this question it is necessary to make some brief remarks about the nature of wrongness in the constructivist account.

---

[16] As might be thought to be recommended in Devlin's attack on the Wolfenden Committee (see Devlin 1959 and Hart 1963).

[17] The best-known defence of expressivism is Feinberg 1965. For a detailed criticism see Skillen 1980.

## FREE-RIDING, DOING WRONG, AND
## DEGREES OF WRONGNESS

It is argued above that the terms of agreement must be acceptable to each agent. Taking up the reflective stance, each agent understands that it is only her commitment together with that of others to accept the terms of agreement as providing reasons that override those of narrow self-interest that grounds the moral community and makes possible stable co-operation for mutual advantage. For such a commitment to be a reasonable one for each agent to make and to sustain, the terms of agreement must be such that each can accept them no matter what his particular features. Impartiality is generated from within the constructivist argument (see Chapter 7 above). Thus, the understanding of wrong on this account is a constructivist version of the Scanlonian one: 'an act is wrong if its performance under the circumstances would be disallowed by any set of principles for the general regulation of behavior that no one [participant] could reasonably reject as the basis for informed, unforced general agreement' (Scanlon 1999: 153).

In Chapters 4 and 5 the deployment of this argument by impartialist theorists was criticized. How then is it possible that the constructivist theory has arrived back at this formulation? The criticisms were, first, that insofar as the impartialists understood this formulation in the light of an assumption of fundamental equality, they did nothing to provide an account of that equality. Thus, the demand to treat others as equals appeared to the agent as an alien constraint on the pursuit of his good to be overcome either by a desire to treat others as equals or by the threat of sanctions. Second, the use of the Scanlonian formula by impartialist theorists concerned to provide an account of the public domain beyond the narrow scope of justice was argued to be incompatible with the impartialist need to maintain justificatory neutrality.

Neither of these criticisms applies to the use of the Scanlonian formula above. First, the theory does not assume agents of equal and objective moral worth. Rather, impartiality is, as already noted, a product of the constructivist procedure. The participants in the construction are interested in what others can accept and reject not because they are assumed to care for those others or to recognize in them some objective value, but because all have reason to seek principles that all have reason to accept (cf. Scanlon 1999: 191; Chapter 7 above). Second, there is no aspiration within constructivism to maintain justificatory neutrality. The participants in the construction must come to agree to rules to govern their interaction that reflect their concern to promote and protect what they have reason to value. Such rules, then, will reflect a common understanding of certain requirements of human flourishing. Thus, those who would oppose these rules because of reasons that not all can accept will find themselves isolated unless they can change their views. Insofar as they refuse participation, reject the understanding of morality offered, and set themselves up in opposition to the moral community they place themselves and the moral community in a state of nature in which moral rules do not apply. Insofar as they participate and act morally for their own reasons, they do not pose a challenge to the moral community and can be accepted within it (Chapter 8 above).

What then can be said prior to actual deliberation between agents about the rules to which all have reason to agree? Given that the parties to the contract are motivated to advance their goods it can reasonably be supposed that they will endorse rules that are designed to protect their lives, liberty, and property. However, the constructivist must accept that what people will have reason to do in choosing principles to regulate their lives will depend, in part, on the circumstances in which they find themselves. What people have reason to want, as Scanlon puts it, 'depends on the conditions in which they are placed, and among these conditions are facts about what most people around them want, believe, and expect' (Scanlon 1999: 341). Given this, different societies will reflectively endorse a range of wrongs within the limits circumscribed by the need for the terms of agreement to advance the goods of those to whom they apply.

However, the issue for the current argument concerns not so much the content of the particular rules, but rather the understanding of wrong and wrongdoing. Specifically, can this account avoid the charge that it reduces all wrongs to acts of free-riding, and can it make sense of the idea of degrees of wrongness, which it must do if it is to generate a plausible theory of punishment? The suspicion that the constructivist account reduces all wrongs to wrongs of free-riding emerges from the way in which the argument is constructed. After all, the fundamental challenge for constructivism is to show that there are reasons to be moral, rather than to treat co-operative norms as merely of instrumental value, and thus as binding only when the advantages of co-operation outweigh those of defection and free-riding. Moreover, given that the argument is not concerned with sincere independents, but with those who claim membership of the moral community it appears as if the failure on the part of the offending agent is a failure to abide by the imperatival force of moral reasons and is thus to free-ride on those with whom the agent co-operates.

There is, indeed, a sense in which all wrongs must be acts of free-riding. For the wrongdoer takes advantage of a system that is made possible only by the restraint of others. The wrongdoer thus promotes his narrow self-interest without regard for those with whom he claims to co-operate on moral terms. However, whilst this is true, this is not the nature of the wrong for which he is held accountable. What informs the choice of principles is agreement on what people have reason to value. Thus, the contracting parties will agree, to recall the example from earlier, to outlaw the intentional harming of one another (outside of certain contexts).[18] They will do so because they have reason to value their lives, capacities, and so on. Thus, as was noted in relation to the impartialist use of Scanlon's account, whilst what it is for something to be wrong is for it to be such that it could be reasonably rejected in Scanlon's test, what makes it wrong is that the act, for example, violates certain interests, causes harm, or whatever (cf. 1999: 391).

This means that the failure on the part of the offending agent is, in part, a failure to restrain the pursuit of his narrow self-interest in accordance with the demands of morality (demands that he claims to recognize as having imperatival force). But, it is also a failure that manifests itself in disregard for a particular rule that is grounded in the some account of what he and his co-operative partners have reason to value. Thus, in condemning the offender for the wrong that he has committed the community can refer both to the failure of self-restraint and to the actual wrong committed (the harm done, the interest violated, or whatever).

It should be clear from this how the constructivist theory can account for the idea of there being degrees of wrong. By this is not meant degrees of responsibility, but differences in the seriousness of different wrongs. For if the contracting parties must choose principles through which to live together based on what they have reason to value, then they can invest such principles with different significance depending on the interest or value being protected or promoted. Here the flexibility of constructivist theory may be most apparent. Given that the reasons the constructing parties have will depend, in part, on the conditions that they face, they will give different significance to different interests and values in part because of different conditions. Thus, to give one example, in a society going through important changes in its economic development it may be that those reflecting on the terms of agreement will have reason to value the protection of property

---

[18] Of course, the actual terms of agreement in a given society are more precise than this. However, this need for precision does not make the theory liable to the problems raised in Ch. 4 as in the constructivist account there is no aspiration to justificatory neutrality.

in relation to wrongs against the person differently from those in a society in which economic relations are established and stable.

Developing this further would require a full-blown constructivist account of the criminal law in different conditions and that is beyond the immediate need of this argument. All that must be shown here is that the account does not treat wrongs only as instances of free-riding, and that the account can provide grounds for differentiating one wrong from another on grounds of seriousness. There is, of course, much more than could be said, but the above is sufficient to show what is needed in response to both challenges.

Given the accounts of punishment and of wrong, it is possible now to return to the problem postponed above concerning the integration of the demands of hard treatment required to solve the assurance problem, the expression of blame, and the requirement to treat people as moral agents. The challenge is to show that these can be integrated into a coherent account of punishment.

## HARD TREATMENT, CENSURE, AND RESPECT FOR AGENCY

The questions addressed in this section arise because of the complex rationale given to punishment above. Given that punishment deters, assures, and censures is there the possibility that in order to perform one function (say deterrence) the system of punishment would have to fail to perform another (to censure appropriately)? Before embarking on a discussion of this two points are worth emphasizing. First, what is under discussion is the punishment of those who claim membership of the moral community. Those who would be independents stand outside of morality. As is pointed out above, when necessary the community will defend itself against them and may coerce them. However, this will not be punishment and nothing need be conveyed by the threat of coercion except a prudential disincentive. These are the equivalent of Locke's 'wild Savage Beasts, with whom Men can have no Society nor Security' (Locke 1988: § 11, 274; cf. Kant 1991: 307–8 ). Second, what can be said about these questions is limited for, as will be seen, much hangs on the particular circumstances of the community in which the system of punishment is to operate and on predictions of the deterrence effects of punishment (which are difficult to measure and which, of course, also vary in different societies). At best, what can be offered are some general guidelines for how the different demands made of the punishment system are to be fitted together.

It might seem as if not merely the demands made of the system of punishment, but also the techniques deployed in punishment can be easily separated. Thus, the communication of censure and the educative role of punishment are performed through moral condemnation and communication (through public trials, symbols, and the like), and the deterrence and assurance functions through hard treatment. However, this is to misunderstand the nature of hard treatment. Whilst the threat of hard treatment can—for example, when directed at a dog (or an independent)—be morally neutral, within punishment hard treatment also conveys censure. As von Hirsch puts it,

> The penal sanction clearly does convey blame. Punishing someone consists of visiting a deprivation (hard treatment) on him, because he supposedly has committed a wrong, in a manner that expresses disapprobation of the person for his conduct. . . . The difference between a tax and a fine does not rest in the kind of material deprivation (money in both cases). It consists, rather, in the fact that the fine conveys disapproval or censure, whereas the tax does not. (von Hirsch 1993: 9)

Hard treatment is, then, a vehicle for censure as well as deterrence.[19] However, this does not make impossible tensions between the censuring and deterrence functions of punishment.

Consider the most obvious case: a crime is relatively easy to get away with and the pay-offs are quite large, yet the degree of censure thought to attach to this crime is small. Take, for example, cheating on public transport by purchasing a ticket for a certain journey and then travelling further than the ticket allows. Assume that the system of sanctions that would be needed to deter those who override would involve the threat of serious penalties. Yet these penalties are such that they convey a degree of censure

---

[19] This fact seems to be overlooked in the common criticism of expressive theories of punishment that if punishment is about communication then we could, in Scanlon's words, just as well ' "say it with flowers" or, perhaps more appropriately, with weeds' (Scanlon 1988: 214). What is odd about this widely held view is that it is not true. We could not just as well say it with flowers because flowers typically say something else. The fact that in, say, the UK people express affection with flowers is no doubt arbitrary—candles, for example, might have taken this role. However, as it happens candles do not typically express affection and flowers do not express censure. Thus, the sister of someone killed by a drunk driver who says, after the driver has been fined £100, that £100 is how the state values the life of her sibling does not express the thought that had the fine been greater perhaps the driver would have thought more carefully (although that might be true), but the thought that the penalty imposed is not sufficiently serious. £100 expresses a minor reprimand; a prison sentence something more serious.

that is thought to be disproportionate given the nature of the offence. In these circumstances it appears as if one demand must give way. Why should reflective agents considering this practice not conclude that, given that those who are tempted to free-ride will not be deterred by minor sanctions (because the chances of being caught are small), and that the failure of some to pay is encouraging others who would pay to believe that their commitment to paying is leading to their being taken advantage of and thus the failure of some to pay is threatening the entire system, therefore, what should be implemented is a more draconian system of penalties?

Part of the reply to this question lies with the initial argument that those who are considering the terms of agreement will choose terms that reflect their status as moral agents and the status of those terms as moral. In thus choosing an institution of punishment that has a communicative and educative function they choose a system that reflects the priority of the moral over the prudential. However, they also recognize the temptations of narrow self-interest and the need for assurance. Thus, the contracting parties can conceive of the need for hard treatment as what Andrew von Hirsch calls a 'prudential supplement' for those who have made the commitment to the moral life (von Hirsch 1990, 1993, 1999; Chapter 3 above). Such people recognize that, although they have accepted the priority of moral reasons over narrow self-interest they will sometimes be tempted by self-interest, and whilst they have reason to endorse their commitment to morality and to act morally, the threat of hard treatment provides an additional reason to quiet the voice of temptation. To give any greater priority to prudential sanctions would be to give up the idea that the penality system addresses the offender as a moral agent and as a member of the community.

In addition, it must be remembered that hard treatment conveys blame and censure. It is in part communicative, and thus speaks to the moral as well as the prudential reason of the offender. The punishment of the offender aims to communicate to him his failure to live by moral standards that apply to him insofar as he claims membership of the moral community, and it aims to call him to account for the particular wrong that he has performed. As Duff puts it, 'An offender's punishment must be such that it appeals to, but does not coerce, his understanding and his will. . . . It must also be proportionate in its severity to the seriousness of his offence: only then can it communicate to him an adequate understanding of the moral character of his offence' (Duff 1986: 278). Thus, the hard treatment imposed must convey the right 'message' to the offender. This will, of course, depend on the nature and conventions of the society in question, but the flavour of the argument is captured in the response that a reader of this book might have to someone who in response to some minor wrong said, ' "I'm not so upset, so I'll only break your arm" ' (this example is borrowed from von Hirsch 1990: 284). The point is that the response is disproportionate and, thus, conveys the wrong degree of censure. The need is to fit the censure to the seriousness of the crime. In addition, in a system of punishment it is the community that speaks and it does so, in part, in support and vindication of the values that have been flouted by the offender. For the state to treat life, liberty, and property as unimportant in its infliction of punishment is for it to undermine by its actions the very things that the system of punishment is meant to uphold.

Thus, in a situation in which penal hard treatment carries with it a message that must be related to the seriousness of the offence and that must be consistent with the values that are upheld by the rules to which they are attached, the demands of censure will ideally take precedence over those of deterrence. The agent must be reminded of his commitment to live a moral life and the relationship of that commitment, together with that of others, to the moral community. Such a reminder can hardly take the form of a revised account of the pay-offs in the calculation that the offender had made of how best to advance his narrow self-interest.

Nevertheless, this does not address the problem of what the contracting parties have reason to do if what is needed in order to convey the appropriate level of censure is insufficient to deter potential offenders. This is particularly serious for the constructivist account for, given that for each agent the commitment to morality is dependent on the like commitment of others, the existence of the moral community is at stake where the condition of sufficient security is thought not to hold. In such circumstances, where the moral commitment is weak and those who would make it are inclined not to do so for fear of being taken for fools, the contracting parties will have little choice but to increase the levels of hard treatment so as to re-establish trust in the system and allow those who would be moral to act once again in accordance with morality's demands. Is increasing the levels of hard treatment in such circumstances incompatible with the above analysis? There are some reasons to think not. For in such circumstances what is regarded as 'serious', both in terms of offences and in terms of sanctions, is likely to be significantly different from what is thought serious in stable societies in which the moral commitment is strong in most people.

Is there then anything that can be said about the levels of punishment in a given society without knowing the details of that society? More importantly, given the above analysis, are there any general reasons to which the contracting parties might appeal in setting upper limits on the punishment for certain offences? The answer to both questions is 'yes', for the contracting parties can appeal to considerations of ordinal and cardinal proportionality in devising systems of punishment.

The principle of ordinal proportionality requires that 'persons convicted of crimes of comparable gravity should receive punishments of comparable severity (save under mitigating or aggravating circumstances altering the harmfulness of the conduct or the culpability of the actor)' (von Hirsch 1990: 282).[20] Imposing a harsh penalty for a particular minor crime, then, would require doing so across the board for such crimes (and this would raise further problems, as discussed below). The requirement of ordinal proportionality can be further unpacked in terms of what von Hirsch calls three 'sub-requirements'. The first is parity: 'when offenders have been convicted of crimes of similar seriousness they deserve penalties of comparable severity.' The second is 'rank-ordering': 'punishing crime Y more than crime X expresses more disapproval for crime Y, which is warranted only if it is more serious. Punishments should thus be ordered on a penalty scale so that their relative severity reflects the seriousness-ranking of the crimes involved.' The third is 'spacing': 'suppose crimes X, Y, and Z are of ascending order of seriousness; but that Y is considerably more serious than X but only slightly less so than Z. Then, to reflect the conduct's gravity, there should be a larger space between the penalties for X and Y than for Y and Z' (all quotations from von Hirsch 1993: 18; cf. 1985: ch. 4, 1990, 1992).

Why should the principle of ordinal proportionality be thought important? The answer is clear. If punishment is the appropriate response to the agent through which the community expresses its censure, then actions that are similarly censured should evoke similar responses, and the sub-requirements follow from this. Of course, these measurements are necessarily very rough, both because judging the similarity of different legal sanctions is difficult (is 100 hours' community service a lesser or greater punishment, in terms of the censure it conveys, than a day in prison?[21]), and because, as is argued above, the response of the community may not necessarily be through the use of law. Where there is no preventive ration-

---

[20] Cf. von Hirsch 1985: ch. 4; Bedau 1984. Of course, the seriousness of a crime is going to depend in part on the frequency of its occurrence. It could, therefore, be argued that a frequently committed minor offence is more serious than a similar offence which is only occasionally performed.

[21] This raises the very interesting question of the difference between types of penalties. However, addressing this will depend on the particular society and its social understandings being examined.

ale the community might use social stigmatization. Nevertheless the point is that the level of stigmatization should be appropriate to the measure of censure, just as, within the legal system, the punishment should also reflect the degree of censure.

Cardinal proportionality concerns 'the overall magnitude and anchoring points of a penalty scale' (von Hirsch 1990: 282). Systems of penalties could meet the requirements of ordinal proportionality and yet vary enormously in the penalties that they impose for particular crimes. One system might construct the scale in accordance with a most serious punishment of death and another with a most serious punishment of, say, six years in prison. Short of examining the particular conditions for which the contracting parties are choosing principles of punishment is there anything that can be said about what considerations should govern their choice? Clearly there is. First, given the imperfect nature of the penality system, the contractors have reason to insist not only on certain protections in the system designed to protect the innocent, but also (in all but the most extreme circumstances) on limits on the kinds and quantities of punishment that can legitimately be imposed. Second, there are the considerations discussed above: that the penalties ought to express a proportionate degree of censure, and that they ought not to be such that they devalue the interests and values that they are designed to protect. Of course, these are matters where the choice of the contractors will influence and not merely reflect the social conditions on which they are supposedly to base their choice. This is because in a society in which six years in prison is chosen as the maximum punishment such a penalty is likely to come to be regarded as a serious one. In another society where the penalty scale is anchored around a maximum penalty of death, the citizens are likely to think six years expresses something a great deal less censorious.[22]

It is in considering cardinal proportionality that the contractors have reason to look at the level of penalties needed to secure the condition of sufficient security. It is, thus, in this area that the tension between the need for hard treatment to deter and the needs for it to express the appropriate degree of censure and for the system to address the offender as a member of the moral community is most evident. The discussion of this tension above provides the framework in which the contractors have reason to operate. Ideally, levels of penalties will be such that they provide a

---

[22] Of course, how serious the censure conveyed by a penalty will be is related to how effective that penalty is in deterring those who would offend. A population that thinks three years in prison an expression of the gravest opprobrium will surely also be a population that regards three years as a significant deterrent.

prudential supplement and such that they allow the offender to understand that she is primarily being addressed as a moral being, one who has committed herself to the priority of moral reasons over those of narrow self-interest. However, where the moral community is threatened the contractors have reason to choose levels of hard treatment that will deter and assure in order to restore the condition of sufficient security and to allow morality once more to re-establish itself.

Finally, in choosing a system of punishment, the contractors have reason (related to both spacing and to cardinal proportionality) to give weight to Jeremy Bentham's argument that punishment ought 'to induce a man to choose always the least mischievous of two offences' by ensuring that 'where two offences come in competition, the punishment for the greater offence must be sufficient to induce a man to prefer the less'. Similarly punishments ought to be such that having 'resolved upon a particular offence' the offender is induced 'to do no more mischief than what is necessary for his purpose' (Bentham 1970: 168; emphasis suppressed).[23] Bentham's argument is compelling: if the punishment for illegal car parking is the same as that for, say, killing a policeman, then an offender of the car parking rule who is apprehended by a policeman may just as well kill the policeman in an attempt to escape.

Although compelling, in itself this objection would not be sufficient, because it would always be possible to counter it by denying that there is an upper limit on punishments. In other words, it might be true that having the death sentence for car parking offences and killing policemen will encourage car parking offenders to kill policemen, and therefore that the penalty for killing policemen should be far greater than the penalty for parking a car illegally, but it does not follow from that alone that the punishment for illegal car parking should necessarily be scaled down. History has demonstrated the amazing capacity of persons to invent hideous and painful treatments for others, and thus it would be possible to respond to this objection by scaling the punishment for police killers up.[24] Indeed, the

---

[23] 'If any man have any doubt about this, let him conceive the offence to be divided into as many separate offences as there are distinguishable parcels of mischief that result from it. Let it consist for example, in a man's giving you ten blows . . . If then, for giving you ten blows, he is punished no more than for giving you five, the giving you five of these ten blows is an offence for which there is no punishment at all: which being understood: as often as a man gives you five blows, he will be sure to give you five more, since he may have the pleasure of giving you these five for nothing. . . . This rule is violated in almost every page of every body of laws I have ever seen' (Bentham 1970: 168).

[24] See the much quoted description of the execution of the regicide Damiens in the opening pages of Foucault's *Discipline and Punish* (1977: 3–5) and the descriptions of

author of the pamphlet *Hanging not Punishment Enough for Murtherers, Highway Men, and House Breakers, etc.* (Anon. 1701) argues that since hanging is punishment for larceny it cannot be sufficient punishment for more serious crimes such as those listed in the title. Having said that, if the punishment for illegal car parking is very severe, even if the punishment for killing the policeman is still more severe, the offender of the car parking rule may think that he has little to lose in trying to do everything in his power to evade capture, including risking the greater penalty for killing the policeman.

The discussion above is necessarily general. The question of what penalties are effective deterrents is a difficult one even for particular societies cf. von Hirsch et al. 1999). It is still more so when what are being considered are the general guidelines that might be adopted by contracting agents in a constructivist situation. The point is, in part, to illustrate the difficulties of designing a system of punishment that can meet the demands that contracting agents have reason, on the constructivist account developed here, to require of it. The discussion is also designed to show that the contracting parties have reason to endorse a system of penalties that will act only as a prudential supplement to the moral appeal and censure that is expressed in punishment. However, where conditions do not allow this, the contracting parties have reason to adopt penalties that may go beyond this (assuming that there are marginal deterrence effects of increases in penalties beyond those that would be compatible with the prudential supplement view). Although it may be that in such dire circumstances the understanding of what counts as a serious penalty is itself such that large penalties can be imposed without violating the need for proportionate censure.

However, these points might be thought insufficient to address the central concern of those critics who allege that any use of threats and hard treatment is incompatible with treating persons as moral and responsible beings; that insofar as punishment addresses the agent with the injunction 'don't do $x$ because otherwise you will suffer', it coerces the agent and fails to respect his status as a moral being. In a phrase from Hegel of which Antony Duff is fond, it treats the citizen 'like a dog instead of with the freedom and respect due to him as a man' (Hegel 1952: 246; Duff 1986: 178–86, 1999).

---

capital punishments in Germany in Evans 1996: 27–64. Evans quotes an English witness to the use of breaking with the wheel ('one of the commonest methods of capital punishment to be employed in Germany' at the time) as writing that ' "The several kinds of torments which they inflict upon offenders in those parts makes me to imagine our English hanging to be but a flea-biting" ' (Evans 1996: 27–8).

The compatibility of any use of hard treatment and the demand to treat persons with the respect due to them is something to which Duff has given a great deal of attention. He argues that any account of punishment that takes seriously the Kantian claim that agents are to be treated as respons- ible, autonomous beings 'rules out, as improperly coercive and manipula- tive, any kind of punishment which (whether by design or in fact) serves to beat, cow or manipulate the offender into submission, instead of commun- icating to him, and trying to persuade him to accept, the reasons which jus- tify his punishment' (Duff 1986: 278; see also 186, 268–77). Here the tension is not between the need for hard treatment and the need to censure appropriately, but between the use of hard treatment for preventive pur- poses and the very theory that underlies the constructivist account of pun- ishment. However, this is only problematic if Duff is right in his insistence that a system of 'punishment as a rational deterrent' 'is still open to the objection that it does not show punishment to be consistent with a proper respect for the citizen as a rational and autonomous agent; that it still por- trays punishment as an improperly manipulative attempt to coerce the citizen into obedience to the law' (1986: 186).

Duff is only right if his objection is aimed at deterrence-only punish- ments and if the agent has a claim not only to be treated as 'rational and autonomous', but also as part of the moral community. However, Duff argues that insofar as punishment employs threats to prevent certain acts then, even if there are other—possibly constraining—ends, the agent is coerced and the state thereby fails to treat her as an equal, autonomous, being (see e.g. 1986: 268–77).

The argument that the *only* way to respond to an offender that is com- patible with treating the offender with due respect is through moral dia- logue depends on a view of persons as essentially rational, moral beings. Duff's self-confessed intention is to 'explore the implications of the Kantian demand that we should respect other people as rational and autonomous moral agents' (1986: 6), and it is this that leads him to the conclusion that any deterrence-based rationale for hard treatment is manipulative and incompatible with the demand of equal respect.

The constructivist theory advanced here, by contrast, has as its strength the compatibility of coercion and moral censure, because of the integration of prudential and moral reason. In endorsing moral reasons as regulative of the pursuit of narrow self-interest, the agent does not forgo prudential reason in favour of moral reasons that he perceives to be grounded in God, or transcendental reason, or whatever. Rather, he integrates prudential and moral reason by committing himself to pursue his good together with others through moral norms. This commitment is partially underwritten by his understanding that he has self-interested reasons to engage in stable co-operation with others. In agreeing to commit with others to live together on moral terms, each agent wills also to coerce those who would take advantage of him by treating him and those norms that govern their co-operation as merely of instrumental value in the pursuit of their narrow self-interest. In agreeing to treat those who sincerely claim to have made the commitment to morality, but who in some instance or other have failed in their moral duty, not as alien free-riders, but as potentially moral beings who have temporarily given in to the temptation of narrow self-interest, the agent recognizes that persons are, in von Hirsch's terms, 'neither . . . perfectly moral agents (. . . angels), nor . . . beasts which can only be coerced through threats' (von Hirsch 1999: 70; Chapter 3 above). This combination does not undermine or subvert the offender's autonomy, rather, it reinforces it. The offender is coerced as a member of a necessarily coercive community in accordance with his prudential reason, and in addition, he is appealed to as a moral being. Insofar as the communication is successful and he realizes his responsibility for organizing the pursuit of his self-interest through binding, moral, terms of co-operation, he becomes a fully morally autonomous being.

To appeal only to prudential reason would be to fail to treat the agent as having made a commitment to the moral life and would be to misrepresent the nature of the rules that govern that agent's co-operation with others. In including a coercive appeal to prudential reason as a supplement to the appeal to moral reason the agent is treated with respect, for the will to coerce free-riders is implicit in the will to co-operate together with others on moral terms. Thus, these terms are correctly represented as being in part grounded in, but as going beyond, prudential reason.

## PENAL JUSTICE IN AN UNJUST SOCIETY

Before concluding, there is one final aspect of punishment theory on which it is worth commenting. This is the question of whether it is possible to do penal justice in an unjust society. Although without a full-blown account of the principles of constructivist justice the comments that can be made in this section can only be brief and general, this is a sufficiently important topic, and the approach of constructivism sufficiently different from that of other approaches, to make a discussion of the topic worthwhile. There are a number of views on this question currently in the literature: von Hirsch writes in general terms of acute social disadvantage as possibly reducing the culpability of the offender (von Hirsch 1993: 106–8); Hudson argues that the law might recognize a defence of acute social disadvantage (Hudson 1995); and Duff that such disadvantage creates a problem of whether the preconditions of criminal liability are met when the unjust state confronts the disadvantaged offender (Duff 1998, 1999).

What these approaches have in common is that they think that the wrongdoer is morally bound not to perform the act that he performs (excluding those extreme cases where, for example, the person steals bread in order to avoid starvation). For von Hirsch and Hudson, the offender commits a wrong, but is less culpable (or can claim some mitigation) in so doing. For Duff, the wrong is committed, but there is a real question of whether the state has the moral standing to call to account, and to judge, the wrongdoer.

These approaches share with *faux* constructivism, then, the view that morality binds independent of self-interest and of the behaviour of others. Where others are immoral, or non-moral, one's motivation to be moral may be weakened, but what is demanded by morality is no less one's duty. Constructivism denies this. According to the constructivist the commitment to morality is conditional on its advancing one's good and on the like commitment of others. Where the state (assuming that is the institutional form given to the moral community) itself fails to treat the agent as a being deserving of his share of the social product—where it displays in its actions that it regards the individual as only of instrumental value, to be engaged or dispensed with depending on his usefulness—the state itself dissolves the moral contract and reduces the relations of it and the individual to those of the state of nature.

This is an important feature of the constructivist argument for the 'real world'. When those who are consistently discriminated against and deprived of their share of the social product form an 'underclass' and set up in alternative societies in which they abide by their own rules and disregard those of the community that surrounds them, they do not reject morality and the moral standards of the community that surrounds them. Rather, they react to the rejection of morality by that community. Denied a reasonable route to moral co-operation, they engage with the wider community as the constructivist would expect; taking advantage of it when they can whilst refusing to abide by its norms or to temper the immediate pursuit of their self-interest in accordance with its demands. Insofar as this is the situation, the state attempts to coerce and to protect itself from them, but it cannot punish them. Given that stable co-operative relations for mutual advantage could exist each side has reason to reconsider its approach. Such reasons do not dictate that they should arrive at morality, for that requires a commitment by both parties to live on moral terms. Nevertheless, there are good reasons for making that commitment. In its absence, there is no morality and there can be no punishment.

## CONCLUSION: JUSTICE AND PUNISHMENT

That completes the account of the rationale of coercion and of the moral justification of punishment, at least for the moment.[25] The argument has given an answer to Tolstoy's question, 'why and by what right, do some people punish others?' It has done so by embedding the account of punishment in a constructivist moral theory. In addition, the problem of punishment has been used to reveal the flaws in contemporary theories of justice; flaws only the correction of which can make possible a moral justification for punishment. In short, punishment secures the condition of sufficient security, it communicates to the offender the wrongs that he has done to his victim and to the community, and it tries in so doing to reinforce in him his commitment to morality. The justification for this appeals to what would emerge from the constructivist situation, and also to the construction of morality itself; to the intrinsic relationship of the commitment to the authority of moral norms and the commitment to coerce free-riders.

The argument has reconciled as demanded the personal perspective (from which morality and coercion seem to be restraints imposed from the outside and against which self-interest strains) and the moral perspective (which demands that the agent accept the authority of moral reasons over

[25] There are some questions that are left unanswered and many that are not addressed at all. Some of these could only be explored by looking at the specific features and conditions of the society to which the constructivist analysis developed here was being applied. Nevertheless, a list of questions not addressed above would be a considerable one. Not least, the argument has not dealt with the issue of what principles should guide the contracting parties in making some norms legal and attaching to them formal punishments. Although I am confident that the account can answer questions such as this, I am less confident that it can generate answers to, say, all of the questions listed by Braithwaite and Pettit in their *Not Just Deserts* (see Ch.1 above). However, this is not a matter of embarrassment. It is an attractive feature of constructivism, I believe, that it can accommodate variations in, say, sentencing or parole practices given that systems of punishment must be implemented in different circumstances.

# REFERENCES

Acton, H. B. (1969) (ed.). *The Philosophy of Punishment* (London: Macmillan).

Alexander, L. (1980). 'The Doomsday Machine: Proportionality, Punishment and Prevention', *Monist*, 63: 199–227.

Anderson, E. (1996). 'Reasons, Attitudes, and Values: Replies to Sturgeon and Piper', *Ethics*, 106: 538–54.

Anon. (1701). *Hanging not Punishment Enough for Murtherers, Highway Men, and House Breakers, etc.* (London: A. Baldwin).

Anscombe, G. E. M. (1957). 'Does Oxford Moral Philosophy Corrupt Youth?', *Listener*, 14 Feb., 266–71.

Aristotle (1957). *The Politics*, trans. T. A. Sinclair, rev. T. J. Saunders (Harmondsworth: Penguin).

Armstrong, K. G. (1969). 'The Retributivist Hits Back', in Acton (1969: 138–58). Originally published in *Mind*, 70 (1961), 471–90.

Arneson, R. (1982). 'The Principle of Fairness and Free-Rider Problems'. *Ethics*, 92: 616–33.

Baier, A. C. (1993). 'Moralism and Cruelty: Reflections on Hume and Kant', *Ethics*, 103: 436–57.

Baier, K. E. (1955). 'Is Punishment Retributive?', *Analysis*, 16: 25–32. Repr. in Acton (1969: 130–7).

Baldwin, T. (1999). 'Punishment, Communication, and Resentment', in Matravers (1999b): 124–32).

Barry, B. (1968). 'Warrender and his Critics', *Philosophy*, 43: 117–37.

—— (1979). 'And Who is my Neighbour?', *Yale Law Journal*, 88: 629–58. Repr. in Barry (1991b: 40–77).

—— (1989). *A Treatise on Social Justice*, i: *Theories of Justice* (Hemel Hempstead: Harvester-Wheatsheaf).

—— (1990). *Political Argument: A Reissue with a New Introduction* (Berkeley and Los Angeles: University of California Press).

—— (1991a). 'Chance, Choice, and Justice', in Barry (1991b: 142–58).

—— (1991b). *Liberty and Justice: Essays in Political Theory 2* (Oxford: Clarendon Press).

—— (1995a). *Justice as Impartiality* (Oxford: Clarendon Press).

—— (1995b). 'John Rawls and the Search for Stability', *Ethics*, 105: 874–915.

—— (1996). 'A Commitment to Impartiality: Some Comments on the Comments', *Political Studies*, 44: 328–42.

—— (1998). 'Something in the Disputation not Unpleasant', in Kelly (1998b: 186–257).

BARRY, B. (n.d.). 'Sustainability and Intergenerational Justice', unpublished manuscript.

—— and MATRAVERS, M. (1998*a*). 'Justice', in E. Craig (ed.), *The Routledge Encylopedia of Philosophy* (London: Routledge).

—— —— (1998*b*). 'International Justice', in E. Craig (ed.), *The Routledge Encylopedia of Philosophy* (London: Routledge).

BAYLES, M. (1968) (ed.). *Contemporary Utilitarianism* (New York: Doubleday).

BECKER, L. (1986). *Reciprocity* (London: Routledge & Kegan Paul).

BEDAU, H. A. (1978). 'Retribution and the Theory of Punishment', *Journal of Philosophy*, 75: 601–20.

—— (1984). 'Classification-Based Sentencing: Some Conceptual and Ethical Problems', *New England Journal on Criminal and Civil Confinement*, 10: 1–26.

BENN, S. I. (1958). 'An Approach to the Problems of Punishment', *Philosophy*, 33: 325–41.

BENTHAM, J. (1970). *An Introduction to the Principles of Morals and Legislation*, ed. J. H. Burns and H. L. A. Hart (Oxford: Clarendon Press).

BINMORE, K. (1993). 'Bargaining and Morality', in Gauthier and Sugden (1993: 131–56).

BLACKBURN, S. (1993). *Essays in Quasi-Realism* (Oxford: Oxford University Press).

—— (1998). *Ruling Passions: A Theory of Practical Reasoning* (Oxford: Clarendon Press).

BRADLEY, F. H. (1927). *Ethical Studies*, 2nd edn. (Oxford: Clarendon Press).

BRAITHWAITE, J. (1989). *Crime, Shame and Reintegration* (Cambridge: Cambridge University Press).

—— (1999). 'Restorative Justice: Assessing Optimistic and Pessimistic Accounts', *Crime and Justice: A Review of Research*, 25: 1–127.

—— and Pettit, P. (1990). *Not Just Deserts: A Republican Theory of Criminal Justice* (Oxford: Clarendon Press).

BROAD, C. D. (1915–16). 'On the Function of False Hypotheses in Ethics', *International Journal of Ethics*, 26: 377–97.

BRUBAKER, S. (1989). 'In Praise of Punishment', *Public Interest*, 97: 44–55.

—— (1990). 'In Praise of Punishment: A Reply to A. Rawls', *Public Interest*, 99: 133–6.

BUCHANAN, A. (1990). 'Justice as Reciprocity versus Subject-Centred Justice', *Philosophy and Public Affairs*, 19: 227–52.

BURGH, R. (1982). 'Do the Guilty Deserve Punishment?', *Journal of Philosophy*, 79: 193–210.

BUTLER, J. (1969). *Fifteen Sermons* (London: Bell).

BYRD, B. S. (1989). 'Kant's Theory of Punishment: Deterrence in its Threat, Retribution in its Execution', *Law and Philosophy*, 8: 151–200.

CANEY, S. (1992). 'Liberalism and Communitarianism: A Misconceived Debate', *Political Studies*, 40: 273–89.

—— (1998). 'Impartiality and Liberal Neutrality', in Kelly (1998*b*: 87–107).

CHARVET, J. (1966). 'Criticism and Punishment', *Mind*, 75: 573–9.

—— (1981). *A Critique of Freedom and Equality* (Cambridge: Cambridge University Press).

—— (1995). *The Idea of an Ethical Community* (Ithaca, NY: Cornell University Press).

—— (1998). 'Fundamental Equality', *Utilitas*, 10: 337–52.

CHRISTMAN, J. (1989) (ed.). *The Inner Citadel: Essays on Individual Autonomy* (New York: Oxford University Press).

CLARK, M. (1997). 'The Sanctions of the Criminal Law', *Proceedings of the Aristotelian Society*, 97: 25–40.

COHEN, G. (1989). 'On the Currency of Egalitarian Justice', *Ethics*, 99: 906–44.

—— (1992). 'Mind the Gap: Review of T. Nagel, *Equality and Partiality*', *London Review of Books*, 14 May, 15–17.

COHEN, M. (1939). 'A Critique of Kant's Philosophy of Law', in G. T. Whitney and D. F. Bowers (eds.), *The Heritage of Kant* (Princeton: Princeton University Press).

COLEMAN, J., and LEITER, B. (1996). 'Legal Positivism', in D. Patterson (ed.), *A Companion to Philosophy of Law and Legal Theory* (Oxford: Blackwell), 241–60.

COOPER, D. (1971). 'Hegel's Theory of Punishment', in Z. A. Pelczynski (ed.), *Hegel's Political Philosophy* (Cambridge: Cambridge University Press).

COPP, D. (1991). 'Contractarianism and Moral Skepticism', in Vallentyne (1991*b*: 196–228).

—— and ZIMMERMAN, D. (1984) (eds.). *Morality, Reason and Truth: New Essays on the Foundations of Ethics* (Totowa, NJ: Rowman & Allanheld).

COTTINGHAM, J. (1979). 'Varieties of Retribution', *Philosophical Quarterly*, 29: 238–46.

CRAGG, W. (1992) (ed.). *Retributivism and its Critics* (Stuttgart: Franz Steiner).

CULLITY, G., and Gaut, B. (1997) (eds.). *Ethics and Practical Reason* (Oxford: Oxford University Press).

DAGGER, R. (1993). 'Playing Fair with Punishment', *Ethics*, 103: 473–88.

—— (1997). *Civic Virtues: Rights, Citizenship, and Republican Liberalism* (Oxford: Oxford University Press).

DAHRENDORF, R. (1985). *Law and Order* (London: Stevens).

DANIELS, N. (1989) (ed.). *Reading Rawls: Critical Studies on Rawls' A Theory of Justice*, rev. edn. (Stanford, Calif.: Stanford University Press).

DARE, T. (1992). 'Retributivism, Punishment, and Public Values', in Cragg (1992: 35–41).

DAVIS, M. (1983). 'How to Make the Punishment Fit the Crime', *Ethics*, 93: 726–52.

—— (1986*a*). 'Why Attempts Deserve Less Punishment than Complete Crimes', *Law and Philosophy*, 5: 1–33.

—— (1986*b*). 'Harm and Retribution', *Philosophy and Public Affairs*, 15: 236–66.

DAVIS, M. (1989). 'The Relative Independence of Punishment Theory', *Law and Philosophy*, 7: 321–50.

—— (1991). 'Criminal Desert, Harm and Fairness', *Israel Law Review*, 25: 524–48.

DAY, J. (1978). 'Retributive Punishment', *Mind*, 87: 498–516.

DENNETT, D. (1987) (ed.). *The Philosophical Lexicon* (www.blackwellpublishers.co.uk/lexicon).

DEVLIN, P. (1959). *The Enforcement of Morals* (London: Oxford University Press).

DOLINKO, D. (1991). 'Some Thoughts about Retributivism', *Ethics*, 101: 537–59.

—— (1997). 'Retributivism, Consequentialism, and the Intrinsic Goodness of Punishment', *Law and Philosophy*, 16: 507–28.

DUFF, R. A. (1977). 'Psychopathy and Moral Understanding', *American Philosophical Quarterly*, 14: 189–200.

—— (1986). *Trials and Punishments* (Cambridge: Cambridge University Press).

—— (1988). 'Punishment and Penance: A Reply to Harrison', *Proceedings of the Aristotelian Society (Supplementary Volume)*, 62: 153–67.

—— (1990). 'Justice, Mercy and Forgiveness', *Criminal Justice Ethics*, 9: 51–63.

—— (1993). 'Introduction', in R. A. Duff (ed.), *Punishment* (Aldershot: Dartmouth Publishing Co.), pp. xi–xvii.

—— (1996). 'Penal Communications: Recent Work in the Philosophy of Punishment', *Crime and Justice: A Review of Research*, 20: 1–97.

—— (1998). 'Law, Language and Community: Some Preconditions of Criminal Liability', *Oxford Journal of Legal Studies*, 189–206.

—— (1999). 'Punishment, Communication, and Community', in Matravers (1999*b*: 48–68).

—— and GARLAND, D. (1994) (eds.). *A Reader on Punishment* (New York: Oxford University Press).

DWORKIN, G. (1970). 'Acting Freely', *Nous*, 4: 367–83.

—— (1971). 'Paternalism', in Wasserstrom (1971: 107–26).

—— (1988). *The Theory and Practice of Autonomy* (Cambridge: Cambridge University Press).

DWORKIN, R. (1977). *Taking Rights Seriously* (London: Duckworth).

—— (1989). 'The Original Position', in Daniels (1989: 16–52). Originally published in *University of Chicago Law Review*, 40 (1975), 500–33.

ELLIS, A. (1997). 'Punishment and the Principle of Fair Play', *Utilitas*, 9: 81–98.

ESTLUND, D. (1996). 'The Survival of Egalitarian Justice in John Rawls's Political Liberalism', *Journal of Political Philosophy*, 4: 68–78.

EVANS, R. (1996). *Rituals of Retribution: Capital Punishment in Germany, 1600–1987* (London: Penguin).

EZORSKY, G. (1972) (ed.). *Philosophical Perspectives on Punishment* (Albany: State University of New York Press).

FARIS, E. (1914). 'The Origin of Punishment', *International Journal of Ethics*, 24: 54–67.

FARRELL, D. (1985). 'The Justification of General Deterrence', *Philosophical Review*, 94: 367–94.

—— (1988). 'Punishment without the State', *Nous*, 22: 437–53.

—— (1989). 'On Threats and Punishments'. *Social Theory and Practice*, 15: 125–54.

—— (1990). 'The Justification of Deterrent Violence', *Ethics*, 100: 301–17.

FEINBERG, J. (1965). 'The Expressive Function of Punishment', *Monist*, 49: 397–423. Repr. in Feinberg (1970: 95–118).

—— (1970). *Doing and Deserving: Essays in the Theory of Responsibility* (Princeton: Princeton University Press).

FINGARETTE, J. (1977). 'Punishment and Suffering', *Proceedings and Addresses of the American Philosophical Association*, 50: 499–525.

FINNIS, J. (1972). 'The Restoration of Retribution', *Analysis*, 32: 131–5.

FISHKIN, J. (1992). *The Dialogue of Justice* (New Haven: Yale University Press).

FLEISCHACKER, S. (1992). 'Kant's Theory of Punishment', in H. Williams (ed.), *Essays on Kant's Political Philosophy* (Cardiff: University of Wales Press), 191–212.

FLEW, A. (1954). 'The Justification of Punishment', *Philosophy*, 29: 291–307. Repr. in Acton (1969: 83–101).

FOOT, P. (1967) (ed.). *Theories of Ethics* (Oxford: Oxford University Press).

FOUCAULT, M. (1977). *Discipline and Punish: The Birth of the Prison*, trans. A. Sheridan (London: Penguin).

—— (1978). *The History of Sexuality*, i: *An Introduction*, trans. R. Hurley (New York: Random House).

FRANKFURT, H. (1971). 'Freedom of the Will and the Concept of a Person', *Journal of Philosophy*, 68: 5–20. Repr. in Frankfurt (1988: 11–25).

—— (1988). *The Importance of What We Care about: Philosophical Essays* (Cambridge: Cambridge University Press).

FREY, R. (1984) (ed.). *Utility and Rights* (Minneapolis: University of Minnesota Press).

—— and MORRIS, C. (1993) (eds.). *Value, Welfare, and Morality* (New York: Cambridge University Press).

FRIEDAN, B. (1965). *The Feminine Mystique* (Harmondsworth: Penguin).

GARDNER, M. (1976). 'The Renaissance of Retribution: An Examination of "Doing Justice" ', *Wisconsin Law Review*, 781–815.

GARLAND, D. (1990). *Punishment and Modern Society: A Study in Social Theory* (Oxford: Clarendon Press).

GAUTHIER, D. (1984). 'Justice as Social Choice', in Copp and Zimmerman (1984: 251–69).

—— (1986). *Morals by Agreement* (Oxford: Clarendon Press).

—— (1988a). 'Morality, Rational Choice, and Semantic Representation: A Reply to my Critics', *Social Philosophy and Policy*, 5: 173–221.

—— (1988b). 'Moral Artifice', *Canadian Journal of Philosophy*, 18: 385–418.

GAUTHIER, D. (1991). 'Why Contractarianism?', in Vallentyne (1991*b*: 13–30).

—— (1993*a*). 'Value, Reasons, and the Sense of Justice', in Frey and Morris (1993: 180–208).

—— (1993*b*). 'Uniting Separate Persons', in Gauthier and Sugden (1993: 176–92).

—— (1993*c*). 'Between Hobbes and Rawls', in Gauthier and Sugden (1993: 24–39).

—— (1994). 'Assure and Threaten', *Ethics*, 104: 690–721.

—— (1997). 'Political Contractarianism', *Journal of Political Philosophy*, 5: 132–48.

—— (1998). 'Mutual Advantage and Impartiality', in Kelly (1998*b*: 120–36).

—— and SUGDEN, R. (1993) (eds.). *Rationality, Justice and the Social Contract* (Hemel Hempstead: Harvester Wheatsheaf).

GEWIRTH, A. (1978). *Reason and Morality* (Chicago: University of Chicago Press).

GIBBARD, A. (1990). *Wise Choices, Apt Feelings* (Oxford: Clarendon Press).

—— (1991). 'Constructing Justice', *Philosophy and Public Affairs*, 20: 264–79.

GOLASH, D. (1994). 'The Retributive Paradox', *Analysis*, 54: 72–8.

GOLDMAN, A. (1979). 'The Paradox of Punishment', *Philosophy and Public Affairs*, 9: 42–58.

—— (1982). 'Toward a New Theory of Punishment', *Law and Philosophy*, 1: 57–76.

GOODIN, R. (1993). 'Equal Rationality and Initial Endowments', in Gauthier and Sugden (1993: 116–30).

—— (1995). *Utilitarianism as a Public Philosophy* (New York: Cambridge University Press).

GRAY, J. (1989). *Liberalisms: Essays in Political Philosophy* (London: Routledge).

GROSS, H., and HIRSCH, A. VON (1981) (eds.). *Sentencing* (New York: Oxford University Press).

GUTMANN, A. (1985). 'Communitarian Critics of Liberalism', *Philosophy and Public Affairs*, 14: 308–22.

HAMPTON, J. (1984). 'The Moral Education Theory of Punishment', *Philosophy and Public Affairs*, 13: 208–38.

—— (1991*a*). 'A New Theory of Retribution', in R. G. Frey and C. W. Morris (eds.), *Liability and Responsibility* (Cambridge: Cambridge University Press), 377–414.

—— (1991*b*). 'Two Faces of Contractarian Thought', in Vallentyne (1991*b*: 31–55).

—— (1992*a*). 'An Expressive Theory of Retribution', in Cragg (1992: 1–25).

—— (1992*b*). 'Correcting Harms versus Righting Wrongs: The Goal of Retribution', *UCLA Law Review*, 39: 1659–702.

HARDIN, R. (1998). 'Reasonable Agreement: Political not Normative', in Kelly (1998*b*: 137–53).

HARE, R. M. (1981). *Moral Thinking: Its Levels, Method and Point* (Oxford: Oxford University Press).

—— (1984). 'Rights, Utility, and Universalization: Reply to J. L. Mackie', in Frey (1984: 106–20).

HAREL, A. (forthcoming). 'Efficiency and Fairness in Criminal Law: The Case for a Criminal Law Principle of Comparative Fault', *California Law Review.*

HARMAN, G. (1977). *The Nature of Morality* (New York: Oxford University Press).

HARSANYI, J. (1982). 'Morality and the Theory of Rational Behaviour', in Sen and Williams (1982: 39–62).

HART, H. L. A. (1955). 'Are There Any Natural Rights?', *Philosophical Review*, 64: 175–91. Repr. in Waldron (1984: 77–90).

—— (1958). 'Legal Responsibility and Excuses', in S. Hook (ed.), *Determinism and Freedom* (New York: New York University Press). Repr. in Hart (1968: 28–53).

—— (1959). 'Prolegomenon to the Principles of Punishment', *Proceedings of the Aristotelian Society*, 60: 1–26. Repr. in Hart (1968: 1–27).

—— (1963). *Law, Liberty and Morality* (London: Oxford University Press).

—— (1968). *Punishment and Responsibility* (New York: Oxford University Press).

—— (1994). *The Concept of Law*, 2nd edn. (Oxford: Clarendon Press).

HEGEL, G. W. F. (1952). *Hegel's Philosophy of Right*, trans. T. M. Knox (London: Oxford University Press).

—— (1974). *Hegel's Lectures on the History of Philosophy*, trans. E. S. Haldane (Atlantic Highlands, NJ: The Humanities Press).

—— (1977). *Phenomenology of Spirit*, trans. A. V. Miller (Oxford: Oxford University Press).

—— (1991). *Elements of the Philosophy of Right*, trans. H. B. Nisbet, ed. A. Wood (Cambridge: Cambridge University Press).

HIRSCH, A. VON. (1976). *Doing Justice: The Choice of Punishments* (New York: Hill & Wang).

—— (1985). *Past or Future Crimes: Deservedness and Dangerousness in the Sentencing of Criminals* (Manchester: Manchester University Press).

—— (1990). 'Proportionality in the Philosophy of Punishment: From "Why Punish?" to "How Much?" ', *Criminal Law Forum*, 1: 259–90.

—— (1992). 'Proportionality in the Philosophy of Punishment', *Crime and Justice: A Review of Research*, 16: 55–98.

—— (1993). *Censure and Sanctions* (Oxford: Clarendon Press).

—— (1999). 'Punishment, Penance, and the State: A Reply to Duff', in Matravers (1999*b*: 69–82).

—— and ASHWORTH, A. (1992). 'Not Not Just Deserts: A Response to Braithwaite and Pettit', *Oxford Journal of Legal Studies*, 12: 83–98.

—— BOTTOMS, A., BURNEY, E., and WIKSTRÖM, P.-O. (1999). *Criminal Deterrence and Sentence Severity* (Oxford: Hart Publishing).

HOBBES, T. (1991). *Leviathan*, ed. R. Tuck (Cambridge: Cambridge University Press).

HOEKEMA, D. (1980). 'The Right to Punish and the Right to be Punished', in H. G. Blocker and E. Smith (eds.), *John Rawls' Theory of Social Justice: An Introduction* (Athens: Ohio University Press), 239–69.

HOLLIS, M. (1993). 'The Agriculture of the Mind', in Gauthier and Sugden (1993: 40–52).

Home Office (1990). *Crime, Justice and Protecting the Public* (London: HMSO).

HONDERICH, T. (1969). *Punishment: The Supposed Justifications*, 1st edn. (London: Hutchinson).

—— (1984). *Punishment: The Supposed Justifications*, 2nd edn. with new post-script (Cambridge: Pelican Press).

—— (1988). *A Theory of Determinism: The Mind, Neuroscience, and Life Hopes* (Oxford: Clarendon Press).

—— (1993). *How Free Are You?* (Oxford: Oxford University Press).

HONIG, B. (1993). *Political Theory and the Displacement of Politics* (Ithaca, NY: Cornell University Press).

HUDSON, B. (1995). 'Beyond Proportionate Punishment: Difficult Cases and the 1991 Criminal Justice Act', *Crime, Law and Social Change*, 22: 59–78.

HUME, D. (1994). 'Of the Original Contract', in D. Hume, *Political Essays*, ed. K. Haakonssen (Cambridge: Cambridge University Press).

IVISON, D. (1999). 'Justifying Punishment in Intercultural Contexts: Whose Norms? Which Values?', in Matravers (1999*b*: 88–109).

KANT, I. (1948). *The Moral Law: Kant's Groundwork of the Metaphysic of Morals*, ed. H. Paton (London: Hutchinson).

—— (1991). *The Metaphysics of Morals*, trans. M. Gregor (Cambridge: Cambridge University Press).

KELLY, P. (1990). *Utilitarianism and Distributive Justice* (Oxford: Clarendon Press).

—— (1998*a*). 'Taking Utilitarianism Seriously', in Kelly (1998*b*: 44–59).

—— (1998*b*). (ed.). *Impartiality, Neutrality and Justice: Re-reading Brian Barry's Justice as Impartiality* (Edinburgh: Edinburgh University Press).

KELSEN, H. (1992). *Introduction to the Problems of Legal Theory*, trans. B. L. Paulson and S. L. Paulson (Oxford: Clarendon Press).

KLOSKO, G. (1992). *The Principle of Fairness and Political Obligation* (Lanham, Md.: Rowman & Littlefield).

KNOWLES, D. (1999). 'Punishment and Rights', in Matravers (1999*b*: 28–47).

KORSGAARD, C. (1997). 'The Normativity of Instrumental Reason', in Cullity and Gaut (1997: 215–54).

KRAUS, J. and COLEMAN, J. (1991). 'Morality and the Theory of Rational Choice' in Vallentyne (1991*b*: 255–90).

KYMLICKA, W. (1989). 'Liberal Individualism and Liberal Neutrality', *Ethics*, 99: 883–905.

—— (1990). *Contemporary Political Philosophy: An Introduction* (Oxford: Clarendon Press).

—— (1991). 'The Social Contract Tradition', in P. Singer (ed.), *A Companion to Ethics* (Oxford: Blackwell Publishers), 186–96.

LACEY, N. (1987). 'Punishment', in D. Miller et al. (eds.), *The Blackwell Encyclopaedia of Political Thought* (Oxford: Blackwell Publishers), 409–12.

—— (1988). *State Punishment* (London: Routledge).

LANE, R. (1991). *The Market Experience* (New York: Cambridge University Press).

LEHNING, P. (1993). 'Right Constraints?', in Gauthier and Sugden (1993: 95–115).

LOCKE, J. (1988). *Two Treatises of Government*, ed. P. Laslett (Cambridge: Cambridge University Press).

LYONS, D. (1965). *Forms and Limits of Utilitarianism* (Oxford: Oxford University Press).

MABBOTT, J. D. (1939). 'Punishment', *Mind*, 48: 152–67. Repr. in Acton (1969: 39–54).

—— (1955). 'Professor Flew on Punishment', *Philosophy*, 30: 256–65. Repr. in Acton (1969: 115–29).

McCLOSKEY, H. J. (1968). 'A Non-utilitarian Approach to Punishment', in M. Bayles (ed.), *Contemporary Utilitarianism* (New York: Doubleday), 239–59.

—— (1972). 'Two Concepts of Rules: A Note', *Philosophical Quarterly*, 22: 344–8.

MacINTYRE, A. (1984). *After Virtue*, 2nd edn. (Notre Dame, Ind.: University of Notre Dame Press).

MACKIE, J. L. (1977). *Ethics: Inventing Right and Wrong* (Harmondsworth: Penguin).

MARSHALL, S. (1992). 'Harm and Punishment in the Community', in Cragg (1992: 75–82).

MATRAVERS, M. (1997). Review of R. Goodin, *Utilitarianism as a Public Philosophy*, *Utilitas*, 9: 261–5.

—— (1998). 'What's "Wrong" in Contractualism?', in Kelly (1998*b*: 108–19).

—— (1999*a*). ' "What to Say?": The Communicative Element in Punishment and Moral Theory', in Matravers (1999*b*: 108–23).

—— (1999*b*) (ed.). *Punishment and Political Theory* (Oxford: Hart Publishing).

—— (1999*c*). Review of Andrew von Hirsch, *Censure and Sanctions*, *Utilitas*, 11: 246–51.

—— (2000*a*). 'Contractualism and the Moral Significance of Human Well-Being', in A. J. Coates (ed.), *International Justice* (Aldershot: Ashgate).

—— (2000*b*). ' "What's In It For Me?" A Critical Comment on T. M. Scanlon's *What We Owe to Each Other*', *Imprints*, 4.

MENDUS, S. (1998). 'Some Mistakes about Impartiality', in Kelly (1998*b*: 176–85).

—— (1999). 'The Importance of Love in Rawls's Theory of Justice', *British Journal of Political Science*, 29: 57–75.

MILL, J. S. (1987). 'Utilitarianism', in Mill and Bentham (1987: 272–338).

—— and BENTHAM, J. (1987). *Utilitarianism and Other Essays*, ed. A. Ryan (London: Penguin).

MONTAGUE, P. (1983). 'Punishment and Societal Defense', *Criminal Justice Ethics*, 2: 31–6.

MOORE, M. (1982). 'Moral Reality', *Wisconsin Law Review*, 1061–156.

—— (1987). 'The Moral Worth of Retribution', in F. Schoeman (ed.), *Responsibility, Character, and the Emotions* (New York: Cambridge University Press), 179–219.

—— (1992). 'Moral Reality Revisited', *Michigan Law Review*, 90: 2424–533.

—— (1993). 'Justifying Retribution', *Israel Law Review*, 27: 15–49.

—— (1997). *Placing Blame: A General Theory of the Criminal Law* (Oxford: Clarendon Press).

MOORE, MARGARET (1993). *Foundations of Liberalism* (Oxford: Clarendon Press).

MORRIS, H. (1968). 'Persons and Punishment', *Monist*, 52: 475–501. Repr, in Gross and Hirsch (1981: 93–109).

—— (1981). 'A Paternalistic Theory of Punishment', *American Philosophical Quarterly*, 18: 263–71.

MULHALL, S., and SWIFT, A. (1996). *Liberals and Communitarians*, 2nd edn. (Oxford: Blackwell).

MURPHY, J. G. (1971). 'Three Mistakes about Retributivism', *Analysis*, 31: 166–69.

—— (1973). 'Marxism and Retribution', *Philosophy and Public Affairs*, 2: 217–43.

—— (1979). *Retribution, Justice, and Therapy* (Dordrecht: D. Reidel).

—— (1985). 'Retributivism, Moral Education, and the Liberal State', *Criminal Justice Ethics*, 4: 3–11.

—— and HAMPTON, J. (1988). *Forgiveness and Mercy* (Cambridge: Cambridge University Press).

NAGEL, T. (1970). *The Possibility of Altruism* (Oxford: Clarendon Press).

—— (1986). *The View from Nowhere* (New York: Oxford University Press).

—— (1991). *Equality and Partiality* (New York: Oxford University Press).

NARAYAN, U. (1993). 'Appropriate Responses and Preventive Benefits: Justifying Hard Treatment and Censure in Legal Punishment', *Oxford Journal of Legal Studies*, 13: 166–82.

NARVESON, J. (1974). 'Three *Analysis* Retributivists', *Analysis*, 34: 185–93.

NIELSON, K. (1971). 'Against Moral Conservatism', *Ethics*, 82: 219–31.

NIETZSCHE, F. (1956). *On the Genealogy of Morals* (New York: Doubleday).

NINO, C. S. (1983). 'A Consensual Theory of Punishment', *Philosophy and Public Affairs*, 12: 289–306.

NORRIE, A. (1999). 'Albert Speer, Guilt, and "The Space Between" ' in Matravers (1999*b*: 133–51).

NOWELL-SMITH, P. (1961). *Ethics* (Harmondsworth: Penguin).

NOZICK, R. (1974). *Anarchy, State, and Utopia* (Oxford: Basil Blackwell Ltd.).

PAUL, E., MILLER, F., and PAUL, J. (1988) (eds.). *The New Social Contract: Essays on Gauthier* (New York: Blackwell).

PETTIT, P. (1997). *Republicanism: A Theory of Freedom and Government* (Oxford: Clarendon Press).

PHILIPS, M. (1986). 'The Justification of Punishment and the Justification of Political Authority', *Law and Philosophy*, 5: 393–416.

PINCOFFS, E. L. (1966). *The Rationale of Legal Punishment* (Atlantic Highlands, NJ: Humanities Press).

PLATO (1969). *The Apology*, in *The Last Days of Socrates*, trans. H. Tredennick (Harmondsworth: Penguin).

PRIMORATZ, I. (1989a). 'Punishment as Language', *Philosophy*, 64: 187–205.

—— (1989b). *Justifying Legal Punishment* (Atlantic Highlands, NJ: Humanities Press).

QUINN, W. (1985). 'The Right to Threaten and the Right to Punish', *Philosophy and Public Affairs*, 14: 327–73.

QUINTON, A. (1969). 'On Punishment', in Acton (1969: 55–64). Originally published in *Analysis*, 14 (1954), 133–42.

RAWLS, A. E. (1990). 'Of Rawls, Responsibility, and Retribution', *Public Interest*, 99: 128–33.

RAWLS, J. (1951). 'Outline of a Decision Procedure for Ethics', *Philosophical Review*, 60: 177–97.

—— (1955). 'Two Concepts of Rules', *Philosophical Review*, 64: 3–32. Repr. in Foot (1967: 144–70).

—— (1964). 'Legal Obligation and the Duty of Fair Play', in S. Hook (ed.), *Law and Philosophy* (New York: New York University Press), 3–18.

—— (1971). *A Theory of Justice* (Cambridge, Mass.: Harvard University Press).

—— (1975). 'Fairness to Goodness', *Philosophical Review*, 84: 536–54.

—— (1978). 'The Basic Structure as Subject', in A. Goldman and J. Kim (eds.), *Values and Morals* (Dordrecht: Reidel).

—— (1980). 'Kantian Constructivism in Moral Theory', *Journal of Philosophy*, 77: 515–72.

—— (1982a). 'Social Unity and Primary Goods', in Sen and Williams (1982: 159–85).

—— (1982b). 'The Basic Liberties and their Priority', in S. McMurrin (ed.), *The Tanner Lectures on Human Values*, vol. iii (Salt Lake City: University of Utah Press). A revised version of this piece appears as Lecture VIII in Rawls (1993).

—— (1985). 'Justice as Fairness: Political not Metaphysical', *Philosophy and Public Affairs*, 14: 223–51.

—— (1987). 'The Idea of an Overlapping Consensus', *Oxford Journal of Legal Studies*, 7: 1–25.

—— (1988). 'The Priority of Right and Ideas of the Good', *Philosophy and Public Affairs*, 17: 251–76.

—— (1989). 'The Domain of the Political and Overlapping Consensus', *New York University Law Review*, 64: 233–55.

—— (1993). *Political Liberalism* (New York: Columbia University Press).

—— (1998). '*Commonweal* Interview with John Rawls', excerpted in Rawls (1999: 616–22).

RAWLS, J. (1999). *Collected Papers*, ed. A. Scheffler (Cambridge, Mass.: Harvard University Press).

RAZ, J. (1985). 'Authority, Law and Morality', *Monist*, 68: 295–324.

—— (1986). *The Morality of Freedom* (Oxford: Clarendon Press).

REED, T. M. (1978). 'On Sterba's "Retributive Justice" ', *Political Theory*, 6: 373–76.

RIPSTEIN, A. (1994). 'Equality, Luck, and Responsibility', *Philosophy and Public Affairs*, 23: 3–23.

ROUSSEAU, J. J. (1968). *The Social Contract*, trans. M. Cranston (Harmondsworth: Penguin).

ROYKO, M. (1981). 'Nothing Gained by Killing a Killer? Oh Yes, There Is', *Los Angeles Times*, 13 Mar.

RUBENSTEIN, C. (1981). 'Money and Self-Esteem, Relationships, Secrecy, Envy, Satisfaction', *Psychology Today*, 15: 29–44.

RYAN, A. (1987). 'Introduction', in Mill and Bentham (1987: 7–64).

SADURSKI, W. (1989). 'Theory of Punishment, Social Justice, and Liberal Neutrality', *Law and Philosophy*, 7: 351–73.

SAGOFF, M. (1988). *The Economy of the Earth: Philosophy, Law and the Environment* (Cambridge: Cambridge University Press).

SANDEL, M. (1982). *Liberalism and the Limits of Justice* (Cambridge: Cambridge University Press).

SAYRE-McCORD, G. (1991). 'Deception and Reasons to be Moral', in Vallentyne (1991*b*: 181–95).

SCANLON, T. M. (1982). 'Contractualism and Utilitarianism', in Sen and Williams (1982: 103–28).

—— (1988). 'The Significance of Choice', in S. McMurrin (ed.), *The Tanner Lectures on Human Values*, vol. viii (Salt Lake City: The University of Utah Press), 151–216.

—— (1992). 'The Aims and Authority of Moral Theory', *Oxford Journal of Legal Studies*, 12: 1–23.

—— (1999). *What We Owe to Each Other* (Cambridge, Mass.: Harvard University Press).

SCHEFFLER, S. (1992). 'Responsibility, Reactive Attitudes, and Liberalism in Philosophy and Politics', *Philosophy and Public Affairs*, 21: 299–323.

SEN, A. (1985*a*). 'Well-Being, Agency and Freedom', *Journal of Philosophy*, 82: 169–221.

—— (1985*b*). 'Rights and Capabilities', in T. Honderich (ed.), *Morality and Objectivity* (London: Routledge).

—— (1993). 'Capability and Well-Being', in M. Nussbaum and A. Sen (eds.), *The Quality of Life* (Oxford: Clarendon Press).

—— and WILLIAMS, B. (1982), *Utilitarianism and Beyond* (Cambridge: Cambridge University Press).

SHER, G. (1987). *Desert* (Princeton: Princeton University Press).

Simmons, A. J. (1979). *Moral Principles and Political Obligations* (Princeton: Princeton University Press).

Singer, P. (1997). *How Are We to Live?* (Oxford: Oxford University Press).

Skillen, A. (1980). 'How to Say Things with Walls', *Philosophy*, 55: 509–23.

Slattery, B. (1992). 'The Myth of Retributive Justice', in Cragg (1992: 27–34).

Smart, J. J. C. (1968). 'Extreme and Restricted Utilitarianism', in Bayles (1968: 99–115).

—— (1973). 'An Outline of a System of Utilitarian Ethics', in Smart and Williams (1973: 3–74).

—— and Williams, B. (1973). *Utilitarianism For and Against* (Cambridge: Cambridge University Press).

Smith, H. (1991). 'Deriving Morality from Rationality', in Vallentyne (1991*b*: 229–53).

Smith, M. B. E. (1973). 'Is There a Prima Facie Obligation to Obey the Law?', *Yale Law Journal*, 82: 950–76.

Sorell, T. (1999). 'Punishment in a Kantian Framework', in Matravers (1999*b*: 10–27).

Sprigge, T. L. S. (1968). 'A Utilitarian Reply to Dr McCloskey', in Bayles (1968: 278–82).

Stephen, J. F. (1883). *A History of the Criminal Law of England* (London: Macmillan).

Sterba, J. P. (1977). 'Retributive Justice', *Political Theory*, 5: 349–62.

Strawson, P. (1982). 'Freedom and Resentment', in G. Watson (ed.), *Free Will* (New York: Oxford University Press), 59–80. Originally published in *Proceedings of the British Academy*, 47 (1962), 1–25.

Sturgeon, N. (1984). 'Moral Explanations', in Copp and Zimmerman (1984: 49–78).

Sugden, R. (1991). 'Rational Bargaining', in M. Bacharach and S. Hurely (eds.), *Foundations of Decision Theory* (Oxford: Blackwell), 294–315.

—— (1993*a*). 'The Contractarian Enterprise', in Gauthier and Sugden (1993: 1–23).

—— (1993*b*). 'Rationality and Impartiality: Is the Contractarian Enterprise Possible?', in Gauthier and Sugden (1993: 157–75).

Taylor, C. (1985). *Human Agency and Language: Philosophical Papers 1* (Cambridge: Cambridge University Press).

—— (1989*a*). *Sources of the Self: The Making of the Modern Identity* (Cambridge: Cambridge University Press).

—— (1989*b*). 'Cross-Purposes: The Liberal-Communitarian Debate', in N. Rosenblum (ed.), *Liberalism and the Moral Life* (Cambridge, Mass.: Harvard University Press).

Ten, C. L. (1987). *Crime, Guilt, and Punishment* (Oxford: Clarendon Press).

Thomson, J. J. (1990). *The Realm of Rights* (Cambridge, Mass.: Harvard University Press).

TOLSTOY, L. (1928). *Resurrection,* trans. L. Maude (London: Oxford University Press).

TUNICK, M. (1992*a*). *Hegel's Political Philosophy: Interpreting the Practice of Legal Punishment* (Princeton: Princeton University Press).

—— (1992*b*). *Punishment: Theory and Practice* (Berkeley and Los Angeles: University of California Press).

VALLENTYNE, P. (1991*a*). 'Contractarianism and the Assumption of Mutual Unconcern', in Vallentyne (1991*b*: 71–5).

—— (1991*b*) (ed.). *Contractarianism and Rational Choice: Essays on David Gauthier's Morals by Agreement* (New York: Cambridge University Press).

VELLEMAN, J. D. (1997). 'Deciding How to Decide', in Cullity and Gaut (1997: 29–52).

WALDRON, J. (1984) (ed.). *Theories of Rights* (New York: Oxford University Press).

—— (1999). 'The Plight of the Poor in the Midst of Plenty: Review of J. Rawls, *Collected Papers*', *London Review of Books*, 15 July, 3–6.

WALKER, N. (1969). *Sentencing in a Rational Society* (Harmondsworth: Penguin).

—— (1991). *Why Punish?* (Oxford: Oxford University Press).

WALZER, M. (1983). *Spheres of Justice: A Defence of Pluralism and Equality* (Oxford: Blackwell).

—— (1990). 'The Communitarian Critique of Liberalism', *Political Theory*, 18: 6–23.

WASSERSTROM, R. (1971) (ed.). *Morality and the Law* (Belmont, Calif.: Wadsworth).

—— (1980). *Philosophy and Social Issues* (Notre Dame, Ind.: University of Notre Dame Press).

WEALE, A. (1993). 'Justice, Social Union and the Separateness of Persons', in Gauthier and Sugden (1993: 75–94).

WICKSTEED, P. H. (1933). *The Common Sense of Political Economy and Selected Papers and Reviews on Economic Theory,* ed. L. Robbins, 2 vols. (London: Routledge).

WILLIAMS, B. (1973). 'A Critique of Utilitarianism', in Smart and Williams (1973: 77–150).

—— (1981). *Moral Luck: Philosophical Papers 1973–1980* (Cambridge: Cambridge University Press).

—— (1985). *Ethics and the Limits of Philosophy* (London: Fontana Press/Collins).

—— (1993). 'Moral Incapacity', *Proceedings of the Aristotelian Society*, 93: 59–70.

WILLIAMS, H. (1983). *Kant's Political Philosophy* (Oxford: Oxford University Press).

WOOD, A. (1990). *Hegel's Ethical Thought* (Cambridge: Cambridge University Press).

# INDEX

Anderson, E. 22 n.
Aristotle 83
Armstrong, K. 6–7
Ashworth, A. 27

Barry, B.:
  agreement motive defined by 137
  and assumption of mutual advantage
    140–1, 216 n.
  and conceptions of the good 116–17
  on constructivism 98–101
  and equality 136
  and externalism 137
  and fair play theory 113–14
  and harm 129–30
  on Hobbes 239 n.
  and justice as mutual advantage 140–1,
    162 n., 165–68, 223
  and restrictions on justice 103–4
  and scope of justice 107, 124, 131 n.
  structure of justice as impartiality
    105 n.
  see also justice as impartiality; construc-
    tivism, faux
Benn, S. 3
Bentham, J.:
  hedonistic theory of 13, 16
  see also under punishment, utilitarian
    theory of
Blackburn, S. 121 n.
Braithwaite, J. and Pettit, P. 23–9
  see also dominion

Caney, S. 127 n.
Charvet, J.:
  and existential commitment 190–4
  and non-tuism 194–5
Coleman, J. 110
consequentialism 12
constructivism:
  faux and genuine contrasted 9, 98–101,
    136–7, 140–1, 162–3, 243
constructivism, faux:
  characterized 136, 140–1
  and motivation 9, 152–4
  see also justice as impartiality

constructivism, genuine:
  and affective morality, distinguished
    195–6, 206–7, 218–20
  and the Aristotelian Principle 186, 192–4,
    211–12
  and assurance problem 238–43
  and authority of self-interest 220
  and autonomy 186, 193–4, 237–8
  characterized 155–6
  and coercion, 10, 178–9, 238–43
  coercive nature of norms in 241–3
  and communitarian challenge 182–3
  and conceptions of the good 208–14
  and co-operation, reasons for 187–8, 220
  and equal recognition 193–4, 221–3
  and free riding 240–3
  role of existential commitment in 190–3,
    214
  failure to accord with intuitions 161–5,
    223–9
  and first-third world relations, 227–8
  Gauthier's see Gauthier, D.; justice as
    mutual advantage
  and independents 220, 222, 243
  compared with Lockean account 188
  and the moral community 214–23, 234–6
  and motivation, 10, 178–9, 214–18
  and non-contributors 223–9
  and non-moral virtues 229–30
  and non-tuism 193–200
  and pluralism 229–34
  and prudence 184–7, 189, 191
  and punishment see punishment,
    constructivist theory of
  and reciprocity 200–4, 216–17
  as a reflective practice 182–4, 222
  subjective value claim in 180–1
  and wrong 253–6
Copp, D. 170, 172
Cottingham, J. 48 n.

Dagger, R. 54, 56, 57 n., 59 n., 62, 63–4,
    69 n., 71 n.
Dahrendorf, R. 28
Davis, M. 2, 252
Dolinko, D. 6 n., 47, 84